Psychological Dynamics of Sport and Exercise
Third Edition

Diane L. Gill, PhD
University of North Carolina at Greensboro

Lavon Williams, PhD
Guilford College

Human Kinetics

Library of Congress Cataloging-in-Publication Data

Gill, Diane L., 1948-
  Psychological dynamics of sport and exercise / Diane L. Gill, Lavon Williams. -- 3rd ed.
    p. cm.
  Includes bibliographical references and index.
  ISBN-13: 978-0-7360-6264-0 (hard cover)
  ISBN-10: 0-7360-6264-5 (hard cover)
  1. Sports--Psychological aspects. 2. Exercise--Psychological aspects. 3. Motivation (Psychology) I. Williams, Lavon. II. Title.
  GV706.4.G55 2008
  796.01--dc22

                          2007043948

ISBN-10: 0-7360-6264-5
ISBN-13: 978-0-7360-6264-0

The Web addresses cited in this text were current as of November 23, 2007, unless otherwise noted.

Acquisitions Editor: Myles Schrag; **Developmental Editor:** Rebecca Johnson; **Managing Editor:** Lee Alexander; **Copyeditor:** Alisha Jeddeloh; **Proofreader:** Erin Cler; **Indexer:** Joan K. Griffitts; **Permission Manager:** Carly Breeding; **Graphic Designer:** Joe Buck; **Graphic Artist:** Denise Lowry; **Cover Designer:** Keith Blomberg; **Photo Asset Manager:** Laura Fitch; **Photo Office Assistant:** Jason Allen; **Art Manager:** Kelly Hendren; **Associate Art Manager:** Alan L. Wilborn; **Illustrator:** Denise Lowry; **Printer:** Sheridan Books

Printed in the United States of America   10   9   8   7   6   5   4   3

The paper in this book is certified under a sustainable forestry program.

Human Kinetics
Web site: www.HumanKinetics.com

United States: Human Kinetics, P.O. Box 5076, Champaign, IL 61825-5076
800-747-4457
email: humank@hkusa.com

Canada: Human Kinetics, 475 Devonshire Road Unit 100, Windsor, ON N8Y 2L5
800-465-7301 (in Canada only)
email: info@hkcanada.com

Europe: Human Kinetics, 107 Bradford Road, Stanningley, Leeds LS28 6 AT, United Kingdom
+44 (0) 113 255 5665
email: hk@hkeurope.com

Australia: Human Kinetics, 57A Price Avenue, Lower Mitcham, South Australia 5062
08 8372 0999
e-mail: info@hkaustralia.com

New Zealand: Human Kinetics, Division of Sports Distributors NZ Ltd., P.O. Box 300 226 Albany,
North Shore City, Auckland
0064 9 448 1207
e-mail: info@humankinetics.co.nz

Contents

Preface

Sport and exercise psychology is an exciting and dynamic scholarly area with countless applications for professionals and participants in a wide range of settings. This book provides an overview of sport and exercise psychology—the scientific study of human behavior in sport and exercise and the practical application of that knowledge in physical activity settings. It cannot provide an in-depth review of all the literature; instead, we highlight key theoretical work and research studies, drawing from that scholarship to provide guidelines for using sport and exercise psychology.

This third edition reflects the tremendous growth of sport and exercise psychology. In the first edition of this text (1986), I (D.G.) noted the growth in the field over 10 years of teaching sport psychology courses. By the second edition (2000), research and professional practice had expanded in many directions, and most of the chapters were greatly expanded with largely new material. Again, with this third edition, sport and exercise psychology has continued to grow, and this text incorporates newer material. However, this time we have not expanded the text but have selectively revised to emphasize content that is relevant to professional practice.

Our goal is to present practical theory—guidelines based on the best available knowledge that can be used by teachers, trainers, consultants, and other kinesiology professionals to enhance sport and exercise experiences for all. Throughout this text, we have pulled together research findings, theories, and consistent themes to provide those guidelines. But, a note of caution is in order. Human behavior is complex and dynamic—one size does not fit all, and you will not find any one correct answer for your many questions about sport and exercise behavior. This text will help you recognize the complexities and find practical theories that you can use.

The book is targeted to upper-undergraduate and graduate courses in kinesiology or exercise and sport science, and the text is organized into five parts representing major areas that might be found in such classes. Part I provides an orientation, with chapters covering the scope, historical development, and current approaches of sport and exercise psychology. Part II focuses on the individual, with chapters on personality, attention and cognitive skills, and self-perceptions. Part III covers the huge topic of motivation, addressing the *why* question of sport and exercise behavior. Part IV covers the broad area of emotion, as well as competitive anxiety and stress management. Part V, on social processes, contains chapters on social influence, social development, and group dynamics, as well as gender and cultural diversity.

Introductions, chapter objectives, and key points are provided to guide your reading, and you can test your understanding with the review questions at the end of each chapter. Summaries follow each chapter, along with key references and recommended resources for readers who want to go beyond the text in their research or professional practice.

As a new feature in this edition, case studies and application points are provided to help you connect the content with real-world application. Application points are included throughout, and each chapter concludes with a case study related to professional practice in physical education and coaching, exercise and fitness, or sports medicine to illustrate the application of practical theory. Each application point is labeled with an icon representing one of the professional areas (PE/coaching, exercise/fitness, or sports medicine/rehabilitation). We have tried to include application points and case studies that reflect the wide range of professional settings. Several cases and application points overlap professional areas, and each one could be modified to apply to the other areas. As you are reading the text, get some extra practice by changing each application point to fit one of the other professional areas.

PE/coaching   **Exercise/fitness**   **Sports medicine/rehabilitation**

We hope this book helps you understand and use sport and exercise psychology. Perhaps you will find information that helps you become a more effective teacher, trainer, or consultant; that encourages and guides your research; or that you can use to enhance your own physical activities and your life. You will not find a prescription, but you will find practical theory—guidelines to use as you move through your sport and exercise psychology study and into professional practice.

Acknowledgments

Many people made important contributions to this text. Rainer Martens has been a continuing source of support and advice throughout my career. Many other people at Human Kinetics have helped with this revision, including developmental editor Becky Johnson and STM division director Myles Schrag, who deserves special thanks for his patient support. In this third edition I especially must acknowledge the contributions of my students, who have taught me much about sport and exercise psychology. Lavon Williams, coauthor of this edition, has made contributions beyond authorship as a valued colleague and friend who challenges me to think in new ways. And, as always, I thank my family for being a consistent source of encouragement and support.

My appreciation is also extended to the people at Human Kinetics who have helped with this revision, and to Diane Gill who gave me the opportunity to contribute to this 3rd edition. Lastly, a million thank yous to my family for all of their love and support—you are the greatest!

Part I

Overview of Sport and Exercise Psychology

Part I of this text provides a framework for the psychological dynamics of sport and exercise. Chapter 1 covers the scope of sport and exercise psychology, and introduces sport and exercise psychology as part of the multidisciplinary, applied field of kinesiology. Chapter 2 explores the roots of sport and exercise psychology and reviews its historical development from isolated studies to the diverse, multifaceted, global field of today.

Chapter 3, on understanding and using sport and exercise psychology, presents perspectives on sport and exercise psychology science and knowledge, as well as applications in professional practice. Physical activity participants and professionals are faced with sport and exercise psychology questions every day. Sound, theoretically driven research provides some answers; in-depth, interpretive approaches offer fresh insights; and real-world questions require an educated, experienced professional who can integrate many sources of knowledge and apply practical theory in the real world.

Chapter 1

The Scope of Sport and Exercise Psychology

Chapter Objectives

After studying this chapter, you should be able to

- describe the focus and scope of sport and exercise psychology,
- explain the relationship between sport and exercise psychology and other kinesiology subfields, and
- describe the role of the person and the environment in sport and exercise behavior.

Teachers, trainers, coaches, fitness directors, consultants, athletes, and exercisers must answer questions about behavior every day. They seek accurate, reliable information about psychology, just as they seek information about physiology and biomechanics. Professionals use the best available information, along with experience and judgment, to enhance sport and exercise for all participants. Sport and exercise psychology is the branch of kinesiology that seeks to answer questions about human behavior in physical activity settings.

To become acquainted with some of the issues in sport and exercise psychology, consider the following questions:

- Should a coach help a junior tennis player psych up for a championship match?
- Will more middle school children participate in an after-school activity program if the physical education teacher sets up a point system with awards for the top students?
- Will the participants in the Fit at Fifty-Plus program exercise longer in a group than alone?
- Should parents encourage their children to play aggressive sports in order to let off steam?
- Is there an *I* in team?

Check *Real-Life Scenarios* on page 8 to see how your answers compare. For this warm-up, the answers given are as straightforward as possible, but they are not absolute. You will not find any one correct answer in this text or in the real world. Instead, you will find guidelines—information on how some characteristics affect some behaviors in some situations. Such information is never complete, but as our understanding of human behavior in sport and exercise advances, the guidelines become clearer. First, though, let's consider the scope of sport and exercise psychology, its place within kinesiology, and its relation to psychology.

KINESIOLOGY: A MULTIDISCIPLINARY, APPLIED FIELD

Sport and exercise psychology is part of the overall study of human movement, also known as *kinesiology.* Kinesiology is multidisciplinary: It incorporates the entire range of sciences as well as scholarly areas from the humanities into a biopsychosocial perspective. Kinesiology is also applied: Knowledge is applied to human movement. As the astute reader has noticed, in this text sport and exercise are merged under one label encompassing varied physical activities. Participants include everyone from 8-year-olds in swimming classes to 75-year-olds in cardiac rehabilitation programs to Olympic athletes. Kinesiology, then, integrates and applies information from the various sciences in the study of human movement and physical activity.

In this text, we use *kinesiology* and *exercise and sport science* interchangeably to refer to the field that encompasses sport and exercise psychology, but academic programs go by many aliases, such as human movement, sport studies, health and human performance, or, more traditionally, physical education. *Kinesiology* (the science of human movement) is preferred by those who focus on the discipline and science of the field, but most departments also include professional programs (e.g., teacher education, fitness management). Kinesiologists apply selected theories, concepts, and methods from the basic disciplines (e.g., physics, sociology) and also develop theories, concepts, and methods to create unique knowledge about human movement.

Within kinesiology, sport and exercise psychology occupies the middle of the physical science–social science continuum and has ties to all other subareas. The most prominent subareas are as follows:

- *Biomechanics,* the subarea closest to the physical sciences, applies principles from physics to human movement.

- *Exercise physiology* is clearly aligned with biology and draws upon anatomy and physiology to understand the biology of human movement and exercise activities.

- *Sport and exercise psychology* fits between, and overlaps with, biology and sociocultural studies, as discussed in the next section.

- *Sociocultural sport studies* includes the scholarly areas sometimes separated into sociology, history, and philosophy of sport.

Many scholars use sport-specific theories and methods to address unique sport and exercise concerns. For example, sport-specific approaches dominate competitive-anxiety research and application (see chapter 11). Although there is considerable psychology research on anxiety, in sport anxiety has unique properties, and several sport-specific models and measures have been used in research and practice. Sport and exercise psychology, then, both borrows selected information from the associated discipline of psychology and develops theoretical models and approaches unique to physical activity.

Sport and exercise psychology also draws from the other exercise and sport sciences. Indeed, a thorough understanding of sport and exercise behavior requires information from all the kinesiology subareas. For example, you will understand the psychological effects of distance running more fully if you also consider the physiological effects. Biomechanical approaches may be particu-

Key Point

A thorough understanding of sport and exercise behavior requires integrating information from all the kinesiology subareas: exercise physiology, biomechanics, sport and exercise psychology, and sociocultural sport studies.

larly useful in the study of skilled movements, and sociocultural constructs are prominent in research on gender relations and group dynamics in sport and exercise.

SPORT AND EXERCISE PSYCHOLOGY AS A SUBDISCIPLINE

Now let's look at sport and exercise psychology as a distinct subdiscipline. Sport and exercise psychology is the branch of kinesiology that incorporates theories and approaches of psychology.

Psychology: Science of Human Behavior

Psychology is about people, and it may be defined as the scientific study of human behavior. The ABCs of psychology are affect (feelings), behavior, and cognition (thought). *A, B,* and *C* are interconnected, and people think, feel, and behave within specific situations and a larger social context—their environment *(E)*. To fill in the alphabet, people and the ABCs are constantly changing—they are dynamic *(D)*. Psychology seeks to understand people's thoughts, feelings, and behavior within the dynamic context of their environment.

Psychology is a diverse field with many subareas. The American Psychological Association (APA), the primary professional organization in psychology, lists more than 50 divisions, including the larger divisions such as clinical, developmental, experimental, and personality and social psychology. It also includes such divergent specialties as military psychology and psychopharmacology, as well as exercise and sport psychology.

Sport and exercise psychology emphasizes certain aspects of psychology, particularly personality and social psychology. Some scholars take psychophysiological or developmental perspectives, and consultants often incorporate counseling and clinical psychology theories and approaches. Some specialty areas within psychology integrate differing perspectives. Sport and exercise psychology is closely related to health psychology, an area that has grown tremendously in the last 10 years. Health psychology includes social, clinical, and psychophysiological perspectives, and health psychologists often work with colleagues from other disciplines in clinical and research settings.

Sport and exercise psychology is particularly in line with the recent positive psychology movement. Traditionally, psychology has emphasized problems and treatment, focusing on negative behavior. During his APA presidential term, Martin Seligman campaigned both within psychology and in the larger public arena to place more emphasis on positive psychology. According to the introduction to a special issue of the *American Psychologist,* by Seligman and Csikszentmihalyi (2000), positive psychology focuses on positive subjective experience, positive health and quality of life, resilience, empowerment, and prevention rather than treatment. A recent handbook (Snyder & Lopez, 2005) contains numerous chapters by leading scholars summarizing research on such topics as flow, positive emotions, resilience, optimism, self-efficacy, coping, meaningfulness, and spirituality. Positive psychology clearly has taken off in psychology. More important, sport and exercise psychology fits well with the movement. Promotion of positive health has long been the focus of sport and exercise psychology, and the field has much to contribute to positive psychology.

Motor Behavior and Sport and Exercise Psychology

Given the wide scope of psychology, it is not surprising that sport and exercise psychology does not draw equally from all areas of psychology. The North American Society for the Psychology of Sport and Physical Activity (NASPSPA), one of the main professional organizations for sport and exercise psychology, includes two other areas under the larger category of motor behavior:

- *Motor learning and motor control* aligns most closely with the area of perception and cognition and the area of learning and performance. Motor-learning specialists focus on cognitive processes involved in learning and performing motor skills, whereas motor-control specialists emphasize the neuropsychological processes and biological mechanisms underlying controlled movements. (See Schmidt & Wrisberg, 2004, or Magill, 2007, for an overview of motor learning and control.)

- *Motor development* focuses on developmental psychology as it relates to sport and motor performance. Motor development overlaps with motor learning and motor control under the more general rubric of motor behavior, and motor-development specialists might investigate the development of motor patterns and skilled performance across the life span. Haywood and Getchell (2005) provide an overview of motor development.

Application Point

Psychological kinesiology includes motor behavior as well as sport and exercise psychology. If you were coaching a soccer team of 10- to 12-year-olds, how could you use information from motor behavior to help you be a better coach? For example, you might consider cognitive and physical developmental stages, motor patterns, cognition, and attention, as well as motor-skill learning.

The three areas within NASPSPA reflect the typical division of psychological kinesiology in North America, with sport and exercise psychology separate from motor learning, control, and development. Similarly, in this text we cover sport and exercise psychology but not motor behavior. Most sport psychology around the world includes cognition, perception, and other aspects of motor behavior. Moreover, international research on motor behavior is more applied and more directly related to sport and exercise than in North America. Indeed, the subareas within psychological kinesiology have much to offer each other. For example, the relationship between attention and performance is a prominent topic in both sport and exercise psychology and motor behavior, and educational programs for youth sport coaches draw upon knowledge from motor development and motor learning, as well as sport and exercise psychology.

Sport and Exercise Psychology: A Definition

As already suggested, the following are key aspects of our definition of sport and exercise psychology:

- Sport and exercise psychology is a branch of kinesiology. Those who have psychology backgrounds may consider sport and exercise psychology to be a branch of psychology, but in this text the scholarly base is in kinesiology and the applications are to sport and exercise settings. Also, *sport and exercise* is understood as one term encompassing a wide range of physical activities and settings.

- Sport and exercise psychology is about people and human behavior.
- Sport and exercise psychology involves scientific study to advance knowledge and understanding of human movement.
- Sport and exercise psychology is an applied field. This text emphasizes moving from research into practice—using sport and exercise psychology in the real world.

So, in this text, sport and exercise psychology is defined in the following way: Sport and exercise psychology is the branch of kinesiology that involves the scientific study of human behavior in sport and exercise as well as the practical application of that knowledge in physical activity settings.

Application Point

How can you use sport and exercise psychology? If you are a kinesiology professional—a physical education teacher, athletic trainer, personal trainer, exercise instructor in a health promotion or rehabilitation program, or coach of the New York Yankees or the Girl Scout jump-rope team—think about that question. Or, think about your own physical activity. List three questions about people and human behavior that apply to your situation. Keep them in mind as you read through this text. The text will not give you absolute answers, but you will find relevant information and guidelines—and probably more questions. Apply that information to your situation and the people in it in order to use sport and exercise psychology to answer your questions.

COMPLEXITY OF SPORT AND EXERCISE BEHAVIOR

In sport and exercise psychology, we try to understand meaningful or whole behavior as it occurs in the real world. This is no easy task—remember the ABCDEs. Human behavior in sport and exercise, as in any situation, is complex. Even when we think we understand a behavior (e.g., why an athlete choked in the big game), our explanation may not hold up a week later.

Consider the following truths about human behavior:

- Everyone is alike.
- Everyone is different.

Or, consider these insights from a sage observer of human behavior, William Shakespeare:

- I am that I am (Sonnet 121, 9).
- Men are as the time is (*King Lear,* 5.3.31).

A modern update of these insights might read as follows:

- Genes and personality determine behavior.
- Environment and learning determine behavior.

Recognizing that all of these statements are correct is a key to understanding and using sport and exercise psychology. All people are alike in some ways, but every person is unique. The last set of truths reflects a basic tenet of social psychology set forth in a formal but simple way by Kurt Lewin (1935):

$$B = f(P, E).$$

That is, behavior is a function of the person and the environment. This text moves from an emphasis on the individual to an emphasis on the social environment. In reality, we cannot separate the person and the environment so easily. As Lewin emphasized, individual and environmental factors do not operate independently; they interact. Personal characteristics influence behavior in some situations and not others; situational factors affect people differently; and perhaps most important, the person affects the situation just as the situation affects the person. Thus, the relationships among person (P), environment (E), and behavior (B) are dynamic, changing over time.

For example, a 10-year-old baseball player may make a costly error. A child who is anxious about competition (P) and then hears critical comments (E) likely will become even more anxious, which leads to more errors and changes the situation for future games. A child who is more confident and receives constructive feedback might be more prepared the next time and develop stronger skills and confidence.

Key Point

The relationships among the person (P), environment (E), and behavior (B) are dynamic, changing over time. Kurt Lewin (1935) stated this tenet in the equation $B = f(P, E)$.

Application Point

Behavior changes as the person and environment change. As a personal trainer working with a businessperson, you may find that one week she comes in energetic, confident, and eager to try everything, but the following week she is tense, distracted, and doesn't respond to your suggestions. What personal or environmental factors might be influencing her behavior? Consider work (e.g., closing a major deal, conflicts with the boss) and personal life (e.g., medical condition, changing family situations). In general, expect change and be ready to adapt.

Any behavior takes place within the context of many interacting personal and environmental factors, and everything changes over time. The dynamic complexity of sport and exercise behavior makes precise prediction nearly impossible. Still, greater understanding of the person, social processes, and the relationships of these factors with behavior leads to informed choices. We may not be able to predict how one child will react to a particular teacher's comments, but we can help the teacher relate to different people and enhance the sport and exercise experience for all participants. Sport and exercise psychology is a relatively young field that is just beginning to answer some of our many questions. As you read this text, use the information as a guide—not a prescription—to help answer your questions about sport and exercise behavior.

Real-Life Scenarios

Should a coach help a junior tennis player psych up for a championship match?

No. Many of us believe that the best athletes prepare for competition by psyching up, and many precompetition coaching techniques aim to increase athletes' arousal levels. However, many athletes, especially those who are young, need to calm down. Exceptions exist; some top athletes do use psych-up strategies effectively to enhance performance. Still, control of arousal is a key psychological skill, and emotional-control methods should be used much more often, especially with younger, less experienced participants. See chapters 11 and 12 for more on arousal and performance, along with practical suggestions on stress management.

Will more middle school children participate in an after-school activity program if the physical education teacher sets up a point system with awards for the top students?

Yes. The chance to receive awards may act as an incentive to some children who would otherwise not participate. However, most children participate in physical activity for intrinsic reasons, such as fun and challenge. If most would participate anyway, using rewards accomplishes nothing and presents problems. Research indicates that when children see themselves as participating to get extrinsic rewards, they lose intrinsic interest. The more we emphasize extrinsic rewards, the more likely it becomes that many children (and adults) will participate only under those circumstances. Rewards and intrinsic motivation are discussed in chapter 8.

Will the participants in the Fit at Fifty-Plus program exercise longer in a group than alone?

Yes. Research on social influence indicates that people usually exercise longer and work harder when others are watching or doing the same thing, and social support often helps people stay with an exercise program. However, the presence of others does not always help, and it may interfere with the learning of complex skills that require coordination. Chapter 13 presents additional discussion of social influence.

Should parents encourage their children to play aggressive sports in order to let off steam?

No. Some people argue that aggressive behavior is a natural response and that we should channel those impulses into nondestructive outlets, such as youth sport. However, the most accepted theories and research indicate that aggression is learned social behavior. Encouraging aggression in sport reinforces aggressive behavior, increasing the likelihood of aggression elsewhere. Aggression and moral behavior in sport and exercise are reviewed in chapter 14.

Is there an *I* in team?

Yes. The standard locker-room slogan, "There is no *I* in team," provides a spelling lesson, but it is unwise psychological advice. It implies that team members should forget about individual goals and focus only on the team; however, research indicates that we elicit the best performance from both individuals and groups when we explicitly recognize and reinforce individual contributions. Many coaches take steps to ensure that individual goals are set and individual achievements are reinforced. Chapter 15 includes more detailed explanations of group performance.

PUTTING IT INTO PRACTICE

Now you are ready to put the content of chapter 1 into practice. Read the chapter summary, discuss the case study, answer the review questions, and enhance your knowledge by researching the recommended readings.

Summary

Sport and exercise psychology is the branch of kinesiology that involves the scientific study of human behavior in sport and exercise, as well as the practical application of that information in physical activity settings. Similar to the other disciplines within kinesiology, sport and exercise psychology can be applied to skilled movements, physical activities, health-oriented exercise programs, physical education, and competitive athletics. Within North America, sport and exercise psychology is differentiated from the related psychological areas of motor learning and control and motor development. It emphasizes personality and social psychology, but it also draws upon many other areas of psychology to focus on the complex relationships among personal characteristics, the social situation, and human behavior in physical activity settings.

Case Study

As the $B = f(P, E)$ model suggests, behavior in sport and exercise depends on both the person and the environment. Assume you are an exercise instructor in a cardiac rehabilitation program. How could you apply that model as you work with the participants? First, remember that all people are alike, but every person is unique. Participants in the program are likely older with more established careers and home lives, and they are dealing with a life-threatening condition, which likely leads to uncertainty and anxiety. At the same time, everyone is different. Some will be new to exercise whereas others will be former athletes; some will be optimistic and confident whereas others will be apprehensive and withdrawn. They will all have different life stories and backgrounds, and they will have different skills and preferences for the exercise program.

How will you structure your program and tailor your instructions to encourage participants to stick with it and to develop healthy exercise behaviors? Consider what you might do to meet the common needs, such as adding relaxation strategies to a session or providing information about typical responses of heart rate and blood pressure to exercise. Also, think about individualizing your approach to clients. For example, one person might do better with encouragement and attention, whereas another might prefer to work on his own. Try to think of other ways that you might consider the person and the environment in your program. Finally, remember that behavior is complex and dynamic—everything changes.

Review Questions

1. Define *sport and exercise psychology* as the term is used in the text.
2. Describe motor control and learning, as well as motor development, and discuss the relationship of sport and exercise psychology to these areas.
3. Explain the dynamic relationships among the person, the environment, and behavior.

Recommended Reading

Lewin, K. (1935). *A dynamic theory of personality.* New York: McGraw-Hill.

In 1935, Lewin presented $B = f(P, E)$, an elegant representation of human behavior. Lewin was committed to understanding behavior in the real world. In his later works, *Resolving Social Conflicts* (1948) and *Field Theory in Social Science* (1951), he moved on to larger social issues and action research. These classics have been reissued (Lewin, 1997). If you want to apply psychology to complex, real-world problems, read Lewin for new insights. If you're not ready to delve into Lewin, that's fine. Most people who have been in sport and exercise psychology for a long time are not at that point either. To get more information about sport and exercise psychology—who's involved, what they do, the big questions in research and practice—go to the most current sources. Check recent issues of the major journals and the Web sites of major organizations.

Journals

The Journal of Sport and Exercise Psychology, The Sport Psychologist, and the *Journal of Applied Sport Psychology* focus on sport and exercise psychology and include current research by major scholars. *The Journal of Sport and Exercise Psychology* emphasizes theory-based research, whereas *The Sport Psychologist* has a more applied focus and includes articles on professional activities as well as applied research. The *Journal of Applied Sport Psychology* is the journal of the Association for Applied Sport Psychology, and it emphasizes applied research. The original *International Journal of Sport Psychology* is still published, but the newer *International Journal of Sport and Exercise Psychology* is now the official journal of the International Society of Sport Psychology. It covers a range of sport and exercise psychology topics with an emphasis on international and cultural concerns.

Web Sites of Sport and Exercise Psychology Organizations

NASPSPA, which includes motor behavior as well as sport and exercise psychology; Division 47 (Exercise and Sport) of the APA (APA-47); the Association for Applied Sport Psychology (AASP), which was the Association for the Advancement of Applied Sport Psychology (AAASP) before 2006; and the International Society of Sport Psychology (ISSP) have Web sites that provide information not only on the organizations themselves but also on conferences, contact people, resources, and current issues. In addition, the international scope of sport and exercise psychology is evident in the number of organizations found around the world, including the well-established Canadian *Societe Canadienne d'Apprentissage Psychomoteur et Psychologie du Sport* (SCAPPS) and the European Federation of Sport Psychology (FEPSAC). Following are the current Web sites:

- AASP: www.aaasponline.org
- APA: www.apa.org
- APA-47: www.apa.org/divisions/div47/
- FEPSAC: www.fepsac.com
- ISSP: www.issponline.org
- NASPSPA: www.naspspa.org
- SCAPPS: www.scapps.org

Chapter 2

History of Sport and Exercise Psychology

Chapter Objectives

After studying this chapter, you should be able to

◆ trace the roots of sport and exercise psychology, beginning with psychology and physical education; and

◆ identify the key stages in the development of sport and exercise psychology as a subdiscipline.

This chapter traces the historical development of today's multifaceted, global sport and exercise psychology. Sport and exercise psychology is relatively young as an identifiable scholarly field, but there are traces of sport and exercise research in psychology and kinesiology going back 100 years. This chapter provides a brief review of that history; for more details, see Gill (1997) and Weiss and Gill (2005).

EARLY ROOTS: 1890 TO 1920

Psychology and kinesiology began to organize around the beginning of the 20th century, and that early work includes evidence of sport and exercise psychology. Both Wiggins (1984) and Ryan (1981) cite an early psychological study of American football by G.T.W. Patrick (1903) and note the words of G. Stanley Hall (1908), founding president of the APA:

Physical education is for the sake of mental and moral culture and not an end in itself. It is to make the intellect, feelings and will more vigorous, sane, supple and resourceful. (pp. 1015-1016)

Norman Triplett's (1898) study of social influence and performance is a widely recognized early contribution. Triplett observed that cyclists seemed motivated to perform better with social influence (pacing machine, competition), and he devised an experiment to test his ideas. As he predicted, performers did better on a lab task when in pairs than when performing alone. Other early scholars from both psychology and physical education espoused the psychological benefits of physical education and conducted isolated studies, including George W. Fitz (1895) of Harvard, who conducted experiments on the speed and accuracy of motor responses.

GRIFFITH'S SPORT PSYCHOLOGY WORK: 1920 TO 1940

Coleman R. Griffith began his systematic sport psychology work in 1918 as a doctoral student at the University of Illinois, and soon caught the attention of George Huff, director of physical education for men, who established Griffith's athletics research laboratory. Griffith was a prolific researcher who developed research measures and procedures focused on psychomotor skills, learning, and personality. He taught sport psychology classes and published numerous articles, as well as two classic texts, *Psychology of Coaching* (1926) and *Psychology and Athletics* (1928).

Griffith also took his research onto the playing field. He used an interview with Red Grange after the 1924 Michigan–Illinois football game, in which Grange noted that he could not recall a single detail of his remarkable performance, to illustrate that top athletes perform skills automatically. In addition, he corresponded with legendary coach Knute Rockne on the psychology of coaching and motivation (see chapter 11 for details). When the lab closed in 1932, Griffith continued as a professor of educational psychology, and eventually provost, at Illinois, but he did not abandon sport psychology. In 1938 he was hired by Philip Wrigley as the sport psychologist for the Chicago Cubs.

Although sport and exercise psychologists most often cite Griffith's applied work with the Cubs, he actually was more concerned with developing the research and knowledge base. In the inaugural volume of the *Research Quarterly,* Griffith (1930) called for a more scientific and experimental approach to psychological topics such as skill acquisition and the effects of emotions on performance. He noted the abundance of anecdotal reports and lack of experimental approaches:

Key Point

Coleman Griffith was the first person in North America to do systematic sport psychology research and practice. He focused on psychomotor skills, learning, and personality. He developed research measures and procedures, and he also took his sport psychology work outside of the lab and onto the playing fields.

> *Many of these popular articles tell interesting stories about psychological problems, but from the point of view of a science they do not get very far, either in the correct envisagement of the problem, or in its solution. (p. 35)*

Griffith went on to discuss his studies of attention, mood, and reaction time with athletes and to outline 25 topics that might be investigated in his lab. The list included several topics that we continue to investigate with (perhaps) more sophisticated methods: the effect of exercise on length of life and resistance to disease, the nature of sleep among athletes, methods of teaching psychological skills in sport, photographic analysis of muscle coordination during fear, sex differences in motor-skill tests, and the effects of nicotine and other toxins on learning—to name just a few.

Griffith maintained his scientific perspective while recognizing the expertise of coaches and athletes. His advice from 1925 still rings true today:

> *A great many people have the idea that the psychologist is a sort of magician who is ready, for a price, to sell his services to one individual or one group of men. Nothing could be further from the truth. Psychological facts are universal facts. They belong to whoever will read while he runs. There is another strange opinion about the psychologist. It is supposed that he is merely waiting until he can jump into an athletic field, tell the old-time successful coach that he is all wrong and begin, then, to expound his own magical and fanciful theories as to proper methods of coaching, the way to conquer overconfidence, the best*

forms of strategy, and so on. This, of course, is far from the truth, although certain things have appeared in the application of psychology to business and industry to lead to such an opinion. During the last few years and at the present time, there have been and are many men, short in psychological training and long in the use of the English language, who are doing psychology damage by advertising that they are ready to answer any and every question that comes up in any and every field. No sane psychologist is deceived by these self-styled apostles of a new day. Coaches and athletes have a right to be wary of such stuff. (pp. 193-194)

Application Point

As Griffith cautioned, coaches should be wary of stories that sound too good to be true. Useful sport and exercise psychology advice is based on evidence. Check out professional resources (e.g., coaching journals, newsletters, and Web sites) and find one or two sources of sport psychology advice that a coach could use that are also supported by references to research or other evidence.

Griffith's research, publications, and thoughtful insights make him one of the most significant figures in the history of sport psychology, and he is widely characterized as the father of sport psychology in North America. However, as Kroll and Lewis (1970) note, Griffith was a prophet without disciples, and *father* is really a misnomer. Sport psychology research and practice did not continue after Griffith's pioneering work. Parallel efforts in Germany by R.W. Schulte and in Russia by Peter Roudik and A.C. Puni continued but did not influence North America.

ISOLATED SPORT AND EXERCISE PSYCHOLOGY STUDIES: 1940 TO 1965

From Griffith's time through the late 1960s, when an identifiable sport and exercise psychology specialization emerged, sustained programs were nonexistent. C.H. McCloy (1930) of the University of Iowa examined character building through physical education, and Walter Miles (1928, 1931) of Stanford studied reaction time, but research was sporadic. After World War II, several scholars developed research programs in motor behavior that incorporated sport psychology topics, including Arthur Slater-Hammel at Indiana, Alfred (Fritz) Hubbard at the University of Illinois, John Lawther at Penn State, and Franklin Henry at Berkeley. Warren Johnson's (1949) study of precontest emotion in football is a notable contribution of this time and a precursor to later studies of competitive emotion.

In the 1960s, more texts that covered sport and exercise psychology began to appear, including Cratty's *Psychology and Physical Activity* in 1967 and Singer's *Motor Learning and Human Performance* in 1968. Bruce Ogilvie and Thomas Tutko published *Problem Athletes and How to Handle Them* in 1966. Their clinical approach and lack of a scientific framework and supporting evidence led to a cold reception from motor behavior and physical education scholars. However, Ogilvie and Tutko's work was popular in the coaching community and foreshadowed the influx of applied sport psychology works in the 1980s.

EMERGENCE OF SPORT AND EXERCISE PSYCHOLOGY AS A SUBDISCIPLINE: 1965 TO 1975

Despite the innovative work during the first half of the 20th century, sport and exercise psychology did not emerge as an identifiable field until the late 1960s, when several scholars developed research programs, graduate courses, and eventually specialized organizations and publications. Simultaneously, many people became sport psychologists in other countries, particularly in Europe, and sport psychology became an established area.

International Organization

The International Society of Sport Psychology (ISSP) formed and held the first International Congress of Sport Psychology in Rome in 1965. Reflecting on the development of the ISSP, Miroslav Vanek (1993) cited the influence of the Soviet-ization of top-level sport in the 1950s. Thus, international sport psychology has a closer alignment with applied psychology and performance enhancement for elite athletes than in North America. Several sport psychologists from Europe and the Soviet Union, including Vanek, were instrumental in forming an international society, along with Ferruccio Antonelli, founding president of the ISSP and organizer of the first international congress.

The second international congress was held in Washington, DC, in 1968, and the proceedings of that congress (Kenyon & Grogg, 1970) provide a nice overview of sport psychology at that time. Antonelli remained ISSP president for several years, and in 1970 he founded the *International Journal of Sport Psychology*, the first sport psychology research journal.

Vanek (1985), who was president of the ISSP from 1973 to 1985, described the field as follows:

> *The psychology of sport has become an institutionalized discipline within the sport sciences. . . . Our membership has grown, we have journals devoted to sport psychology, national and international societies, coursework and text-books, specific courses for training in sport psychology, increasing research efforts, and so on. In fact, sport psychology has become a profession in many countries. (p. 1)*

The ISSP has continued to expand, holds meetings every 4 years, and serves as the primary international forum for the field today.

North American Organization

As international sport psychology was organizing, North American scholars also began to organize, forming the North American Society for the Psychology of Sport and Physical Activity (NASPSPA). Loy (1974) reported that a small group began discussions at the 1965 AAHPER (now the American Alliance for Health, Physical Education, Recreation and Dance, or AAHPERD) conference, and that the first meeting of NASPSPA was held at the 1967 AAHPER conference; NASPSPA officially incorporated just after that meeting. The first independent meeting of NASPSPA was held at Allerton Park, Illinois, in 1973, and the proceedings of that conference (Wade & Martens, 1974) marked the start of Human Kinetics Publishers as well as a milestone for sport and exercise psychology.

The organization of the NASPSPA reflected the overlapping of sport and exercise psychology and motor behavior with subareas of motor learning, motor development, and social psychology of physical activity (now sport and exercise psychology). A separate Canadian organization, the Canadian Society for Psychomotor Learning and Sport Psychology (CSPLSP; now known as *Societe Canadienne d'Apprentissage Psychomoteur et Psychologie du Sport,* or SCAPPS) was founded in 1969 and became an independent society in 1977.

Publications

Key Point

The formation of sport psychology organizations, including the ISSP in 1965 and the official incorporation of NASPSPA in 1967, marks the organization of sport and exercise psychology as a field of study.

As sport and exercise psychology research, graduate programs, and organizations developed, scholarly publications emerged. Earlier studies appeared in psychology journals and in the *Research Quarterly* (later renamed the *Research Quarterly for Exercise and Sport),* which continues to publish sport and exercise psychology research. As research expanded, sport and exercise psychologists developed specialized publications.

The *International Journal of Sport Psychology* began publishing in 1970, but for North American scholars, the most important publication during the 1970s was the NASPSPA proceedings, which were published from 1973 to 1980 as *Psychology of Motor Behavior and Sport.* With the 1979 appearance of the *Journal of Sport Psychology,* NASPSPA stopped publishing full papers in proceedings. The *Journal of Sport Psychology* (known as the *Journal of Sport and Exercise Psychology* since 1988) was immediately recognized, as it is today, as the leading publication outlet for research on sport and exercise psychology.

DEVELOPMENT OF THE SUBDISCIPLINE: 1975 TO 1999

From the 1970s through the 1990s, scholars of sport and exercise psychology established research labs and graduate programs, held successful annual conferences, developed a respected research journal, and gradually became the largest and most diverse of the three areas within the NASPSPA. Rainer Martens' (1975) text, *Social Psychology and Physical Activity,* reflects the content and orientation of those early years. Major psychological theories (e.g., inverted-U hypothesis, achievement motivation theory) framed the content, most supporting research was from psychology, and the sport psychology work cited seldom involved sport but more likely involved laboratory experiments with motor tasks such as rotary-pursuit and stabilometer tasks.

Key Point

In the mid-1980s, sport and exercise psychology moved to more applied issues and approaches, and it made a strong move to sport relevance with the development of sport-specific models and measures.

By the mid-1980s, sport and exercise psychology had grown in new directions. Martens' 1979 article in the *Journal of Sport Psychology,* which he presented as "From Smocks to Jocks" at the 1978 CSPLSP conference, marked the beginning of a move toward more applied research and sport-specific concerns. Field research and applied issues moved to the forefront and captured the attention of students, psychologists who had previously ignored sport, and the public. Before 1980, sport psychology application largely referred to physical education, but with the 1980s, it came to imply psychological skills training of elite competitive athletes.

With more diverse students and researchers coming into sport psychology, the NASPSPA no longer fit all interests. John Silva initiated an organizational meeting at Nags Head, North Carolina, in October 1985, marking the beginning of the Association for the Advancement of Applied Sport Psychology (AAASP), which shortened its name to the Association for Applied Sport Psychology (AASP) in 2006. As summarized in the first issue of the *AAASP Newsletter* (1986), the AASP provides a forum for people interested in research, theory development, and application of psychological principles in sport and exercise. The first conference of the organization took place at Jekyll Island, Georgia, in 1986; annual conferences continue with the three areas that were set in 1985: intervention and performance enhancement, health psychology, and social psychology.

Martens' keynote address at that first AAASP conference challenged sport psychology to accept alternative approaches to science in order to develop truly useful knowledge. That widely cited paper (Martens, 1987b) was published in the inaugural issue of *The Sport Psychologist,* which focused on the emerging literature on applied sport psychology. With *The Sport Psychologist* emphasizing applied research and professional concerns, the *Journal of Sport Psychology* concentrated on strong research, and in 1988, during my editorial term, added *Exercise* to the title and more explicitly sought research on health-oriented exercise as well as sport. Also, the AAASP started its *Journal of Applied Sport Psychology* in 1989. This journal serves many of the same purposes as *The Sport Psychologist* and also provides AASP information, publishes major addresses from the conference, and develops instructive theme issues.

Several people trained in traditional psychology programs moved into sport and exercise psychology in the 1980s. Bruce Ogilvie, whose earlier applied work had not been accepted in exercise and sport science in the 1960s, was recognized for those pioneering efforts when applied sport psychology organized in the 1980s. Richard Suinn, clinical psychologist and former president of the APA, and APA colleagues, including Steve Heyman and William Morgan, organized an interest group, and in 1986, Division 47—Exercise and Sport Psychology—became a formal division of APA.

The NASPSPA, AASP, and APA Division 47 are the primary organizations in the United States, but sport and exercise psychology also has a presence in other organizations. AAHPERD, the initial home of the NASPSPA, includes a Sport and Exercise Psychology Academy. The American College of Sports Medicine (ACSM), a large organization traditionally dominated by exercise physiology and sports medicine, has expanded its psychology constituency in recent years. Suinn's work with Olympic skiers in 1976 helped the U.S. Olympic Committee (USOC) recognize the potential role of sport psychology. In 1983, the USOC established an official sport psychology committee and a registry, and many sport psychologists have worked with athletes, coaches, and training programs through the organization since then. In 1987, the USOC hired Shane Murphy as its first full-time sport psychologist, and it continues to support sport psychology specialists.

Applied sport psychology caught the attention of students and the public, creating a market for more publications and resources. Few sport psychology texts existed when I wrote the first edition of this text (Gill, 1986), but the literature quickly expanded. Many applied sport psychology books appeared, including Robert Nideffer's *The Inner Athlete* (1976a) and *Athlete's Guide to Mental Training* (1985); Dorothy Harris and Bette Harris' *The Athlete's Guide to Sport Psychology* (1984), Terry Orlick's *In Pursuit of Excellence* (1980), Rainer Martens' *Coaches Guide to Sport Psychology* (1987a), and Jean Williams' *Applied Sport Psychology* (1986; now in 5th edition, 2006).

Application Point

Sports medicine professionals recognize that injury and rehabilitation have psychological aspects, but they seldom have training in sport and exercise psychology. If you were a sports medicine professional, how might you learn more about sport and exercise psychology and how to use psychological skills and strategies in rehabilitation programs? Check the sport and exercise psychology organizations and resources for educational opportunities that a sports medicine professional might pursue. Look for specific courses, conference programs and workshops, and continual learning and graduate programs that could provide information on useful sport and exercise psychology.

SPORT AND EXERCISE PSYCHOLOGY TODAY: 2000 TO PRESENT

In this new millennium, sport and exercise psychology has grown up and moved in many directions. Traces of its roots and development are evident—we still have theory-based experiments on social influence, and consultants do psychological skill training with Olympic athletes. However, sport and exercise psychology today is multifaceted and diverse in research and practice, and it is now truly global.

During the 1980s and 1990s, attention shifted to sport and applied work with athletes. Attention has now shifted back to exercise in response to the public concern for health and fitness, with a strong move toward increased research on exercise and applied emphasis on physical activity and health. Indeed, some programs and publications intentionally separate exercise psychology from sport psychology, reflecting that newer emphasis. In this text, however, sport and exercise psychology is a single area—one that is large and diverse, to be sure.

Today's sport and exercise psychology is multifaceted, diverse, and global. Professionals include psychologists and kinesiologists in both academic research and in private practice who take varying scholarly approaches. Participants vary in gender, age, ability, and cultural background. Multiple organizations, publications, and Internet sites provide resources to participants, professionals, and the public. Settings are diverse. Sport and exercise psychology is found in training rooms, community youth programs, senior centers, and clinics, as well as on playing fields and in gymnasiums. Professional and personal goals are diverse, including education, health promotion, life skills development, community development, and performance enhancement.

Application Point

The popular perception of sport and exercise psychology is that it provides psychological skills for Olympic athletes, but it also is useful in health promotion and youth development programs. List two or three ways sport and exercise psychology could be used in an exercise program for older adults. (Check sport and exercise psychology or health promotion Web sites for ideas.)

Most notably, sport and exercise psychology is global. The ISSP, which formed before any North American organizations, has regained prominence. In addition to the ISSP and the North American organizations, there are established sport and exercise psychology organizations in Europe, Asia, and Australia, with South American and African scholars developing sport and exercise psychology programs and joining the international sport and exercise psychology community.

Benchmarks in the History of Sport and Exercise Psychology

1898

Norman Triplett conducts the first social psychology experiment, confirming his observations that people perform tasks faster in the presence of others.

1925

The Board of Trustees at the University of Illinois establishes the Athletics Research Laboratory with Coleman R. Griffith as director.

1965

The International Society of Sport Psychology (ISSP) is formed and holds the first International Congress of Sport Psychology in Rome in 1965.

The North American Society for the Psychology of Sport and Physical Activity (NASPSPA) is officially incorporated on March 13, 1967.

1979

The first issue of the *Journal of Sport Psychology* (*Journal of Sport and Exercise Psychology* since 1988) is published by Human Kinetics with Dan Landers as editor.

1985

The Association for the Advancement of Applied Sport Psychology (AAASP) is formed in 1985 with John Silva as president. (In 2006, the name is changed to the Association for Applied Sport Psychology, or AASP.)

Division 47, Exercise and Sport Psychology, becomes a formal division of the American Psychological Association (APA) in 1986.

PUTTING IT INTO PRACTICE

Now you are ready to put the content of chapter 2 into practice. Read the chapter summary, discuss the case study, answer the review questions, and enhance your knowledge by researching the recommended readings.

Summary

Although sport and exercise psychology is a relatively young field, we can trace its roots back over 100 years. We can identify isolated early studies, but apart from Coleman Griffith's still-enlightening work, sport and exercise psychology was not organized until the late 1960s, as marked by the official incorporation of the NASPSPA in 1967. Sport and exercise psychology expanded rapidly during the 1970s, creating a knowledge base and specialized publications. During the 1980s, sport and exercise psychology turned toward applied research and practice. Through the 1990s and into this century, sport and exercise psychology expanded in many directions, particularly addressing health-related exercise and physical activity. Today, sport and exercise psychology is multifaceted, diverse, and global.

Case Study

Many years ago, before sport and exercise psychology was an established area of study, Coleman Griffith was doing research and consulting with athletes and coaches. As a high school coach who wants to use sport and exercise psychology today, what history lessons could you take from Coleman Griffith? Be wary of advice that sounds like the magic key to success. Remember that Griffith started a lab, conducted research, and consulted with coaches and athletes before offering his services. Be sure that the advice is supported by evidence. Since Griffith did his pioneering work, sport and exercise psychology has developed organizations, publications, and Web sites. Today's coaches can look to organizations such as the AASP, APA, ISSP, and countless other resources for advice. Still, as we learned in chapter 1, behavior is complex and dynamic. Despite tremendous growth in the research base, sport and exercise psychology does not have the magic key to replace the insights and experience of the successful coach.

Review Questions

1. Name the first person to do systematic sport psychology research in North America, and discuss his work.
2. Discuss the beginnings of sport and exercise psychology.
3. Discuss the development of applied sport psychology.
4. Describe the diverse topics, settings, and professionals in sport and exercise psychology today.

Recommended Reading

McCullagh, P. (Ed.). (1995). Sport psychology: A historical perspective. *The Sport Psychologist, 4.*

This special issue contains several articles by scholars who know their history and want to communicate that historical knowledge to others. Read Gould and Pick's (1995) article on the Griffith years (1920-1940) to learn more about Coleman Griffith's remarkable work. Read at least two other articles and you will have a much better understanding of sport and exercise psychology.

Weiss, M.R., & Gill, D.L. (2005). What goes around comes around: Re-emerging themes in sport and exercise psychology. *Research Quarterly for Exercise and Sport, 76,* S71-S87.

This article, which appeared in the 75th anniversary issue of the *Research Quarterly for Exercise and Sport,* covers 75 years of sport and exercise psychology research, reflecting on its roots and development and noting dominant themes, such as emotion and moral development, as well as more recent themes such as exercise adherence.

Chapter 3

Understanding and Using Sport and Exercise Psychology

Chapter Objectives

After studying this chapter, you should be able to

◆ discuss the relationships among theory, research, and practice;
◆ identify paradigms that have shaped the field of sport and exercise psychology;
◆ describe the scientific method and how it is used in sport and exercise psychology research; and
◆ describe the professional roles in sport and exercise psychology.

To answer sport and exercise psychology questions such as those raised in chapter 1, professionals seek good information that they can use. For example, the tennis coach wants good information on anxiety and emotional control to help the junior tennis player prepare for competition. Good information is not only scientifically sound; it is also relevant and useful in professional practice. This chapter will help you understand and use sport and exercise psychology knowledge. First, we review theories, research methods, and paradigms that have shaped the knowledge base of sport and exercise psychology, and we emphasize practical theory as the key link between research and practice. We then focus on using sport and exercise psychology in professional roles.

UNDERSTANDING SPORT AND EXERCISE PSYCHOLOGY

This chapter draws upon the work of other scholars, including Martens' (1979, 1987) influential calls for changes in our approaches to science and knowledge; Dzewaltowski's (1997) call for an ecological model focusing on context; Mahoney's (1991, 2005) provocative calls for a more complex, dynamic, and constructivist approach to human behavior and change; and Kurt Lewin's (1935, 1948, 1951) classic work, which becomes more insightful with each rereading. This blended approach frames the presentation of sport and exercise psychology knowledge in this text. We emphasize the person and behavior in context (as Lewin proposed), and we strive to communicate practical theory to provide unifying principles to use within the ever-changing context of sport and exercise.

Theory, Research, and Practice

Theory, research, and practice are necessarily interconnected. Competent professionals in any area must understand the knowledge base, and familiarity with current research and theory is the hallmark of a professional. *Evidence-based practice* is the phrase commonly used to describe effective professional practice, particularly in health-related professions. The APA recently approved a policy statement on evidence-based practice in psychology, and that statement provides a clear, concise guide to professional practice in sport and exercise psychology. As the APA (2006, p. 273) policy states, "Evidence-based practice in psychology (EBPP) is the integration of the best available research with clinical expertise in the context of patient characteristics, culture, and preferences."

All components of that definition are critical. First, professionals use the best available research. As the policy notes, the best research comes from a variety of methods and is both clinically relevant (practical) and internally valid (scientifically sound). Competent professionals use clinical (professional) expertise as well as research evidence. Professional knowledge comes from experience, training, and ongoing education, and expertise includes competencies in assessment, decision-making, and interpersonal skills. Research and professional expertise must be integrated within the context of individual characteristics, preferences, and culture.

Clearly, research and practice are connected in evidence-based practice, and most discussions of science emphasize research–practice connections. The real world offers research ideas, and research results are ultimately tested for usefulness in the real world. To complete the picture, theory must be included. Theory is the critical link in the triad of theory, research, and practice.

Theory is both the guide and goal of research. Theory, which is a systematic explanation of a phenomenon based on sound scientific evidence, is our goal because it explains behavior. For example, catastrophe theory, discussed in chapter 11, explains the relationship between anxiety and performance. And, as you will discover, catastrophe theory is a good example of how theories incorporate multiple constructs in a complex network of interrelationships. Theories are never final but are constantly revised or replaced with new information.

Thus, theory also serves as a source of questions and guide for research. As Forscher (1963) pointed out in "Chaos in the Brickyard," a classic gem of scientific wisdom, theory is the key to useful research. Research without theory as a guide gives us piles of bricks (facts) but no useful structures. Theory is also the key to effective practice. Too often practitioners look for a quick fix to a problem rather than searching for common themes and unifying principles that apply in varying contexts.

> **Key Point**
>
> Theory is the critical link in the triad of theory, research, and practice. It is both the guide and goal of research—it serves as a source of questions to research and it explains behavior.

Setting the Direction: Identifying Research Questions

At a symposium and in a subsequent article (Gill, 1997), I was asked to identify measurement, statistics, and design issues in sport and exercise psychology—a formal way of asking, "How do we answer our questions?" But first we must ask, "What are our questions?" My main point at the symposium, and a central theme in this chapter, is that identifying our questions is the essential step. When research has a defined purpose and guiding framework, when constructs are clearly defined, and when clear, relevant questions are asked, we solve problems.

My favorite research advice was originally published in 1865 in *Alice's Adventures in Wonderland* (Carroll, 1865/1992). Alice (the searching researcher or student) asks the Cheshire Cat (the resident expert) for advice: "Would you tell me, please, which way I ought to walk from here?" The cat returns the question (as do all expert advisors): "That depends a good deal on where you want to get to." When Alice replies that she doesn't much care where, the sage responds, "Then, it doesn't matter which way you walk." If you don't know where you want to get to, no one can tell you how to get there.

PARADIGMS AND SOURCES OF KNOWLEDGE

Just as there are many questions in sport and exercise psychology, there are many ways to answer those questions. Indeed, many questions are best answered with multiple approaches. Most often, professionals look to science, and researchers use the scientific method (also known as *normal science* or *positivistic methods)* to answer questions. So, we will first outline the scientific method. See Thomas, Nelson, and Silverman (2005) for details on science and research methods in kinesiology.

Scientific Method

Science is a process, and the scientific method is a systematic way to solve problems. Sport and exercise psychology developed as a discipline by following psychology and its reliance on traditional scientific methods. As described by Thomas, Nelson, and Silverman (2005), the scientific method is a series of steps.

1. Developing the problem. In the scientific method, the researcher must be specific, typically identifying independent and dependent variables. The independent variable is manipulated to determine the effect on the dependent variable.

2. Formulating the hypothesis. The hypothesis is the prediction or expected result. The hypothesis must be testable.

3. Gathering the data. The researcher must first plan the methods to maximize internal and external validity and then make observations to gather data. *Internal validity* means you are certain the results can be attributed to the treatment. For example, if the choice group adhered to the exercise program more than the no-choice group, you are sure that choice was what increased adherence—you can rule out other alternatives. *External validity* refers to the generalizability of results. If choice increased adherence in the study, choice should increase adherence in other studies and settings.

4. Analyzing and interpreting the results. Most studies involve statistical analyses. The researcher must then interpret the results to support or refute the hypothesis and compare results with other research, theories, or other sources of information.

Science is one way to answer questions, but we do not devise an experiment to answer all questions in life, or even in sport and exercise. Nonscientific sources of knowledge include the following:

- Tenacity—Means clinging to beliefs, the way it's always been done, or superstitions.

Key Point

The scientific method is a systematic way to solve problems. It includes the following four steps:

1. Developing the problem
2. Formulating the hypothesis
3. Gathering the data
4. Analyzing and interpreting the results

- Intuition—Includes commonsense or self-evident truths.

- Authority—Refers to accepting the authority's truth (e.g., that of teachers, experts, rule books).

- Rationalistic method—Uses logic, such as the classic syllogism: All men are mortal; Socrates is a man; therefore, Socrates is mortal.

- Empirical method—Includes experience, observation, and data gathering.

Application Point

Physical education teachers and other professionals use many sources of knowledge every day. Give an example of how a physical education teacher might use each of the nonscientific sources (tenacity, intuition, and so on) in trying to motivate students and promote participation and skill development.

We might use any of these sources to understand sport and exercise psychology. Both the rationalistic (logic) and empirical methods are key parts of the scientific method; logic is critical in developing the problem and interpreting results, and gathering data is the empirical method. Even the most careful researcher is wise to rely on intuition in some cases, and professionals must rely on some authority in addition to their own judgment. The scientific method has helped us develop a knowledge base and gain credibility, and it continues to dominate both psychology and kinesiology. However, several scholars argue for alternative methods and a wider acceptance of real-world knowledge. Those scholars challenge paradigms—the larger meta-theories about knowledge and understanding.

Paradigm Challenges in Sport and Exercise Psychology

Martens' (1979, 1987) influential papers are often interpreted as methodological critiques, but they go beyond methods to challenge our paradigms. In his paper titled "Smocks and Jocks," Martens (1979) criticized sport psychology research for its lack of relevance to the real world and called for more research in the field. Although many interpreted that call as an excuse to abandon scientific rigor and theory, Landers (1983)—a strong advocate of theory testing—pointed out that Martens did not call for abandoning theory, but for using relevant theory, or theory that is relevant to the real world.

Martens' 1987 paper on science and knowledge in sport psychology prompted many sport and exercise psychologists not only to move to the field but also to abandon other aspects of science in favor of more subjective forms of knowing. Martens' concern was not simply methodological but a challenge to our assumptions about good research and what it means to know in sport and exercise psychology. Martens drew upon other criticisms of traditional science, and other sport and exercise psychologists have extended the critical analyses (see Brustad, 2002, for more detail).

Traditional science is objective, deterministic, and reductionistic—all assumptions that have been challenged. Science assumes there is an objective truth to be discovered. It is deterministic, assuming that we can discover causes or determinants and therefore predict behavior. And it is reductionistic in that scientists are constantly trying to find underlying mechanisms to explain behavior. Critics challenge all these assumptions, arguing that truth and knowledge are subjective.

Dewar and Horn (1992), and more recently Brustad (2002), echoed many of Martens' concerns, but they extended the critical analysis with a stronger plea for contextualizing knowledge. Science is not neutral, and more to the point, sport and exercise psychology reflects the values and interpretations of the dominant culture. Dewar and Horn argued that we must interpret results in ways that are sensitive to social and political contexts in order to develop a more inclusive knowledge.

Dzewaltowski (1997) moved beyond critique to propose an alternative ecological meta-theory. First, Dzewaltowski described the existing meta-theories that guide our work:

> **Key Point**
>
> Dzewaltowski's ecological model stresses behavior and people in context, emphasizing the specific sport or exercise environment.

- **Biological-dispositional.** These approaches emphasize person characteristics or physiological mechanisms as the source of behavior and regulation. They are closely tied to traditional science methods.

- **Cognitive-behavioral.** These approaches focus on the social and physical environment as a source of behavioral regulation and also rely on natural science, but they stress cognition (thought) rather than individual characteristics.

- **Cognitive-phenomenological.** These approaches are similar to the cognitive-behavioral, but follow the Gestalt tradition to focus more on the whole than on isolated behaviors.

- **Social constructionist.** These approaches are the farthest removed from the scientific method and consider all knowledge as socially constructed and subjective.

The key to Dzewaltowski's ecological model is the focus on the environment, specifically the person in the environment. This approach focuses on the relationship between people and their environment and uses various descriptive, exploratory, and experimental methods. The environment is not static; the person transforms the environment (note that this is not the same as the view that the person constructs the environment) just as the environment transforms the person. Dzewaltowski's model stresses behavior and people in context, emphasizing the specific environment. That emphasis seems critical if we are to answer questions about sport and exercise behavior in the real world.

Application Point

The ecological model suggests that people's behaviors differ according to the context. Think about your own behavior and reactions (effort, aggression, emotional reactions, and so on) in various physical activity contexts. List some ways your behaviors and reactions might differ across the following three settings: a competitive volleyball match, recreational volleyball with friends, and a volleyball class.

Multiple Research Methods and Knowledge Sources

The scientific method fits the assumptions of traditional science, but as the paradigms and approaches to knowledge have been challenged, alternative methods have become more widespread. Most researchers, and certainly most practicing professionals, realize that multiple sources of knowledge are useful. The scientific method is strong on internal validity—we can be confident that the results are reliable, but the results may not fit the real world. Other methods may provide less reliable but more relevant knowledge. Martens (1987) cited the DK continuum (see box) to illustrate the degree of confidence we have in sources of knowledge:

DK Continuum

Damn Konfident
> Scientific method
> Systematic observation
> Single case study
> Shared public experience
> Introspection
> Intuition

Don't Know

Research methods courses and texts in psychology and kinesiology cover a range of methods along the DK continuum. Many researchers and publications focus on qualitative methodology, which includes a wide range of approaches such as ethnography and clinical case study. For example, Thomas, Nelson, and Silverman's text (2005) lists the following major types of research:

- **Analytic research**—Includes historical and philosophical research as well as integrative reviews.
- **Descriptive research**—Includes surveys, interviews, case studies, developmental research, correlational research, and epidemiological research, which are becoming increasingly popular in sport and exercise psychology.
- **Experimental research**—This is the classic scientific method with experimental manipulation and control.
- **Qualitative research**—Includes a variety of methods emphasizing narrative data and interpretive analyses rather than numerical data and statistics.

Toward a Dynamic Model of Complexity

We extend Dzewaltowki's (1997) ecological model by emphasizing the dynamic complexity of the sport and exercise environment. Some aspects of chaos and complexity models seem particularly relevant. First, complexity models are nondeterministic. We cannot specify all determinants of behavior, and we cannot predict behavior no matter how much we improve our measures. The best we can do is develop guidelines and descriptive patterns. Human behavior is far more complex than most of the phenomena that fit complexity models. We will not identify a pattern that fits all behavior or even all behavior in a very limited setting.

Not only is behavior complex, it is dynamic. Conditions constantly change, and seemingly trivial conditions can have tremendous impact later, as in the classic example of the butterfly flapping its wings to affect distant storm patterns—or when an elementary physical education teacher makes one hurried comment to a child that affects the child's activity patterns as an adult. Moreover, that one comment is part of a limitless set of comments and events. Each combination is unique, and even under identical circumstances, people interact with their circumstances in unique ways.

One response might be to give up, to assume we cannot predict anything and therefore cannot use sport and exercise psychology. That is not at all the case. Instead of trying to find elusive answers to such questions as "How do I stick to an exercise program?" or "How can I help a soccer player control emotions?", look to the literature and other sources of knowledge to find guidelines and patterns. Research and theory provide those unifying principles that practitioners can adapt according to their experience and the immediate situation and thus move toward practical theory.

Practical Theory

Practical theory is not an oxymoron. Practical theory is theory—guidelines rather than facts—that is relevant to the real world. Lewin's (1951) statement, "There is nothing so practical as a good theory," reflects this view. Practitioners must look for theories rather than facts. Facts continually change in the real world; today's fact is tomorrow's outdated practice.

Lewin's line comes from a larger statement (1951) addressed to researchers:

> *This can be accomplished . . . if the theorist does not look toward applied problems with highbrow aversion or with a fear of social problems, and if the applied psychologist realizes that there is nothing so practical as a good theory. (p. 169)*

Key Point

Because facts continually change in the real world, practitioners must look for theories rather than facts. Scholars must ask real-world questions with an eye on the person in context.

Boyer (1990) made the same point in noting that the scholarship of application is not a one-way street:

> *It would be misleading to suggest knowledge is first discovered and then applied . . . the process is far more dynamic. . . . New understandings can arise out of the very act of application—whether in medical diagnosis, serving clients, shaping public policy or working with the public schools. In activities such as these, theory and practice vitally interact, and one renews the other. (p. 23)*

Scholars must ask real-world questions with an eye on the person in context. Researchers as well as practitioners must stop searching for facts and aim for practical theory.

USING SPORT AND EXERCISE PSYCHOLOGY

Now that you understand approaches to knowledge and the key role of practical theory, we will turn to using sport and exercise psychology in professional practice. This section covers major professional roles for those who specialize in sport and exercise psychology, as well as the use of sport and exercise psychology by other kinesiology professionals.

Who Uses Sport and Exercise Psychology?

Obviously sport and exercise psychology specialists use sport and exercise psychology. Most specialists have doctoral training and may apply sport and exercise psychology in consulting with athletes or exercisers, conducting workshops for coaches or teachers, teaching future professionals in undergraduate and graduate kinesiology programs, and conducting research to contribute to the knowledge base. However, one does not need a PhD to use sport and exercise psychology. As noted in chapter 1, kinesiology professionals use sport and exercise psychology every day. Physical education teachers, exercise instructors, and sports medicine professionals all deal with people in sport and exercise settings. Understanding behavior in sport and exercise and using that knowledge to more effectively relate to people is the essence of evidence-based professional practice. Specialists have more training and likely are more familiar with the most current research. However, teachers, exercise instructors, and other kinesiology professionals have more experience and are more familiar with the specific context in which they practice. Understanding of the participants and the setting allows professionals to use practical theory more effectively.

 Application Point

Theories and guidelines based on research can help professionals, but the best professionals also use their experience and insights. As an exercise instructor with a water aerobics class, what experiences and insights about the class and participants could help you use sport and exercise psychology theories so that participants gain optimal benefits from the class?

Professional Roles in Sport and Exercise Psychology

Sport and exercise psychology specialists work in three main professional areas—research, education, and consulting. Research and teaching are the primary roles for most specialists, who typically work in colleges and universities. In the research role, specialists develop the knowledge base, as discussed in the previous section. Most specialists are heavily involved in the teaching role, teaching sport and exercise psychology courses, advising, and supervising student research. Most often, sport and exercise psychology is taught in kinesiology departments, and faculty may teach other courses, such as motor behavior or sociology of sport. Many sport and exercise psychology specialists who teach in colleges and universities also engage in consulting. In addition, some counselors and clinical psychologists extend their practice to sport and exercise psychology consultation, and a few specialists devote their entire professional practice to consulting.

Educational and Clinical Sport and Exercise Psychology

In the consulting role, the distinction between educational and clinical practice is important. Clinical practice requires extensive training in understanding and treating clinical concerns such as depression or eating disorders. Clinical psychologists have extensive graduate training and supervised experience, and they must be licensed by state boards in order to offer their services. Educational practice is just that—education. An educational sport and exercise psychology consultant might be considered a mental coach. Most often educational consultants provide psychological skills training to participants for performance enhancement or personal development.

Professional Standards in Sport and Exercise Psychology

Unlike clinical psychology, sport and exercise psychology is not a licensed specialty, and it is not immediately obvious where one could find information on qualified educational consultants. Competent sport and exercise psychology consultants will not profess to solve all problems or turn you into the next Olympic medalist. Instead, they might emphasize your responsibility and point out that psychological skills require just as much time and effort as physical skills.

Sport and exercise psychology organizations are concerned about maintaining standards and credibility amid the growing popularity of the specialty. Most notably, the AASP published certification guidelines in 1989. Members of AASP may apply for certification as consultants; see the AASP Web site for details on the certification process and criteria (www.aaasponline.org). Generally, the guidelines require graduate work in both kinesiology and psychology, as well as supervised practical experience. Certification is not a license; rather, it indicates that the person has met certain competency standards. For background information and a more thorough discussion of certification in relation to professional practice and licensing, see Zizzi, Zaichowski, and Perna (2002).

The APA, the primary professional organization for psychology, certifies clinical and counseling psychology programs, and licensing as a clinical psychologist follows APA standards. The APA also has long had ethical standards for all psychology training and professional practice. Although clinical psychology licensing is not required for educational sport and exercise psychology practice or AASP certification, the APA provides an established model that has been adopted for sport and exercise psychology training and professional practice.

Application Point
Many athletes seek professional help in developing psychological skills as well as physical skills. As a high school coach, you may have a young athlete who has the talent to move to the intercollegiate level and wants to work on the mental game. Review the resources at the AASP and APA Web sites and develop a list of guidelines that you could use to help the athlete find an appropriate sport psychology consultant. Consider the skills and credentials you would look for, as well as the services and outcomes you and the athlete would expect.

Recently the AASP adopted an ethical code, which is based on APA ethical standards, to accompany its certification guidelines. The introduction to the code begins thus:

> *AASP is dedicated to the development and professionalization of the field of sport psychology. As we establish ourselves as a profession, we must attend to both the privileges and responsibilities of a profession.*

The AASP certification guidelines represent one step toward professionalization in that they establish criteria for designating qualified individuals. The ethics code is an important step toward taking professional responsibility. Whelan, Meyers, and Elkin (2002) provide an excellent discussion of ethics in professional practice, as well as background on the events leading up to the development of the AASP ethics code. The Ethical Principles and Standards of the Association for Applied Sport Psychology includes an introduction and preamble, six general principles, and 25 standards that specify the boundaries of ethical conduct. The six general ethical principles are summarized in the following box. The AASP Web site has the ethics code, and readers might also go to the APA Web site (www.apa.org) to check the more extensive and well-established APA ethics code, most recently updated in 2003.

AASP General Ethical Principles

From the Ethical Principles and Standards of the AASP (www.aaasponline.org)

- **Principle A: Competence.** AASP members maintain the highest standards of competence in their work. They recognize the boundaries of their professional competencies and the limitations of their expertise.
- **Principle B: Integrity.** AASP members promote integrity in the science, teaching, and practice of their profession.
- **Principle C: Professional and scientific responsibility.** AASP members are responsible for safeguarding the public and AASP from members who are deficient in ethical conduct.
- **Principle D: Respect for people's rights and dignity.** AASP members accord appropriate respect to the fundamental rights, dignity, and worth of all people.
- **Principle E: Concern for others' welfare.** AASP members seek to contribute to the welfare of those with whom they interact professionally.
- **Principle F: Social responsibility.** AASP members are aware of their professional and scientific responsibilities to the community and the society in which they work and live.

The AASP certification guidelines provide a framework for identifying professional competencies, and the ethics code contains general guidelines for professional practice. These guidelines and the ethical codes were developed to meet the needs of professionals in consulting roles. However, the guidelines are applicable for all who practice sport and exercise psychology.

PUTTING IT INTO PRACTICE

Now you are ready to put the content of chapter 3 into practice. Read the chapter summary, discuss the case study, answer the review questions, and enhance your knowledge by researching the recommended readings.

Summary

Understanding the theory–research–practice triad and the key role of theory is critical to continuing progress. Sport and exercise psychology has advanced largely by using traditional science, but the scientific method has shortcomings. To advance sport and exercise psychology knowledge and provide practical theory to guide professional practice, we must continually reconsider the guiding paradigms and methods. The most promising routes to relevant, useful knowledge recognize the powerful influence of the social environment, focus on people in context, and stay mindful of the complex dynamics of sport and exercise behavior.

Both sport and exercise psychology specialists and kinesiology professionals use sport and exercise psychology. Sport and exercise psychology specialists work in research, education, and consulting roles. The APA has well-established standards for psychology practice, and clinical sport and exercise psychologists must meet APA and state licensing standards. Most sport and exercise psychology consultation follows an educational model. The AASP certification criteria and the ethics code provide guidelines for all who use sport and exercise psychology.

Case Study

As an athletic trainer, you may well want sport and exercise psychology information and strategies that you can use to help athletes with rehabilitation. But how do you find good information? As discussed in this chapter, we can be confident in information that comes from sound scientific research. So, you could search research journals or publications aimed at professionals that draw from the research. Many professional journals, newsletters, and Web sites draw from research, and professionals should look for evidence that the information is indeed based on the best available evidence.

Busy professionals cannot read all the research or check all the sport and exercise psychology resources, however. One alternative is to look for a consultant who specializes in sport and exercise psychology. An athletic trainer who seeks a consultant to offer a workshop or program will want to know the consultant's credentials and experience. For example, if you are seeking a consultant on psychological skills for injury rehabilitation, you might look for someone who has graduate training in sport and exercise psychology and who is an AASP-certified consultant. Remember that science is not the only source of useful information, and not all questions can be addressed through the scientific method. As an athletic trainer, you will often rely on advice from others, trial and error, and your experiential knowledge. However, the more you can use logic and observation to move up the DK continuum toward valid, scientific knowledge, the better.

Review Questions

1. Define *theory* and explain why it is the critical link in the theory–research–practice triad.
2. Explain what is meant by *evidence-based practice* and describe how it applies to kinesiology professionals.
3. Describe the scientific method and list its steps.
4. Explain the statement, "There is nothing so practical as a good theory."
5. Discuss the three main professional roles in sport and exercise psychology.

Recommended Reading

APA Presidential Task Force on Evidence-Based Practice. (2006). Evidence-based practice in psychology. *American Psychologist, 61,* 271-285.

   The APA policy statement is a great resource describing how competent professionals integrate research and professional expertise in professional practice.

Forscher, B.K. (1963). Chaos in the brickyard. *Science, 142,* 3590.

> Forscher's short and entertaining article is a classic must-read for any graduate student. It reads like a fable, and like most fables, it has a clear message. Using the analogy of bricks and buildings, Forscher makes the point that theory (the blueprint) is the key difference between a useful building and a pile of bricks.

Martens, R. (1987). Science, knowledge and sport psychology. *The Sport Psychologist, 1,* 29-55.

> Martens' influential article urges changes in sport and exercise psychology to make research more relevant and to connect academic work to practicing sport psychology. The issues Martens raised 20 years ago remain; rereading the article and continual reconsideration of the issues will help you understand and use sport and exercise psychology knowledge.

Whelan, J.P., Meyers, A.W., & Elkin, T.D. (2002). In J.L. Van Raalte and B.W. Brewer (Eds.), *Exploring sport and exercise psychology* (pp. 503-524). Washington, DC: APA.

> Whelan and his colleagues discuss ethics in sport and exercise psychology and the AASP ethics code and its relationship to the APA code. Anyone who intends to practice in any setting (research, teaching, consultation) must understand and follow professional ethical standards. Go to the APA (www.apa.org) and AASP (www.aaasponline.org) Web sites for more information on the ethics codes.

Zizzi, S., Zaichkowsky, L., & Perna, F. (2002). In J.L. Van Raalte and B.W. Brewer (Eds.), *Exploring sport and exercise psychology* (2nd ed., pp. 459-478). Washington, DC: APA.

> This chapter provides an overview of the AASP certification guidelines, including information on the development of the guidelines, the role of certification, and continuing issues in sport psychology practice.

Part II

The Person in Sport and Exercise Psychology

Sport and exercise psychology is about human behavior in physical activity, and we begin by focusing on the person—individual characteristics. That is, we focus on the person in the classic formula defining behavior as a function of the person and the environment (see chapter 1). Chapter 4 emphasizes enduring personality dispositions and reviews personality research and application. As the chapter reveals, general personality models and measures have been widely used, but they have not been very useful in sport and exercise psychology. Sport-specific individual characteristics and approaches combining person and environmental factors have been more useful.

Chapter 5 addresses individual differences in attention and cognition, as well as cognitive skills, such as imagery, that may be useful in sport and exercise. Chapter 6 covers self-perceptions, starting with self-concept and recent work on multidimensional, physical self-perceptions. Chapter 6 also looks at self-confidence and the extensive sport and exercise psychology work on self-efficacy.

Chapter 4

Personality

Chapter Objectives

After studying this chapter, you should be able to

◆ define *personality*,

◆ describe the major theoretical perspectives and models of personality,

◆ trace the sport and exercise psychology research on personality, and

◆ discuss the development and use of sport-specific personality and psychological skills measures.

Personality plays a big role in sport and exercise behavior, and kinesiology professionals use personality information every day. Individual differences are obvious. One third grader relishes performing on center stage during physical education whereas a classmate moves further to the back of the line; one person goes on long, solo runs whereas a neighbor socializes at the fitness center; one gymnast rises to the challenge of competition, whereas another chokes and performs far below expectations.

Such individual differences reflect personality. Not only do we recognize these differences, but we assess personality when we size up opponents, consider how different students might react to feedback, or evaluate our own strengths and weaknesses. Those personality assessments in turn affect our behavior. Consider a diver awaiting the first dive of the competition. The diver who thinks, "Yes! I'm confident and ready to hit that first dive," will probably perform differently than one who is hesitant or worried about mistakes. We also use personality judgments when interacting with others. Instructors do not make the same comments to the student they consider fragile or sensitive as to the student they view as mentally tough.

 ## *Application Point*

Professionals often evaluate personality and adjust their behavior when working with clients. As a personal trainer, list two or three ways that your clients might differ in personality. Then, describe how your behavior and interactions might differ based on those differences.

The goal of personality research in sport and exercise psychology is to provide accurate, reliable information about individual differences and the relationship of such differences to sport and exercise behaviors. This chapter first covers general personality psychology and then focuses on research and role of personality information and measures in sport and exercise psychology.

PERSONALITY DEFINED

As discussed earlier, psychology is about the person, and personality is about what it means to be a person. Friedman and Schustack (2003) define personality psychology as the study of forces that make people unique. Thus, the term *personality* denotes characteristic or consistent differences in behavior. The personality characteristic of aggressiveness is attributed to a person who consistently displays aggressive behavior (e.g., often argues, easily angers, initiates fights). We commonly think of personality as including social characteristics, such as introversion or aggressiveness, but it also includes perceptual and cognitive characteristics, such as the ability to concentrate. Personality is the overall pattern of these characteristics that make each person unique.

In describing personality, Friedman and Schustack (2003) list eight key aspects or underlying forces, ranging from unconscious forces to the interactive forces of the person and the environment. These aspects parallel the major perspectives on personality and represent the typical categories of major theories (see the following box on perspectives and related forces).

Perspectives and Related Forces

Perspective	Aspect or Forces
Psychoanalytic	Unconscious
Neoanalytic	Ego (self)
Biological	Biological
Behavioral	Conditioned by environment
Cognitive	Cognitive
Trait	Traits, skills, predispositions
Humanistic	Spiritual
Interactionist	Interaction of person and environment

Key Point

Personality is the overall pattern of psychological characteristics that make each person unique.

No doubt individual differences have been obvious as long as people have interacted, and explanations can be found as far back as there are records. Personality theories range from simple, commonsense explanations to complex, sophisticated models and vary from the purely biological to purely environmental. Traditionally, personality theories may be categorized as psychodynamic, trait, and social learning or environmental theories. As Friedman and Schustack's list shows, current personality psychology encompasses a broader range of theories. In addition, some personality psychologists go beyond traditional theoretical categories with integrative models that incorporate multiple perspectives. Trait perspectives dominate sport and exercise psychology, and more recent work takes an interactionist perspective. Before covering that work, we will consider personality perspectives, starting with early biological models.

EARLY THEORIES AND CURRENT BIOLOGICAL PERSPECTIVES

The ancient Greeks, who gave us the Hippocratic oath and early medicine, linked biology and behavior to explain individual differences. According to the Greeks, everyone had four basic body fluids or humors, and varying individual temperaments (personalities) were due to differing proportions of these humors. Blood was associated with a sanguine or cheerful temperament, yellow bile was associated with a choleric or irritable temperament, black bile was associated with a melancholic or sad temperament, and phlegm was associated with a phlegmatic or indifferent, apathetic temperament.

Today's theorists do not refer to the four body fluids, but we can find some biological influence in current personality research. Many biological explanations of individual differences have considerable credibility; however, even proponents of biological explanations do not claim a biological basis for all behaviors. Two current lines of research on biology and temperament merit discussion. First, Jerome Kagan's work on the genetic aspects of temperament, specifically shyness versus outgoingness, is widely respected and has considerable support. Similarly, Marvin Zuckerman's work on sensation seeking emphasizes biological factors and has relevance to sport and exercise behavior.

Kagan (1995) titled his book *Galen's Prophecy,* reflecting ties to Hippocrates and the later views of Galen, a second-century physician. Like Hippocrates and Galen, Kagan defines temperament as "any moderately stable, differentiating emotional or behavioral quality whose appearance in childhood is influenced by an inherited biology, including differences in brain neurochemistry" (p. xvii). Kagan has focused on the inhibited–uninhibited or shy–bold temperament and has amassed considerable evidence supporting a biological basis for this temperament. However, he also makes it clear that temperament cannot be reduced to biology but requires both biological and experiential conditions acting together over time.

Zuckerman (1994) raises similar issues in his text on sensation seeking, and he devotes a chapter to risk taking in sport. For Zuckerman, sensation seeking is part of a broader impulsive sensation–seeking trait, which represents the optimistic tendency to approach novel stimuli and explore the environment (p. 385). Sensation seeking has a high biological or genetic basis, but similar to Kagan, Zuckerman does not argue for a purely biological basis. Instead, he advocates incorporating biological and experiential factors in a psychobiological context.

Sport and exercise psychology researchers seldom take biological perspectives on personality, but some models combine biological characteristics, learning, and other individual characteristics. Dishman (1982, 1984) proposed a psychobiological model of exercise adherence that includes biological factors (such as body composition) and psychological factors (specifically, the personality characteristic of self-motivation). Research on exercise adherence has expanded greatly, as we will discuss in later chapters, and most models take a biopsychosocial perspective, incorporating social as well as biological and psychological components.

Although few personality theorists explore biological factors, most would agree with Kagan. Personality is determined by multiple, interdependent factors,

Key Point

Most personality theorists agree that personality is determined by multiple, interdependent factors, and we are not likely to identify simple biological or experiential factors.

and we are not likely to identify simple biological or experiential sources. If we look for a biological or experiential base, we can find it, but we will understand personality and behavior better if we investigate their complexities and interdependent relationships.

PSYCHOLOGY MODELS OF PERSONALITY

Much current research focuses on personality structure and identifying the dimensions that define one's personality. This work includes trait theories (personality is a collection of traits), as well as more current interactionist approaches. Before discussing these models, we'll briefly note two other traditional approaches to personality: clinically oriented psychodynamic theories and social learning theories.

Psychodynamic Theories

Clinically oriented theories, including psychoanalytic and humanistic theories, are particularly prominent in therapeutic and counseling settings. Psychoanalytic theories often stem from clinical observations, focus on psychopathology, and offer few testable predictions, especially about healthy personalities. Humanistic theories are more optimistic and posit self-change or growth. Sport and exercise psychologists who consult with clients may find the more holistic and optimistic approach useful in helping people develop healthy lifestyles, but these perspectives have little impact on research and practice.

Social Learning Theories

Social learning theories might be considered antipersonality theories in terms of traditional personality perspectives. In an often-cited critique, Mischel (1968) pointed out that even the most psychometrically sound trait measures predict only a small proportion of behavior. The aggressive soccer player does not display aggressive behavior in every situation and may even be quite nonaggressive in other settings. The inability of trait measures to predict behavior led many psychologists to renounce personality theories and adopt a social learning approach, which focuses on the situation and learned behaviors. Bandura (1977b) described a social learning perspective as follows: "Psychological functioning is explained in terms of a continuous reciprocal interaction of personal and environmental determinants" (pp. 11-12). An extreme view such as B.F. Skinner's behaviorism discounts personality altogether. According to Skinner, a soccer player exhibits aggressive behavior because the situation calls for it and because it has been reinforced in the past; any person in the same situation would display the same behavior.

Personality Traits or Dispositions

Most personality research and most common personality measures (e.g., Cattell 16PF, Minnesota Multiphasic Personality Inventory [MMPI]) are based on trait approaches. Traits are relatively stable, highly consistent attributes that exert generalized causal effects on behavior (Mischel, 1973). Trait theories imply consistency and generalizability of behavior; for instance, the person with a high level of shyness consistently displays shy behavior in varied situations, such as classes, team meetings, and activities. These theories assume that once we identify traits, we can predict behavior. Thus, many personality psychologists have worked on developing psychometrically sound personality measures.

Interactionist Approaches

Key Point

Most personality psychologists prefer an interactionist approach. However, the approach does not provide simple predictions because any behavior is the function of a seemingly limitless number of personality and environmental factors.

Today, most personality psychologists prefer an interactionist approach that considers the interrelated roles of personality factors and situational factors as co-determinants of behavior. Certain personality characteristics predict behavior in some, but not all, situations. For instance, a tennis player might consistently become anxious when facing competition but not when facing other challenges, such as academic tests or verbal presentations.

$B = f(P, E)$, the formula presented in chapter 1, is a simple representation of the interactionist approach, but the interactionist approach is not simple. Any behavior, such as aggressive behavior in ice hockey, is the function of a seemingly limitless number of personality and environmental factors. An opponent's insult may provoke an aggressive response from a player in one situation but not from another in the same situation, and perhaps not even in the same player in a slightly different situation (e.g., perhaps a lack of sleep or problems outside sport facilitated the aggressive response). The interactionist approach is more complex, but also more realistic, than the extreme trait and situational approaches. As noted in chapter 1, we should not expect simple answers to questions about human behavior.

Big Five Model of Personality

Psychologists continue to debate the structure of personality, but the literature suggests consensus. Most personality psychologists accept the Big Five model and its five major dimensions (see figure 4.1): neuroticism, extraversion, openness to experience (culture or intellect in some versions), agreeableness, and conscientiousness. Most models of personality reflect some aspects of the Big Five. Today's theorists cite Sir Francis Galton's (1883) attempts to categorize the many descriptive terms for people as one of the first dimensional models. With the advantage of statistical analyses, Cattell used factor analysis to develop his

Figure 4.1
Personality dimensions: the Big Five.

1. Neuroticism
Nervousness, anxiety, depression, anger versus emotional stability

2. Extraversion
Enthusiasm, sociability, assertiveness, high activity level versus introversion

3. Openness to experience
Originality, need for variety, curiosity, artistic sensitivity

4. Agreeableness
Amiability, altruism, modesty, trust versus egocentrism, narcissism, skepticism

5. Conscientiousness
Constraint, achievement striving, self-discipline

model and the widely used 16PF measure of 16 key personality factors. Eysenck (1991), on the other hand, argued for fewer dimensions. His early three-factor model of psychoticism, extraversion, and neuroticism served as the basis for much five-factor work. Although debate continues, the general five-factor structure is accepted, and corresponding measures have been developed. Specifically, the NEO (which originally stood for neuroticism, extraversion, and openness) Personality Inventory (NEO PI; Costa & McCrae, 1985) is widely used today.

Integrative Models

Recent perspectives on personality go beyond the Big Five model and the interactionist approaches to take a more integrative approach to understanding the person. Both Mayer and McAdams and Pals recently offered integrative models that encompass multiple perspectives. Mayer (2005) takes a systems approach:

> Personality is the organized, developing system within the individual that represents the collective action of his or her motivational, emotional, cognitive, social-planning, and other psychological subsystems. (p. 296)

Mayer incorporates cognitive, emotional, and social factors that are not typically included in personality. He contends that personality connects the biological and social on a continuum and suggests that this systems framework might unify the broader discipline of psychology.

Like Mayer, McAdams and Pals (2006) incorporate biological and social perspectives into an integrative model. They define personality in terms of five key principles that outline an integrative view of the whole person:

> Personality is conceived as (a) an individual's unique variation on the general evolutionary design for human nature, expressed as a developing pattern of (b) dispositional traits, (c) characteristic adaptation, and (d) self-defining life narratives, complexly and differentially situated (e) in culture and social context. (p. 204)

McAdams and Pals thus acknowledge basic human nature that exists in all people, but they emphasize the complex, dynamic relationships among dispositional traits (e.g., the Big Five), characteristic adaptations (e.g., goals, values, coping strategies), and integrative life narratives (i.e., stories that give life meaning, unity, and purpose), as well as the continuing influence of cultural systems and practices within the social ecology of daily life. McAdams and Pals' view is more complex, dynamic, and realistic in representing the person than the personality trait measures and perspectives that have been used most often in sport and exercise psychology.

Key Point

McAdams and Pals (2006) incorporate biological and social perspectives into an integrative model that emphasizes the complex, dynamic relationships among dispositional traits, characteristic adaptations, and integrative life narratives, as well as the continuing influence of cultural systems and practices within the social ecology of daily life.

PERSONALITY MEASURES

Personality assessment in sport and exercise psychology usually involves personality inventories, but it can also take the form of life histories, projective measures, in-depth interviews, case histories, or behavioral observations. Objective personality inventories, the most common measures, involve structured responses (e.g., multiple-choice or true–false items), are easily administered and scored, and they can be compared with norms and other samples because they are widely used. Several of the most common personality measures, such as the Cattell 16PF, MMPI, and Eysenck Personality Inventory (EPI), as well as personality measures assessing single traits, such as Spielberger's (1966) State-Trait Anxiety Inventory (STAI), have been used with sport and exercise participants.

One of the most popular personality measures, the Myers-Briggs Type Indicator (MBTI), has seldom been used in research but is commonly found in training and educational settings. The MBTI, which may be interpreted from a five-factor perspective (McCrae & Costa, 1989), reports preferences on four scales:

1. Extraversion (E)–Introversion (I)
2. Sensing (S)–Intuition (N)
3. Thinking (T)–Feeling (F)
4. Judging (J)–Perceiving (P)

With the MBTI, you can classify yourself on each dimension and determine your overall personality type. Descriptions are available in reports on various forms of the MBTI, including popular versions available in books and at Web sites. Although the MBTI is widely used, many personality psychologists express reservations. The profile descriptions reflect normal (versus clinical or pathological) samples, which certainly has advantages, but the descriptions tend to be intuitively obvious, and the dichotomous classifications encourage stereotypes and labels. The MBTI may be a useful icebreaker for discussion of interpersonal styles, but relationships to specific sport and exercise behaviors are elusive.

Taking a more positive perspective on personality, Seligman (2005) advocates assessing positive psychological characteristics and emphasizing strengths rather than focusing on problems. Seligman's Values in Action (VIA) Signature Strengths Survey parallels the *Diagnostic and Statistical Manual of Mental Disorders, Fourth Edition (DSM IV)*, which is widely used to identify psychological problems and pathologies. However, the VIA measure, which is available at Seligman's Web site (www.authentichappiness.org), assesses 24 positive strengths, including creativity, courage, intimacy, fairness, self-control, and spirituality.

PERSONALITY RESEARCH IN SPORT AND EXERCISE PSYCHOLOGY

Personality is a consistently popular topic in sport and exercise psychology. Perhaps the unique physical characteristics of athletes prompt a search for analogous psychological profiles. Most of the research involves questions such as these: Is there an athletic personality? Are runners more introverted than volleyball players? Can we predict success from personality information? Or, in reverse: How does physical activity affect personality? We might claim that sport fosters leadership, moral development, or teamwork. More recently, exercise has been promoted as an avenue to improved mental health. Claims of general personality changes have not been supported, but research on specific relationships between sport behaviors and moral development, as well as exercise effects on specific self-perceptions and emotions, is promising (such work will be discussed in later chapters).

Personality Profiles of Athletes

As part of his pioneering sport psychology work, Coleman Griffith (1926, 1928) examined the personality profiles of successful athletes. Through observations and interviews, Griffith identified the following characteristics of great athletes: ruggedness, courage, intelligence, exuberance, buoyance, emotional adjustment, optimism, conscientiousness, alertness, loyalty, and respect for authority.

Many athletes have filled out many personality inventories since Griffith's time. In reviewing the literature, Ogilvie (1968) concluded that certain traits are associated with successful athletes. With colleagues, Ogilvie developed the Athletic Motivation Inventory (AMI) to measure those traits, which include drive, determination, leadership, aggressiveness, guilt proneness, emotional control, self-confidence, conscientiousness, mental toughness, trust, and coachability (Tutko, Lyon, & Ogilvie, 1969). You may notice the similarity between the AMI list and Griffith's list. As discussed in the following section, most scholars do not find such consistency in the sport personality research.

Mental Health Model

Morgan's (1978, 1980) mental health model represents the most systematic work on personality and sport. According to the model, positive mental health is directly related to athletic success whereas psychopathology and success are inversely related. In studies with college and Olympic wrestlers, national-team rowers, and elite distance runners, Morgan demonstrated that successful athletes possessed more positive mental health characteristics and fewer negative mental health characteristics than the general population. That pattern, depicted in figure 4.2, has been termed the *iceberg profile*. On the Profile of Mood States (POMS; McNair, Lorr, & Droppleman, 1971), successful athletes typically score above the waterline (population norm) on vigor but below on the negative moods of tension, depression, anger, fatigue, and confusion.

Although Morgan's model is widely cited and the iceberg profile has been replicated with other athlete samples, cautions are in order. First, the model is general. Not every successful athlete fits the iceberg profile, and many less-than-successful athletes do match the profile. It is not surprising that psychopathology is negatively related to success in athletics; it is negatively related to success in most endeavors. Furthermore, we cannot assume that the iceberg profiles of athletes necessarily imply that positive mental health (personality) leads to success—success in sport may lead to more positive mood profiles and enhanced mental health.

Morgan's clearest results are with the POMS, a measure of moods, rather than with global personality inventories. Rowley, Landers, Kyllo, and Etnier (1995) conducted a meta-analysis of POMS research and found that although athletes tended to show the iceberg profile, the effect size was a meager 0.15, accounting for less than 1% of the variance, raising questions about the usefulness of POMS in predicting athletic success. However, an offshoot of that POMS research offers more promise. The POMS assesses mood, and mood varies over time and situations. Morgan and colleagues (e.g., Morgan, Brown, Raglin, O'Conner, & Ellickson, 1987) used POMS to track mood changes in athletes over a competitive season, and Raglin (1993) summarized that research. Generally, variations in the iceberg profile reflect overtraining: The profile of swimmers flattens in the midseason overtraining period, reflecting greater mood disturbance. The mood disturbances, which may be useful for tracking athletes, may reflect par-

Figure 4.2
POMS summaries for elite wrestlers, distance runners, and rowers.

Reprinted from W.P. Morgan and M.L. Pollock, 1977, "Psychological characterization of the elite distance runner," *Annals of the New York Academy of Sciences*, 301(1): 382-403, by permission of Blackwell Publishing Ltd.

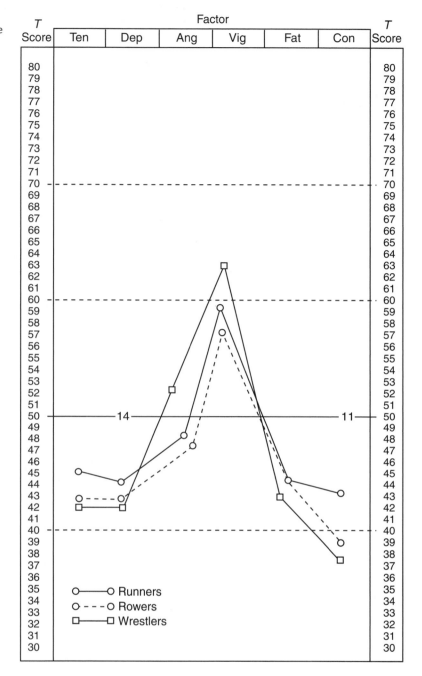

allel physiological changes, but Raglin reported that physiological monitoring of cardiovascular, metabolic, or hormonal measures has not pinpointed clear mechanisms. Indeed, many questions remain open, but the relationships of mood (personality), physiological measures and processes, and performance are certainly worthy of further research.

Application Point

Athletic trainers are in a good position to recognize overtraining. As an athletic trainer, how could you use personality information to identify overtraining and help athletes adjust training levels for optimal performance and health?

Problems With Sport Personality Research

Despite Morgan's work, most scholars see little value in global personality measures. Fisher, Ryan, and Martens (1976) concluded that global personality traits relate slightly, if at all, to sport participation or performance, and this skeptical view still holds today. The findings are as varied as the studies; studies show different traits that characterize athletes, and some findings are contradictory. For every study indicating that runners are more introverted than volleyball players, another shows no difference. Little evidence supports a general athletic personality type, a personality profile that separates elite athletes from everyone else, or specific personality profiles associated with specific activities.

With such vast quantities of sport personality research yielding such meager information, it seems that personality information cannot be of much help to participants and professionals. Although the literature tells us little, individual differences play a crucial role in human behavior in sport and exercise. Unfortunately, many studies were undertaken because they were easy to conduct rather than to answer meaningful questions.

If sport and exercise psychologists address relevant questions and do quality research, personality information can have value. First, we might remedy conceptual, methodological, and interpretive problems with the previous research.

Conceptual Problems

The major conceptual problem in sport personality research is that many studies were done without a good reason. As Ryan (1968) stated,

> The research in this area has largely been of the "shot gun" variety. By this I mean the investigators grabbed the nearest and most convenient personality test, and the closest sport group, and with little or no theoretical basis for their selection fired into the air to see what they could bring down. It isn't surprising that firing into the air at different times and at different places, and using different ammunition, should result in different findings. In fact, it would be surprising if the results weren't contradictory and somewhat contrary. (p. 71)

Without meaningful questions, research cannot provide meaningful answers.

Methodological Problems

Once researchers identify meaningful questions, they must follow sound methodology.

Too often, sport personality researchers have used inappropriate samples (such as a single basketball team to represent all basketball players) or inappropriate measures (such as the MMPI, which was designed for clinical diagnoses, to assess nonclinical athlete samples).

Interpretive Problems

Even if research is conceptually and methodologically sound, we must be cautious in interpreting findings. The most common interpretive error is overgeneralization—trying to make too much of the findings. For example, suppose someone conducted a sound study and found that intercollegiate volleyball players were more independent than the norm. Should we assume that players scoring high on independence are better volleyball players? No! First, we cannot assume that independence makes a person a better volleyball player; the data are correlational. Correlations indicate a relationship, but not necessarily a cause–effect relationship. Perhaps the experience of playing volleyball leads to higher independence scores or some other factor influences both independence scores and volleyball participation. From a practical perspective, why would a coach want high independence scores? What does high independence mean in terms of actual performance or behavior in volleyball? Are high scores on independence (or any other personality factor) likely to override the influence of coaching, strategies, training, or team norms? Professionals should ask such questions and use their professional judgment when analyzing personality information.

Elite Performance and Personality

In reviewing the work on elite performance and personality, Vanden Auweele, De Cuyper, Van Mele, and Rzewnicki (1993) noted the limited information from earlier sport personality research. For example, a meta-analysis of 25 studies on introversion and extraversion of athletes showed an overall effect size of –0.100, indicating no difference between athletes and the norm. Vanden Auweele and colleagues offered three specific directions or shifts that hold promise for personality research:

- A shift from traditional personality assessment to behavioral assessment
- A shift from interindividual to intraindividual (e.g., idiographic, case, wholistic) research
- A shift from deterministic models to probabilistic models (e.g., we cannot perfectly predict behavior because we cannot possibly identify all antecedents)

Use of Personality Measures to Screen Athletes

Key Point

Sport and exercise psychologists and all kinesiology professionals must be cautious in using and interpreting personality measures. Selection on the basis of personality measures is indefensible since reliable relationships are not established.

Unfortunately, some personality measures have been used to select participants, and one of the earliest sport personality measures, the AMI (Tutko, Lyon, and Ogilvie, 1969), is an especially notable—or notorious—example. Even if the AMI or another personality measure predicted certain behaviors, that would not justify dropping athletes. Height is related to success in volleyball; the relationship between height and volleyball success is doubtless stronger and more reliable than that between any personality trait and success. Also, the relationship has a logical basis. But even given this strong, logical relationship, most coaches would not automatically select one starter over another because of a 1-inch (2.5-centimeter) height difference. Selection on the basis of personality measures is indefensible since reliable relationships are not established. After much criticism, as well as advances in sport and exercise psychology, the AMI no longer is widely used. Sport and exercise psychologists and all kinesiology professionals must be similarly cautious about using and interpreting more current measures.

RELEVANT PERSONALITY CHARACTERISTICS AND SPORT-SPECIFIC PSYCHOLOGICAL SKILLS

More valid and useful personality measures focus on specific, relevant characteristics and psychological skills and can be used within an interactionist perspective that considers the context of physical activity. Sport and exercise psychology consultants often assess personality to provide a guide for psychological skills training for performance enhancement and personal development. Similar to researchers, consultants seldom use global personality measures, instead focusing on characteristics and sport-specific skills relevant to the particular setting.

Specific Personality Measures

Specific personality constructs and measures are more promising than the more global personality measures such as the Big Five. For example, researchers have used personality constructs and measures of perceived locus of control, optimism, perfectionism, coping style, motivational orientation, and especially anxiety to help explain sport and exercise behavior. In most cases, these personality measures have been developed within conceptual frameworks that emphasize the interaction of personality with situational factors to influence behavior. Measures include both dispositional traits (e.g., trait anxiety) and characteristic adaptations (e.g., values, coping strategies) from McAdams and Pals' (2006) personality model, and most have gone through considerable development and revision to be more useful in applied settings.

Several models and measures have proven particularly useful in health settings, and that work is often applied in sport and exercise psychology research and practice. For example, Ken Wallston and colleagues developed the Multidimensional Health Locus of Control (MHLC) scales that have been widely used in health psychology and behavioral medicine research and practice for more than 25 years. *Locus of control* refers to the degree to which you see events as behaviors within your control (internal) or controlled by others (external). Perceived internal control is linked with a number of positive health outcomes, as well as motivational models. The MHLC scales were first described by Wallston, Wallston, and DeVellis in 1978, and they are available at Ken Wallston's Web site (www.vanderbilt.edu/nursing/kwallston/mhlcscales.htm).

Similarly, optimism has been linked to health outcomes, and dispositional optimism measures, such as the Life Orientation Test (LOT; Scheier, Carver, & Bridges, 1994) and Trait Hope Scale (THS; Snyder, Harris, et al., 1991), have been widely used in health psychology and behavioral medicine. See Carver and Sheier (2005) and Snyder, Rand, and Sigmon (2005) for recent updates on the uses of that work. Perceived control and optimism are in line with the positive psychology movement, and such dispositional measures have been related to positive health behavior, resiliency, and intrinsic motivation. Sport and exercise psychologists have used these measures in their research and practice. Several have gone further to develop measures or relevant personality constructs specifically for sport and exercise settings, most notably in the area of anxiety.

Sport Competition Anxiety Test

Competition creates some anxiety in nearly everyone, and intense anxiety keeps people from performing well or enjoying themselves. Individual differences in competitive anxiety are obvious, and many consultants spend considerable time helping participants learn to control anxiety. Much of that work stems from Martens' (1977) competitive anxiety model and the Sport Competition Anxiety Test (SCAT), which set a model for sport-specific personality measures. Martens began with real-world observations and built upon existing psychological work following four guidelines:

1. *Interaction approach.* Individual differences in competitive anxiety are easy to see, and situational factors also play a role. Close, important games create more anxiety than less important contests. Even the calmest athlete becomes anxious under some conditions. To understand competitive anxiety, we must consider the person, the situation, and the ongoing interactive process.

2. *State-trait anxiety distinction.* Spielberger (1966) distinguished the relatively stable personality characteristic of trait anxiety from the immediate, changeable feelings of state anxiety. Trait anxiety is the tendency to become anxious in stressful situations (a personality disposition). State anxiety is the actual state of apprehension and tension at any given moment (an emotional response). A high trait-anxious person might see an upcoming tennis match as a threat and respond with high state anxiety, whereas another might perceive it as a challenge and remain relatively calm.

3. *General versus specific anxiety.* High trait-anxious people may not become equally anxious in all stressful situations. One person may become overly anxious in competitive sport but remain calm in academic exams. Another might never become anxious in competition but panic in social settings. Psychology researchers had demonstrated that situation-specific measures of trait anxiety predict state anxiety more accurately than more general anxiety measures. Following that line of thought, Martens proposed the personality construct of competitive trait anxiety, defined as "a tendency to perceive competitive situations as threatening and to respond to these situations with feelings of apprehension or tension" (1977, p. 23).

4. *Competition process.* The final step places competitive anxiety within the context of the competition process. The primary situational source of anxiety in competition is evaluation. We want to do well and we worry about performing poorly. But people do not worry to the same extent. Competitive trait anxiety affects our perceptions and subsequent anxiety through the cognitive appraisal process that is central to all emotion.

Martens developed the SCAT to measure the sport-specific personality disposition of competitive trait anxiety. To determine your competitive anxiety, take the SCAT (appendix A). If you score high (above the 75th percentile), you probably tend to be quite nervous and tense in competition; if you have a low score, you probably control anxiety well and seldom choke in competition. The test items are simple and straightforward, but extensive psychometric testing indicates that those items best identify high- and low-anxious competitors. Details on the development of the SCAT with reliability and validity data are published elsewhere (Martens, 1977; Martens, Vealey, & Burton, 1990). In brief, the SCAT meets all generally accepted standards for psychological tests, and considerable research demonstrates that it predicts state anxiety in sport competition.

The SCAT quickly became one of the few useful personality measures in sport and exercise psychology, and Martens' extensive research set a model that others have followed in developing sport-specific measures. The SCAT, a valuable research tool, also has practical value in identifying competitors who might benefit from training in anxiety management. Still, the SCAT remains a personality measure that should not be used without considering the situation and interactive processes.

Key Point

Although the SCAT meets all generally accepted standards for psychological tests, and considerable research demonstrates that it predicts state anxiety in sport competition, it remains a personality measure that should not be used without considering the situation and interactive processes.

Sport Anxiety Scale

Research on competitive anxiety has progressed since Martens developed the SCAT, and multidimensional models dominate research today. Smith, Smoll, and Schutz (1990) used the multidimensional anxiety model to develop a sport-specific measure of cognitive and somatic trait anxiety, the Sport Anxiety Scale (SAS). The SAS includes two cognitive anxiety scales—worry and concentration disruption—as well as a somatic anxiety scale. In addition to providing good psychometric evidence for the SAS, Smith et al. (1990) reported that the concentration disruption scale was negatively related to college football players' performance. That finding suggests that multidimensional approaches may provide insights into the anxiety–performance relationship. The expanding literature that follows a multidimensional approach, discussed in later chapters on emotion, confirms the suggestion.

Application Point

Both the SCAT and SAS are sport-specific personality measures developed through considerable research. If you were a coach or consultant working with athletes in an Olympic development program, would you use the SCAT or SAS to select athletes for a final team, identify athletes who might benefit from anxiety management training, or tailor your instructions and training sessions? Why or why not?

More Sport-Specific Personality Measures

Many other sport and exercise psychology researchers have developed sport-specific measures for use in research and practice. Several measures have been developed that relate to motivational orientation. Dishman and Ickes (1981) developed the Self-Motivation Inventory (SMI) that addresses exercise motivation and adherence from a biopsychosocial perspective. Recently a version of the SMI was developed for children and shown to be related to physical activity behavior among adolescent girls (Motl, Dishman, Felton, & Pate, 2003). We will cover other motivational orientation measures used within social-cognitive and developmental models in the chapters on motivation.

Perfectionism has been of interest for some time, and the leading psychology researchers have extended their research to sport and exercise settings. Flett and Hewitt (2005), who developed one of the most widely used measures of perfectionism, the Multidimensional Perfectionism Scale (MPS; Hewitt & Flett, 1991), reviewed the literature on perfectionism in sport and exercise. They concluded that perfectionism is a maladaptive factor in sport and exercise that often undermines performance and fosters dissatisfaction. Although some scales and models refer to adaptive perfectionism, and it seems that striving for perfection could be beneficial in sport, there is no evidence to support any benefits. However, the relationship between perfectionism and maladaptive outcomes may be mediated by several factors. The recent development of sport-specific perfectionism measures (Araki, 2004; Dunn, Causgove Dunn, & Syrotuik, 2002) may help advance our understanding of perfectionism and its role in sport and exercise.

Sport-Specific Psychological Skills Measures

In one of the first attempts to assess the psychological skills of elite athletes, psychologist Michael Mahoney and collaborator Marshall Avener used interviews, surveys, and observations at the tryouts for the 1976 U.S. Olympic gymnastics team. Their study (1977) on Olympic qualifiers and nonqualifiers showed that qualifiers were more self-confident, were more likely to think and dream about gymnastics, were more likely to use self-talk and internal mental imagery, and were able to control worry and concentrate on the task at the time of performance.

Others replicated many of these findings, especially the higher confidence of more successful athletes (Gould, Weiss, & Weinberg, 1981; Highlen & Bennett, 1979; Meyers, Cooke, Cullen, & Liles, 1979); and, as chapter 11 will relate, the ability to control anxiety seems to characterize successful performers. The work did not establish a personality profile for elite athletes; nevertheless, the initial findings encouraged similar investigations and set a direction for sport personality research.

Mahoney and colleagues continued their investigations of psychological skills and used the results to develop the Psychological Skills Inventory for Sports (PSIS; Mahoney, Gabriel, & Perkins, 1987). The PSIS parallels the skills identified in earlier work, with subscales for concentration, anxiety control, confidence, mental preparation, motivation, and team emphasis. Mahoney et al. (1987) assessed several groups of elite (national and international teams), pre-elite (junior national teams), and non-elite (intercollegiate teams) athletes, and also asked several sport psychologists to describe the ideal athlete on the PSIS measure. As expected, elite athletes reported stronger psychological skills than did the pre-elite and non-elite athletes, providing some validity evidence for the PSIS. Specifically, elite athletes

- experienced fewer problems with anxiety,
- were more successful at deploying their concentration,
- were more self-confident,
- relied more on internally referenced and kinesthetic mental preparation,
- were more focused on their own performance than that of the team, and
- were more highly motivated to do well in their sport.

Still, the elite athletes' self-reports were not quite up to the profiles provided by the sport psychologists; the ideal athlete was more confident, motivated, and team focused; had fewer anxiety and concentration problems; and used more internal mental preparation. The results suggest that even elite athletes have varying psychological strengths and can benefit from continued mental training.

Although the PSIS and initial comparisons among athletes provide information, caution is in order. The sample presented several confounds (e.g., elite athletes were older, different activities were represented at the three levels), and Mahoney and colleagues cautioned readers not to draw solid conclusions from preliminary results with measures lacking psychometric testing. Subsequent work by Chartrand, Jowdy, and Danish (1992) revealed problems with the PSIS and confirmed these cautions.

More recent measures of psychological skills for sport fare better. Smith, Schutz, Smoll, and Ptacek (1995) developed and validated a multidimensional measure of sport-specific psychological skills, the Athletic Coping Skills Inventory-28 (ACSI-28), as part of a project on coping with athletic injury. The ACSI-28 assesses psychological skills similar to those assessed with the PSIS, but it has superior psychometric properties. The refined 28-item ACSI contains seven subscales:

- Coping with adversity
- Peaking under pressure

- Goal setting and mental preparation
- Concentration
- Freedom from worry
- Confidence and achievement motivation
- Coachability

Smith and colleagues (1995) demonstrated the factorial validity of the seven ACSI-28 subscales, which can be summed to yield a score for personal coping resources. They also provided evidence for validity of the ACSI-28 in measuring personal coping resources as a multifaceted construct with seven facets of underlying coping skills.

Thomas, Murphy, and Hardy (1999) developed the Test of Performance Strategies (TOPS), which, similar to the ACSI-28, is a self-report measure of psychological skills and strategies used by athletes. Thomas et al. provided evidence supporting the reliability and validity of eight subscales each for practice and competition. The subscales are similar, reflecting common underlying skills, but in competition negative thinking replaced attention control as a factor, with attention control linked to emotional control. As Thomas and colleagues noted, this reflects the reality that concentration is difficult without emotional control. The TOPS subscales are as follows:

- Goal setting
- Relaxation
- Activation
- Imagery
- Self-talk
- Emotional control
- Automaticity
- Attention control (practice) and negative thinking (competition)

Key Point

Performance profiling, which involves people identifying and rating themselves on relevant psychological skills, is one way to engage athletes in the process of psychological skill development.

Performance profiling (Butler & Hardy, 1992) is a technique that can help athletes identify and assess psychological skills, such as those measured with the ACSI-28 or TOPS. Rather than complete an inventory, an athlete or a team, perhaps with the guidance of a consultant, first identifies relevant psychological skills and characteristics (physical skills could also be identified). Those skills are used as labels for segments on a circle (as in the example in figure 4.3). Athletes then rate themselves on each skill by darkening segments to create a profile or visual representation of their strengths and potential areas for improvement. Performance profiling is one way to engage athletes in the process of psychological skill development while also connecting the person and the situation in their physical activity context.

Sport psychology consultants continue to work on assessment, and many use the ACSI-28, TOPS, or alternative measures in applied work. Some personality comparisons have been confirmed in other research. Self-confidence, in particular, clearly relates to success in athletics and to successful performance of many sport and exercise behaviors. We will explore self-confidence in greater detail in chapter 6. Similarly, concentration, anxiety control, and mental preparation (e.g., imagery, goal setting) are consistently identified as

Figure 4.3
Performance profiling can help athletes
identify and assess psychological skills.

Adapted, by permission, from P. Butler and L.
Hardy, 1992, "The performance profile: Theory
and application," *The Sport Psychologist* 6(3):
257.

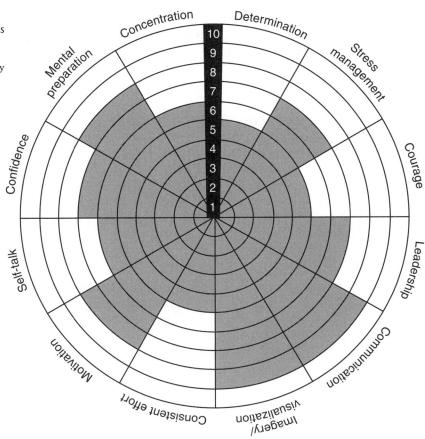

important psychological skills for sport and exercise participants. When we
cover those topics in later chapters, we will highlight the critical role of individual differences.

PUTTING IT INTO PRACTICE

Now you are ready to put the content of chapter 4 into practice. Read the chapter
summary, discuss the case study, answer the review questions, and enhance
your knowledge by researching the recommended readings.

Summary

Personality is the overall pattern of psychological characteristics that make
each person unique. Individual differences are obvious in physical activity
settings, and personality plays a key role in nearly all sport and exercise
behaviors. The vast research on personality, conducted throughout the
history of sport and exercise psychology, has yielded little useful information;
global personality measures are poor predictors of specific sport and exercise
behaviors. This summary has changed little since the 1986 edition of this
text. However, sport and exercise psychology has advanced greatly in the
understanding of individual differences. Those advances involve more specific
characteristics and psychological skills, sport-specific measures, and more

clearly delineated relationships among individual differences, situational factors, and specific behaviors. We will continue to look at many of these insights in later chapters.

Case Study

You are coach of the high school boys' basketball team. Your colleague, the coach of the girls' team, picked up information at a recent coaches' meeting on a new personality measure—the Basketball Personality Scale (BPS)—that is purported to assess characteristics matching those of top professional players. She is considering using the BPS with her team this season and asks for your advice. What do you say? Think about the information in the chapter, reread sections, and use your judgment in forming advice to give to your colleague.

D.G.'s advice: Do not use the BPS. But, do consider the personalities on your team, and try to get more information on each player's psychological skills and characteristics. First, though, what psychological skills are important? Do all players need the same skills? How might different individual characteristics fit together? As a coach, how can you help develop the strengths of different players? (I advise emphasizing strength building more than working on problems—the positive approach.)

After you have given some thought to the relevant psychological skills, consider whether a measure such as the ACSI-28 or TOPS would be helpful. Most likely such measures would be of little help with a high school team and might even create problems. You already know a lot about your players' psychological skills from observing their reactions in games and practices. You might consider using a performance profiling technique or having players do self-evaluations. If you do, encourage them to think about skills they believe are important, strengths they can bring to the team, and skills they would like to develop further. Then, after getting more personality information, be sure you have a plan to use it. You might plan some practice time for developing skills such as anxiety management or concentration for helping players work on skills that are important for them.

Please note that my advice changes with the participants and the situation—so should yours.

Review Questions

1. What is personality?
2. Describe the Big Five model of personality and list the dimensions.
3. Describe Morgan's mental health model, as well as related sport and exercise psychology research.
4. Discuss the advantages of sport-specific personality and psychological skills measures for research and practice, using the SCAT as an example.
5. Describe performance profiling and discuss its use with sport and exercise participants.

Recommended Reading

McAdams, D.P., & Pals, J.L. (2006). A new Big Five: Fundamental principles for an integrative science of personality. *American Psychologist, 61*, 204-217.

McAdams and Pals' article gives an overview of their model, which goes beyond traditional personality perspectives to provide a comprehensive framework for understanding the whole person.

Rowley, A.J., Landers, D., Kyllo, L.B., & Etnier, J.L. (1995). Does the iceberg profile discriminate between successful and less successful athletes? A meta-analysis. *Journal of Sport & Exercise Psychology, 17* (2), 185-199.

Morgan's description of the iceberg profile, which suggests that highly successful athletes score high on positive mental health characteristics and low on negative moods, prompted considerable research. Rowley and colleagues conducted a meta-analysis of that work and concluded that there is little support for the model.

Smith, R.E., Schutz, R.W, Smoll, F.L., & Ptacek, J.T. (1995). Development and validation of a multidimensional measure of sport-specific psychological skills: The Athletic Coping Skills Inventory-28. *Journal of Sport & Exercise Psychology, 17,* 379-398.

Those who work directly with athletes find sport-specific measures much more helpful than global personality measures. Smith and colleagues have developed one of the stronger measures of sport-specific skills, the ACSI-28.

Chapter 5

Attention and Cognitive Skills

Chapter Objectives

After studying this chapter, you should be able to

◆ define *attention* and describe individual differences in attentional style,

◆ discuss sport and exercise psychology research on attention and expertise,

◆ identify guidelines for effective goal setting in sport and exercise,

◆ describe several attentional control and concentration techniques, and

◆ explain the use of imagery in psychological skills training.

Attention and cognitive skills are prominent in sport and exercise psychology research and practice. Most kinesiology professionals and sport psychology consultants devote considerable time to cognitive skills and strategies. You often hear professionals saying "Concentrate" and "Focus" in fitness clubs and physical education classes. Coaches tell 10-year-olds, "Keep your eye on the ball," and Olympic divers use imagery to mentally perform the dive while standing on the platform. However, individual differences in attention and cognitive skills are obvious. Some 10-year-olds are better than others at keeping their eye on the ball. Diver Greg Louganis reported that imagery helped him perform, but other athletes find imagery to be more trouble than help. Sport and exercise psychology research includes such individual differences as well as situational factors and development of cognitive skills.

Cognitive skills, such as the ability to focus, have clear implications for performance and behavior. To date, interest in and use of cognitive skills have outpaced the related research, but research is beginning to address many questions about the role of attention and cognition in sport and exercise behavior.

ATTENTION MODELS AND MEASURES

As Abernethy (2001) notes, interest in attention is at least as old as experimental psychology itself. In *The Principles of Psychology*, William James (1890) described attention as follows:

Key Point

Attention is "taking possession by the mind, in clear and vivid form, of one out of what seems several simultaneously possible objects or trains of thought" (James, 1890, pp. 403-404).

> *Everyone knows what attention is. It is taking possession by the mind, in clear and vivid form, of one out of what seems several simultaneously possible objects or trains of thought. Focalization, concentration or consciousness are its essence. It implies withdrawal from some things in order to deal effectively with others. (pp. 403-404)*

We still understand attention much as James described it, but today's cognitive psychologists have more to say about attention, learning, and memory for motor skills.

Nideffer's Attentional Model

Attentional style came to the attention of sport and exercise psychology largely through the work of Robert Nideffer (1976a), who proposed a two-dimensional model of attention (see figure 5.1). Width ranges from narrow to broad, focusing on a limited or wide range of cues. Direction may be internal, focused on one's own thoughts and feelings, or it may be external, focused on objects and events outside the body.

Figure 5.1
Nideffer's model of attentional focus.
Adapted from R. Nideffer, 1976, *The inner athlete* (New York, NY: Crowell), 49.

Nideffer posited that using the appropriate attentional focus can enhance performance. A broad-internal focus is an analytical style useful for planning strategies or analyzing previous performances; coaches and teachers often need a broad-internal style. Many activities, especially highly interactive team sports and games, call for a broad-external attentional style, which involves taking in a great deal of information. A quarterback trying to pick out secondary receivers or a child trying to keep track of everyone in a game could use a broad-external focus. A narrow-external focus is useful for activities requiring concentration on a ball or target, such as bowling, archery, and golf. A narrow-internal focus is appropriate for mentally rehearsing a task, and focusing internally may be helpful for distance running or weightlifting.

Although all attentional focuses are useful, problems arise when people rely too heavily on one style or use a style inappropriately. Most activities require shifting of attention. For example, a soccer goalie might use a broad-external focus in preparing for a shot, shift to a narrow-external focus to make the save, and use some broad-internal analysis to set up the shift to the offense.

Measuring Attentional Style

Attentional style and the ability to use varying styles effectively are part of personality. Nideffer (1976b) developed the Test of Attentional and Interpersonal Style (TAIS) in order to assess individual tendencies to direct broad and narrow attention to internal and external information. The specific attentional subscales of the TAIS, along with sample items, are listed in figure 5.2. Nideffer provided preliminary information on the reliability and validity of the TAIS, and some initial work suggested that attentional styles relate to performance and behavior. However, continued research challenges the value of the TAIS.

Van Schoyck and Grasha (1981) reasoned that a sport-specific measure might be more valid than the general TAIS and thus developed a tennis-specific version (T-TAIS). The T-TAIS was more reliable, and more importantly, more consistently related to tennis ability and match scores compared with the TAIS. Dewey, Brawley, and Allard (1989) reported that TAIS subscores did not relate

Figure 5.2

TAIS attentional subscale definitions and sample items.

Adapted from R. Nideffer, 1976, *The inner athlete* (New York, NY: Crowell), 116-118.

BET (Broad-External)

The higher the score, the more the answers indicate that the person deals effectively with a large number of external stimuli. The person has an effective broad-external focus.

- In a room filled with children or on a playing field, I know what everyone is doing.

OET (External Overload)

The higher the score, the more the person makes mistakes because of external overload and distraction and has difficulty narrowing attention when needed.

- When people talk to me, I find myself distracted by the sights and sounds around me.

BIT (Broad-Internal)

The higher the score, the more the person is able to think about several things at once and has a broad-internal focus.

- It is easy for me to bring together ideas from a number of different areas.

OIT (Internal Overload)

The higher the score, the more the person makes mistakes because of thinking about too many things at once.

- I have so many things on my mind that I become confused and forgetful.

NAR (Narrow Effective Focus)

High scorers are able to narrow attention effectively when the situation calls for it.

- It is easy for me to keep sights and sounds from interfering with my thoughts.

RED (Errors of Underinclusion)

High scorers have chronically narrowed attention. They make mistakes because they cannot broaden attention when necessary.

- In games I make mistakes because I am watching what one person does and I forget about the others.

to behavioral tests of attention as expected, casting further doubt on the validity of the measure.

These studies not only demonstrated the superiority of sport-specific measures but also raised questions about Nideffer's model. Van Schoyck and Grasha (1981) supported the width (narrow–broad) but not the direction (internal–external) dimension. Instead, they described a bandwidth dimension with two components, scanning and focusing. Landers (1981) concluded that the TAIS does not differentiate attentional direction, is a poor predictor of performance, and has limited value in sport.

Association, Dissociation, and Performance

One of the most widely cited works on attentional style and performance is Morgan and Pollock's (1977) study of marathon runners. Many runners use a dissociative style, which means they focus on external objects or thoughts, perhaps replaying the day's events or playing songs in their minds—they focus on anything other than running and internal sensations. Surprisingly, elite marathoners did not use dissociation but instead reported using an associative strategy. They focused on their breathing, paid attention to the feelings in their leg muscles, adopted an internal focus, and monitored their bodily sensations.

Morgan and Pollock's observations were widely cited to support the claim that an associative or narrow-internal focus is desirable for endurance events. However, Morgan and Pollock did not claim that association is advantageous for all runners at all times, and other evidence argues against such a blanket conclusion. In our study (Gill & Strom, 1985), female athletes performed an endurance task for as many repetitions as possible using either a narrow-internal focus on feelings in their legs or a narrow-external focus on a collage of pictures. Not only did the external focus lead to more repetitions, but nearly all participants preferred that style. Our study is not unique; Morgan's own research (Morgan, 1981; Morgan, Horstman, Cymerman, & Stokes, 1983) revealed that dissociation resulted in superior performance on a treadmill task, and that even elite marathoners sometimes use dissociation while running. Dissociation may reduce perceptions of pain or fatigue and help a performer keep going, as in jogging or training tasks. However, elite runners usually have goals (time or place) beyond simply maintaining performance. The runners in Morgan and Pollock's study apparently monitored bodily sensations to pace themselves and achieve performance goals.

Schomer (1987) had runners use two-way radios to report attentional focus during their runs. Content analysis confirmed that runners used both association and dissociation, with considerable variation during the run. Silva and Applebaum (1989) reported similar results based on retrospective reports of Olympic trial marathoners. Smith, Gill, Crews, Hopewell, and Morgan (1995) found that the most economical distance runners reported less use of dissociation and more use of relaxation than the least economical runners, but they did not differ in use of association. The results suggest that although relaxation strategies may benefit runners, association per se is not the source of the benefits. Continuing investigations may help us understand how varying individual attentional styles interact with situational factors to influence attentional processes and performance, as well as how attentional styles are developed through instructions, training, or experiences.

RESEARCH ON ATTENTIONAL PROCESSES

Boutcher (2002) categorized the literature on attention and performance into three perspectives—information processing, social psychological, and psychophysiological, but advocated a synthesis of the three perspectives for research and practice. As Boutcher noted, most of the limited research on attention in sport has been done by motor-behavior researchers taking the information-processing perspective and focusing on attentional selectivity, capacity, and alertness, as outlined here.

- **Attentional selectivity** is the ability to selectively attend to certain cues, events, or thoughts while disregarding others. James recognized the importance of selective attention, and the ability to selectively attend to cues, events, or thoughts while disregarding others is a key skill in sport and exercise.

- **Attentional capacity** refers to limits in the amount of information that a person can process at one time. We can't look at two things or think two thoughts at exactly the same time. Cognitive psychology theories differ on mechanisms and explanations, but all point to limited capacity. For example, listening for both the starter's gun and a coach's command could strain capacity and interfere with performance.

- **Attentional alertness** refers to the influence of arousal on information processing and attention.

The three attentional processes are interrelated—because of attentional capacity, attention must be selective, and arousal or alertness affects processing. Landers (1980) applied Easterbrook's (1959) cue utilization model to explain that as arousal increases, some attentional narrowing enhances performance, but further arousal increases and narrowing impair performance because important cues are lost.

Control and Automatic Processing

> ### Key Point
>
> Control processing is deliberate, slow, and effortful. Automatic processing, which typically occurs with well-learned skills, is fast, effortless, and not under conscious control. Although control processing requires great attention, effort, and awareness, automatic processing does not and thus is not so limited by attentional capacity.

The distinction between control and automatic processing is particularly relevant. Control processing, or conscious thought (as when a golfer decides which club to use), is deliberate, slow, and effortful. Automatic processing, which typically occurs with well-learned skills, is fast, effortless, and not under conscious control. Although control processing requires great attention, effort, and awareness, automatic processing does not and thus is not so limited by attentional capacity. Skilled performers do complex tasks that would be impossible if they had to consciously process all information. Control processing eventually gives way to automatic processing and effortless skilled performance. Professionals working with people who are learning and practicing skills must consider the implications of capacity limits to advance to more automatic skilled performance.

As Coleman Griffith observed in his interview with football star Red Grange (see chapter 2), elite athletes often make skilled moves without thinking. More recently, Beilock and colleagues (Beilock & Carr, 2001; Beilock, Wierenga, & Carr, 2003) referred to *expertise-induced amnesia* to describe experts' tendency to remember less detail of a specific performance (episodic memory) due to automated processing. As Beilock and Carr (2001) confirmed, events that make the experts think about what they're doing disrupt automatic processing and impair performance, which is one explanation for choking under pressure. Beilock and colleagues are continuing to investigate the role of cognitive processes in sport and motor performance and have extended the work in many directions. For example, the same cognitive processes that underlie choking under pressure may partially explain stereotype threat effects—when capable members of minority groups do not perform up to their capabilities (see chapter 16 for more information on stereotype threat).

Dijksterhuis and Nordgren (2006) suggest that unconscious thought uses information (as opposed to no thought), but in a less structured way than conscious thought. They argue that unconscious thought can be more effective in more complex decisions, and that a gut-feeling decision is often superior to more structured conscious thought when it is impossible to consciously consider all information. Although they refer to decisions rather than motor performance, their reasoning parallels the control–automatic processing reference. It is not possible to consciously attend to or control all aspects of skilled performance, and automatic (unconscious) processing is more effective.

Boutcher (2002) advocates a multilevel model in which enduring dispositions, demands of the activity, and environmental factors determine initial arousal. During performance, arousal may be channeled into control or automatic processing to reach optimal attention. The model is complex, with feedback loops and multiple interconnections; practical implications are not obvious, and few aspects of the model have been tested. Still, Boutcher's framework, which considers the individual, environment, and behavior in continual, dynamic interaction, reflects the general approach to sport and exercise behavior described in part I. Most sport and exercise psychology research focuses on individual differences in attentional style, but a few scholars are incorporating cognitive psychology and psychophysiological approaches.

Psychophysiological Approaches

Some researchers have taken a psychophysiological perspective to explore attention and performance. Hatfield, Landers, and Ray (1984) assessed right- and left-brain electroencephalogram (EEG) activity of elite rifle shooters and found systematic patterns suggesting that these performers reduced unnecessary conscious mental activity of the left hemisphere at the time of the shot. Landers, Christina, Hatfield, Doyle, and Daniels (1980) found heart rate deceleration in elite shooters just before the shot, and subsequent studies showed similar deceleration on a golf putting task (Boutcher & Zinsser, 1990; Crews & Landers, 1991).

Janelle and Hillman (2003) and Hatfield and Hillman (2001) reviewed the increasingly sophisticated research on the psychology of expertise from a psychophysiological perspective. Research continues to advance our understanding of brain–behavior links. Psychophysiological perspectives are particularly prominent in emotion (see chapter 12), and Janelle and colleagues have linked that work with attention (Janelle, 2002; Janelle, Singer, & Williams, 1999).

ATTENTION AND EXPERTISE

Operating from an information-processing perspective and using a paradigm that originated with studies of chess experts (Chase & Simon, 1973), several sport and exercise psychology and motor-behavior scholars have examined individual differences and cognitive processes in sport expertise and motor performance. For example, in one of the early studies, Allard, Graham, and Paarsalu (1980) found that basketball players were better than nonplayers at remembering slides from structured (basketball) situations but not unstructured situations, confirming Chase and Simon's findings that experts have better recall accuracy for specific game situations. Subsequent studies revealed similar perceptual and cognitive superiority for experts in field hockey, volleyball, and many other sports, as well as in nonsport activities.

Studies using occlusion techniques with varied sport tasks (Abernethy, 2001; Abernethy & Russell, 1987) indicate that advance cues (e.g., racket position) can help predict ball flight, that experts are better at picking up this advance information, and that differences relate to selective attention. McPherson has taken a different approach from the visual information-processing protocols and used verbal protocols to examine the role of knowledge and tactical decision making. McPherson's research with tennis players (McPherson, 2000; McPherson & Kernodle, 2003) indicates that experts have a greater declarative (knowing what to do) and procedural (doing it) knowledge base, and they have action-plan profiles in memory to match current conditions, allowing them to make superior tactical decisions.

Janet Starkes and Anders Ericsson, who have each done much research on attention and expertise, have compiled an excellent text with chapters by many leading researchers (Starkes & Ericsson, 2003). Overall, that research confirms differences between experts and nonexperts, with experts demonstrating superior attentional skills and using more automatic processing. Abernethy (2001) and Starkes, Helsen, and Jack (2001) provide more detail in their reviews of that research.

Quiet Eye

Joan Vickers of the University of Calgary has been conducting research related to attention and cognition in kinesiology for several years, and her work on the so-called quiet eye is particularly relevant. As discussed in her recent book (Vickers, 2007), the quiet eye has four characteristics: It is directed to a critical location or object in the performance space, its onset occurs before the final movement common to all performers of the skill, its duration tends to be longer for elite performers, and it is stable, confirming the need for an optimal focus before the final execution of the skill.

Vickers uses sophisticated eye-tracking technology in her research to monitor gaze and visual attention. She first identified the quiet eye with basketball free-throw shooters (Vickers, 1996), and since then the quiet eye has been found in expert performers in several sports by several researchers. For a real-world sport example, read Vickers' January 2004 *Golf Digest* article, where she refers to lab research demonstrating that the quiet eye differentiates good and poor putters. Good putters fixate on the back of the ball where the putter will contact it. They use rapid shifts of gaze to connect the contact point to the spot on the golf hole and then maintain that quiet-eye fixation for 2 or 3 seconds. Poorer putters are unable to maintain the quiet eye and have a more erratic gaze.

At her Web site (www.kin.ucalgary.ca/nml), Vickers states that the processing of quiet-eye information and the ability to self-regulate cognitive and emotional activity are key to the successful execution of motor skills, not only in sport but also in everyday skills like locomotion and in disorders such as attention-deficit/hyperactivity disorder (ADHD). Furthermore, stress interferes with normal attention and has negative effects on quiet eye and performance.

Development of Expertise

As well as examining differences between experts and nonexperts, recent research has focused on the development of expertise. Several studies suggest that expertise and related cognitive skills are developed and that training may help. As Starkes and Ericsson (2003) and others report, consistent research indicates that expertise is developed over 10 years or 10,000 hours of deliberate practice. That is, experts engage in deliberate practice of increasing challenge and activities that improve performance. Other research suggests that with training, novices can become more like experts. Perceptual training is used successfully with many skilled professionals, such as pilots and surgeons, and some have tested similar programs with sport performers. Williams, Ward, and Chapman (2003) found that novice field-hockey goalkeepers who received perceptual training improved their decision time over those who did not receive such training.

> **Key Point**
>
> Research indicates that expertise is developed over 10 years or 10,000 hours of deliberate practice with increasing challenge to improve performance. Other research suggests that with training, novices can become more like experts.

Chambers and Vickers (2006) applied Vickers' decision-training model to investigate the role of coaches' feedback and questioning on swimmers' times and technique. Decision training involves training perceptual and cognitive abilities and emphasizes bandwidth feedback. That is, rather than receiving precise feedback on every trial, performers receive feedback only when performance is outside a larger bandwidth. Bandwidth feedback is effective, particularly in transfer and retention. Based on related research, the combination of bandwidth feedback and questioning by instructors should promote active learning, problem solving, performance awareness, confidence, and control. Chambers and Vickers indeed found greater gains in technique and more improved times during transfer, suggesting that bandwidth feedback and questioning have positive effects on performance, coach–athlete relationships, and overall development.

Development and training bring up questions related to youth sport and early specialization. Cote and colleagues' developmental perspective on expertise is particularly relevant (Cote, Baker, & Abernethy, 2003; Soberlak & Cote, 2003). They confirm that deliberate practice is important in the development of expertise, but they caution against overly early specialization and structured practice. Their research indicates that experts spend more time in deliberate play from ages 6 to 14, but they emphasize multiple activities and do not shift the majority of time to deliberate practice until later. Cote et al. (2003) conclude:

> *Early sport diversification, high amounts of deliberate play, child-centered coaches and parents, and being around peers who are involved in sport all appear to be essential characteristics of environments for young children that encourage their later investment in deliberate practice. (p. 110)*

 Application Point

Research indicates that deliberate practice is important, and many people believe that early specialization in a sport is necessary to develop expertise. Considering the research on youth development and sport expertise, how would you advise youth sport coaches and parents who want to start young children on the path to becoming sport experts?

IMAGERY MODELS AND MEASURES

Individual differences are prominent in the work on attentional styles, but they have received less attention in relation to imagery. Instead, sport and exercise psychology focuses on the use of imagery techniques for performance enhancement.

Individual Differences in Imagery Ability

As early as 1883, Sir Francis Galton discussed imagery extensively and reported that he had given a questionnaire on imaging ability to a diverse sample. Many books on imagery have been written, and the *Journal of Mental Imagery* has been published for some time. Individual differences in imagery abilities and the role of such differences in imagery processes are prominent in the cognitive psychology literature.

Individual differences in imagery can be assessed with many measures (Sheehan, Ashton, & White, 1983), including objective, performance-based assessments, but most measures are self-report questionnaires. Many measures are multidimensional, recognizing that people have several imagery abilities. For instance, a person might be adept at picking out specific aspects of an image (e.g., seeing the position of a bat during a swing) but may develop grainy images rather than sharp, detailed images.

Craig Hall has done some of the most extensive sport and exercise psychology research on imagery. Hall and colleagues (Hall, Pongrac, & Buckolz, 1985) developed the Movement Imagery Questionnaire (MIQ) and later the Imagery Use Questionnaire (IUQ) (Hall, Rodgers, & Barr, 1990) to assess athletes' use of imagery. More recently, Hall and colleagues developed the Sport Imagery Questionnaire (SIQ; Hall, Mack, Paivio, & Hausenblas, 1998), which measures five types of imagery:

- Motivational specific (relates to specific goals and motivation)
- Motivational general-mastery (relates to coping and mastery of challenges)
- Motivational general-arousal (relates to emotional focus and control of anxiety or confidence)
- Cognitive specific (relates to the common use of imagery to develop and maintain skills)
- Cognitive general (relates to cognitive plans and strategies)

Hausenblas, Hall, Rodgers, and Munroe (1999) extended the SIQ model to exercisers and developed the Exercise Imagery Questionnaire (EIQ) with similar types and uses. They found that, similar to athletes, exercisers used imagery for both motivational and cognitive purposes. The EIQ structure is somewhat different from the SIQ and has three factors (energy, appearance, and technique).

Other than the SIQ and related EIQ, sport and exercise psychologists have few measures of individual differences in imagery, but many consultants use some form of imagery assessment. For example, Vealey and Greenleaf (2006) present a sport imagery evaluation that may be useful for self-assessment or for consultants working with athletes.

Sport and Exercise Psychology Research: Mental Practice Model

Much of the support for imagery use comes from early work comparing mental practice with physical practice. Feltz and Landers (1983) have provided the most thorough review of the literature on mental practice. Using meta-analysis, they reached several conclusions:

- Mental practice effects are primarily associated with cognitive-symbolic rather than motor elements of the task. Mental practice is especially useful for tasks involving movement sequences, timing, or cognitive problem solving.

- Mental practice effects are not limited to early learning; they are found in both early and later stages of learning and may be task specific. Imagery may be useful both in early learning and with more familiar tasks but may operate differently at various stages of learning.

- It is doubtful that mental practice effects are produced by low-gain innervation of muscles to be used during actual performance. Although Suinn (1983) and others report muscle activity during imagery, Feltz and Landers found no evidence for the claim that low-gain neuromuscular activity accounts for mental rehearsal effects. Instead, imagery appears to elicit general muscle innervation.

- Mental practice assists the performer in psychologically preparing for the skill to be performed. The general muscle innervation might set appropriate tension levels and attentional focus.

Recent research has generally been more descriptive in reporting athletes' imagery use and describing the role of imagery in psychological skills training.

Key Point

Feltz and Landers' (1983) meta-analysis led to several conclusions, including the conclusion that mental practice primarily affects cognitive-symbolic elements of the task and that the effects are not limited to early learning.

Imagery Theory

Although research is limited, several theories provide guidance and direction. Before the Feltz and Landers (1983) review, the psychoneuromuscular theory and the symbolic learning theory were dominant. Since then, several sport and exercise psychologists have adopted Lang's (1979) bioinformational theory or have focused on psychological states (Gould, Damarjian, & Greenleaf, 2002; Vealey & Greenleaf, 2006).

- **Psychoneuromuscular theory.** Psychoneuromuscular theory, alluded to in Feltz and Landers' third conclusion, is also referred to as *muscle memory.* Jacobson (1931) first reported that imaginary movements produced muscle innervation similar to those produced in the actual movement. Suinn (1983) observed muscle activity (EMG) patterns during imagery that paralleled those during a ski run, but generally there is little support for the psychoneuromuscular theory.

- **Symbolic learning theory.** According to symbolic learning theory, imagery works like a blueprint to develop a mental code for movements. Much sport and exercise psychology research on imagery is consistent with symbolic learning, but we have no convincing tests of the theory.

- **Bioinformational theory.** Lang's (1977, 1979) psychophysiological information-processing theory assumes that an image is a functionally organized set of propositions. When imaging, we activate stimulus and response propositions, which implies that imagery training should include not only conditions of the situation (e.g., the setting), but also the behavioral, psychological, and physiological responses in that situation. Thus, we might think of response sets (Vealey & Greenleaf, 2006) rather than simple responses.

- **Psychological states.** Psychological states or mental sets do not refer to a specific theory but explain imagery effects by referring to optimal arousal or attentional states. As we will discuss in later chapters, imagery may be effective for controlling emotions to maintain an optimal psychological state, but that is not a theory to explain how imagery might affect performance.

Despite the prominence of imagery in the sport and exercise psychology literature, we can draw few conclusions about how it works. Generally, imagery seems to be one way to facilitate skill learning and performance. Many participants in physical activity find imagery effective, and sport and exercise psychology research on imagery training is accumulating.

Model for Imagery Use

Martin, Mortiz, and Hall (1999) reviewed the literature and offered a model that provides a guide for imagery use in sport (see figure 5.3). The model incorporates the sport situation, the type of imagery used, and imagery ability as factors that influence imagery use. Martin et al. discuss three broad categories of imagery use: skill and strategy learning and performance, cognitive modification, and arousal and anxiety regulation. We usually think of imagery as mental practice for skills. However, imagery is also useful for developing cognitive skills, as discussed in the previous sections, as well as for emotional control. Moreover, as the model suggests, competitive sport is not the only situation in which imagery may be useful. Training and rehabilitation are specifically included in the model, and both practice and rehabilitation settings are promising but underused settings for imagery and cognitive skill use. The imagery types are those from the SIQ, and Martin and colleagues also include individual differences in imagery abilities.

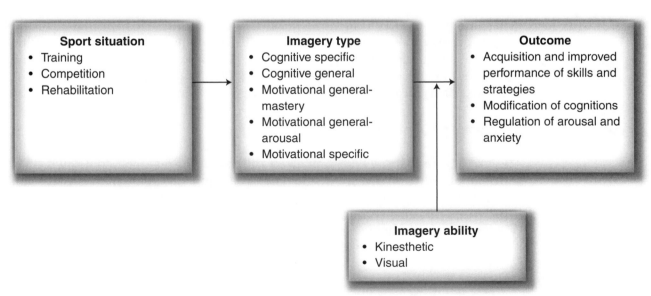

Figure 5.3
Applied model of mental imagery use in sport.

Application Point

Imagery can be used for practicing mental skills and emotional control as well as for practicing sport skills, and it has been underused in exercise and rehabilitation. List two or three ways that a client in a rehabilitation program could use imagery to facilitate rehab exercises, return to full activity, or enhance psychological control.

USING COGNITIVE SKILLS

As discussed in the preceding sections, attention and cognition are key aspects of sport and exercise behaviors, and the use of cognitive skills can help people control their thoughts in order to enhance their physical activity experiences. This section focuses on using cognitive skills, starting with goal setting. After considering goal setting, we'll turn to strategies for attention and thought control, and then we'll return to imagery, one of the most popular cognitive techniques.

GOAL SETTING

Goals are so common that they are almost unavoidable. Participants usually hold multiple goals, and even if they do not form goals, teachers, coaches, exercise instructors, family, or friends will often set goals for them. Common as they are, though, goals are not automatically effective; it is much easier to set goals than to make them work effectively.

Simply, a goal is something that a person is trying to accomplish. Typically goals set a standard of excellence, such as a performance level or time limit. For example, you might set a goal to cut three strokes off your golf game, to walk 1 mile (1.5 kilometers) every day next week, or just to finish your first 10K run. Not only are goals common, they work. Goal setting has been a popular research topic since the 1960s, when Locke began his influential studies. The extensive literature reviewed by Locke et al. in 1981 indicated consistent benefits of goal setting for performance. The literature has continued to accumulate, and updated reviews (e.g., Locke & Latham, 1990) continue to confirm the benefits. Several sport and exercise psychologists have investigated goal setting using Locke's model; see reviews by Weinberg (2002), Burton and Naylor (2002), or Gould (2006) for more details on that work.

Locke and Latham's Model of Goal Setting

Locke and Latham's (1990) review of the extensive research confirmed their primary prediction that specific, difficult goals enhance performance more than vague, easy (e.g., "Do your best") goals or no goals at all. Locke and Latham proposed that goal setting enhances performance by directing attention, mobilizing effort, enhancing persistence, and developing new learning strategies.

Burton and Naylor (2002) applied the Locke and Latham model to sport, listing five attributes that influence goal effectiveness:

- **Goal difficulty.** Locke and Latham argue that more difficult goals lead to better performance, and reviews and meta-analyses consistently confirm this prediction (e.g., Mento et al., 1987).

- **Goal specificity.** Locke and Latham further argue that specific difficult goals are even better. Specific easy goals do not enhance performance.

- **Goal valence.** Valence refers to positivity versus negativity, and positive goals are more effective. Goals should specify what you want to accomplish rather than what you want to avoid.

- **Goal proximity.** Proximity refers to short-term and long-term goals. Most scholars advocate short-term goals, which are more flexible and controllable and help develop confidence. However, long-term goals also have an important role.

- **Goal collectivity.** Locke and Latham suggest that group goals enhance performance just as individual goals do.

Locke and Latham's model includes four moderator variables as well as the main attributes. Specifically, goal effectiveness may depend on the following:

- **Ability.** If difficult goals are impossible for a person with low ability, they are ineffective. Difficult goals are more effective for people with high ability.

- **Commitment.** Highly committed people match their goals, whether the goals are difficult or easy. Therefore, high commitment helps only with difficult goals.

- **Feedback.** Both goals and feedback are necessary for performance enhancement. Feedback may enhance confidence or allow for the adjustment of strategies.

- **Task complexity.** The mechanisms are not clear, but more complex tasks may require developing new task strategies before motivational effects can make new strategies work.

Goal Setting in Sport

Sport and exercise psychology research suggests that goal setting is popular and often effective in sport. Gould, Tammen, Murphy, and May (1989) reported that goal setting was the psychological intervention most often used by sport psychologists working with U.S. Olympic athletes. Similarly, Orlick and Partington (1988) reported extensive goal setting by Canadian Olympic athletes. Weinberg, Burton, Yukelson, and Weigand (1993) surveyed athletes at three universities to determine actual goal-setting practices and views. Virtually all the athletes set goals, and most considered goal setting to be moderately to highly effective. Athletes rated overall performance goals as most important, followed by winning, fun, and skill development; they rated conditioning, psychological skills development, social affiliation, and strategy goals as less important.

Burton and Naylor (2002) and Weinberg (2002) both conclude that specific, difficult, challenging goals improve performance more than vague or no goals, but other results are inconsistent. Kyllo and Landers (1995) used meta-analysis techniques and concluded that setting goals generally has a small effect on performance and that moderate, absolute, and combined short- and long-term goals are associated with the greatest effects.

Weinberg (2002) suggested differences in motivation, commitment, task conditions, and competition that might explain inconsistent results in sport settings. Burton (1989), emphasizing individual orientation and perceived ability, conducted a 5-month goal-setting program emphasizing performance goals (improvement) over outcome goals (winning) with swimmers. Athletes who were better at meeting performance goals were less anxious and performed better, demonstrating that goal-setting skills can be learned and developed through practice.

Goal-Setting Principles

The extensive research on goal setting, the more limited sport and exercise psychology research, and the reports of consultants who have conducted goal-setting interventions provide guidelines for setting goals effectively. The following principles, from Weinberg (2002), are representative:

- **Set specific goals.** One of the most consistent research findings is that specific goals enhance performance more than vague or no goals. Set specific goals such as improving from 70% to 85% on free throws or walking 1 mile (1.5 kilometers) 5 days next week.
- **Set realistic but challenging goals.** Goals should be challenging but attainable.
- **Set both short- and long-term goals.** Athletes and exercisers typically have long-term goals, which provide a destination. However, short-term goals are needed to provide feedback about progress, allow for adjustment of goals, and generally keep people on track to meeting their long-term goals.
- **Set goals for both practice and competition.** Practice goals can help focus attention and effort, develop strategies, and create a more realistic and motivating situation.
- **Ink it, don't think it.** Many authors advocate writing down and recording goals. Moreover, the goals should be placed where they will be visible and salient.
- **Develop goal-achievement strategies.** Participants should identify strategies for reaching goals. For example, how might they improve their free-throw percentage? Perhaps they could change their technique or perform specific practice drills.
- **Prioritize process, performance, and outcome goals.** Focus on process and performance rather than outcomes. The best way to win the gold (reach a desired outcome) is to focus on performance and process goals.
- **Set individual and team goals.** Individual goals have a place in team activities, as long as they do not conflict with team goals but focus on the person's contribution.
- **Provide support for goals.** Social support plays a role in goal attainment; coaches and instructors who show a genuine concern for participants provide goal support.
- **Evaluate goals.** Coaches, instructors, and trainers should provide feedback on goal effectiveness as well as on actual performance.

Common Goal-Setting Problems

Of course, no intervention is perfect. Some common problems in goal setting, again from Weinberg (2002), are as follows:

- **Failure to monitor goal progress and readjust goals.** People often start off strong but then fade. Reevaluation can help keep people motivated and on track.

- **Failure to recognize individual differences.** People differ, and goal setting should differ from person to person.

- **Failure to set specific, measurable goals.** People often set general goals (e.g., "Improve my game"); consultants can help identify more specific and effective goals.

- **Setting too many goals.** People often set too many goals and have difficulty monitoring and tracking them. Help participants focus on priorities and set only a few initial goals.

COGNITIVE-CONTROL STRATEGIES

Nideffer's (1976a) model of attentional styles is the basis for some popular attentional control interventions, and Nideffer himself was among the first to use cognitive interventions in sport psychology. This section covers strategies for attentional control and concentration, including Nideffer's (1993) attentional control training as well as self-talk and cognitive restructuring techniques.

Attentional Control and Concentration

Concentration implies control of attention. Instructors often tell participants, "Keep your eye on the ball" or "Focus on the feelings." As with most psychological skills, it is much easier to tell someone to concentrate than to convey how to do it. Concentration is not an innate ability but a skill acquired through training and practice.

Key Point

ACT involves assessing individual attentional strengths and weaknesses, the attentional demands of the sport, the situation and personal characteristics that affect arousal and behavior under pressure, and situation-specific problem areas, and then developing an intervention program.

Nideffer (1993) proposed that people can improve their ability to use and shift attentional styles through attentional control training (ACT). The main technique in ACT is centering, which involves relaxing the muscles, breathing deeply, and focusing on feelings with exhalation. ACT also involves assessing individual attentional strengths and weaknesses (with the TAIS), the attentional demands of the sport, the situation and personal characteristics that affect arousal and behavior under pressure, and situation-specific problem areas, and then developing an intervention program. ACT takes training, but there are many simpler concentration strategies that are also useful.

Wilson, Peper, and Schmidt (2006) list several strategies that physical activity participants could easily use. These strategies, listed next, are grouped as external (avoiding distractions) or internal (staying centered). Wilson and colleagues refer to athletics, but these strategies can also be applied to children in physical education, adults in fitness programs, or clients in rehabilitation programs.

External Strategies to Keep Concentration

- *Dress rehearsal.* Dress rehearsal, with such elements as music, uniforms, announcements, and lights matching competition conditions, is particularly effective.

- *Rehearsal of simulated competition experiences.* As with dress rehearsal, athletes practice concentrating and dissociating from disruptive stimuli. Simulated competition might involve tapes of competition sounds or crowd noises.

- *Mental rehearsal.* Mental rehearsal, visualization, and imagery are some of the most widely used and useful cognitive strategies. Imagery, which is covered in more detail in the next section (see page 75), may be used for controlling attention and practicing concentration.

Internal Strategies to Stay Centered

- *Attentional cues and triggers.* Many athletes use verbal or kinesthetic cues to focus concentration or retrigger lost concentration. For example, a free-throw shooter may focus on the rim, or a swimmer might focus on the feel of the hand pulling through the water.

- *Tic-toc. Tic* is any thought that is irrelevant to what you need to do (e.g., thinking about the previous event). Switch to *toc*—actions needed right now.

- *Turning failure into success.* With this strategy, participants mentally rehearse a successful performance immediately after a failure. After a disastrous free exercise routine, for instance, a gymnast might immediately visualize the great routine of the previous meet.

- *Biofeedback.* Biofeedback may be used to show how thoughts affect the body, to monitor relaxation, to identify stressful points during imagery, and to facilitate concentration training. For example, biofeedback might be used while an athlete is thinking of an anxiety-provoking situation to illustrate the effects of thoughts on the body. Biofeedback is common in rehabilitation settings and might easily be used to practice cognitive control.

- *Increasing focusing and refocusing skills.* Focus training involves bringing attention back when it starts to wander, as in meditation. Wilson, Peper, and Schmidt, (2006) suggest four techniques.

1. First, using mindfulness, the person sits quietly and tries to stay focused on a single thought for as long as possible. Mindfulness and related techniques are often incorporated into exercise programs. Not only can mindfulness training enhance the exercise itself, but it can help participants develop useful attentional and emotional-control skills.

2. With the technique called *one pointing,* the person looks at an action photo or an object (e.g., a tennis ball) and keeps the focus on that point.

3. The third technique, the grid exercise, is used in several psychological skills programs. The grid (see figure 5.4) is a 10-by-10 block of numbers ranging from 00 to 99 in random locations. The task is to mark off consecutive numbers from 00 to as high as possible within a given time, such as 2 minutes. The exercise can be varied by using distracting background sounds or different instructions (e.g., going backward). The point is to practice scanning and focusing (e.g., in soccer, players scan the field of play and then focus on the pass). However, as with most concentration exercises, the transfer value from practice to competition is questionable.

4. Wilson, Peper, and Schmidt (2006) suggest video games as a fourth technique for focusing and refocusing, and we might include varied computerized concentration exercises. As with other focusing exercises, the transition from the computer to the playing field can be a big leap. Exercises that incorporate some of these focusing techniques in the actual sport or exercise setting are likely to be more effective than exercises that do not have transitional steps to tie the skills to the activity.

- *Developing performing protocols.* Wilson, Peper, and Schmidt (2006) suggest that athletes might tune in to their ideal performance by associating concentration with certain performance rituals. Others refer to pre-performance routines, suggesting that consistently practiced protocols will automatically trigger focused attention that leads to good performance. For example, Boutcher and Crews (1987) demonstrated that the use of a preshot concentration routine improved putting performance.

These are just a few examples; many athletes and exercisers have developed their own cognitive strategies and exercises.

Figure 5.4
Grid concentration exercise.

Reprinted, by permission, from D.V. Harris and B.L. Harris, 1984, *The athlete's guide to sports psychology: Mental skills for physical people* (New York, NY: Leisure Press), 189.

84	27	51	78	59	52	13	85	61	55
28	60	92	04	97	90	31	57	29	33
32	96	65	39	80	77	49	86	18	70
76	87	71	95	98	81	01	46	88	00
48	82	89	47	35	17	10	42	62	34
44	67	93	11	07	43	72	94	69	56
53	79	05	22	54	74	58	14	91	02
06	68	99	75	26	15	41	66	20	40
50	09	64	08	38	30	36	45	83	24
03	73	21	23	16	37	25	19	12	63

Directions: Beginning with 00, put a slash through each number in the proper sequence.

Self-Talk

Self-talk occurs whenever a person thinks—whether the self-talk is spoken aloud or silently—and makes perceptions and beliefs conscious. Most athletes and exercisers use self-talk, often as self-coaching, but there is little research or guidance on the technique. See Zinsser, Bunker, and Williams (2006) or Williams and Leffingwell (2002) for more details.

Uses of Self-Talk

Williams and Leffingwell (2002) list the following uses of self-talk:

- **Correcting bad habits.** Self-coaching or self-instruction (e.g., "Keep your eye on the ball, follow through") can help correct bad habits that have become automatic.

- **Focusing attention.** Cue words or statements such as "Be here" and "Track the ball" can help maintain attention.
- **Modifying activation.** Self-talk (e.g., "Easy," "Get pumped") can help athletes modify activation to reach an optimal emotional state.
- **Building self-confidence.** As discussed in chapter 6, self-confidence is a psychological key to excellence. As in the classic children's book *The Little Engine That Could,* if you keep repeating "I think I can," eventually you will make it up the hill.

Although most sport and exercise literature on psychological skills and self-talk focuses on athletes, self-talk is equally applicable to exercise. As noted in chapter 6, self-efficacy is central in exercise adoption and adherence, and self-talk that builds confidence can help exercisers. Gauvin (1990) reports that persistent exercisers use positive and motivational self-talk, whereas dropouts and sedentary people use self-defeating and negative self-talk.

Effective Self-Talk

For self-talk to be effective, the user first must be aware of the self-talk and its effects and then see whether it needs to be modified. Williams and Leffingwell (2002) suggest that self-talk may be identified through retrospection (reflect on exceptionally good or poor past performances and recall the self-talk), imagery, observation (instructor or other observer records while person goes through self-talk out loud), and self-talk logs (daily records of self-talk that include details of the situation and the performance).

After identifying effective and ineffective self-talk patterns, one can modify them. Zinsser et al. (2006) and Williams and Leffingwell (2002) offer similar lists of common techniques for modifying self-talk:

- **Thought stopping.** The person uses a cue to interrupt unwanted thoughts as they occur. A common technique is to quickly and clearly say (or yell) "Stop!" as soon as that unwanted thought comes into mind. Some people use visual cues (e.g., visualizing a red stoplight) or physical cues (e.g., snapping the fingers). Thought stopping is a great wake-up call, but you must then substitute a positive thought.
- **Changing negative thoughts to positive ones.** Switch from the negative thought to a constructive one. For example, after thinking, "I always hit into the lake on this hole," you would say "Stop!" Then you might think, "But when I take a smooth, easy backswing, I have a solid, straight drive." When standing at the tee, it's not easy to think of those positive substitute thoughts. Many consultants suggest making a list of typical negative thoughts and writing a positive substitute next to each one to make it easier to retrieve the replacement thoughts in stressful situations.
- **Countering.** Changing negative thoughts to positive ones is not effective if you don't believe what you're thinking. Countering is an internal debate, using reason to directly challenge self-defeating thoughts. For example, when the heart pounds and muscles tighten, saying "I am calm" is not likely to be effective. To counter the negative self-talk, you might say, "This happens to everyone; when I breathe easily and focus on my shot, I do fine."
- **Reframing.** People often view the world in narrow, rigid terms, and reframing changes that perspective. For example, the college freshman who starts

off with a less-than-stellar season after a glorious high school record might reframe the situation as one for learning new skills and developing strategies for the higher-level play.

Application Point

Self-talk requires no special equipment or skills and can be used in many sport and exercise settings. It may be particularly useful for young children, and it can also be fun. Assume that you are the teacher for a children's beginning swimming class. Suggest several self-talk strategies the children could use to build confidence and develop skills.

Negative Self-Talk and Cognitive Restructuring

Key Point

Positive self-talk has positive effects whereas negative self-talk interferes with performance, but it's not easy to get rid of negative thoughts. Affirmations (positive thoughts) and cognitive restructuring, where participants first recognize that negative thoughts are irrational and then identify constructive thoughts to replace them, can help.

Many relatively simple techniques for modifying self-talk and developing concentration relate to cognitive restructuring. According to Ellis (1982), among others, the many irrational or distorted thoughts that we all hold are debilitating. In therapeutic settings, irrational thinking might be the basis of depression or other clinical disorders. In sport and exercise, such thinking can interfere with performance and detract from the overall experience. Irrational thinking in sport and exercise might include such distorted thoughts as, "I'm nothing if I don't win this tournament," "I can't run well if it's raining," or "I'll never be able to do this skill." Such thoughts are irrational and may lead to excessive fear of failure and impaired performance.

The obvious answer is to get rid of negative thoughts, but that's not so easy. In cognitive restructuring, participants first recognize that such thoughts are irrational, identify constructive thoughts to replace them, and then practice rational self-statements. Zinsser and colleagues (2006) suggest several strategies, including cognitive prestructuring, which involves writing out events that trigger negative thoughts, specific negative self-talk, resulting feelings, and behaviors, and then rebutting the negative talk. A simpler strategy, affirmations, involves constructing positive attitudes or thoughts (e.g., "I've got a smooth backswing," "I fly down the stretch"). Coping and mastery self-talk tapes, which essentially are affirmations and restructured thoughts, can also be used. For a mastery tape, the athlete might imagine the ideal performance or recall a previous great performance and then write out a script of all the positive thoughts. After reviewing and modifying the script, an audiotape program can be made. The tape might include music that elicits appropriate emotions, and the pace of the text should permit visualization of the scenes. A coping tape is similar but is designed to help the person deal with anxiety or get through a difficult situation.

IMAGERY

As discussed earlier, imagery involves using all the senses to mentally create or recreate an experience. As we have already seen, imagery can be effective for practicing other psychological skills such as modifying self-talk, practicing concentration, and building confidence. Now we will consider imagery in more detail. Gould et al. (2002) and Vealey and Greenleaf (2006) reviewed the literature and drew upon their experiences to provide guidelines and exercises for imagery training; see those sources for more detailed information.

Guidelines for Using Imagery Effectively

For effective use of imagery, Gould and colleagues (2002) suggest the following:

- *Practice imagery regularly.* Like other psychological skills, imagery is developed through training and continued practice.

- *Use all senses to enhance image vividness.* Imagery is more than vision, and it is more effective when the image recreates all the sensations. Kinesthetic sense is particularly relevant for physical activities.

- *Develop imagery control.* Control is the key to psychological skills; practice controlling images.

- *Use both internal and external perspectives.* When Mahoney and Avener (1977) reported that elite gymnasts used more internal (performer's perspective) imagery than external (observer's perspective) imagery, many consultants advised athletes always to use an internal perspective. Most now recognize that advice should vary with the person, the activity, and the situation.

- *Facilitate imagery through relaxation.* As with concentration, imagery combined with relaxation is more effective than imagery alone.

- *Develop coping strategies through imagery.* Generally, positive imagery is preferable, but imagery can also be used to develop coping strategies and skills (e.g., coming back after injury).

- *Use imagery in practice as well as competition.* Athletes are more likely to use cognitive techniques for competition than in practices. However, physical practice is the place to practice psychological skills, and these skills can make practice more fun and more effective.

- *Use videotapes or audiotapes to enhance imagery skills.* Tapes may be helpful and may add novelty to practices.

- *Use triggers or cues to facilitate imagery quality.* Words, phrases, or objects may aid imagery, just as cues may aid concentration.

- *Emphasize dynamic kinesthetic imagery.* Dynamic imagery focusing on the kinesthetic feel of the movements may help recreate the physical experience.

- *Imagine in real time.* Slowing down or speeding up may be useful in imagery training, but most imagery should match real time and speed.

- *Use imagery logs.* Logs can help people monitor progress, remember cues, or stay with a training program.

These guidelines can help anyone develop more effective imagery strategies, whether in extensive training or in occasional sport and exercise activities.

Imagery, attention skills, and cognitive-control skills are increasingly used in training and rehabilitation. In one of the first investigations of imagery with injured athletes, Ievleva and Orlick (1991) found that imagery helped athletes cope with pain, as well as stay motivated and positively involved in their sport and in the rehabilitation process. Other researchers and sports medicine professionals suggest that imagery may even help in the healing process. In their chapter on psychological strategies in Ray and Wiese-Bjornstal's (1999) text on counseling in sports medicine, Shaffer and Wiese-Bjornstal (1999) note possible roles of cognitive restructuring and goal setting. They suggest that imagery has several roles for injured athletes: Injury imagery helps in reading the body and reactions to the injury, skill imagery helps in the practice of skills, and rehabilitation imagery helps in the healing process by promoting a positive mindset, keeping the athlete engaged in the rehabilitation process, and even influencing physiological function.

For consultants helping athletes develop an imagery training program, Gould et al. (2002) suggest a four-phase model (keep in mind that any training must be adjusted for the individual and the situation):

1. **Awareness, realistic expectations, and basic education.** Imagery is no quick and easy road to success—it takes practice. It is not a substitute for physical practice but a skill to enhance practice and performance.

2. **Imagery skill evaluation and development.** People vary in their imagery skills and styles. Consultants might evaluate imagery skills (see Vealey & Greenleaf, 2006). Assessment can increase awareness of skills and help the consultant work with the person to develop appropriate training strategies. Training strategies typically follow three steps. First, sensory awareness training helps people become more aware of all sensations (sounds, smells, feelings) and use them in imagery. Second, vividness training might start with simple exercises, such as imagining a childhood bedroom, to develop clearer, more vivid images. Finally, with controllability training, participants learn to regulate images, such as speeding up and slowing down while imagining running. Vealey and Greenleaf (2006) provide several excellent examples of exercises, as well as guidelines for imagery training and use.

3. **Using imagery.** Once imagery skills are developed, they can be used for many purposes, including practicing physical skills or strategies, correcting errors, practicing emotional control, and developing confidence.

4. **Imagery evaluation, adjustment, and refinement.** The final step is evaluating whether imagery training has met its goals and whether refinements and adjustments are needed. It is best to evaluate and consider modifications throughout the program. No two people are alike, and variations and adjustments are expected in imagery training. Moreover, imagery does not automatically work, even with the best of intentions and adherence to guidelines.

PUTTING IT INTO PRACTICE

Now you are ready to put the content of chapter 5 into practice. Read the chapter summary, discuss the case study, answer the review questions, and enhance your knowledge by researching the recommended readings.

Summary

Attention and cognitive skills are prominent in sport and exercise psychology, but research is limited. The expanding research from a psychophysiological perspective and the work on cognition and expertise are beginning to add to our understanding of cognitive processes in physical activity. Cognitive-control strategies are popular and often effective in sport and exercise. Goal setting is effective, and the literature indicates that specific, challenging goals are more effective than vague, do-your-best goals. Sport and exercise psychologists consistently emphasize the importance of controlling attention and thoughts, and participants use techniques such as thought stopping, cognitive restructuring, and imagery. Most sport and exercise psychologists advise individual assessments, evaluation, and modifications with cognitive skill training.

Case Study

You are an athletic trainer for an intercollegiate athletics program, and you are working with a volleyball player who is now in rehabilitation after anterior cruciate ligament (ACL) surgery. The physicians estimate that she can return to practice in 6 to 8 weeks. You have a plan for exercises and activities. Will you incorporate any cognitive skills in your program? If so, which ones, and how will you accomplish that?

D.G.'s advice: Of course I will use cognitive strategies during rehabilitation. I know the athlete is thinking; cognitive control can help her use her thinking to make rehabilitation more effective so that she will be better prepared to return to play. I would start with some simple assessments (talking to the athlete) to find out what she is thinking about the injury, about the rehab process, and about returning to play. Then, using some guidelines for goal setting and self-talk, I would help the athlete set goals, particularly short-term goals for rehab activities. I would not set up an extensive psychological skills program immediately, and I might not add anything else. But, if the athlete finds the initial cognitive strategies helpful, I'd suggest some other self-talk or imagery exercises that she could try to see what works for her. That's my general advice to get you started. Consider the case and describe how you would incorporate cognitive skills.

I did not include much detail. Details vary with the case and situation, and details change over time. You will be more effective in your own practice if you do not set up one plan but have multiple options that can be adapted for the individual, setting, and time.

Review Questions

1. Define *attention*.
2. Describe Nideffer's two-dimensional model of attention.
3. Explain the relationships of association and dissociation to performance.
4. Explain how experts differ from nonexperts in attention and cognitive skills.
5. Discuss the theories used to explain how imagery works.
6. Discuss Locke and Latham's model of goal setting.
7. Identify guidelines for effective goal setting.
8. Describe two specific concentration strategies that could be used in sport and exercise.
9. Identify common guidelines for using imagery effectively.

Recommended Reading

Abernethy, B., Maxwell, J.P., Masters, R.S.W., van der Kamp, J., & Jackson, R.C. (2007). Attentional processes in skill learning and expert performance. In G. Tenenbaum & R.C. Eklund (Eds.), *Handbook of sport psychology* (3rd ed., pp. 245-263). Hoboken, NJ: Wiley.

> Abernethy has conducted considerable research on the role of attention and cognitive strategies of elite performers. This chapter summarizes work by motor behavior and sport psychology scholars, and it provides a solid review with suggestions for continuing work.

Janelle, C.M., & Hillman, C.H. (2003). Expert performance in sport: Current perspectives and critical issues. In J.L. Starkes & A. Ericsson (Eds.), *Expert performance in sports* (pp. 19-48). Champaign, IL: Human Kinetics.

The Starkes and Ericsson book includes several chapters by leading scholars, and the Janelle and Hillman chapter provides a nice overview of the current perspectives and research on expertise.

Vealey, R.S., & Greenleaf, C.A. (2006). Seeing is believing: Understanding and using imagery in sport. In J.M. Williams (Ed.), *Applied sport psychology: Personal growth to peak performance* (5th ed., pp. 306-348). Boston: McGraw-Hill.

In the fifth edition of Williams' applied sport psychology book, Vealey and Greenleaf update earlier chapters on imagery and sport. The chapter provides a good overview of research and theories to help you understand imagery, as well as helpful guidelines for using imagery.

Weinberg, R. (2002). Goal setting in sport and exercise: Research to practice. In J.L. Van Raalte & B.W. Brewer (Eds.), *Exploring sport and exercise psychology* (2nd ed., pp. 25-48). Washington, DC: APA.

Weinberg is a leading researcher on goal setting in sport, and his chapter provides ideas and guidelines on goal setting for both research and practice.

Zinsser, N., Bunker, L., & Williams, J.M. (2006). Cognitive techniques for building confidence and enhancing performance. In J.M. Williams (Ed.), *Applied sport psychology: Personal growth to peak performance* (5th ed., pp. 349-381). Boston: McGraw-Hill.

This chapter presents an up-to-date overview of cognitive strategies, emphasizing self-talk, along with helpful suggestions for practice.

Chapter 6

Self-Perceptions

Chapter Objectives

After studying this chapter, you should be able to

◆ define the different approaches to the study of self-perceptions,

◆ describe the multidimensional views of the self and the related sport and exercise psychology work on physical self-concept, and

◆ trace the development of self-efficacy theories and apply them to the promotion of self-esteem.

People's perceptions of themselves and what they believe they can accomplish in sport, academics, work, and life explains their performance, feelings, and thoughts. More positive feelings about oneself are associated with more positive outcomes. For example, higher self-esteem is associated with lower anxiety and greater optimism, adaptability, life satisfaction, happiness, and ability to cope with stress, whereas lower self-esteem is associated with depression, suicide ideation, disordered eating, and delinquency (Horn, 2004). These results parallel those found in physical activity, where people who reported more positive thoughts about themselves also tended to report higher levels of performance, motivation, physical activity, self-pride, and happiness and less boredom and anxiety (Craft, Magyar, Becker, & Feltz, 2003; Crocker & Kowalski, 2000; Georgiadis, Biddle, & Chatzisarantis, 2001; Tremblay, Inman, & Willms, 2000; Weiss & Ferrer-Caja, 2002).

Given this, it is not surprising that physical activity specialists such as teachers, coaches, athletic trainers, and personal trainers are interested in helping their students, athletes, and clients feel good about themselves so that they will have more positive attitudes toward physical activity and be more motivated to be physically active. Take a moment and consider how you might the help following people.

1. Chris, a 10-year-old girl, began playing soccer two years ago when she asked her parents if she could join the local recreational soccer league. Her parents were thrilled and were hopeful that the experience would help build her self-esteem. Although she voluntarily plays soccer each year and is as capable as most of the other players in the league, she exhibits low self-confidence and has an overall unhappy demeanor when it comes to actually playing in a game. In practice and in games, she gives up easily. Her parents are convinced that soccer will never do anything for their daughter's self-esteem. If you were the soccer coach, what would you do to help Chris view herself in a more positive light, both as a person and as a soccer player?

2. Rob, a top tennis recruit at a nationally ranked university, was playing his first college match. Up two sets and ahead 4–2 in the third set, Rob was

on top of the world feeling competitive at the college level. Racing to return a shot, Rob felt a sudden snap in his lower leg—he had ruptured his Achilles tendon and had to forfeit the match. His postsurgery rehabilitation program was effective but slow. Over time, Rob began to question his ability to recover and his worth as an athlete. He wonders aloud who he will be and what he will do without tennis. If you were a therapist, what would you do to help Rob overcome his despair and continue his rehabilitation efforts?

3. A recent medical checkup revealed that Jordan's blood pressure and cholesterol levels are rising. Her doctor, who had been suggesting that she increase her physical activity, is now warning Jordan that if she doesn't attempt to control her health through physical activity, she will be on medication within three months. With this wake-up call, Jordan wants to start exercising. As one of the best personal trainers in town, she comes to you for help. A former college athlete, Jordan is extremely disappointed in herself for letting her health and fitness levels get this bad, and she doubts that she will ever be able to regain what she once had. How will you help Jordan have a more positive view of herself and feel more confident about her ability to be physically fit?

Now that you have generated some solutions for helping the people described in these scenarios, the next step is to explain why these solutions will work. This is where greater knowledge of self-perceptions is helpful. A working knowledge of the self will give you insight into how people evaluate their abilities and their self-worth. It will also provide you with an understanding of how external factors such as significant others can affect the self-evaluation process. It is this knowledge that will allow you to evaluate the effectiveness of the solutions you generated and, if needed, to refine or discard the ideas that you have generated in order to create more effective ones.

SELF-PERCEPTIONS

Self-perceptions are most broadly defined as peoples' thoughts, attitudes, and feelings about themselves in general or about their skills, abilities, and characteristics in a particular achievement domain (Horn, 2004). The term *self-system*, also known as *integrated self-knowledge structures* (Markus, Cross, & Wurf, 1990), is conceptually similar to self-perceptions. Two of the earliest self-perceptions studied were self-esteem (a.k.a., self-worth) and self-concept. William James (1890, 1892) discussed the development of a sense of global self-worth from more specific self-judgments. C.H. Cooley (1902), on the other hand, proposed that self-concept was formed through social interaction, and he introduced the notion of reflected appraisal and the term *looking-glass self.*

Although often used interchangeably, self-concept is the overall perception, the descriptive aspect, of the self (e.g., I am compassionate, I am talented, writing is my strength, free-throw shooting is my weakness), whereas self-esteem is the evaluative aspect of the global self. These evaluations can be positive or negative (e.g., I am worthy, I am a failure). The distinction between self-concept and self-esteem is convenient for discussing the various aspects of the self, but in reality, these terms are difficult to separate because peoples' descriptions of themselves are so emotionally charged (Harter, 1999). The evaluative component usually is the key for study of the self. In the following sections, we will explore the two ways of viewing the self.

MARKUS' DYNAMIC SELF-SYSTEM

According to Markus (1977), self-concept is a complex, multifaceted, dynamic system that consists of unique collections of cognitive representations of the self, called *schemata,* that represent self-beliefs related to domain-specific attributes and abilities (e.g., athlete schema). Self-schemata are active, dynamic self-representations that are derived from past experiences and that organize and direct behaviors. Self-schemata allow for information retrieval and processing, as well as reaction to information.

People have many self-schemata that work together in a self-system. We can have schemata relative to exercise, body weight, independence, and academic performance (see Stein, Roeser, & Markus, 1998). Some self-schemata are more salient than others. For example, the athlete schemata may be highly salient and a dominant influence for some but not for others. Schemata that are less salient and less elaborate have less influence. We are more apt to find a person with a stronger exercise schema than athlete schema in the gym working out rather than on the playing field.

Application Point

Kim and John are both athlete and math schematics. They are both on the school basketball and math teams. Kim's athlete schematic is stronger than her math schematic, whereas the opposite is true for John. They discover that the math bowl is scheduled on the same day as a basketball game. What event do you think Kim attended? What about John?

Although people possess numerous self-schemata, it is unlikely that everyone possesses self-schemata relative to every attribute in a domain. People can be schematic, aschematic, or nonschematic for a particular attribute in a domain (Kendzierski, 1988). Schematics view the attribute or behavior as highly and personally descriptive and as important to their overall sense of self. Aschematics moderately identify with the attribute and do not believe the attribute is important to their self-concept. Nonschematics do not identify with the attribute, but they do believe that the attribute is important to their self-concept. People's schema types are related to their behavior. For example, diet schematics are likely to diet more than diet aschematics.

Schemata are conceptions of the self in the present and are thought to influence behavior and future-oriented self-conceptions, called *possible selves* (Markus & Nurius, 1986). Possible selves are positive and negative self-images already in a future state (Oyserman, Bybee, & Terry, 2006). Markus & Nurius (1986) discuss possible selves as important motivators that bridge the present to the future. For example, a golfer who conceives of becoming a professional golfer (hoped-for self) may develop a more elaborate golfer schema, a sense of mastery and confidence, and specific goals and strategies. A person who fears losing motor functioning (feared self) may do home exercises. Various conditions are needed to maximize the relationship between possible selves and behavior. For example, possible selves are thought to be most effective when the hoped-for and feared selves are balanced (Oyserman & Markus, 1990). A person who hopes to be active and fears becoming sedentary may be more likely to exercise than one who only hopes to be active but does not fear being a couch potato.

Whaley (2004) suggests that possible selves influence behavior when people are confident that they can successfully execute the behavior and believe that achievement of the possible self is likely. The more elaborate and accessible the possible selves are, the more effective they are thought to be (Ruvolo & Markus, 1992). Imagery is a viable method for developing elaborate, accessible, possible selves in order to develop competence. Imagery helps when it is specific, or detailed, and we can see ourselves doing it—it's possible.

Markus (1977) contends that only a subset of the self, not all self-knowledge, is active at any given time. This concept of the working self continually varies as it regulates behavior (controls and directs actions). The immediate social situation affects the working self, which in turn affects behavior. For example, take Bobby, an athlete schematic who has the opportunity to play recreational softball after years of not competing but chooses not to play because he fears looking unathletic. The invitation itself evokes Bobby's athlete schematic, and since he hasn't played for years it evokes the feared unathletic self. His decision is a function of his working self-concept. Perhaps if the invitation had been made by family at a reunion, Bobby would have played. Understanding the working self helps to explain that the self is dynamic without being inconsistent.

Social influence extends to social groups or culture. Markus (1977) discussed two views of the self that differ across cultures—independent and interdependent. The independent view (e.g., individual achievement, self-focused, private, direct) dominates North American culture, including its sport culture. Other cultures, such as most in Asia, take an interdependent view and see the self in relation to others (e.g., linked, relational, indirect, cooperative). In the United States, the typical athlete and exerciser schema fit the independent view. We see athletes as independent, competitive, individual achievers, and if that does not fit with your gender or cultural identity you may not easily see yourself as an athlete—it's not a possible self. This exerciser schema may not be competitive, but it is independent as well as white and middle class, and exercise may be seen as self-indulgent to cultures with more community identity.

Exercise Schemata

Researchers have adopted Markus' views to focus on self-identity as an exerciser or athlete. Kendzierski (1994) has used the approach to study exercise schemata and exercise behaviors. In initial studies and using a scale adapted for the physical domain, Kendzierski classified people as exerciser schematics (they identified as exercisers), nonexerciser schematics (they identified as nonexercisers), or aschematics (no relevant exerciser identity) and found that exerciser schematics process information differently from others.

Subsequent studies with predominantly college-aged students showed that exerciser schematics exercised more frequently, performed more exercise activities, were more likely to report exercising three times per week, and were more likely to start an exercise program than were nonexerciser schematics and aschematics. Exerciser schematics also plan to exercise, strategize overcoming obstacles to exercise, report more exercise-related behavior, and exercise more, expend more calories, and perceive themselves as more fit than those with a schemata for nonexercise (Estabrooks & Courneya, 1997; Kendzierski, 1988; Kendzierski, Furr, & Schiavoni, 1998; Yin & Boyd, 2000; see also Whaley, 2004, for a review).

Whaley (2004) reported that only 6 of 13 older adults who had been exercising for more than 2 years were schematic for exercise. Six of the remaining 7 did not fall into any of the three categorizes defined by Kendzierski. All 6 considered their exercise to be important to their self-concept, but *exercise* was only moderately descriptive. They explained that exercisers are younger or exercise all the time. Whaley explained that their exercise behavior did not fit into how society views an exerciser. These results highlight the influence of social context on self-concept.

Athlete Identity

Brewer, Van Raalte, and Linder (1993) defined athletic identity as the degree to which a person identifies with the athletic role and looks to others for acknowledgment of that role. A person with a strong athletic identity has an athlete self-schema and processes information from an athletic perspective. For example, people with strong athletic identities might think about how their eating and sleeping habits affect performance. Brewer, Van Raalte, and Linder developed the Athletic Identity Measurement Scale (AIMS), and initial findings suggested that people establish strong athletic identities through the development of skills, confidence, and social interactions during sport. Further, a strong, exclusive athletic identity may predispose athletes to emotional difficulties when they cannot participate. A more recent study has shown that marathon runners with higher athlete identities are more committed and better performers but are not more likely to neglect other aspects of their life than runners with lower athlete identities (Horton & Mack, 2000). Having a strong athletic identity is not always advantageous, however. For example, strong athletic identities can interfere with planning for life beyond college (Lally & Kerr, 2005).

As conceived by Brewer and colleagues (1993), athletic identity is multifaceted, inclusive of (1) social identity, or the strength with which athletes identify with the athletic role, which may be further subdivided into self-identity (views of the self as an athlete) and social identity (others' views of them as athletes in samples of athletes with disabilities); (2) exclusivity, or the degree to which athletes rely solely on the athletic setting for identity; and (3) negative affectivity, or negative emotional responses to not being able to train or compete. Anderson (2004) argues that measures like the AIMS focus too narrowly on strength and exclusivity and thus are unidimensional. Arguing for the multidimensional nature of the self and dynamic processes and social aspects involved in self-knowledge, she proposed the Athletic Identity Questionnaire (AIQ). The AIQ assesses four aspects of the self: athletic appearance, importance of physical activities to the self, competence, and encouragement from others. Initial validation studies revealed that athletic identity was related to physical activity in the form of exercise behavior stages and frequency of exercise.

The social group in which one is a member (i.e., culture) is important to consider when considering athletic identity. Research has also shown that males have stronger athletic identities than females, and Mexican Americans are more likely to have stronger athletic identities than Caucasians and African Americans (see Weise-Bjornstal, 2004). Further, a recent study demonstrates that not only do black athletes have stronger athletic identities than white athletes (Brown et al., 2003), race and athletic identity converge in given situations and influence cognitions. Although black and white Division I college athletes had similar believes about racial discrimination (which is in contrast to most public opinion findings), there were differences in beliefs when considering athletes' racial and athletic identities. When comparing white and black athletes with high and low athletic identities, black athletes with high athletic identities were the most likely to believe that racial discrimination was no longer a problem, and black athletes with low athletic identities were the least likely to think this. In addition to highlighting the social nature of the self, these findings likely demonstrate the concept of the working self. Athletes' thoughts about racial discrimination were a function of their racial and athletic identities (see also Lally & Kerr, 2005).

Application Point

Rebecca is an exercise schematic and has a strong athletic identity. Given this, create a profile for Rebecca that describes her most likely social identity and behaviors. What would her probable social identity and behaviors be if she were a nonexercise schematic with a relatively weak athletic identity?

Self-schema theory is helpful in practice because it forces us to recognize that the dimensions of the self do not work in isolation of each other (i.e., the self is dynamic and whole) and the self does not function in isolation of its social context (i.e., the self is a social construct). With an understanding of the working self, it may be easier to accept that behavior is a reflection of the working self and all that comes with it. The complex, dynamic, fluid, and social aspects of the self will be important as we turn our attention to the structure of the self.

MULTIDIMENSIONAL SELF-ESTEEM

Key Point

From a multidimensional perspective of self-esteem, people do not value all domains equally. Rather, self-evaluation of each domain combines in a unique way to form self-esteem.

Early perspectives emphasized a unidimensional, global view of the self where aspects contributing to one's global self-esteem could not be differentiated. For example, Coopersmith (1967) viewed self-concept as a unitary construct, and his widely used measure combines items reflecting self-evaluations across many life domains as though they contributed equally to self-esteem. Others (e.g., Harter, 1983) have criticized this approach, arguing for a multidimensional approach. They argue that people do not value all domains equally; rather, self-evaluation of each domain combines in a unique way to form self-esteem.

In what areas of life do your accomplishments mean the most to you—when you excel academically, athletically, socially, in your work, in relationships, in creative arts? How might you have answered this question 5 years ago? Do you think you will answer any differently 5 years from now? Understanding the multidimensional nature of self-esteem enables practitioners to better understand what life domains contribute to self-esteem and how these change over time.

Harter's Model of Perceived Competence: A Multidimensional Approach

Susan Harter (1990), who advocates a multidimensional and developmental approach to self-perceptions, has been particularly influential in our discipline. From a multidimensional and developmental perspective, the relationship between the domains and global self-esteem, the number of domains contributing to overall self-esteem, and the content of these domains change throughout life (Harter, 1999; Horn, 2004). Children as young as 4 to 7 years make self-judgments in five domains: cognitive competence, physical competence, physical appearance, social acceptance, and behavioral conduct. However, children are not capable of making overall judgments of their global self-worth. In this way, young children have a unidimensional perspective of self (see figure 6.1). With greater cognitive maturity, children aged 8 to 12 make more reliable judgements in the domain areas and are able to form an overall judgment of self-worth. In this way, older children have developed a multidimensional perspective and the domains are linked with, but independent from, global self-esteem (see figure 6.1).

Harter (1990) suggests further developmental changes in self-perceptions, adding close friendship, romantic appeal, and job competence domains for adolescents. According to Harter, college students make clear differentiations among scholastic competence, intellectual ability, and creativity, but for slightly older adults, a single dimension of intelligence suffices.

Relative to the physical self, physical appearance remains a relevant subdomain throughout the life span. In contrast, athletic competence is replaced by leisure activities and health status in late adulthood (see Harter, 1999; Horn, 2004). Without multidimensional models such as Susan Harter's, explaining such variations of self-esteem would not be possible.

> ### Key Point
>
> Harter's approach is both developmental and multidimensional. Throughout the course of life, the number of domains contributing to overall self-esteem, the relationship between the domains and global self-esteem, and the content of these domains change.

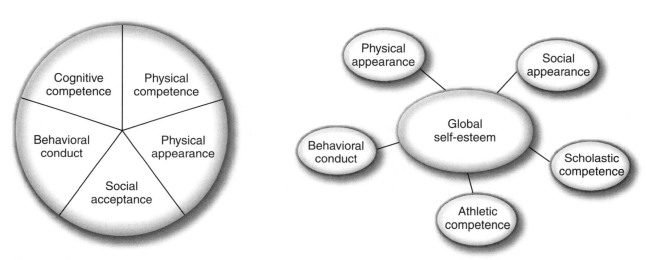

Figure 6.1
Unidimensional and multidimensional perspectives of self.

Hierarchical Models of Self-Concept and Self-Esteem

> ### Key Point
>
> Hierarchical models of self-concept and self-esteem are multifaceted and multilevel. Global self-esteem or self-concept, at the top level, is relatively stable and resistant to external change. Each lower level includes subdomains that are less stable and less resistant to external forces.

Multidimensional models have been expanded to include a hierarchical structure. Shavelson, Hubner, and Stanton (1976) proposed a multifaceted, hierarchical model with global self-concept at the top level, which is the most stable and resistant to the influence of external forces (see also Harter, 1999; Horn, 2004; Marsh & Craven, 2006). At the next level, academic self-concept and three nonacademic components—social self-concept, emotional self-concept, and physical self-concept—form the basis of the global self-concept. These lower-level, domain-specific self-concepts are less stable and resistant to external forces than the global self-concept. Each of these four components, in turn, includes subdomains based on evaluations of behavior in specific situations. For example, academic self-concept includes subdomains of language arts, history, math, and science, and physical self-concept includes physical ability and physical appearance.

FOCUSING ON PHYSICAL SELF-CONCEPT

Herbert Marsh argues for a focus on the specific domain of interest rather than on global self-concept (Marsh & Craven, 1997). Marsh (Marsh, 1997; Marsh & Craven, 2006) and Ken Fox (Fox, 1990, 1998; Fox & Corbin 1989) have contributed substantially to our understanding of the physical self. Both used the Shalverson model as a blueprint but found the physical self to be more complex than that which can be captured with two subareas. In Fox's three-tier hierarchical model, global self-esteem is at the top. Physical self-worth, at the next level, is based on the four subdomains of sport competence, attractive body, physical strength, and physical condition. Physical self-worth mediates the relationship between self-esteem and the four subdomains. Although the hierarchical structure of self-concept is a pervasive perspective today, some research questions it (e.g., Kowalski, Crocker, Kowalski, Chad, & Humbert, 2003).

Fox developed a measurement tool, the Physical Self-Perception Profile (PSPP), for assessing the physical self. It includes the following subscales:

- **Sport competence (sport):** Perceptions of sport and athletic ability, ability to learn sport skills, and confidence in the sport environment

- **Physical condition (condition):** Perceptions of physical condition, stamina, and fitness; ability to maintain exercise; and confidence in the exercise and fitness setting

- **Body attractiveness (body):** Perceived attractiveness of figure or physique, ability to maintain an attractive body, and confidence in appearance

- **Physical strength (strength):** Perceived strength, muscle development, and confidence in situations requiring strength

- **Physical self-worth (PSW):** General feelings of happiness, satisfaction, pride, respect, and confidence in the physical self

The inclusion of physical self-worth underscores that the physical subdomains cannot be summed to obtain the physical self-worth score. Fox and Corbin (1989) provided evidence for the sensitivity, reliability, and stability of the subscales; confirmed the subscale factor structure; and reported associations of the subscales with physical activity involvement to provide initial validity support. Sonstroem, Speliotis, and Fava (1992) subsequently found that the PSPP showed strong internal consistency, separated exercisers from nonexercisers, and predicted degree of exercise involvement among adults, and they recommended its continued use.

Marsh (Marsh, 1996; Marsh, Richards, Johnson, Roche, & Tremayne, 1994) used psychometric techniques to develop the Physical Self-Description Questionnaire (PSDQ), a multidimensional physical self-concept measure with 11 scales: strength, body fat, activity, endurance and fitness, sport competence, coordination, health, appearance, flexibility, global physical self-worth, and global esteem. Marsh and colleagues provided good psychometric support for the measure; they confirmed its validity by correlating PSDQ subscales with external criterion measures of body composition, physical activity, endurance, strength, and flexibility.

Consistent with the hierarchical models (e.g., Shavelson et al., 1976), Fox and Marsh contend that the subdomains are further divided into more situation-specific areas. For example, sport competence can be divided into a facet (e.g., basketball ability), a subfacet (e.g., shooting ability), and self-efficacy or situation-specific confidence (e.g., "I can make this free throw"). Further, these more dynamic, lower-level self-perceptions affect their more stable, higher-order counterparts. These lower-level self-perceptions (e.g., confidence and self-efficacy) are discussed later in the chapter.

Sonstroem and Morgan (1989) made the nature of the relationship among the higher- and lower-order self-perceptions more explicit in their model, similar to that of Fox (1990) and Marsh (1990). They proposed the following:

1. Physical fitness is more highly related to physical self-efficacy than to physical competence, physical acceptance, and global self-esteem.

2. Physical self-efficacy is more highly related to physical competence than to physical acceptance or global self-esteem.

3. Physical competence is more highly related to global self-esteem than is physical self-efficacy or physical fitness.

Further developing the understanding of self-esteem, Marsh and colleagues (Marsh, Chanal, & Sarrazin, 2006; Marsh & Craven, 2006) argue that achievement is influenced by both a domain-level self-worth (e.g., physical self-worth) and performance, which are mutually reinforcing. Thus, physical performance influences physical self-worth and physical self-worth influences performance.

 ## *Application Point*

Alexis, who is only 10 years old, suffers from an overall poor self-concept. Because she is well-coordinated and likes to dance, her parents think that dance classes will bolster her low self-esteem. Considering the nature of self-esteem and the structure of the physical self, what do you think of her parents' idea, and why? How might this happen, and why would it be likely to happen?

Research on Physical Self-Concept

Earlier reviews of research on psychological benefits of physical activity (e.g., Folkins & Sime, 1981) suggested that vigorous exercise and enhanced fitness might positively affect mood and self-concept. Recent multidimensional self-perception measures allow consideration of more specific relationships among self-perceptions and physical activity, and they may be especially useful with the growing interest in health-oriented exercise and the psychological benefits of physical activity.

Studies on the relationship between self-concept and exercise indicate a positive relationship (e.g., Asci, 2003; Taylor & Fox, 2005). Consistent with the hierarchical model of self-esteem, body esteem shows stronger relationships with fitness than global self-concept, and physical strength and body-fat percentage are two physical measures that particularly relate to self-concept. Berger and McInman (1993) report that longitudinal or intervention studies on exercise are more mixed. Again, characteristics of the program may be relevant. For example, weightlifting and outdoor adventure programs appear effective in enhancing self-concept (e.g., Brone & Reznikoff, 1989; Tucker, 1987). Berger, Pargman, and Weinberg (2007) suggest that the neuropsychological, biochemical, and social cognitive characteristics of aerobic activities are the reason for their effectiveness. They also suggest that exercisers' motives play a role. They cite research revealing that exercisers with health and fitness motives experienced increases in self-esteem more than those with physical appearance motives.

Overall, sport, exercise, and physical activity programs do not have strong effects on global self-worth. As noted in previous chapters, general personality is not likely to change with short-term programs. However, activity programs may well influence specific perceptions of physical competence or body concept, and multidimensional measures may help us investigate such effects. More specific perceptions of self-efficacy for specific tasks are even more amenable to change; we will consider those self-perceptions later in this chapter. Also, quality of life and psychological well-being encompass mood and emotion, as well as personality and self-concept, and we will consider emotion in more depth in chapter 12.

Body Image

Before exploring the structure of the self, let's look at a specific self-perception related to physical activity that remains salient throughout the life span. Perceptions of the physical body are part of self-concept. Body perceptions are particularly relevant to physical self-concept, and both Fox (1990) and Marsh (1990, 1996) include body image in their models. Moreover, body image is particularly relevant to sport and exercise psychology work on eating disorders and related concerns with participants in physical activity.

Body perceptions and measures of body image have been associated with self-concept for some time. Early measures include the Body Cathexis Scale (BCS; Secord and Jourard, 1953) and the Body-Esteem Scale (BES). More recent research on body image is grounded in self-presentation (Leary, 1992) and self-esteem literature. Self-presentation theory suggests that as social beings, people desire to make a positive impression and are selective in the self-information they present to others (see Martin Ginis, Lindwall, & Prapavessis, 2007; Prapavessis, Grove, & Eklund, 2004). When people want to present a favorable body image but fear negative evaluation by others, they experience social physique anxiety (SPA). Hart, Leary, and Rejeski (1989), who developed the Social Physique Anxiety Scale (SPAS), provided evidence that the SPAS demonstrates good internal consistency, test–retest reliability, and correlations with other body image and esteem measures and public self-consciousness.

In a review, Rodin and Larson (1992) concluded that cultural and social factors emphasize unrealistic body shapes and that thinness is joined by fitness within the body shape ideal. Developmental factors conspire against females since physical maturation conflicts with the prevailing cultural imperative. Rodin and Larson further concluded that athletes particularly face extraordinary cultural and psychological pressures to maintain an ideal body and that such pressures may lead to eating disorders and substance abuse. Eating disorders are primarily female phenomena (cf. Martin Ginis et al., 2007). Reel and Gill (1996) found strong relationships between both SPAS and body dissatisfaction and eating behavior, suggesting body image as an important predictor. In "The Real Swimsuit Issue," Barbara Ehrenreich (1996) discussed body image and self-concept for women, saying, "Where is the FDA [Food and Drug Administration] when you need it? There should be warning labels on every suit: this product may be hazardous to your self-esteem" (p. 68).

Body-image concerns are not unique to females. Male bodybuilders with higher SPA were more likely to use anabolic steroids than those with lower SPA (cf. Martin Ginis et al., 2007). Nonetheless, females generally are more concerned with body image than males (Hart et al., 1989) and have been found to have greater SPA (cf. Prapavessis et al., 2004). This is not surprising given the societal image of the ideal female body and the emphasis on physical attractiveness in media coverage of women's sport (see Gill, 2002, 2007).

SELF-CONFIDENCE AND SELF-EFFICACY

Self-confidence and self-efficacy may be the most critical self-perceptions in sport and exercise psychology. Many top athletes exude confidence, and male athletes are more likely to be boastful publically. Muhammad Ali and Joe Namath were known for their colorful and convincing boasts, and recently Barry Bonds proclaimed, "I was born to hit a baseball. I can hit a baseball" (www.baseball-almanac.com). When commenting about his status as a top wide receiver in 2001, the controversial Terrell Owens said, "To be honest, I think I'm a little better than [Randy] Moss. I bring a lot more to the table than he does" (Kroichick, 2001). Phil Davis, a wrestler at Penn State, didn't hide his confidence when he stated, "I'm making a pretty strong case [for the No.1 spot]. There's very little evidence to argue against it" (Reis, 2007).

Athletes recognize the value of a positive attitude, and we tell performers, "Think like a winner" or "Believe in yourself." As noted in chapter 4, the most consistent difference between elite athletes and those who are less successful is that elite athletes possess greater self-confidence (e.g., Gould, Weiss, & Weinberg, 1981; Mahoney & Avener, 1977). Is self-confidence really that important? If so, can we enhance an athlete's confidence? If confidence increases, will athletes perform better, enjoy the activity more, or experience other benefits? Sport and exercise psychologists have applied Bandura's self-efficacy model and social-cognitive theory to address these questions, and the work continues to advance in many directions.

Bandura's Self-Efficacy Theory

Albert Bandura (1977b, 1982, 1986, 1997) proposed an elegant model of self-efficacy and behavior. Consistent with models of self-esteem, self-efficacy is a situation-specific form of self-confidence, or the belief that one is competent and can do whatever is necessary to achieve expected outcomes. Self-efficacy may fluctuate greatly, whereas self-confidence is a more global and stable personality characteristic. A high school wrestler in a tournament might feel confident or efficacious going into the first match. If he goes into the final period behind on points, feeling tired, and seeing the opponent looking fresh and eager, he may quickly feel much less confident.

> **Key Point**
>
> Self-efficacy is a situation-specific form of self-confidence, or the belief that one is competent and can do whatever is necessary to achieve expected outcomes. Self-confidence is a more global and stable personality characteristic, whereas self-efficacy may fluctuate greatly.

For Bandura, self-efficacy predicts actual performance when necessary skills and appropriate incentives are present. He suggests that efficacy expectations are the primary determinants of choice of activity, level of effort, and degree of persistence. High-efficacious people seek challenges, try hard, and persist, whereas low-efficacious people tend to avoid challenges, give up, and become more anxious or depressed when faced with adversity. Self-efficacy theory implies that various strategies used by coaches, instructors, and performers affect performance and behavior because they affect self-efficacy—the critical mediating variable.

So far we have considered self-efficacy as an individual characteristic, but Bandura has also suggested the possibility of a collective form of efficacy.

Collective efficacy is the shared belief of group members in their joint capabilities as a group to execute a task successfully. It involves the coordinated use of individual resources. Such a notion seems particularly applicable to sport teams. Bandura suggests that aggregating individual members' judgments about the group's capabilities is appropriate when assessing collective efficacy in groups requiring greater coordinated efforts (e.g., a football team), whereas an aggregate of individuals' self-efficacy is sufficient for groups requiring less coordinated efforts (e.g., a wrestling team). However, in a review of the literature on collective efficacy in sport, Meyers and Feltz (2007) conclude that the aggregate of athletes' individual self-efficacy is not appropriate for highly interdependent tasks.

Research on Sources of Self-Efficacy

Efficacy expectations develop through six primary types of information: performance accomplishments, vicarious experiences, emotional and physiological states, verbal persuasion, and imaginal experiences. Changes in self-efficacy, in turn, influence actual behavior. Performance accomplishments, or mastery experiences, provide the most dependable information and have the most powerful effects on self-efficacy. In practicing your serve, if you repeatedly view yourself successful, self-efficacy will increase, whereas repeatedly viewing yourself as unsuccessful will result in lower self-efficacy. Feltz and Lrigg (2001) contend that the power of performance accomplishments depends on the perceived difficulty of the task, effort expended, guidance received, and degree to which the performer views the required ability as innate versus learned.

Vicarious experiences involve watching someone else accomplish the skill (a model). Demonstrations are often used to teach sport skills, and seeing someone else perform can give athletes confidence. Several studies have demonstrated the effectiveness of modeling (see McCullaugh & Weiss, 2001), particularly models who are similar to the observer (George, Feltz, & Chase, 1992; Weiss, McCullaugh, Smith, & Berlant, 1998). Self-modeling, or watching your own correct performance or the best parts of your performance, is also thought to affect self-efficacy. Although research shows a positive association between self-modeling and performance, it does not seem to enhance self-efficacy (e.g., Ram & McCullaugh, 2003; Starek & McCullaugh, 1999; Winfrey & Weeks, 1993).

Bandura suggests that physiological and emotional states, or more precisely, perceptions of arousal, affect behavior through efficacy expectations. A person's physiological state is a function of the autonomic response associated with fear or readiness. If you notice your heart pounding and your knees shaking just before a match, you likely will feel less confident than if your heart were beating strongly and you felt steady. Emotional state, or mood, is associated with self-efficacy. Treasure, Monson, and Lox (1996) found that the higher a wrestler's positive emotional states were (e.g., determined, excited, inspired), the greater the self-efficacy; the higher the negative emotional states, the lower the self-efficacy. Further, the higher the precompetition self-efficacy, the better the wrestler's performance.

Verbal persuasion is often used to boost confidence. Teachers and coaches encourage performers with statements such as, "You've got the talent; I know you can do it." Others' evaluations or expectations, as well as self-talk, are forms of verbal persuasion. Positive imaginal experiences, such as imaging a successful performance, have also been found to increase self-efficacy (Feltz & Riessinger, 1990).

Key Point

There are five sources of self-efficacy: performance accomplishment, vicarious experiences, physiological and emotional states, verbal persuasion, and imaginal experiences.

In discussing sources of collective efficacy, Feltz and Lrigg (2001) suggest that self-efficacy and collective efficacy might share similar sources. At the group level, these sources include performance accomplishment, vicarious experience, physiological states, emotional states, and verbal persuasion. For example, if team members repeatedly and collectively perceive team success, the efficacy of the group will probably increase. Likewise, seeing another team beat an upcoming opponent may enhance the group's collective efficacy. In addition, leader effectiveness may influence collective efficacy through minimization of coordination losses and verbal persuasion. Booing or cheering fans and positive or negative press have also been suggested as possible sources of collective efficacy.

Research on Self-Efficacy in the Physical Domain

Over the last 15 years, self-efficacy theory has been applied more widely in exercise activities and sport. Based on Feltz and Lrigg's (2001) cogent review of self-efficacy in sport settings, we conclude the following. First, most of the studies show a significant or at least a moderate relationship between self-efficacy and performance. Second, self-efficacy is a stronger predictor of performance than other variables. Third, self-efficacy predicts performance, but performance is a stronger predictor of self-efficacy. Finally, self-efficacy is associated with anxiety, emotions, win orientation, and sport confidence. Collective efficacy may predict team performance more than self-efficacy.

In rehabilitation settings, self-efficacy is a determinant of physical activity behavior. For example, Ewart, Taylor, Reese, and DeBusk (1983) reported that postmyocardial infarction (PMI) patients who were more efficacious about their physical capabilities exerted more effort, recovered faster, and returned to normal activities more quickly. Ewart et al. (1986) also demonstrated that PMI patients' efficacy predicted exercise compliance, whereas physical capabilities did not. Taylor, Bandura, Ewart, Miller, and DeBusk (1985) reported that not only patients' efficacy but also their spouses' efficacy predicted cardiac function.

Many studies support strong links between self-efficacy and physical activity. McAuley and his colleagues have conducted several leading studies in this area, and his reviews (McAuley, 1992, 1993; McAuley, Pena, & Jerome, 2001) summarize that work. Self-efficacy predicted exercise behavior in college undergraduates (Dzewaltowski, 1989; Dzewaltowski, Noble, & Shaw, 1990); it predicted exercise adherence for middle-aged adults (McAuley, 1993); and it related to physical activity in a community sample (Sallis et al., 1986). These studies suggest that self-efficacy theory may contribute substantially to our understanding of exercise behavior in both asymptomatic and diseased populations (McAuley, 1993). Physical activity also influences self-efficacy. Acute (e.g., McAuley et al., 1999; McAuley, Lox, & Duncan, 1993; Rudolph & McAuley, 1995) and chronic (Kaplan, Atkins, & Reinsch, 1984; Kaplan, Ries, Prewitt, & Eakin, 1994; Ries, Kaplan, Limberg, & Prewitt, 1995) exposure to exercise resulted in increased self-efficacy.

Application Point

Bobby is in rehabilitation after surgery to repair his ACL. He has expressed doubts in his ability to fully recover and fears he will never return to game play. How do you think Bobby's attitude will affect his recovery, and why? Also, give three suggestions for bolstering Bobby's confidence.

Self-Efficacy Measures

Self-efficacy by definition is unstable and situation-specific. Bandura (1977a, 1986) argued (and most researchers agree) that self-efficacy measures should be microanalytic, assessing efficacy along three dimensions: level, strength, and generality.

- **Level** reflects the expected performance attainment or number of tasks that can be completed. For example, in Feltz's (1984) diving studies, performing the back dive from the board was the highest level, whereas jumping feet first from the side of the pool was a lower level. Components of a complex skill, or lead-up activities, might reflect levels.

- **Strength** represents the certainty with which the person expects to attain each level successfully. Typically, strength of efficacy is measured on a percentage scale, with 100% reflecting absolute certainty. On the diving task, a person might be 100% certain of successfully jumping off the side of the pool but only 20% certain of successfully completing a back dive from the board.

- **Generality** refers to the number of domains in which people consider themselves efficacious. For example, gymnastics efficacy might generalize from efficacy for floor exercise to efficacy for the balance beam and uneven parallel bars.

Because self-efficacy measures refer to specific tasks and situations, they vary widely across studies. Strength is usually the key measure, and most studies use the percentage format. Levels are also common, but they are not as critical as strength. For example, Feltz (1984a) focused on the strength of efficacy for the ultimate task (back dive from the board) for her main tests of self-efficacy theory. Generality is even rarer in self-efficacy measures and research. Feltz and Chase (1998) discuss the measurement of self-efficacy and suggest that the Physical Self-Efficacy Scale (PSES; Ryckman, Robbins, Thornton, and Cantrell, 1982) is more similar to a self-concept scale than self-efficacy.

> ### Key Point
> Bandura (1977a, 1986) argued that self-efficacy measures should assess efficacy along three dimensions: level, strength, and generality.

Sport Confidence

Robin Vealey (1986) drew on self-efficacy theory and other self-perception work, as well as the research on sport personality, in the development of a sport confidence model. Sport confidence was initially conceptualized as two separate, related constructs: trait (SC-T) and state (SC-S) sport confidence. She reconceptualized her model by taking into account social and cultural influences on sources and levels of sport confidence, viewing sport confidence on a continuum from trait to state-like and reexamining the sources of self-confidence (Vealey, 2001). She has identified nine sources of self-confidence that fall in three general categories: (1) sources of achievement include *mastery* and *demonstrating ability,* (2) self-regulation includes *physical and mental preparation* and *physical self-presentation,* and (3) social climate includes *social support, vicarious experiences, coach leadership, environmental comfort,* and *situational favorableness.*

Based on her reconceptualized model, Vealey identifies three strategies for enhancing self-confidence: enhancing the quality of training and perceived achievement; using self-regulatory strategies such as goal setting, imagery, and self-talk; and providing a supportive climate through effective feedback, team-building activities, and effective modeling. Given what you have learned about self-efficacy, how might you enhance the self-confidence among the people with whom you work and play?

PUTTING IT INTO PRACTICE

Now you are ready to put the content of chapter 6 into practice. Read the chapter summary, discuss the case study, answer the review questions, and enhance your knowledge by researching the recommended readings.

Summary

Self-perception is one of the most active research areas in sport and exercise psychology today. The work on physical self-concept has adopted the multidimensional and sport-specific frameworks that have advanced other areas of personality and individual differences. That approach provides stronger conceptual frameworks and sounder measures that allow us to investigate multifaceted relationships among self-perceptions and sport and exercise behaviors. Self-efficacy theory has been useful in the investigation of many behaviors, and sport and exercise psychology has moved from self-efficacy work with sport to a wide range of exercise and activity settings. Moreover, self-efficacy theories and research findings offer practical suggestions for enhancing performance and exercise as well as maintaining health-related activities.

Case Study

This chapter highlights approaches for understanding self-perceptions. For this case, we will use the scenarios from the beginning of the chapter for applying your understanding of self-perceptions.

Select one of the three cases introduced in the beginning of the chapter—Chris, Rob, or Jordan—and describe how you would help that person. Consider the structure of self-esteem and the different levels of self-perceptions. For example, which is more malleable: global self-esteem, physical self-worth, or self-efficacy? Be sure you explain why you would take this approach and why it should be effective, and look to the research to find support for the effectiveness of your approach.

Review Questions

1. Define *self-perceptions.*
2. Define *self-schemata* and explain what it means to be schematic, aschematic, and nonschematic.
3. Explain the significance of Harter's model of perceived competence.
4. Describe hierarchical models of self-concept and explain the characteristics of and relationships among the levels.
5. Define and contrast *self-efficacy* and *self-confidence.*
6. Describe the three dimensions along which self-efficacy should be analyzed.

Recommended Reading

Harter, S. (1999). *Construction of the self: A developmental perspective.* New York: Guilford Press.

> This book traces changes in the structure and content of self-concept in children from a young age through adolescence. It focuses on the progression of individuals' competency-related self-assessment and how factors including significant others, gender, and culture shape these self-assessments.

Kendzierski, D., Furr, R.M., & Schiavoni, J. (1998). Physical activity self-definitions: Correlates and perceived criteria. *Journal of Sport & Exercise Psychology, 20,* 176-193.

> Grounded in self-schema theory, this article investigates the criteria for self-definitions in a variety of physical activities (e.g., weightlifting, basketball, exercise) and factors associated with these self-definitions. Results reveal that participants described themselves based on behavioral criteria more than affective criteria.

Kowalski, K.C., Crocker, P.R.E., Kowalski, N.P., Chad, K.E., & Humbert, M.L. (2003). Examining the physical self in adolescent girls over time: Further evidence against the hierarchical model. *Journal of Sport & Exercise Psychology, 25,* 5-18.

> This study examines the hierarchical nature of self-concept as measured by the PSPP among adolescent girls. It is worth reading because the results provide evidence against the hierarchical model of self-concept.

Part III

Motivation

In part III we turn to motivation, a broad and pervasive topic that defies definition. In general terms, *motivation* refers to the intensity and direction of behavior. Motivation refers to why people behave as they do—and that is the essential question in sport and exercise psychology. As seen in other chapters, behavior is determined (or motivated) by both personal characteristics and environmental factors. Part III covers the major theories and approaches to sport and exercise motivation. First, chapter 7, co-authored by David Topor, gives us the basics of behavioral motivation with an emphasis on reinforcement and behavior management. Then we turn to the major social-cognitive theories and models in the motivational literature of sport and exercise psychology. Chapter 8 focuses on motivational orientation, including research on achievement and goal orientations in sport and exercise. Chapter 9 focuses on intrinsic motivation and the social-cognitive models that dominate the research. Finally, chapter 10 brings the behavioral and cognitive models together to focus on maintaining participation in lifestyle physical activity.

Chapter 7

Behavioral Approaches

David Topor and Diane L. Gill

Chapter Objectives

After studying this chapter, you should be able to

- define basic behavior terminology, including *reinforcement, punishment,* and *shaping;*
- explain the steps in implementing a behavioral plan; and
- understand how kinesiology professionals can help athletes and exercisers develop skills, strategies, and other desired behavior patterns through effective behavioral approaches.

Consider these scenarios. The star athlete breaks her leg and needs months of rehabilitation exercises. The man at risk for a heart attack is told by his physician that he must start going to the gym. The young gymnast is overwhelmed by having to perform in front of a large audience and doesn't live up to expectations.

How does the trainer help the athlete follow the prescribed rehabilitation regimen? How does the exercise instructor motivate the client to keep going to the gym? How does the coach help the gymnast maintain focus on her performance? As explained in this chapter, one answer is using principles of behavior theory. Behavioral change and the use of reinforcement are among the most widely researched and accepted concepts of modern psychology. Behavioral approaches emphasize changing environmental circumstances because behavior is determined primarily by its consequences. In other words, behavior is strengthened when rewarded and weakened when punished or ignored.

WHAT IS BEHAVIOR?

Key Point

Classical conditioning involves learning by association with existing involuntary, reflective responses, whereas operant conditioning involves learning new skills and maintaining conditions.

As defined by Malott and Suarez (2004), behavior is a muscular, glandular, or electrical activity. It is anything an animal does, including movement and thoughts. Put another (perhaps a little more gruesome) way, behavior is anything a dead person can't do. Dead people don't walk, talk, play tennis, or go to rock concerts.

Behavior is learned and maintained through two processes, classical conditioning and operant conditioning. Classical conditioning involves learning by association with existing involuntary, reflective responses, whereas operant conditioning involves learning new skills and maintaining conditions. Operant conditioning is the more relevant process for sport and exercise behavior and thus most of this chapter will deal with operant techniques.

Classical conditioning is widely known through the work of Ivan Pavlov. A Nobel Prize–winning Russian physiologist, Pavlov made his name in psychology somewhat serendipitously after noticing that his dogs began to salivate at the sound of an assistant approaching with food. Pavlov then set up his classical-conditioning experiment. Classical conditioning begins with an existing stimulus–response connection. In this case, the dog naturally salivates in response to food; conditioning has not yet occurred. Food is the unconditioned stimulus and salivation is the unconditioned response. To begin classical conditioning, Pavlov sounded a tone immediately before presenting the food. After several trials, the dog began to salivate at the tone regardless of whether the food followed. We now have a conditioned stimulus–response connection, developed by the association of the conditioned stimulus with the unconditioned stimulus. The tone is the conditioned stimulus and the salivation response to the tone is the conditioned response.

For instance, perhaps you are sitting in an evening class and getting hungry. The professor brings in pizza for the students to eat, but she first rings a bell before letting the class see and smell the pizza, at which time you begin to salivate. After repeated trials, you will salivate at the sound of the bell only, which is now a conditioned response to what previously was an unconditioned stimulus. Classical conditioning is seldom used intentionally as an instructional strategy, but it certainly occurs in sport and exercise, as well as in everyday life. For instance, after a poor performance in a game, an athlete may sit at a press conference in front of several microphones, which may increase his anxiety answering questions about his performance. If this occurs several times, the athlete's anxiety will increase simply as a result of sitting in front of the microphones, even in the absence of a poor performance.

Today, techniques associated with behavioral change are primarily based on principles of operant learning. There are many benefits to using behavioral change or performance management with athletes and exercisers. It is effective, gives the person control, has a learning emphasis, is collaborative, is individualized, and is relatively easy to administer. There are numerous techniques to choose from, many of which will be discussed here along with practical applications.

Operant Conditioning

Key Point

Reinforcement is any stimulus, event, or condition whose presentation immediately follows a response and increases the frequency of that response. Positive reinforcement occurs when behaviors are reinforced through provision of something positive. Negative reinforcement occurs when behaviors are strengthened by eliminating something negative.

To understand operant behavioral approaches, we need to establish basic terminology. The key to behavior change is reinforcement. *Reinforcement* is any stimulus, event, or condition whose presentation immediately follows a response and increases the frequency of that response (Malott & Suarez, 2004). Common reinforcers include tangible rewards such as trophies, certificates, T-shirts, and scholarships, as well as nontangible rewards such as praise from a coach, cheers from the crowd, or peer comments on one's fit and healthy look. Successful performance itself is a common reinforcer; seeing the ball go through the basket, serving an ace, or jogging that extra mile may reinforce specific behaviors. In these examples, behaviors are reinforced through the provision of something positive such as praise or awards; this is termed *positive reinforcement.*

Behaviors also can be strengthened by eliminating something negative or aversive; this is called *negative reinforcement.* For example, a coach may stop playing loud, annoying music only after the athletes have completed the required number of sit-ups. Negative reinforcement is less obvious than positive reinforcement, but it does occur. If you learned to dive into the water the way most beginners do, you probably took some painful belly flops. When you finally performed the dive correctly, you did not feel the usual pain. Removal of the pain negatively reinforced the correct diving technique. People may find negative reinforcement confusing because we often use terms incorrectly, saying *negative reinforcement* when we mean *punishment.* Remember, negative reinforcement is reinforcement—an operation that increases the strength of a behavior.

Punishment Principle

Punishment is an aversive condition that follows a behavior and decreases rather than increases the strength of the behavior. Punishment can occur through the presentation of something negative or aversive or through the withdrawal of something positive. Critical comments on poor play, penalties for improper behavior, and being faked out by an opponent may punish the preceding behaviors. Parents often withdraw privileges or something rewarding, such as the use of a car, after an adolescent breaks a household rule. This aversive condition of not having a car will decrease the strength of the adolescent's noncompliant behavior. Similarly, coaches may bench a player for not attending practice sessions. Although punishment is effective in certain situations, a system involving reinforcements is preferable.

As shown in figure 7.1, the two basic behavioral operations are reinforcement and punishment. Reinforcement entails presenting something positive (positive reinforcement) or taking away something negative (negative reinforcement) in order to increase the preceding behavior. Punishment entails presenting something negative or taking away something positive in order to decrease the preceding behavior.

Figure 7.1
Reinforcement and punishment.

Action	Positive events (praise, award)	Negative/aversive events (criticism, pain)
Present	Positive reinforcement	Punishment
Remove	Punishment	Negative reinforcement

IMPLEMENTING A BEHAVIOR PLAN

As with all of the psychological skills and techniques discussed in this book, the context and interpersonal relationships between teacher and student, client and trainer, or athlete and consultant are important. A comfortable, trusting relationship allows for successful implementation and monitoring of a behavioral plan.

There are seven steps to implementing a behavioral plan with an athlete or client (adapted from Spiegler & Guevremont, 2003).

1. Clarify the problem.
2. Formulate goals for the consultation.

3. Design target behaviors.
4. Identify the maintaining conditions of the target behavior.
5. Design a treatment plan.
6. Implement the plan.
7. Evaluate the success of the plan.

Clarify the Problem

Many times people come to a consultant and describe their problems in vague terms (i.e., "I can't concentrate on the game," "I can't stay motivated to train"). The first step is to get specific. By specifying the problem, both the athlete and the consultant will be working on the same challenge. For instance, when an athlete describes difficulties with concentration, what does that really mean? Is the athlete having difficulty focusing at the beginning, middle, or end of the game? What exactly is the athlete having problems focusing on? By clearly defining the problem, the athlete and the consultant are able to tailor the intervention to address the athlete's concerns.

Formulate Goals

Once the problem is clarified, specific goals need to be formulated. For instance, a client might want to build endurance to run a marathon or get in shape for the summer swimming season. Participants should personally set their own performance goals because this increases their commitment to achieve the goals. There are a few instances, however, when the consultant might want to take a more active role in the goal setting. One example might be when the athlete's goals are clearly unrealistic or when the goals are likely to have negative consequences, such as when an athlete wants to double her rehabilitation schedule so that she can return to the game sooner, against the advice of her trainers. Goals may be reevaluated at any time and can be changed based on an ongoing assessment of the athlete's progress.

Design Target Behaviors

A target behavior is a specific aspect of the problem that is clearly defined and easily measured. A client might walk into your office and say he is having trouble completing a moderately stressful workout three times a week. A skilled consultant will first sit down with the client and define what a moderately stressful workout is. For instance, a specific target behavior might be completing 2 sets of 15 repetitions on each station of a weight training circuit during a workout. These behaviors are narrow in scope, clearly defined using unambiguous language, and appropriate for the person. Therefore, a good behavioral goal defines a completed set (we all have different definitions), how much time the client has to do the set, at what point during the workout each set should be done, and so forth. The more specific the goal is, the better.

The behavior must also be measurable, whether it is the frequency, the duration, or the intensity that is measured. Measurement must begin before the intervention is put into place so that both the consultant and the athlete understand the baseline of the identified behavior. The baseline is how often the behavior occurs in a natural setting, that is, before the intervention begins.

For instance, the client who wants to increase the number of sets during each workout would first have to monitor the number of sets performed before implementing a plan developed with the consultant.

When designing a target behavior, it is important to select a behavior that the athlete or exerciser can actively work toward rather than a behavior that the person should not do. For example, rather than a goal of not focusing on the crowd during a game, a more effective goal would be to focus on a particular spot in the stadium each time the athlete becomes distracted. Simply telling a person not to do something does not suggest what should be done instead. Make your target behaviors ones that the athlete can actively perform.

Identify Maintaining Conditions of the Target Behavior

The next step is understanding why the person maintains the maladaptive behaviors. For instance, why does the cardiac rehabilitation client not follow through on his exercise routine? This step requires in-depth knowledge of the client and the behavior.

The basic way of understanding behaviors is through the ABC model. The *A* stands for the antecedents, or the events that occur before the person performs the behavior. The *B* stands for the behavior itself. The *C* stands for the consequences of a behavior, or the events that occur as a result of the behavior. Both antecedents and consequences can maintain a behavior. Maintaining antecedents are responsible for the behavior being performed in the first place. For instance, think about how your behavior differs when you are sitting in class, at a party, or on the sport field. Each environment is an antecedent for specific behaviors. Maintaining consequences determine whether the behavior will occur again. If the consequences of a behavior are not favorable to the person, the behavior is less likely to be repeated. Conversely, if the consequences are positive, the behavior is likely to occur again in the future. Consequences may occur immediately or be delayed, and they can happen directly to the person, to other people, or to the physical environment as a result of the person's behavior. For instance, a consequence of being late to practice might mean the whole team has to do push-ups.

 Application Point

Understanding the ABC model is a first step in behavior management. As a physical education teacher with the behavioral goal of having all students actively participating in a games class, you will likely find some students are active and eager whereas others are withdrawn or avoiding activity. What are some of the possible antecedents and consequences that maintain those differing behaviors?

A thorough assessment of the behavior is key in understanding the maintaining antecedents and consequences. This assessment can be done in a variety of ways and is most effective when multiple reporters are used and multiple aspects of the behavior are accounted for. Multiple reporters of the behavior could include the athlete, the coach, the sport consultant, the athlete's teammates, or even the athlete's friends and family. Multiple aspects of the behavior may include recording overt behavior (e.g., number of sets), inner thoughts and emotions (e.g., "I'm feeling distracted right now"), and perhaps even physiological responses (e.g., heart rate). For example, the baseball player who is unable to focus his attention in the batter's box might need to record what he is paying attention to, what thoughts are going through his mind, what he is feeling, and what bodily sensations (such as sweating) he is experiencing.

There are several ways of assessing behaviors. The first is through an interview with the athlete. Questions emphasizing the *what, when, where, how,* and *how often* of the behavior are most beneficial. In addition to the interview, the consultant may ask the client to complete self-report inventories about current behaviors. These inventories include questions requiring simple *yes* or *no* responses or asking the athlete to rate the accuracy of statements. We all have taken these types of inventories when filling out customer satisfaction surveys or when filling out medical paperwork at a doctor's office. These inventories are highly efficient, provided that the person answers the questions honestly and that the inventory actually measures what you want it to measure (e.g., anxiety in a game situation).

Another method of assessing behavior is to actually observe the behavior. Consultants might watch the athlete before the game, during the game, during practice, or even during the athlete's daily routine. Consultants might note the athlete's activities or use checklists and behavior rating scales to record what behaviors the athlete partakes in, as well as the frequency of those behaviors. Again, these observations can occur in real games, practice, or simulated environments.

Finally, athletes can record their own behaviors. Self-monitoring, or self-recording, is when people record the occurrences of their own behaviors (Polaha, Allen, & Studley, 2004). Self-monitoring has several advantages over the other assessment techniques. For one, it allows the athlete to record both overt and covert behaviors, including thoughts as to why she is not completing the requested exercise regimen. For example, the athlete might write down each time she loses focus, or what anxiety coping skills she is using. The consultant would then be able to examine these behaviors and use them to set up a specific plan for behavioral change.

 ## *Application Point*

Self-monitoring is helpful in trying to manage one's own behaviors. Think about your exercise behavior over a week. What were your behaviors? What events reinforced your exercise behaviors? What events punished your exercise behaviors? How could you monitor your exercise behaviors over the next week in order to identify reinforcing and punishing events so that you could better manage your behavior and stick to your exercise routine?

There is evidence that simply the act of self-recording has a positive impact on an athlete's performance. McKenzie and Rushall (1974) found that self-recording increased attendance at practices and the number of practice laps taken by young swimmers. Critchfield and Vargas (1991) found the same result. Additionally, they found that self-recording had a greater efficacy than other interventions used in the study. In their investigation of self-recording with swimmers, Polaha and colleagues (2004) concluded that self-monitoring is one of the simplest and most effective methods of behavioral change. Their study found that self-monitoring was effective in the development of swimming skills as measured by fewer strokes per lap.

A drawback to having an athlete self-monitor behavior is the chance the athlete may not be accurate in the reporting. For instance, if you were trying to record each time you bite your nails in the span of an hour, errors and biases might occur. You might begin to bite your nails and forget to record it each time, or you might actually start biting your nails less because recording each time you bite is annoying or because you are now more aware of the nail biting and are better able to regulate the behavior. In any case, the recording is not an accurate snapshot of how often the behavior is actually occurring before any type of intervention is put into place. These limitations may hamper the effectiveness of self-recording if they are not attended to. Overall, however, self-recording is a valid and reliable way to obtain data.

At this point, you have clarified the athlete's problem, formulated treatment goals, designed a target behavior, and identified maintaining conditions. But how do you actually achieve behavior change?

Design a Treatment Plan

The target behavior is changed by altering the conditions that maintain it. Many conditions may maintain a behavior, which is why it is crucial that those conditions are thoroughly and carefully identified. For instance, the cardiac patient stays late at work, spends more time with family or friends, or perhaps views the gym as punishing and thus does not follow through on his workout regimen. All of these other activities are viewed as more rewarding than going to the gym. Therefore, the consultant works with the patient to make the gym experience more rewarding, which will increase compliance. There are multiple methods for achieving this.

Reinforcement

One method is reinforcement of the desired behavior. Again, reinforcement is any stimulus, event, or condition whose presentation immediately follows a response and increases the frequency of that response. Positive reinforcers are the most effective. So, if the cardiac patient finds money to be rewarding, giving him $10 immediately after each workout will increase compliance with the workouts. It is important to choose rewards that are reinforcing to the person and to administer them in effective ways. For instance, money might not be rewarding for some people, and it might have other drawbacks. As a consultant you can never assume that a potential consequence can serve as a reinforcer. For some participants, material rewards such as T-shirts or snacks may be effective. For others, improved fitness and appearance after adherence to the exercise routine for 3 months is a more powerful reinforcer. Perhaps the cardiac client finds spending time with friends more rewarding than going to the gym. The consultant may then encourage the client to bring friends with him to the gym.

Several categories of positive reinforcers can be used to change behavior. The first is to use objects that are valuable to the person. These might include money, food, tickets to a game, or another object the athlete finds rewarding. It is crucial to keep in mind that the reinforcer must be decided upon before the treatment begins, and it must be of worth to the person. Providing the athlete with movie tickets or music CDs to maintain the rehabilitation regimen may be ineffective if the athlete does not enjoy movies or music.

Another type of reinforcer is social, such as positive attention, verbal praise, and acknowledgment from other people. It may be given verbally, through a written note, or even through gestures such as a smile or a thumbs-up. For instance, the coach who announces to the rest of the team the progress an athlete has made in rehabilitation following her surgery is socially reinforcing her compliance to the rehabilitation regimen. Similarly, when the leaders of an exercise class announce those with perfect attendance for the month, they are socially reinforcing participants for adherence.

Coaches can take advantage of this reinforcer by having athletes make a public commitment to their team to comply with the training regimen, or even having the athletes sign a behavioral contract and putting it in the locker room. Several studies have found this type of public posting to be an effective reinforcer. Brobst and Ward (2002) found that public posting, along with goal setting and oral feedback, was effective in improving athletic performance both during and after the intervention was in place. Social reinforcers are easy to administer and are unlimited. Try them out next time your roommate cleans up the bathroom and see what happens!

Finally, you can schedule rewarding activities following completion of a task that is less rewarding. This strategy, termed the *Premack principle,* allows people to engage in behaviors they want to do only after doing behaviors they do not want to do. For instance, after completing a challenging new exercise routine, a personal trainer might ask the client to pick a favorite exercise to finish the session.

Effective administration of reinforcers is also important. The reinforcer may be immediate, such as receiving $5 following one workout, or longer term, such as receiving $50 after achieving the goal of three workouts a week. Generally, immediate reinforcers are more effective, but consultants usually use both immediate and long-term reinforcers in a behavior plan. For instance, the consultant could write a behavioral contract with the patient that includes a list of the behaviors the patient needs to accomplish, how many tokens the patient earns for each behavior, a list of rewards, and how many tokens the patient needs to earn a reward. For every 10 minutes the heart patient stays in the exercise class, he might earn 10 tokens. These tokens may be eventually exchanged for movie tickets, exercise clothes, or other rewards the patient has chosen.

Similar to the view of many behaviorists, Kauss (1980) advocates that teachers and coaches use positive reinforcement extensively. Positive reinforcement is more than standing by and saying, "Nice work." It is effective only when applied immediately and consistently, and only when both the teacher and student know what specific behaviors are being reinforced. Kauss lists several guidelines for effective reinforcement (see the following box).

Guidelines for Effective Reinforcement

- *Reinforce immediately.* The more immediate the reinforcement, the stronger its effect. Do not wait for the next break or until after several others have performed.

- *Maintain consistency.* Reinforce correct behaviors every time they occur, especially when teaching new skills. Athletes often change tactics until something is reinforced. If coaches do not reinforce desired behaviors, athletes may turn to easier moves or ones that attract attention.

- *Respond to effort and behavior, not to performance outcome alone.* Beginners seldom perform a skill 100% correctly. Coaches should not wait for the perfect complete skill but should reinforce efforts and behaviors that move toward the desired performance. Responding to behavior rather than to performance outcome is critical. Coaches can help students focus on proper technique by reinforcing correct moves even when the outcome is not perfect. Successful outcomes are also powerful reinforcers; most sport skills have specific desirable outcomes such as making the putt, scoring a goal, or stopping an opponent.

- *Remember that learning is not entirely cumulative; it has its ups and downs.* Neither athletes nor coaches should panic at occasional mistakes or performance slumps. Unless an athlete has slipped into an incorrect pattern, coaches should continue to reinforce correct skills without putting undue pressure on the athlete. Extra pressure may increase anxiety and further aggravate performance difficulties.

- *Use reinforcement to maintain desired behaviors once they are learned.* Frequent and consistent reinforcement is critical during early learning, and reinforcement remains important even after a skill has been well learned. Coaches need not praise every performance, but occasional or intermittent reinforcement helps to maintain desired behaviors. Failure to reinforce correct behaviors, on the other hand, may lead to their extinction. Teachers often focus on incorrect skills and behaviors and ignore students who create no problems or make no obvious mistakes. Those students may change their behaviors, resulting in the deterioration of desirable skills and behaviors. Teachers who rely on positive reinforcement likely will have fewer problems maintaining desirable behaviors.

Reprinted, by permission, from D.R. Kauss, 1980, *Peak Performance* (Englewood Cliffs, NJ: Prentice-Hall), 99-101.

Using reinforcers over time to gradually shape an athlete's behavior is called *shaping*. Shaping is the reinforcement of successive approximations of the final desired performance. It is a key technique in sport and exercise because most physical skills, plays, and routines develop gradually through progressive steps. For instance, shaping can help a tennis player learn the mechanics of delivering a serve or a batter learn how to bunt. Effective teachers recognize successive steps and reinforce athletes as they move toward the correct performance.

Providing specific details about the target behavior is effective in helping athletes meet their target goal. Komaki and Barnett (1977) found that athletes improved their performance an average of 20% after being given specific instruction about how to execute each target behavior. Specifically, the coach modeled the correct movements for the athletes and provided detailed instruction. Similarly, Fitterling and Ayllon (1983) found that detailed behavioral instruction helped ballet students increase the time they met target behaviors from 13% to 88% for the skills that were measured. Coaches may stand next to the athlete and provide detailed instruction or videotape performances and provide instruction after the fact.

Application Point

Shaping is a particularly useful behavioral technique for developing skills, maintaining exercising behaviors, or progressing through rehabilitation exercises. As a therapist, how could you use shaping to help a client recovering from knee surgery progress through an exercise program leading to recovery of full range of motion and normal activity? Identify steps in the program and reinforcement strategies you might use.

Relaxation

In addition to reinforcers, other behavioral techniques address the target behavior. Sport consultants have used relaxation and imagery to enable athletes to reduce anxiety while working toward behavioral goals. Many times athletes pair a stressful reaction with behavior. For instance, an athlete might concentrate on the crowd rather than focus on his own performance. Relaxation training is effective for associating feelings of relaxation with the target behavior. An athlete can use imagery to picture a pleasurable scene, such as lying on the beach, rather than focusing on the crowd. Athletes can also use muscle relaxation to pair their behavior with a less stressful atmosphere. Muscle relaxation entails tensing and relaxing various muscle groups, with the goal of being able to quickly relax the body in a stressful situation. Martin, Vause, and Schwartzman (2005) examined several studies that used imagery and relaxation techniques and found that participants in 14 of the 15 studies showed improvement, with participants in 9 of the studies showing substantial improvement in their sport-related behavior.

Implement the Plan

Once the athlete and the consultant agree on the goals and the behavior plan, the treatment begins on an agreed-upon date. The treatment plan is continually monitored and adjusted over time. For instance, if the goals for treatment change or life circumstances occur that prevent certain activities, the goals and activities would need to be revised.

Evaluate the Plan

Following implementation of the behavioral plan, consultation with the sport consultant should focus on revising the plan to ensure that the athlete continues to meet the target goal. If the target behavior has not been met, the consultant may need to reexamine the variables maintaining the behavior and perhaps find another strategy to help the athlete. Again, assessment is necessary to ensure that progress is occurring. Whether that progress is evident in a higher batting average, more times going to the gym each week, or successful progression through rehabilitation, the athlete should be able to track the success of the intervention. Consultations may taper off following successful attainment of the target behavior, but follow-up meetings may need to take place months or even years later.

Behavior change is very effective in the fields of sport and exercise science. Detailed skill instruction and positive reinforcement for gains are crucial in helping athletes attain their target goals. The following section will examine how coaches can successfully employ these techniques through their coaching styles and techniques.

Tharp and Gallimore's Research on Coaching Style

One of the first attempts to assess coaching behavior was Tharp and Gallimore's (1976) observational study of John Wooden, perhaps the most successful coach in college basketball. Before retiring in 1975, Wooden coached the UCLA (University of California, Los Angeles) men's basketball teams to 10 national championships in 12 years, a record no one else has approached. Tharp and Gallimore's coding system incorporated standard teaching behavior categories such as reward, punishment, and modeling, as well as a few categories created for Wooden's behavior, such as hustles. The authors observed 2,326 teaching behaviors over 30 hours of practice in the 1974-75 season. Table 7.1 lists the percentage of behavioral acts falling into each category.

Table 7.1   Distribution of John Wooden's Coaching Behaviors

Code	Category	Description	Percent of total communications
I	Instructions	Verbal statements about what to do or how to do it	50.3
H	Hustles	Verbal statements to activate or intensify previously instructed behavior	12.7
M+	Modeling-positive	Demonstration of how to perform	2.8
M–	Modeling-negative	Demonstration of how not to perform	1.6
V+	Praises	Verbal compliments, encouragements	6.9
V-	Scolds	Verbal statements of displeasure	6.6
NV+	Nonverbal reward	Nonverbal compliments or encouragements (e.g., smiles, pats, jokes)	1.2
NV–	Nonverbal punishment	Scowls, gestures of despair, and temporary removal of a player from scrimmage, usually to shoot free throws by himself	Trace
W	Scold/reinstruction	Single verbal behavior that refers to a specific act, contains a clear scold, and reasserts a previously instructed behavior (e.g., "How many times do I have to tell you to follow through with your head when shooting?")	8.0
O	Other	Any behavior not falling into the above categories	2.4
X	Uncodable	Behavior not clearly heard or seen	6.6

The most striking finding was the predominance of instruction. Despite the UCLA team's experience and high skill level, more than 50% of Wooden's behaviors were specific instructions to players. Counting other informational acts, such as modeling and reinstruction, about 75% of Wooden's behaviors provided instruction, most of which involved basic basketball skills.

The authors found that Wooden seldom used praise, scolding, or nonverbal punishment. Keep in mind that the UCLA basketball players received tremendous praise and public acclaim, and certainly their many successes were rewarding. Most students and athletes do not have this history of success and rewards, and we should not assume that limiting praise is an effective coaching technique. The most extensive research on coaching behavior indicates that effective coaches give considerable praise and encouragement and rarely use punitive behaviors (Smith & Smoll, 1997; Smoll & Smith, 1984).

Gallimore and Tharp (2004) recently revisited Wooden's remarks to better understand the qualitative aspect of his coaching rather than simply counting his behaviors. The analysis showed that Wooden employed many of the aforementioned behavior strategies. He had an extensive, detailed plan for daily practices that he based on continual evaluation of individual and team development and performance. He made specific individual and team goals, allowing him to anticipate and understand what his players would do or fail to do.

Wooden went to practices with note cards describing the details of a skill the players needed to work on. Examples include moves for a particular position on the court and specific offensive and defensive mechanics that each player needed to master. He explained to the researchers, "I could track the practice of every single player for every single practice session he participated in while I was coaching him" (p. 126). He looked for small improvements over time, understanding that big improvements do not happen quickly.

Wooden was also skilled at providing instructional feedback in a positive way through the feedback sandwich. In this three-step approach, a positive, action-oriented instruction is sandwiched between two encouraging statements. For example, after your shortstop has bobbled a grounder, immediately give a sincere, encouraging statement: "Nice try; you got into position well." Then, give a corrective instruction: "Next time, put your glove on the ground and look the ball into it." Finally, finish off with another encouraging statement: "Hang in there; you'll get it." It is clear that Wooden used detailed skill training, positive reinforcement, and constant reevaluation of both player and team goals, making him a successful coach.

Coaching Behavior Assessment System

Smith, Smoll, and Hunt (1977) took the first step toward understanding the coaching process by developing an observational system, the Coaching Behavior Assessment System (CBAS), to quantify coaching behaviors. After observing and analyzing the behaviors of coaches in several sports, Smith and colleagues generated the 12 categories of coaching behaviors listed in table 7.2.

Coaching behaviors fall into two major classes: reactive behaviors, which respond to players' behaviors, and spontaneous behaviors, which the coach initiates. To use the CBAS, observers check the appropriate category for each observed behavior. The proportions of behaviors in the 12 categories are used to measure coaching style. Smith et al. (1977) demonstrated that the CBAS is easy to use, includes most coaching behaviors, has good reliability, and shows individual differences among coaches. In general, coaches use considerable reinforcement and instruction, but styles differ, most notably in the amount of instruction and proportion of positive behaviors and punitive behaviors.

The CBAS enabled researchers to investigate intriguing practical questions, such as whether differences in coaching behaviors affect players, and if so, whether coaches can be trained to use effective behaviors. In their research program, Smith, Smoll, and Curtis addressed these questions. They used the CBAS to assess behaviors of Little League coaches and compared those behaviors with players' attitudes, enjoyment, and self-esteem (Smith, Smoll, & Curtis, 1978). Researchers recorded behaviors with the CBAS, asked coaches to recall their behaviors, asked players to recall coaches' behaviors, and interviewed players to assess their liking for the coach, activity, and teammates, as well as their self-esteem.

In general, the coaches took a positive approach, using a great deal of reinforcement, technical instruction, and general encouragement. The players perceived coaching behaviors accurately, but the coaches' perceptions of their own behaviors were not accurate; they did not know which behaviors they used most often. The low correlations between CBAS results and coaches' perceptions imply that the first step in a coach training program should be to make coaches aware of their actual behaviors. That knowledge alone may be sufficient to positively modify the behaviors of many well-intentioned coaches who do not realize how much reinforcement or instruction they actually provide.

Table 7.2   Response Categories of the CBAS

Classification	Definition
CLASS I. REACTIVE BEHAVIORS	
Responses to desirable performance	
Reinforcement	A positive, rewarding reaction, verbal or nonverbal, to a good play or good effort
Nonreinforcement	Failure to respond to a good performance
Responses to mistakes	
Mistake-contingent encouragement	Encouragement given to a player following a mistake
Mistake-contingent technical instruction	Instructing or demonstrating to a player how to correct a mistake
Punishment	A negative reaction, verbal or nonverbal, following a mistake
Punitive technical instruction	Technical instruction that is given in a punitive or hostile manner following a mistake
Ignoring mistakes	Failure to respond to a player mistake
Response to misbehavior	
Keeping control	Reactions intended to restore or maintain order among team members
CLASS II. SPONTANEOUS BEHAVIORS	
Game related	
General technical instruction	Spontaneous instruction in the techniques and strategies of the sport (not following a mistake)
General encouragement	Spontaneous encouragement which does not follow a mistake
Organization and administrative	Behavior that sets the stage for play by assigning duties, responsibilities, positions, etc.
Game irrelevant	
General communication	Interactions with players unrelated to the game

Reprinted, by permission, from F. Smoll and R. Smith, 1980, Psychologically-oriented coach training programs: Design, implementation and assessment. In *Psychology of motor behavior and sport-1979,* edited by C.H. Nadeau et al. (Champaign, IL: Human Kinetics), 115.

Understanding effective coaching behaviors is essential before implementing a behavioral plan. Smith and colleagues (1978) found that coaching behaviors relate to player attitudes. As you might expect, coaches who used more reinforcement and encouragement and fewer punitive behaviors were better liked. Contrary to the belief that children just want to have fun and don't care about skill development, coaches who used more instruction also were better liked. A positive approach combining instruction with encouragement related not only to participants' liking for the coach but also to their liking for the activity and teammates and to a greater increase in self-esteem over the season. In a more recent study, Coatsworth and Conroy (2006) found that coach training following Smith and Smoll's approach was associated with self-esteem gains for some youth swimmers, particularly girls and younger swimmers. They concluded that coach training was an effective way to alter coach behavior and enhance the coach–athlete relational context.

The impact of coaching behaviors on win–loss records has also been examined. You might think that coaches who used the positive approach won more games and that success led to positive player attitudes. However, coaching behaviors did not relate to win–loss records and players did not like winning coaches any better than losing coaches. The best-liked coaches actually had a slightly, but not significantly, lower win percentage (.422) than the least-liked coaches (.545). Although win–loss records were not related to players' liking for the coach or activity, players on winning teams thought that the coach liked them more and that their parents liked the coach more than did players on losing teams. As Smoll and Smith (1984) commented, winning apparently made little difference to the children, but they knew it was important to the adults.

Coach Effectiveness Training

From their findings, Smoll and Smith developed a behavioral intervention program for youth sport coaches, coach effectiveness training (CET; Smith, Smoll, & Curtis, 1979). Smith and Smoll (1997) summarized CET guidelines in the following core principles:

- *Developmental model.* Emphasize the important differences between the professional sport model, in which winning and financial gain are the bottom line, and a developmental model, which focuses on providing a positive developmental context. Coaching behaviors that combine instruction and encouragement have a positive effect on children's enjoyment of sport. Winning is defined in terms of giving maximum effort and improving. The primary focus of a youth sport program is having fun, deriving satisfaction from being on the team, learning sport skills, increasing self-esteem, and reducing fear of failure.

- *Positive approach.* The positive approach includes liberal use of positive reinforcement, encouragement, and sound technical instruction. Punitive or hostile responses are discouraged. The positive approach should be applied not only to skill development but also to desirable responses such as teamwork and sportsmanship. One effective way to implement the positive approach is through the aforementioned feedback sandwich.

- *Mutual support.* Establish norms that emphasize athletes' mutual obligations to help one another. When coaches are supportive models and reinforce behaviors that promote team unity, they are likely to develop a "We're in this together" norm.

- *Involve the athletes.* Involving athletes in team decisions and reinforcing compliance are more effective in achieving compliance with team roles and responsibilities than is punishing noncompliance.

- *Self-monitoring.* Coaches are urged to obtain behavioral feedback and engage in self-monitoring to increase awareness and encourage compliance with the guidelines. A typical CET workshop lasts 3 hours and includes a verbal presentation and a manual (Smoll & Smith, 1997), specific suggestions, modeling and role-playing, and a brief self-monitoring form coaches can complete after practices.

Application Point

Smith and Smoll's (1997) research with CET supports the positive approach, but it's not always easy to use this approach in practice. You are coaching a community soccer team of 10- to 12-year-olds. Several players are out of position and missing passes. How could you use the feedback sandwich with these players?

Smith et al. (1979) did an intervention study to evaluate whether CET training would modify behaviors and affect player attitudes. The program included discussion of the research results and follow-up observation for 2 weeks, including self-monitoring and feedback to coaches. Differences in coaching behavior and player attitudes between CET coaches and untrained coaches paralleled the earlier research findings. Trained coaches used more reinforcement and encouragement, and players perceived the trained coaches as using more positive behaviors. Children who played for the trained coaches reported more positive attitudes, liked the coaches more, perceived the coaches as knowledgeable, liked their teammates more, had a higher level of enjoyment in the activity, and reported increased self-esteem. Overall, CET was effective in increasing positive supportive behaviors. In turn, those behaviors elicited more positive player attitudes.

Smith and Smoll (1997) have continued their research and CET programs with consistent results for 20 years. More than 13,000 youth sport coaches have participated in CET workshops, and CET has been applied at the high school, college, and professional levels. This research has influenced others; many youth sport programs have adopted the research-generated guidelines and positive approach. Most of all, Smith and Smoll's work provides a model that begins with a systematic research program, progresses to application of empirical findings in an intervention program, and continues with ongoing evaluation of both the practical intervention and related research.

PUTTING IT INTO PRACTICE

Now you are ready to put the content of chapter 7 into practice. Read the chapter summary, discuss the case study, answer the review questions, and enhance your knowledge by researching the recommened readings.

Summary

Behavioral techniques, which emphasize the role of the environment and behavioral contingencies, are the basics of behavior management. Operant conditioning and related behavior modification techniques can be highly effective with specific sport skills and targeted behaviors. Seven steps to implementing a behavioral plan with an athlete were discussed:

1. Clarify the problem.
2. Formulate goals for the consultation.
3. Design target behaviors.
4. Identify the maintaining conditions of the target behavior.
5. Design a treatment plan.
6. Implement the plan.
7. Evaluate the success of the plan.

Overall, the most effective way to achieve behavior change is through specific skill instruction and positive reinforcement.

The most effective behavioral approaches in sport and exercise psychology, such as exercise behavior management programs and Smith and Smoll's CET, are more comprehensive behavioral programs with considerable variation, modification, and individualization over time. Behavioral techniques are the basics of effective practice needed by every teacher, coach, and consultant. But no practitioner can be effective in a multifaceted sport or exercise setting with only the basics. Behavioral basics are adapted, modified, and used in conjunction with other approaches that accommodate a dynamic social context.

Case Study

Behavioral techniques are helpful tools for any kinesiology professional working with athletes, students, or clients, and they can also be used by students, athletes, or clients themselves to self-regulate their behaviors. If you can help participants develop effective self-regulatory behavioral skills, they will have skills they can use beyond the immediate program. Self-regulation is not only effective, but the sense of control is likely to be more motivating than if all reinforcement comes from the professional. To help you understand self-regulation, set up a behavioral management program for your own exercise behavior. No doubt you engage in some type of exercise or physical activity, and most likely you do not always stick to your routine. Refer to the steps in implementing a behavioral plan, the principles of reinforcement, and the guidelines in this chapter. Identify your target behaviors and goals, as well as reinforcers and contingencies for your behaviors (ABC model). Set up a plan that you could follow over the next week that involves monitoring your behavior and using reinforcement. For added benefits and insights, follow your plan and regulate your exercise behavior over the week. It's not easy, and you will want to evaluate and revise your plan. Good luck!

Review Questions

1. Explain the steps in implementing a behavior plan with an athlete or exerciser.

2. Define *reinforcement* and identify possible reinforcers for athletes and exercisers.

3. Define *punishment*. Explain why experts are cautious about using punishment.

4. Discuss guidelines for using reinforcement effectively.

5. Define *shaping* and give an example of how it might be used with a sport or exercise activity.

6. Summarize the findings of behavior modification research in sport and exercise settings.

7. Describe how Smith, Smoll, and colleagues used the Coaching Behavior Assessment System (CBAS) to quantify the behaviors of youth sport coaches, and discuss their research findings on coach behaviors and player attitudes.

8. Discuss Smith and Smoll's guidelines for Coach Effectiveness Training (CET).

Recommended Readings

Malott, R.W., & Suarez, E.T. (2004). *Principles of behavior, fifth edition.* Upper Saddle River, NJ: Pearson.

> This text provides an excellent overview of various behavior mechanisms in easy-to-understand language.

Martin, J.E., & Dubbert, P.M. (1984). Behavioral management strategies for improving health and fitness. *Journal of Cardiac Rehabilitation, 4,* 200-208.

This article provides an overview of behavioral approaches that can be used in exercise settings, such as cardiac rehabilitation. The authors outline techniques for various settings and participants at various stages of exercise adoption and maintenance. The suggestions are based on several research studies, and you can check Martin et al. (1984) for details on the research.

Smith, R.E., & Smoll, F.L. (1997). Coaching the coaches: Youth sports as a scientific and applied behavioral setting. *Current Directions in Psychological Science, 6,* 16-21.

Smith and Smoll's extensive research and related coach development training are a model of sport and exercise psychology research and practice. They have combined research on coaching behaviors with training programs from their beginning work in the 1970s, and they continue to provide new ideas and inspiration. This article summarizes their extensive work and provides an overview of their CET program.

Chapter 8

Motivational Orientations: Achievement and Competitiveness

Chapter Objectives

After studying this chapter, you should be able to

♦ explain the role of goal orientation in the motivation of physical activity, and

♦ explain the relationship between individual motivation characteristics and environmental conditions.

People participate in physical activity for a host of reasons. Adults report exercising for reasons related to physical health and psychological well-being. They also participate because it is fun and they want to be with others, reasons that aren't so different from the reasons children participate in sport. Most participants in sport and exercise are interested in achievement. We may wonder why some people take on challenges, work hard, and persist whereas others avoid challenge, exert little effort, and give up easily. We may also question why some athletes are devastated by a loss and others take it in stride, or why some people eagerly approach competition and others avoid it. Achievement behavior is central to sport and exercise endeavors, and understanding individual differences in motivational orientations is a key to understanding achievement.

PARTICIPATION MOTIVATION

In the 1970s and 1980s, sport psychologists focused on reasons for participating in and withdrawing from sport (see Weiss and Ferrer-Caja, 2002, for a review). Using the Participation Motivation Questionnaire (PMQ) to assess why young athletes participate in sport, Gill, Gross, and Huddleston (1983) found that the most important reasons for participating were to improve skills, have fun, learn new skills, be challenged, and be physically fit. Several others used this measure or a modified version with other youth sport samples and found similar results (e.g., Gould, Feltz, & Weiss, 1985; Klint & Weiss, 1986; Passer, 1988). Studies with college-aged and adult participants and participants in other countries reveal that although variations have emerged, the general pattern of important reasons is consistent (e.g., Weingarten, Furst, Tenenbaum, & Schaefer, 1984; White & Coakley, 1986).

Primary motives for withdrawing from youth sport involve negative experiences such as lack of fun and playing time, coach-related problems, time requirements, overemphasis on winning, and other things to do (see Weiss & Caja-Ferrer, 2002, for a review). Sapp and Haubenstricker (1978) found that negative experiences were cited only 15% of the time. More often potential dropouts cited other interests as the reason.

Other studies suggest that dropouts may not really be dropouts. Klint and Weiss (1986) found that 95% of former competitive gymnasts were participating in another sport or in gymnastics at a less competitive level. Gould, Feltz, Horn, and Weiss (1982) found that 68% of the young people who withdrew from competitive swimming were active in other sports, and most planned to reenter swimming. Similarly, White and Coakley (1986) concluded that *dropout* and *nonparticipant* were inappropriate descriptors and that discontinuation of a sport often was a good decision from a developmental perspective. Dishman (1986) suggested similar concerns for exercise participation and adherence. Specifically, when considering dropouts, we must look beyond organized exercise programs to unstructured exercise activities. Exercisers who drop out from one program might be compliers in another.

This early descriptive research on participation motivation laid a foundation for the more theoretical research on achievement motivation seen in the last two decades. Current research focuses on why people approach success and strive to avoid failure. To understand how achievement motivation is conceptualized today, we start with Atkinson's (1964, 1974) theory of achievement motivation—an earlier theory that has given rise to the theories of today.

ATKINSON'S THEORY OF ACHIEVEMENT MOTIVATION

Many explanations for individual differences in achievement behavior exist. Some emphasize personality and others stress perceptions and interpretations, but nearly all stem from the classic work of Atkinson (1964, 1974). Atkinson's theory of achievement motivation is an interaction model that specifies personality and situational factors as determinants of achievement behavior in precise, formal terms.

Personality Factors

Murray (1938) first discussed achievement motivation as a personality factor, defining the need to achieve as the desire

> to accomplish something difficult. To master, manipulate or organize physical objects, human beings, or ideas. To do this as rapidly and as independently as possible. To overcome obstacles and attain a high standard. To excel one's self. To rival and surpass others. To increase self-regard by the successful exercise of talent. (p. 164)

Extending Murray's work, Atkinson (1964, 1974) delineated achievement motivation as a combination of two personality constructs: the motive to approach success (or the capacity to experience pride in accomplishment) and the motive to avoid failure (or the capacity to experience shame in failure). Everyone has both; we all feel good when we accomplish something and bad when we fail. But we do not all have the two motives to the same degree, and personality is the key to the difference between the two motives. We commonly refer to people as high or low achievers. People with a high motive to approach success and low motive to avoid failure are the high achievers who seek out challenging achievement situations without worrying about possible failures. Low achievers worry about failure a great deal and avoid achievement situations.

Situational Factors

Atkinson's theory does not predict solely on the basis of the motives but incorporates situational factors as well. The main situational factor is task difficulty, or the probability of success, and another situational factor is the incentive value of success—the lower the probability of success, the greater the incentive value. An average tennis player has a slim chance against top professional Roger Federer but would be elated to win a game; the incentive value is high. At the other extreme, the professional player would not be inspired by the prospect of playing the average player.

Behavioral Tendencies Related to Achievement

According to Atkinson (1964, 1974), the tendency to approach success is a function of the person's motive to approach success as well as the situational factors. High achievers are most likely to strive to achieve when their motive for success is high and there is a 50% chance of success, which would make the victory the most rewarding. People with a strong motive to avoid failure tend to avoid these situations. When forced into an achievement situation, a low achiever will choose either very easy (high probability of success) or very difficult (low probability of success) tasks.

Cognitive Approaches to Achievement Motivation

Many theorists have built on Atkinson's foundation by developing multidimensional approaches that consider personality, development, and environment. Over the last 25 years, cognitive approaches have dominated achievement research. Bernard Weiner (1974) sparked a dramatic change in the study of motivation when he proposed that high and low achievers think differently and therefore act differently. Since then, several multidimensional, goal-perspective approaches have emerged to explain achievement behaviors such as task choice, behavioral intensity, and persistence (e.g., Dweck, 2000; Elliot, 1999; Maehr & Nicholls, 1980; Nicholls, 1989; Spence & Helmreich, 1983). Although each theorist has a distinct perspective, they all contend that people use goals to evaluate an experience as a success or failure. In achievement settings, people experience feelings of success when they demonstrate high ability (i.e., meet their goal) and failure when they do not. Therefore, success and failure are subjective experiences. Early research found that people's perceptions of success and failure were not synonymous with winning and losing (e.g., Spink & Roberts, 1980). Success and failure depend on how one defines ability, which in turn depends on personal, developmental, and situational factors.

IMPORTANCE OF ABILITY

Sport and exercise psychology research has relied heavily on Nicholls' (1989) achievement goal theory to investigate achievement behaviors, cognitions, and affect in sport and exercise settings. Also, sport and exercise psychology researchers have applied Dweck's (2000) (e.g., Martinek & Griffith, 1994;

Martinek & Williams, 1997) and Elliot's (1999) (e.g., Carr, 2006; Cury, Da Fonseca, Rufo, & Sarrazin, 2002) theories of achievement motivation to the physical education setting. Diane Gill (Gill & Deeter, 1988) used the theoretical concepts of Spence and Helmreich (1983) to ground her work on competitiveness.

The primary goal in achievement situations is to demonstrate ability (Nicholls, 1989). But the key to understanding people's achievement behavior is to understand what *ability* means. When people believe they are demonstrating ability via learning and improving, they are said to be task involved. When people believe they are demonstrating ability when they are outperforming others, they are ego involved. Task and ego involvement are situational characteristics and can change from moment to moment. Have you even been engaged in an activity with your focus on accomplishing personal goals (i.e., task involved) when someone else approached and suddenly you found yourself competing with that person (ego involved)?

Goal orientations are the dispositional counterpart to goal involvement. They reflect a person's tendency to be ego or task involved across various situations. People who tend to be ego involved in most situations are more ego oriented, whereas those who tend to be mostly task involved are more task oriented. Situations involving competition are more ego involving than situations that emphasize skill mastery (Ames, 1992; Dweck & Leggett, 1988; Nicholls, 1989). Suppose, for example, that Katie is predominantly task oriented: She defines ability as learning, improving, and trying hard, and she feels successful when she demonstrates these characteristics. However, if we put Katie into a competitive junior tennis program that emphasizes winning and rankings, she is likely to adopt an ego-involving perspective in which ability can be demonstrated and success experienced only by outperforming others. This example highlights the importance of understanding goal orientations and the influence of the environment on them. These will be discussed in more detail in the following sections.

Key Point

Both the task goal orientation, in which goals are based on learning or task mastery, and the ego goal orientation, in which goals focus on outperforming others or on performing equally with less effort, are relatively stable personal orientations.

GOAL ORIENTATIONS

Regardless of goal orientation, people are motivated to pursue their goal of demonstrating their ability when they believe themselves able to do so. Task-involved people perceive themselves as able when they learn and improve, so their progress provides them with competence information that sustains their motivation. Thus, there is wisdom in being task oriented (Nicholls, 1989). Task orientation is associated with more motivationally adaptive patterns. It is associated with the belief that hard work leads to success and that sport promotes a strong work ethic. It is also associated with adaptive learning strategies such as practice; positive emotions such as enjoyment, satisfaction, and interest; and motivated behavior such as persistence, effort, and performance (Biddle, Wang, Kavussanu, & Spray, 2003; Duda, 2005).

When ego is involved, people perceive themselves as able only when they perform better than others. Because of this, ego orientation has been viewed by some as motivationally maladaptive (see Duda, 1997, and Hardy, 1997, for a discussion). However, the research findings have been mixed, indicating that ego orientation is associated with some maladaptive outcomes but not others. Research indicates that ego orientation is associated with the belief that people achieve because they have high ability and that social status is a primary purpose of sport participation. It is also associated with performance strategies that are designed to make one look able. Yet, ego orientation is not associated with positive or negative emotions or motivated behavior (Biddle et al., 2003; Duda, 2005).

One explanation for the mixed results may be that people can be both ego and task oriented (Duda & Whitehead, 1998); task and ego orientations are independent constructs. People can be high or low in both goal orientations or higher in one than in the other. Thus, predominantly ego-oriented people may be protected from the negative outcomes of that orientation if they are also high in task orientation. Research has shown that a high task orientation is adaptive regardless of one's level of ego orientation (Fox, 1998; Standage, Duda, & Ntoumanis, 2003; Standage & Treasure, 2002; Stephens, 2000; Wang & Biddle, 2001).

Another explanation for the mixed results may be that people who are ego oriented only experience negative motivational effects if they have low perceived ability and don't believe they have the ability to outperform others (Nicholls, 1989). Ego orientation is motivationally adaptive when people perceive themselves as able, and it is debilitating when they perceive themselves as unable. If the goal is to outperform your opponent and you have a good chance of doing so, you are motivated to engage in the activity. If you think your chances are not so good, you are not so motivated (see table 8.1). Although this role of perceived competence is critical to Nicholls' theory, only a few researchers have attempted to examine the moderating effects of perceived competence on the relationship between ego goal orientation and motivation-related outcomes (e.g., Cury, Sarrazin, & Famose, 1997; Ommundsen & Pedersen, 1999; Williams & Gill, 1995), and the results have been mixed.

Table 8.1 Task and Ego Orientation

Orientation	Perceived competence	Motivational patterns
Task	High	Adaptive
	Low	Adaptive
Ego	High	Adaptive
	Low	Maladaptive

Recent reconceptualization by Elliot (1999; Elliot & Church, 1996) in the area of achievement motivation may help shed greater light on the complex relationships among goal orientations, perceived competence, and motivation. Using Dweck's (2000) terminology of mastery (task) and performance (ego) goals, Elliot suggested that people who are performance-approach oriented are focused on demonstrating their superiority, whereas people who are performance-avoidance oriented are focused on avoiding demonstrating their incompetence. Research has shown that performance-approach goal orientations are more motivationally adaptive and performance-avoidance orientations are less so (Cury, Da Fonseca, Rufo, Peres, & Sarrazin, 2003; Cury, Da Fonseca, Rufo, & Sarrazin, 2002; Ommundsen, 2004). Not surprisingly, performance-avoidance goal orientations are negatively associated with perceived competence, and performance-approach and mastery goal orientations are positively associated with it (Cury, Da Fonseca, Rufo, & Sarrazin, 2002). It appears that people do wish to maximize the probability of demonstrating their ability and minimize the demonstration of inability.

Application Point

Consider the motivational patterns of Marsha and Bobby, who are in the same class. Today's activity involves a free-throw competition. The teacher has asked students to pair up for a one-on-one competition. Marsha is highly task oriented (mastery or performance approach), whereas Bobby is predominantly ego oriented (performance avoidance). To make matters worse, basketball is his worse sport and he is not very good at any of them. How might they feel about today's lesson, what type of partner might they choose, and how might they behave during the activity? Explain your answers.

Key Point

Unlike the task goal perspective, in which feelings are not constrained by the performance of others, the ego goal perspective maintains that only one person can be the best.

Developmental and environmental factors are thought to be two primary determinants of goal involvement and goal orientations. A greater understanding of these can assist physical activity specialists who desire to promote an adaptive goal orientation.

DEVELOPMENTAL ASPECTS OF GOAL PERSPECTIVES

According to Nicholls (1989), cognitive development relates to people's goal perspectives. Children think of ability differently than do adults. Adults have a mature conception of ability in which they differentiate ability from the difficulty of the task, luck, and effort, whereas young children do not. Young children (around 5 years of age) have an undifferentiated conception of ability and construe ability in a self-referenced manner. If they are trying hard, they are able, regardless of outcome. Around 8 or 9 years of age, children begin to rely on normative criteria, and ability begins to depend on how many other people can do a task. At this time, children partially differentiate effort and ability, and they understand that someone who does not exert much effort to succeed at a task must be more skilled.

By age 11 or 12, children have a mature conception of ability and can completely differentiate ability and effort. Ability is stable, and it limits the impact of effort. Children at this age understand that when two players perform equally well on a task, the player who exerts the least effort is the most able. A person's cognitive development, as well as the conception of ability, is partly a function of relatively stable personal orientations.

The undifferentiated conception of ability is associated with a task goal orientation; that is, goals are based on learning or task mastery. People who set self-referenced goals that are focused on improvement and greater mastery are task oriented. The differentiated conception of ability is associated with ego goal orientation. People who set norm-referenced goals that focus on outperforming others or performing equally with less effort are ego oriented.

Research in the physical domain has shown that children's conceptions of ability mature from being undifferentiated to differentiated as they approach adolescence (Fry, 2000a, 2000b; Fry & Duda, 1997; Lee, Carter, & Xiang, 1995; Xiang, Lee, & Shen, 2001) and that children and adolescents who have a more mature (differentiated) conception of ability are more likely to be high in ego orientation compared with those who have an undifferentiated conception (Xiang & Lee, 1998; Xiang, Lee, & Williamson, 2001). However, it also demonstrates that a mature conception of ability is not necessary to be ego oriented

From a practical standpoint, the influence from multiple significant others is important because young children rely on information from significant adults and it is not until later childhood and adolescence that they rely primary on information from peers (Horn, 2004). However, not enough is known about how parent- and peer-initiated climate may influence goal orientation or motivational patterns, to draw any firm conclusions.

Application Point

For discussion purposes, create a scenario involving different motivational climates. How might the climates affect one's goal orientation and perceptions of ability? Make sure you provide enough information for adequate discussion.

COMPETITIVE ORIENTATION IN SPORT

Thus far, this chapter has focused on achievement and taken the view that the primary goal in achievement settings is to demonstrate ability. Another important component of achievement in the physical domain involves competition. The work of Diane Gill and her colleagues (Gill, 1993; Gill & Deeter, 1988; Gill & Dzewaltowski, 1988) examines achievement behavior in competitive sport. Using the theoretical underpinnings advanced by Spence and Helmreich (1978, 1983), she conceptualized achievement motivation as multidimensional, with mastery, work, and competitiveness dimensions. This implies that some people approach achievement situations with the desire to strive for excellence, others emphasize competition, and still others desire to outperform other people.

Gill (1993) suggests that people's achievement orientation toward sport may differ from their orientation in other achievement settings. To illustrate, how would you rate yourself on the motive to approach success and the motive to avoid failure in competitive sport versus academics? First, do you consider yourself higher or lower than the average student on the motive to approach success in sport? Is success in sport important to you? Do you seek challenges? Does intense competition bring out your best performance? Next, do you consider yourself high or low on the motive to avoid failure in sport competition? For example, do you become tense and anxious in close competitions? Do you worry about how you will perform? Do you make more errors in highly competitive contests?

Now rate yourself in the same way for academic achievement. Are you higher or lower than the average student on your motive to approach success in academics? For example, is success in school important to you? Do academic challenges bring out your best? Finally, do you consider yourself high or low in the motive to avoid failure in academics? Do you choke before important tests or presentations? Do you worry about poor grades?

How do your motives toward sport and academics compare? Usually about half of the students in a typical class find themselves in different classifications for these two areas. Even if you classify yourself the same for both, you may find that your motives are more intense or differ in some other way from one setting to the other. If we extend the illustration further, perhaps to social achievement or artistic achievement, you might find even greater diversity in your motives.

The point is that most achievement motivation models were not developed for sport or exercise, and their value in explaining competitive behavior may be limited. In her study of competitive orientation in sport, Gill blended Spence and Helmreich's (1978, 1983) framework with Martens' work on competitive anxiety (Martens, Vealey, & Burton, 1990). According to Martens (1977), competition is a social process. He offers the following definition:

> *Competition is a process in which the comparison of an individual's performance is made with some standard in the presence of at least one other person who is aware of the criterion for comparison and can evaluate the comparison process. (p. 14)*

The competitive process begins with the objective competitive situation—it is reality. For example, this situation could be the first at bat in the first inning of the game or the last at bat of the game with bases loaded and two strikes. Stage 2 is the subjective competitive situation and involves the participant's perception or appraisal of the objective competitive situation. Stage 3 is the person's response to the perception. Some people will perceive batting first as threatening—all eyes are on them—whereas others will perceive it as mundane. Some players will perceive being the last at bat with two strikes and the bases loaded as terrifying and others as a place in which to thrive. The different ways people react will influence their behavior in competitive situations—stage 4.

Key Point

According to Veroff (1969), achievement motivation develops through three stages: autonomous competence, social comparison, and integrated achievement motivation.

Developing a desire to engage in competitive situations requires a certain level of achievement motivation. There are three stages of achievement motivation: autonomous competence, social comparison, and integrated achievement motivation (Veroff, 1969). People in the autonomous competence stage use internal standards to evaluate success. A child might decide to set up a row of blocks and try to knock them over with a ball. The child sets the goal, attempts to reach it, and decides whether the performance was successful. In the autonomous competence stage, other people have little to do with setting the goals or evaluating success, and competition is not involved.

A child who has had some success in the autonomous stage may advance into the social comparison stage, usually during the early school years. Social comparison involves social standards or competition. A person who succeeds in social comparisons may advance to the final stage of integrated achievement motivation. The integrated stage involves both autonomous competence and social comparison. People in this stage use either autonomous, internal standards or social standards, depending on the situation. A golfer, for example, might set personal goals and work toward those goals in practice rounds and informal play but attend to competitive standards in a round of match play.

Not everyone progresses through the three stages, and some people never master the autonomous stage. Those people are low achievers who do not attempt any achievement tasks, either competitive or noncompetitive. People who successfully master the autonomous stage but are unsuccessful in social comparison will not be competitive. They might be high achievers when personal goals are involved, but they probably avoid competition. People who are successful at social comparison and advance to the integrated stage will be comfortable in competitive situations, but they might also work hard toward personal, noncompetitive goals.

According to Veroff (1969), a person must use social comparison for informative purposes to evaluate skills and abilities in order to advance into the integrated stage of achievement motivation. A person who uses social comparison for what Veroff terms *normative purposes* focuses on winning and uses competition as an ego boost. That person cannot be satisfied with autonomous achievement and will not advance to the integrated stage. Such people may be supercompetitors who turn every situation into a competition.

Application Point

What orientation do you prefer? Does this differ in various situations, or is there one orientation that fits all situations?

Scanlan (1988) identifies those in the social comparison or integrated stages as competitive. Those in the social comparison stage strive for success only in competitive settings and compete to win. Those in the integrated stage strive for success in competitive situations but might also strive for mastery goals. Scanlan's initial work provided a general framework for the study of competitiveness as a sport-specific achievement construct (Gill, 1993).

Competitive Orientations in Sport

Competitiveness reflects enjoyment of competition and the desire to strive for success in competitive situations. Gill identified three competitive orientations in sport: win, goal, and ego. A win orientation reflects an emphasis on interpersonal comparison and winning. A goal orientation emphasizes personal performance standards. You may be tempted to think that competitiveness is the same as ego orientation, but think again. Why wouldn't a highly task-oriented person (even if he were low in ego) enter and strive for success in competitive situations? For the predominantly task-oriented person, competitive situations provide the opportunity to demonstrate personal improvement and learning, whereas for the predominantly ego-oriented person such situations provide the opportunity to demonstrate superiority. Albeit modest, Skorkilis and colleagues (Skorkilis, Sherrill, Yilla, Koutsouki, & Stavrou, 2002) have made initial claim for this.

Research in this area has focused on comparing the competitive orientations of different groups, including groups based on gender, athlete status, and disability status (e.g., Gill & Dzewaltowski, 1988; Kang, Gill, Acevedo, & Deeter, 1990; Skorkilis, 2003). Overall, the results are fairly consistent. Although males are more competitive and win oriented and females are more goal oriented, these differences seem to be related to the competitive experience (see Gill, 1993, for a review). Additionally, athletes tend to be more competitive than nonathletes; however, athletes are more likely than nonathletes to endorse performance goals and less likely to emphasize winning outcomes. Although this may be surprising, it confirms current sport psychology practice, which emphasizes a mastery orientation and focuses on performance goals.

Gill (1993) concluded that although athletes generally score higher on both general and sport-specific achievement motivation, the orientation that best distinguishes athletes from nonathletes is sport-specific competitiveness. Interestingly, athletes do not uniformly emphasize a win orientation; they put greater emphasis on performance than on outcome. Athletes are competitive, but winning isn't the only thing. Lastly, although athletes generally differ from nonathletes, there also is substantial variation among athletes.

PUTTING IT INTO PRACTICE

Now you are ready to put the content of chapter 8 into practice. Read the chapter summary, discuss the case study, answer the review questions, and enhance your knowledge by researching the recommended readings.

Summary

To understand achievement behavior, we must consider individual differences. Cognitive motivation theorists focus on people's perceptions in achievement settings. Several approaches incorporate personal definitions of success and failure. Some people focus on winning and outperforming others (ego orientation), whereas others focus on task mastery (task orientation). Other approaches involve competitive orientations, or the desire to engage in competitive situations (competitiveness), to win (win orientation), and to attain goals (goal orientation). Task or goal orientation leads to greater motivation, achievement, and positive self-perceptions than ego or win orientation. Using TARGET principles to create a mastery climate has shown promise in fostering adaptive goal orientations. Continued research may provide a greater understanding of the role of individual differences and contextual factors in people's motivation in sport and exercise settings.

Case Study

This chapter highlights achievement motivation and focuses on goal orientations, motivational climates, and competitive orientations. Use your knowledge of these concepts to address the following case of Kate and Robin.

Kate and Robin, two ninth-graders, are best friends and do everything together, except when it comes to being physically active. Although Robin is more capable in a variety of activities, Kate embraces physical activity. In physical education, Kate is always eager to participate, chooses personally challenging tasks, tries hard, and persists in the face of objective failure (i.e., losing a game, being one of the slowest to pick up a skill). It seems that Kate likes physical activity, and regardless of her poor showing relative to her peers, she anticipates future success. In contrast, Robin, who could experience greater objective success, avoids participation. When obligated to play, she chooses either the easiest task possible or tasks that no one could do. For example, when given time to practice basketball, Robin spends most of her time dribbling and passing the ball to others. She usually only attempts half-court shots. When encouraged to shoot a variety of shots, she shoots bank shots about 2 feet (.5 meter) from the basket. She expects to fail and seems to dread physical education. Create an achievement motivation profile for each girl, and provide suggestions to their physical education teacher for encouraging Kate's adaptive motivational profile and fostering a more adaptive motivational profile for Robin.

Review Questions

1. Explain Atkinson's theory of achievement motivation and describe the personality and situational factors that interact to determine achievement behavior.

2. Explain one key tenet held by several multidimensional, goal-perspective approaches to achievement motivation.

3. Define, compare, and contrast the task goal orientation and the ego goal orientation.

4. Compare and contrast competitive reward structures and individualistic reward structures.

5. Define *motivational climate*.

6. Compare and contrast mastery and performance climates.
7. Explain Marten's definition of competition.
8. Differentiate among win, goal, and competitive orientations.

Recommended Reading

Carr, S. (2006). An examination of multiple goals in children's physical education: Motivational effects of goal profiles and the role of perceived climate in multiple goal development. *Journal of Sports Sciences*, *24*, 281-298.

> This two-study article examines achievement goal orientations in physical education. The author finds that mastery climates and having a high mastery orientation lead to adaptive motivational responses.

Elliot, A.J. (1999). Approach and avoidance motivation and achievement goals. *Educational Psychologist*, *34*, 169-189.

> In this article, Elliot overviews his reconceptualization of achievement motivation, which tackles the complex relationships among goal orientations, perceived competence, and motivation with greater deliberation than earlier achievement motivation theories. Elliot discusses the motivational correlates of mastery, performance-approach, and performance-avoidance orientations.

Weiss, M.R., & Williams, L. (2004). The *why* of youth sport: A developmental perspective on motivational processes. In M.R. Weiss (Ed.), *Developmental sport and exercise psychology: A lifespan perspective* (pp. 223-268). Morgantown, WV: Fitness Information Technology.

> This book chapter overviews motivation in physical activity and emphasizes developmental theories. The authors first discuss the descriptive literature regarding reasons for participation, and then they discuss four theories highlighting developmental aspects of motivation, including Harter's competence motivation, Harter's mediational model of global self-esteem, Eccles' expectancy value model of achievement motivation, and Nicholls' achievement motivation theory.

Chapter 9

Cognitive Approaches to Motivation

Chapter Objectives

After studying this chapter, you should be able to

◆ describe the relationship between extrinsic rewards and intrinsic motivation,

◆ trace the development of theories concerning expectations and self-confidence, and

◆ discuss attribution theory in relation to achievement behavior in sport and exercise.

Behavioral approaches assume that all behavior is determined by past reinforcements and present contingencies. In contrast, cognitive approaches assume that people are active perceivers and interpreters of information and that cognitive processes are the key to understanding motivation and behavior.

People participate in physical activity for intrinsic reasons. For example, they enjoy the competition, they like the action, they feel good when they perform well, and they simply have fun. Extrinsic rewards such as trophies, T-shirts, and praise are also common reasons for participating. The practical question concerns what happens when we combine these extrinsic rewards with intrinsic motivation. At first glance, the answer is the more motivation, the better. Extrinsic rewards can be powerfully motivating. If we add extrinsic rewards to an activity that is already intrinsically motivating (e.g., giving special awards to all children who compete in an intramural track meet), those rewards should increase the total motivation.

We assume that at worst, extrinsic rewards would have no effect and that they certainly could do no harm. Such conventional wisdom held until the mid-1970s, when researchers shocked the psychological community with studies on rewards and intrinsic motivation. In one study subtitled "Turning Play Into Work," Lepper and Greene (1975) demonstrated that extrinsic rewards can actually undermine intrinsic motivation. Additionally, Deci and Ryan's (1985) research has demonstrated that both working for rewards and working under threat of punishment reduce intrinsic motivation. Both of these conditions are common in physical activity settings—some young people play sport to gain approval of a parent, older adults often adhere to exercise regimes under doctors' orders, and many college athletes rise before the sun to train for the weekend victory. If the goal is to foster intrinsic motivation, should we award certificates when students reach physical fitness test standards? Should we give T-shirts to everyone who finishes the 5K run–walk at the fitness fair? Should we pay people to play? Such questions do not have simple yes-or-no answers. Rewards may undermine intrinsic motivation, but they can also modify behaviors and performance in positive ways.

INDIVIDUAL DIFFERENCES AND MOTIVATION

To understand the effects of rewards and other external events on intrinsic motivation, we need to consider how the reward is interpreted by the individual. Two people in identical situations can have two different motivational experiences. For example, Tom and Sam were both rewarded with Division I scholarships. Both were recruited from small towns to play for a large Big Ten school. Both were top players at their high school, were excited to get their scholarship, and looked forward to playing Division I ball. After 2 years at college, Tom and Sam get about the same amount of playing time, have comparable abilities, and have similar team demands. However, Tom continues to approach practice and games with enthusiasm, whereas Sam's love of the game has dwindled. He complains about the coaches' demands and talks about quitting if he only could. The reward is the same, but the meaning of the reward is different for Tom and Sam.

Understanding motivation requires consideration of individual differences and situational factors. The work by Deci and Ryan (1985, 2000) and subsequent research will help you gain an understanding of the relationship between these factors and motivation. Armed with this information, you will be able to generate strategies for creating motivating environments.

Application Point

How might the meaning of the scholarship be different for Tom and Sam? This example involves a socially prestigious and educationally valuable reward. What if they had simply been rewarded with a certificate noting their excellent play at the high school level or with the opportunity to play ball (without the financial support of a scholarship)?

COGNITIVE EVALUATION THEORY

Key Point

Intrinsic motivation requires feeling competent along with two other conditions. First, the task must be interesting and challenging, and second, the participant must have choice in the activity.

Key Point

The higher the controlling aspect of a reward, the more intrinsic motivation is undermined. If the controlling aspect of the reward is low, then participants do not see the reward as affecting their behavior and thus self-determination is high.

Deci and Ryan (1985) postulate that people have a propensity to seek out interesting ventures and engage in optimally challenging tasks. People are by nature intrinsically motivated, and this motivation is grounded in the psychological need to feel competent and autonomous. To develop fully, all people need to perceive themselves as effective in their environment and acting freely. According to this theory, intrinsic motivation exists where people feel competent when engaging in an interesting, challenging task on their own volition.

As noted earlier, individual interpretation of external events is a critical factor in motivation—it is not the event itself, but the person's interpretation of it that matters. Deci and Ryan (1985) propose that events have both a controlling aspect and an informational aspect. The controlling aspect can undermine autonomy. If the controlling aspect of an event is high, then the person perceives it as controlling. When running a race for a T-shirt, exercising to please another person, or adhering to a home exercise program to avoid feelings of guilt, the T-shirt, the other person, or the guilt is controlling the action; thus, the controlling aspect is high and feelings of autonomy are low. On the other hand, if the T-shirt, pleasing the other person, or staying guilt free is not the controlling force, the controlling aspect is low and feelings of autonomy are high.

The informational aspect affects feelings of competence. An event with high informational value can provide either positive information about skills, abilities, and behaviors that enhances feelings of competence or negative information that detracts from such feelings. For example, receiving a patch for attaining a certain level on a physical fitness test provides positive information and enhances feelings of competence. In most sport and exercise situations, however, tangible rewards are given to a select few, and those who strive for but do not receive rewards may receive negative information that decreases their feelings of competence and thus their intrinsic motivation.

Most events have both controlling and informational aspects, but the two aspects vary in salience. For example, tangible rewards, such as trophies and money, tend to have a highly salient controlling aspect, whereas verbal feedback seems less controlling. Rewards given for specific performance standards have more informational value than rewards distributed on the basis of ambiguous criteria. Additionally, the same event can be viewed differently by different people. For example, one person may perceive a reward primarily as informational, whereas another may perceive the reward primarily as controlling.

Application Point

Think of different motivational outcomes for two 14-year-old boys who both receive an expensive pair of basketball shoes after showing equal promise on their high school varsity team. John is from an upper-class home in which one parent works one full-time job. Kevin is from a lower-class home and both of his parents work full time. In addition, his father works a second job and his mother takes all the overtime she can get.

Rewards and Intrinsic Motivation in Sport

The research indicating the undermining effect of rewards on intrinsic motivation is quite robust (Frederick & Ryan, 1995; Ryan, Vallerand, & Deci, 1984; Weinberg, 1984; Weiss & Ferrer-Caja, 2002). Taking this research out of the laboratory and out into the playing field, Ryan (1977, 1980) conducted thought-provoking studies comparing the intrinsic motivation of scholarship and nonscholarship athletes (see table 9.1). In the first study, scholarship athletes reported less intrinsic motivation than nonscholarship athletes, with the difference between the two groups increasing over 4 years of school. Wagner, Lounsbury, and Fitzgerald (1989) found similar results, with more scholarship athletes perceiving their sport as work.

Ryan (1980) then conducted a similar, larger survey of both male and female athletes in various sports at several Division I and III schools. The basic finding of the first study was replicated; scholarship football players reported less

Table 9.1 Intrinsic Motivation of Scholarship and Nonscholarship Athletes

Are college athletics as much fun as you had expected?					
	Freshmen	**Sophomores**	**Juniors**	**Seniors**	**Average**
Scholarship	3.6	4.8	4.6	4.8	4.45
Nonscholarship	3.7	3.6	3.8	2.8	3.48

Responses are on a scale of 1 to 7, with 1 indicating much more and 7 indicating much less.

Reprinted, by permission, from R. Helmreich and J.T. Spence, 1977, Sex roles and achievement. In *Psychology of motor behavior and sport-1976 (Volume 2)*, edited by R.W. Christina and D.M. Landers (Champaign, IL: Human Kinetics), 42.

intrinsic motivation than nonscholarship football players. However, for male wrestlers and female athletes in all sports, scholarship athletes showed greater intrinsic motivation than nonscholarship athletes. These results showed that not all rewards undermine intrinsic motivation and that salience of the controlling and informational aspects of the reward may play a role. Ryan suggested two possible reasons for the results. First, if virtually all good football players received scholarships, then the scholarships provided little competence information. However, if only the top wrestlers and top female athletes received scholarships, then the scholarships provided positive information about competence and were more intrinsically motivating. Second, Ryan suggested that football coaches may use scholarships in a more controlling manner than coaches in other sports.

A more recent study by Amorose and Horn (2000) found that scholarship athletes were more intrinsically motivated than nonscholarship athletes. One reason may be the different ways intrinsic motivation was measured, and another may be the way the coaches used the scholarship.

Competition and Competitive Success

Competition and competitive success are two other external events that involve the influence of informational and controlling aspects on intrinsic motivation via autonomy and competence. Some suggest that competition, and especially a focus on winning, can act as an extrinsic reward to reduce intrinsic motivation. Deci, Betley, Kahle, Abrams, and Porac (1981) compared people competing among themselves with those competing against a standard of excellence. Subjects in face-to-face competition later exhibited decreased intrinsic motivation in a noncompetitive, free-choice situation. This effect was especially strong for females. However, Weinberg and Ragan (1979) found that competition enhanced intrinsic motivation for males. It should be noted that the free-choice activity in Weinberg and Ragan's study involved competition whereas Deci and colleagues used a noncompetitive setting, and the question of how competition affects intrinsic motivation remains unsettled.

Fortunately, the effects of competitive success and failure on intrinsic motivation are much clearer. Weinberg and colleagues (e.g., Weinberg & Ragan, 1979) consistently showed greater intrinsic motivation after a win than after a loss. However, perceived success and failure are not always synonymous with winning and losing, and perceived success has a more dramatic effect on intrinsic motivation than objective success (e.g., McAuley & Tammen, 1989). For example, Tammen and Murphy (1990) found that although both objective and subjective success affect intrinsic motivation, perceived success has a greater effect than objective success. This influence of success on motivation is logical because of the high informational value of competitive success or failure.

Feedback and Intrinsic Motivation

As noted by Weiss and Ferrer-Caja (2002), several studies have shown positive relationships among feedback, perceived competence, and intrinsic motivation (Goudas, Biddle, & Fox, 1994; Rutherford, Corbin, & Chase, 1992; Whitehead & Corbin, 1991). Vallerand (1983) observed that positive comments about performance enhanced youth hockey players' intrinsic motivation, and in a second study Vallerand and Reid (1984) reported that with undergraduates performing a novel task, intrinsic motivation increased with positive feedback and decreased with negative feedback. Further analysis revealed that the feedback affected perceived competence, and perceived competence in turn affected intrinsic motivation. Similar results were found in a study with children given norm-based fitness feedback (Whitehead & Corbin, 1991). Together, these results demonstrate informational effects that fit with Deci & Ryan's (1985) cognitive evaluation theory.

Intrapersonal Events and Intrinsic Motivation

Key Point

The question of how competition affects intrinsic motivation is still unsettled, though some studies have shown that people have greater intrinsic motivation after a win than after a loss. Other studies have shown that intrinsic motivation increases with positive feedback and decreases with negative feedback.

As explained by Weiss and Ferrer-Caja (2002), intrapersonal events are similar to external events in that they have informational and controlling aspects (see also Deci & Ryan, 1985). For example, approaching tasks with a focus on learning and improving (i.e., task involvement or orientation) offers a sense of internal control and an opportunity for high perceptions of competence because people have control over their personal progress and everyone can progress simultaneously. In contrast, an emphasis on outperforming others (i.e., ego involvement or goal orientation) functions as an external factor and only the top players walk away feeling competent. Extending this logic to cognitive evaluation theory, several researchers have found a relationship between goal orientations and intrinsic motivation (Duda, Chi, Newton, Walling, & Catley, 1995; Ferrer-Caja & Weiss, 2000; Goudas et al., 1994; Williams & Gill, 1995). These studies have generally found a positive relationship between task orientation and intrinsic motivation, but the relationship between ego orientation and intrinsic motivation has been inconsistent.

People's perceptions of their environment and others' behaviors have also been shown to relate to intrinsic motivation (Amorose & Horn, 2000; Black & Weiss, 1992; Hollembeak & Amorose, 2005). Hollembeak and Amorose (2005) found that male and female athletes who viewed their coaches as focusing more on training and instruction rather than mistakes and as not very autocratic were more intrinsically motivated than those who perceived their coaches as less instructive, more mistake oriented, and more autocratic. In addition, female athletes who perceived their coaches as more democratic and rewarding and less punishing were more intrinsically motivated.

THEORY OF SELF-DETERMINATION

Cognitive evaluation theory is a branch of self-determination theory (Deci & Ryan, 1985, 2000). Grounding research in this broader theory in more recent years has allowed researchers to investigate the impact of satisfying all three needs on a continuum of self-determined motivation and behavior.

In addition to the need for competence and autonomy, people have a need for relatedness, or social connectedness or belonging. According to theory, the degree to which one's needs are satisfied is related to self-determined behavior via motivation reflected on a continuum ranging from amotivation to extrinsic motivation to intrinsic motivation (see figure 9.1). In addition, perceptions of need satisfaction, which has been operationalized as people's perceptions (i.e., perceived competence, autonomy, and relatedness), mediates the relationship between the social context and motivation. This mediating role of perceptions has been well supported in the physical domain (e.g., Ferrer-Caja & Weiss,

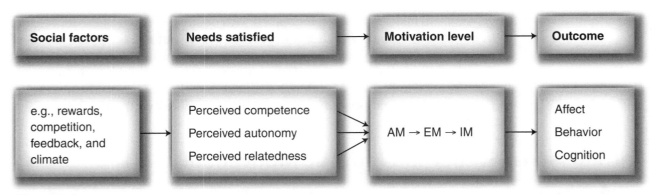

Figure 9.1
Self-determination theory.

2000; Hollembeak & Amorose, 2005; Whitehead & Corbin, 1991). Building on this, Vallerand (2007) forwarded a hierarchical model of intrinsic and extrinsic motivation, suggesting that motivation exists at three levels of generality: situational, contextual, and global.

Amotivation reflects a lack of intention, regulation, and self-determination regarding a behavior. It is akin to feelings of helplessness (Deci & Ryan, 2000). Extrinsic motivation is intentional and controlled by external forces, but its strength varies relative to the degree to which the external force is personally valued or internalized.

- *External regulation.* This is extrinsic motivation in the classic sense, where behavior is controlled by external forces such as rewards or punishment.

- *Introjected regulation.* The contingent consequences regulating the behavior are partially internalized. The behaviors are often performed for ego-involving reasons (e.g., pride, self-presentation) or to avoid guilt.

- *Identified regulation.* The participant accepts the value of the behavior. This behavior is internally regulated, but it is not fully assimilated into the participant's sense of self.

- *Integrated regulation.* This is the most internalized form of extrinsic motivation. It cannot be equated with intrinsic motivation because of the external regulators associated with the behavior, despite the fact they have been fully internalized and assimilated.

With intrinsic motivation, the regulatory process is completely intrinsic. Behaviors are fully assimilated with one's sense of self in the absence of any separable consequences. Intrinsic motivation is associated with the most self-determined forms of behavior.

Research grounded in self-determination theory extends earlier research on intrinsic motivation by providing information on the relationship between perceptions of competence, autonomy, and relatedness with more and less self-regulated forms of motivation, as well as the relationship between these forms of motivation and subsequent outcomes. For example, Standage, Duda, and Ntoumanis (2003) found that autonomy-supportive climates positively related to perceived competence, autonomy, and relatedness. In turn, perceived competence and autonomy were more strongly and positively related to internally regulated forms of motivation than external or nonregulated forms. Finally, self-determined motivation was related to the intention to engage in behavior. Anne Cox (2006) found that perceptions of competence, autonomy, and relatedness mediated the relationship between teacher-directed climate and more self-determined forms of motivation. Furthermore, enjoyment mediated the relationship between self-determined motivation and physical activity. Collectively, these results provide initial support for self-determination theory.

Rewards do not automatically undermine intrinsic motivation any more than they automatically enhance motivation. The practical question, then, is not whether we use rewards and reinforcers but how we should use them. The individual's interpretation of the reward is critical.

In practice, we should use small rewards that are not too salient or controlling, and we should phase out rewards as intrinsic motivation develops. Rewards cannot undermine intrinsic motivation if no intrinsic motivation exists. Carefully chosen rewards may encourage people to participate in new activities in which they can develop a sense of competence and intrinsic motivation. Rewards may also provide valuable competence information in ongoing activities, especially if they are given for the attainment of clearly specified goals that are perceived as within reach of all participants. Coaches and instructors who rely on encouragement and reinforcement, emphasize the process rather than the outcome, and use rewards as symbols of accomplishments rather than to control behavior may find extrinsic rewards useful.

Key Point

In practice, we should use small rewards that are not too salient or controlling, and we should phase out rewards as intrinsic motivation develops.

ATTRIBUTIONS AND SPORT

Key Point

Attributions are the perceived causes of events and behaviors. Attribution theories focus on people's interpretations of the reasons for behaviors. The attributions we make about ourselves and about others affect our behaviors and interactions with others.

Attributions—the perceived causes of events and behaviors—also affect motivation. Attribution theories focus on people's interpretations of the reasons for behaviors. The attributions we make about our successes and failures affect our effort and persistence, as well as our thoughts and feelings about our performance. If you are unable to do the shot put in physical education class, you behave differently depending on why you think you cannot do it. For instance, if you think you need practice, you might keep trying. If you think you need instruction, you might ask the teacher for guidance. Or if you think you are just too weak and uncoordinated, you might give up and try the long jump instead.

The attributions we make about others and that others make about us also affect our behaviors and interactions. If you go up for a rebound and get elbowed by an opponent, you react differently depending on whether you think the elbowing was intentional or accidental. A teacher who thinks you cannot make the shot because you are not strong enough responds differently than a teacher who thinks you are lazy and not paying attention. Coaches think about the reasons their teams win and lose, and they act on the basis of those attributions in preparing for future contests.

Weiner's Model of Achievement Attributions

Although he was not the first person to propose a theoretical model of attributions, Weiner (1986, 1992) has done the most to bring attribution theory to prominence. Weiner suggested that people make attributions about their successes and failures and that those attributions influence achievement motivation and behavior via their affect and expectations for future success and failure. For example, Jane attributes her progress (i.e., a success) to her hard work, feels a sense of pride, and expects continued success. As a result, she strives to improve in her rehabilitation program. Ben attributes his failure to a lack of ability. He is frustrated and sees no hope for improvement; thus he rarely comes to rehab and when he does, he doesn't work very hard. The essential difference between high and low achievers such as Jane and Ben is a difference in attribution patterns.

The first step to understanding the effects of attributions on motivation is identifying the attributions that people actually make. What reasons do people give for success and failure in sport? Try the following exercise. Think about the last time you performed successfully in your favorite sport or exercise activity. What was the main reason for your success? Now think about the last time you had an unsuccessful performance. What was the main reason for your lack of success?

According to Weiner, your responses will probably fall into one of four categories: ability, effort, luck, and task difficulty. Ability includes attributions such as "I'm not very good at tennis" or "I'm a naturally gifted." Effort might include statements such as "We were really up for the game" or "I never gave up when it got tough." Luck attributions include random events and environmental factors (e.g., "We got the breaks," "They had the ref on their side"). Task difficulty includes attributions to the opponent (e.g., "They were a ranked team") and to the task itself (e.g., "The moves were just too complicated"). Although other attributions exist, particularly in sport (Holt & Morley, 2004; Roberts & Pascuzzi, 1979), these four categories cover most reasons.

The four attributions themselves are not the critical consideration; their personal meaning is the driving force of motivation. Weiner's original model classified attributions along two dimensions—locus of causality and stability (table 9.2). *Locus of causality* refers to whether the cause is internal or external to the performer. Generally we view natural ability and effort as personal characteristics and therefore internal attributions, whereas luck and task difficulty are considered more environmental or situational characteristics and thus external attributions. *Stability* refers to whether the cause is relatively stable and unlikely to change over time. Ability and task difficulty are stable; your tennis ability does not change much from one match to the next, and the height of the net will not change. On the other hand, effort and luck may change; you might be more up for the next match and try harder, or you might get the breaks on line calls. Natural ability is an internal, stable factor; effort is internal and unstable; task difficulty is external and stable; and luck is external and unstable.

Table 9.2   Weiner's 2×2 Classification Scheme for Causal Attributions

	Internal	External
Stable	Ability	Task difficulty
Unstable	Effort	Luck

Later, Weiner added a third dimension—controllability—to distinguish between factors that are internal but uncontrollable and those that are internal and controllable. Table 9.3 illustrates this three-way classification. We have all known people who had a natural ability for a particular activity, such as the person who picks up a golf club for the first time and swings it as though he has done it all his life. This natural ability is internal, but not something we can control. Personal effort, on the other hand, is an internal quality we can control. Effort is controllable, but since we cannot control someone else's effort, it can be either an internal or an external attribution.

Table 9.3 Weiner's 2×2×2 Classification Scheme for Causal Attributions

	LOCUS OF CAUSALITY			
	Internal		External	
Controllability	Stable	Unstable	Stable	Unstable
Controllable	Stable effort	Unstable effort	Others' stable effort	Others' unstable effort
Uncontrollable	Ability	Mood	Task difficulty	Luck

Go back to the reasons you gave for your last success and failure and see where your attributions fit in Weiner's classification. Often people make internal attributions for success and external attributions for failure. If you monitor the comments of winning and losing players and coaches for a while, you will notice that external attributions (e.g., lucky breaks, officials' calls, weather) usually come from the losing side. You will likely never hear a winning coach state that the team won because of a referee's decision. This tendency to attribute success internally and failure externally is usually interpreted as a self-serving bias, meaning that those attributions help us. For example, you probably will feel better about winning the 800-meter run if you think you won because of your own effort than if you think you won because your chief rival had the flu.

According to Weiner, the internal–external dimension relates to feelings of pride and shame. Internal attributions elicit stronger feelings. People take more pride in successes that they earn than in those that are due to external factors, and they feel greater shame when failure is their fault. It does not feel as bad to lose because of poor officiating as it does to lose because you gave up at the end. Thus, attributing success internally and failure externally is self-serving because it maximizes feelings of pride and minimizes feelings of shame. The self-serving bias is one of the most consistent findings in the attribution literature and in sport and exercise psychology research (e.g., McAuley & Duncan, 1989).

The stability dimension also has implications for achievement behavior. Specifically, stability relates to expectations. Stable attributions lead us to expect the same outcomes, whereas unstable attributions lead us to expect different outcomes. If you think your team won the volleyball match because yours is the best team in the league, you will expect to keep on winning. If you think you failed to do the high jump because the skill is too complicated for you, you will expect to continue failing. Conversely, if you had to play over your head to win the match, you cannot be confident of future victories, and if you think you were unable to do the high jump because you did not concentrate well, you can change your behavior and maintain hope for future success.

Just as the locus and stability dimensions affect feelings and expectations, the controllability dimension affects behavior. Weiner suggests that controllability affects moral judgments and reactions to others. We tend to reward and punish people on the basis of controllable attributions: We praise those who give extra effort and criticize those who do not try. We are more apt to criticize a student who slacks off than one who performs poorly because of physical disability.

In general, then, the attributional dimensions affect behavior as follows:

- Locus of causality relates to feelings of pride and shame. We experience stronger feelings with internal attributions than with external attributions.
- Stability relates to future expectations. We expect similar outcomes with stable attributions and changeable outcomes with unstable attributions.

Key Point

People tend to attribute success internally and failure externally. This tendency is called the *self-serving bias* because it maximizes feelings of pride and minimizes feelings of shame.

- Controllability relates to moral judgments and responses to others. We praise people for effort and controllable successes, and we criticize lack of effort and controllable failures.

Application Point

Why might a person who attributes his success to luck expect to fail in the future? Why might he lack a sense of satisfaction with his success? Why might a person who attributes her success to her training regime expect to be successful in the future and happy about her success? Consider someone who attributes his failure to lucky events that day or to lack of ability. How might he feel about his success, and why?

Weiner's model has been refined and expanded; Weiner himself has made several modifications. Researchers often interpreted the four basic attributions of ability, effort, luck, and task difficulty as the only attributions. But Weiner (1979) pointed out that those were never intended to be the only attributions, and others have found that participants gave many attributions that did not fall into the four categories (Bukowski & Moore, 1980; Gill, Ruder, & Gross, 1982; Roberts & Pascuzzi, 1979). Luck and task attributions are rare, and attributions to the team (e.g., teamwork), which are not easily classified, are quite common. In any case, the specific attributions themselves are not of primary importance. As Weiner and several reviewers of the sport and exercise attribution literature (e.g., Biddle, Hanrahan, & Sellars, 2001) have noted, the dimensions of attributions are the critical considerations.

Attribution Research in Sport and Exercise

Research on attributions of winners and losers in sport are equivocal. Some studies have shown that winners make more internal, stable, and controllable attributions than losers (e.g., Hamilton & Jordan, 2000; McAuley & Gross, 1983). However, others have shown that winners make more stable and controllable but not more internal attributions (Grove, Hanrahan, & McInman, 1991; Mark, Mutrie, Brooks, & Harris, 1984). As already discussed, it may be that objective success (i.e., winning or losing) misrepresents athletes' perceived success and failure.

Spink and Roberts (1980) showed that winners made more internal attributions than losers. However, they found two types of winners: satisfied winners who felt they had earned the win through ability and effort (internal attributions) and dissatisfied winners who felt that the task was not difficult (external attribution). Likewise, satisfied losers attributed their loss to task difficulty, whereas dissatisfied losers attributed their loss to low ability. Additionally, McAuley (1985) found perceived success to be a better predictor of internal, stable, controllable attribution than objective success.

In addition to the relationship between attributions and achievement behavior, a popular area in both psychology and sport is attributions and emotions—originally, pride and shame. Later, Weiner (1986) expanded the dimensions to include a greater variety of emotions. In the early study of attributions and emotional reactions to academic success and failure, Weiner and his colleagues (Weiner, Frieze, Kukla, Reed, Rest, & Rosenbaum, 1972) found outcome-dependent and attribution-dependent emotions. Outcome-dependent emotions are associated with the outcome, whereas attribution-dependent emotions are related to the reason for the outcome. It appears that different emotions relate to different

Key Point

Outcome-dependent emotions are associated with the actual outcome, whereas attribution-dependent emotions are related to the reason for the outcome.

attributional dimensions (Biddle, Hanrahan, & Sellars, 2001). Vallerand and Blanchard (2000) have suggested that people's appraisal of their performance is both intuitive and reflective. Intuitive appraisal occurs immediately after performance and enacts one's initial emotion. Reflective appraisal often modifies the emotion state associated with one's intuitive appraisal. Research has supported the role of intuitive and reflective appraisals (see Biddle et al., 2001).

As summarized by Biddle (1993), research in sport shows that performance satisfaction, or subjective appraisal, is one of the best predictors of emotion and that attributions play a role. For example, when Robinson and Howe (1989) surveyed 756 male and female high school students, they found that perceived performance consistently predicted emotions, and attributions added to the prediction. Specifically, people who perceived themselves as successful made more internal (e.g., ability), stable (e.g., likely to happen again), and controllable (e.g., "I can make it happen again") attributions, and they experienced emotions that were more positive than those who perceived themselves as failing. Vlachopoulus, Biddle, and Fox (1996) also found that internal attributions for success emerged as a significant, albeit weak, predictor of positive emotion.

McAuley and Duncan (1989) put an interesting twist on the study of attribution and emotions. Instead of assessing perceptions of success, they manipulated outcomes so that people who expected to win lost and those who expected to lose won. Among those who succeeded, feelings of confidence were the strongest for those who made internal attributions. Among those who failed, depression was the greatest for those who attributed the loss to stable, external factors. These results support the concept of self-serving bias. Attributing losses to stable factors also related to more intense feelings of guilt and shame, and attributing losses to external factors also increased feelings of surprise and incompetence. Despite supporting the self-serving bias, this research also suggests that unexpected outcomes result in intense emotions—whether positive or negative.

More recently, Graham, Kowalski, and Crocker (2002) found that among youth soccer players, positive emotions were positively related and negative emotions were negatively related to more stable and personally controllable attributions. As with previous studies, these relationships were weak and are in concert with Vallerand and Blanchard's (2000) conclusion that although attributions have been shown to be related to emotions, as theorized by Weiner, there is no evidence that attributions cause emotion. Further, attributions have been shown to explain only limited amounts of variance in emotions. Vallerand and Blanchard suggest this as a potential area for future research.

Other Attributional Approaches to Achievement Behavior

As noted earlier, Weiner's attributional theory of achievement behavior, similar to Atkinson's (1974) theory (chapter 8), considers differences between high and low achievers in choice, effort, and persistence on achievement tasks. Atkinson's theory uses a personality characteristic, the need to achieve, to account for individual differences within a drive framework. In contrast, Weiner adopts a cognitive approach, asserting that high and low achievers differ in their attribution patterns and that those attribution differences account for behavior differences.

Carol Dweck and her colleagues (see Dweck, 2000) describe a cognitive model of achievement behavior that combines many ideas we have already discussed about expectations, attributions, and behavior. According to Dweck, initial expectations affect behavior. Higher expectations lead to superior performance and greater persistence on achievement tasks. The performance is evaluated with a score, as a win or loss, or perhaps with verbal feedback from a teacher or coach. The performer then makes an attribution, and that attribution leads to revised expectancies for future performances.

Learned Helplessness

Dweck is well known for her work on learned helplessness. Learned helplessness is the acquired belief that one has no control over negative events or that failure is inevitable. It is an attributional interpretation of extreme low achievement. According to Dweck, learned-helpless people differ from mastery-oriented people (high achievers) in their expectancies and attributions in achievement situations, and especially in their failure attributions. Such people attribute failure to stable, uncontrollable factors—especially lack of ability—and give up after initial failure because they see no hope of future success. In contrast, mastery-oriented people tend to see failure as a temporary setback due to unstable, controllable factors. Thus mastery-oriented people persist in the wake of failure, often with extra effort; they try and try again.

Earlier in her career, Dweck (1975) worked with extremely helpless children in two treatment conditions. Half of the children experienced only successes, a treatment often used with low achievers in which they are given easier tasks that guarantee success. The other half received attribution retraining in which they were successful most of the time but failed on several trials. On the failure trials, the experimenter explicitly attributed the failure to the child's lack of effort. Overall, the attribution retraining was much more effective in changing children's responses to failure and improving performance. Children in the success-only group did not improve performance and did not learn to cope effectively with failure. Curtis (1992) found attributional retraining effective among physical therapists experiencing role strain. Generally, the goal of attributional retraining is to foster positive emotional states and expectations by getting people to avoid making ability-based attributions for failures (an internal, stable, uncontrollable attribution) and instead to make controllable attributions for failure—except maybe effort. People who try hard but still fail will come to attribute their failure to a lack of ability (see Biddle et al., 2001).

> **Key Point**
>
> Attributional training attempts to get people to attribute successes to their ability and failures to lack of sufficient effort or poor strategy.

Learned Helplessness in the Physical Domain

Despite an excellent paper on learned helplessness in the physical domain by Robinson in 1990, research in the area is limited. Nonetheless, a few researchers have studied learned-helpless children in physical education and sport settings. Johnson and Biddle (1988) first investigated learned helplessness in the physical domain by examining attributions for success and failure on a balancing task. People who gave up easily were more likely to make negative self-statements and to attribute their failure to lack of ability and to task difficulty than those who persisted longer. Those who persisted longer made more strategy-related statements. Similar results have been found with middle school students in physical education (Martinek & Griffith, 1994; Martinek & Williams, 1997; Walling & Martinek, 1995) and sport participants (Prapavessis & Carron, 1988). Moreover, recent research has demonstrated a link between perceptions of success and failure (i.e., goal orientations) and attributions.

Certainly we encounter learned-helpless participants in sport. The most obvious cases are children in physical education classes and youth sport programs who believe they are too slow, uncoordinated, and unathletic to do well in sport. Occasionally even skilled athletes can become helpless when they suddenly encounter failure after continued success. Dweck's work suggests that we can best help such people by encouraging them to attribute their failures to unstable, controllable factors, including not only effort but strategies, practice, techniques, or anything else that could be changed. Of course, we should not tell a 10-year-old girl who has poor balance, flexibility, and strength that she can do a back flip on the balance beam if she only tries harder. But we should encourage her to persist in achieving attainable goals.

Application Point

Sara is learning to play tennis. In times of failure, she laments that she can't do it, throws down her racket and sits down on the court. When she is successful, she shrugs it off, noting that it will never happen again. What type of attributions do you think she makes when she is successful and when she fails?

Attributional Training in the Physical Domain

We are not familiar with any attribution retraining programs conducted with learned-helpless children or adults involved in sport or exercise, but there is research demonstrating the efficacy of attribution training programs among sport and therapeutic recreation participants (Dieser & Ruddel, 2002; Orbach, Singer, & Murphey, 1997; Orbach, Singer, & Price, 1999). For example, Orbach et al. (1999) investigated the influence of an attribution training program for novice tennis players who were making dysfunctional attributions. Participants were placed into one of three groups. One group was taught to make more adaptive attributions for their poor performances. Specifically, they were told that their poor performances were based on controllable and unstable factors such as effort or game strategy used; thus their performance could be improved over time. The other group was taught more maladaptive attribution. They were told that their performances were based on uncontrollable and stable factors such as innate (natural) ability; thus some people would just naturally perform better than others.

The results showed that those who learned more adaptive attributions had higher expectations for success and experienced more positive emotions than those who made more maladaptive attributions. Further, participants made these attributions for other tennis tasks and continued to make adaptive attributions for at least 3 weeks after the study. These results demonstrate that physical activity leaders can help people make motivationally adaptive attributions.

Application Point

You have learned that Sara, whom you met in the previous application point, attributes her successes to the poor play of her opponents and her failures to her lack of ability. How would you help Sara make more adaptive attributions?

PUTTING IT INTO PRACTICE

Now you are ready to put the content of chapter 9 into practice. Read the chapter summary, discuss the case study, answer the review questions, and enhance your knowledge by researching the recommended readings.

Summary

Cognitive motivation is one of the most prominent areas in sport and exercise psychology. Considerable research indicates that perceptions and interpretations are critical to understanding participation and behavior. People participate in physical activities for intrinsic reasons, and intrinsic motivation is a key influence on sport and exercise behavior. Cognitive constructs, such as perceived competence, autonomy, relatedness, and attributions, appear to be critical mediators between teaching and coaching strategies and participants' behaviors. In general, the collective work on intrinsic motivation and attributions suggests that we should help participants to set challenging, realistic goals and encourage performers to stress effort and personal control. With the use of these approaches, participants' accomplishments will elicit feelings of competence, personal control, and the desire to continue pursuing sport and exercise activities.

Case Study

With Ben's prodding, Jack and Ben have started working out. To get the help they need, they have hired Rudy as their personal trainer. During the first 2 months, both men have come to gym at least five times a week, been diligent in their workouts, and shown amazing and equal progress. Fortunately, the fact that Jack has made greater gains hasn't bothered Ben. Although Jack has inquired about group aerobic workouts, their workouts have been as a pair and focused solely on weight training, at Ben's insistence. During the last month, Rudy has noticed that Jack's motivation has changed. Jack doesn't seem as happy about working out, he doesn't push himself like he did in the beginning, and his progressed has slowed compared with Ben's. When asked, Jack says things like, "I guess I've reached the limits of my ability," and, "I just can't do any better." Unsure of how to proceed with Jack, Rudy asks your advice. What do you think is behind the change in Jack's motivation and behavior? What recommendations do you give Rudy, and why?

Hints: Use your knowledge of cognitive evaluation theory and self-determination theory to speculate about Jack's needs and his individual perceptions relative to those needs. Consider motivations, attributions, and the effect of these on cognitions, behavior, and affect. Is attributional retraining appropriate here?

Review Questions

1. Explain how extrinsic and intrinsic rewards relate to the reasons why people participate in physical activities.
2. Explain the controlling and informational aspects of rewards and how they each affect intrinsic motivation.

3. Trace the research findings relating intrinsic motivation to competition, winning or losing, positive feedback, and perceived control.
4. Explain the relationship between individual needs and the continuum of motivation.
5. Explain attributions and their role in motivation.
6. Describe the relationships among internal attributions, external attributions, success, and failure.
7. Contrast outcome-dependent emotions with attribution-dependent emotions.
8. Describe learned helplessness.
9. Explain the purpose of attributional retraining programs.

Recommended Reading

Amorose, A.J., & Horn, T.S. (2000). Intrinsic motivation: Relationships with collegiate athletes' gender, scholarship status, and perceptions of their coaches' behavior. *Journal of Sport & Exercise Psychology, 22,* 63-84.

> This article extends the early work of E.D. Ryan's (1977, 1980) work on the relationship between scholarship status and intrinsic motivation. The article highlights the influence of coach behavior on intrinsic motivation.

Biddle, S.J.H., Hanrahan, S.J., & Sellars, C.N. (2001). Attributions: Past, present, and future. In R.N. Singer, H.A. Hausenblass, & C.M. Janelle (Eds.), *Handbook of sport psychology* (2nd ed., pp. 444-471). New York: Wiley.

> Biddle has done considerable work on social-cognitive approaches, and in this chapter he and his colleagues provide an excellent overview of attribution theory and research. This book chapter is a valuable resource for anyone interested in attribution theory and the research conducted in this area.

Whitehead, J.R., & Corbin, C.B. (1991). Youth fitness testing: The effects of percentile-based evaluation feedback on intrinsic motivation. *Research Quarterly for Exercise and Sport, 62,* 225-231.

> This is a classic study that examined the effects of norm-based evaluation on children's intrinsic motivation. Children who received negative norm-based feedback reported decreased intrinsic motivation, whereas those who received positive evaluations reported higher intrinsic motivation. Further, the researchers demonstrated that feedback indirectly influences intrinsic motivation via perceived competence.

Chapter 10

Participation Motivation

Chapter Objectives

After studying this chapter, you should be able to

- ◆ discuss the health benefits of physical activity;
- ◆ describe physical activity patterns in the general population and differences in patterns across age and gender;
- ◆ identify the characteristics of exercise dependence and discuss the health risks of excessive exercise;
- ◆ discuss the motivational theories and models that have been applied to exercise behavior;
- ◆ understand the role of the physical and social environment in the development and maintenance of physical activity behavior; and
- ◆ explain how integrative models, such as the transtheoretical model, can be used to promote physical activity as a lifestyle behavior.

This chapter focuses on motivation for continued participation in physical activity—why people begin and stay involved in sport and exercise. We will focus on physical activity as a lifestyle behavior, which is essential in health promotion and fitness programs, important in physical education and youth sport, and relevant even in competitive athletics. Highly competitive athletes may emphasize achievement and performance, but they also maintain training activities and are developing activity patterns that they will continue when they leave their competitive sport.

Maintenance of physical activity, rather than peak performance, is the overriding goal, and participants typically engage in varied activities rather than focusing on one sport or event. Indeed, that variation often is intentional in order to achieve health and fitness goals. Just as activities are varied, participants are much more diverse than the athletes in select sports. This chapter focuses on typical adult fitness participants, a diverse population in itself, as well as children, older adults, and clients in a variety of clinical and health promotion programs.

PHYSICAL ACTIVITY FOR HEALTH AND WELL-BEING

Lifestyle physical activity is increasingly promoted in the media, as well as in health and kinesiology resources. The U.S. Department of Health and Human Services (USDHHS) published the Surgeon General's report on physical activity and health in 1996 and the Healthy People 2010 objectives in 2000, and both are widely circulated as publications and on the Internet. For example, the Centers for Disease Control and Prevention (CDC) Web site (www.cdc.gov) has a section that offers resources and information on physical activity.

Physical inactivity has been linked to nearly all major health problems, including heart disease, diabetes, osteoporosis, and negative psychological conditions such as depression and anxiety (USDHHS, 1996). In a consensus statement, Kesaniemi et al. (2001) concluded that regular physical activity is associated with a reduction in all-cause mortality, fatal and nonfatal total cardiovascular disease, coronary heart disease, obesity, and type 2 diabetes. Further benefits include improved physical function and independent living, as well as less likelihood of depressive illness.

> **Key Point**
>
> Physical inactivity has been linked to most major health problems, including heart disease, diabetes, osteoporosis, and negative psychological conditions such as depression and anxiety.

The interest in physical activity and health promotion is not limited to the United States. The World Health Organization (WHO) includes physical activity as a public health priority, and the WHO Web site (www.who.int) contains information on physical activity and health that parallels U.S. reports. Physical inactivity is a major health problem around the world, and the WHO estimates that 60% of the world's population does not get enough physical activity to achieve even the modest recommendation of 30 minutes per day, with adults in developed countries most likely to be inactive. Like the CDC, ACSM, and many governmental and professional organizations in North America, the WHO promotes physical activity and offers recommendations for both individuals and public policies.

SPORT AND EXERCISE PSYCHOLOGY FOR PHYSICAL ACTIVITY AND HEALTH

> **Key Point**
>
> The CDC and ACSM recommend at least 30 minutes of moderate physical activity most days of the week. More than 50% of the U.S. population is sedentary, with older adults and members of racial and ethnic minority groups participating in less physical activity than the overall population.

Sport and exercise psychology may be the most important discipline for professionals and participants in health-related physical activity programs. Much of the interest in physical activity motivation stems from increasing public recognition of the health benefits of exercise coupled with the fact that most people do not act on that recognition.

The CDC and ACSM (Pate et al., 1995) recommend at least 30 minutes of moderate physical activity most, if not all, days of the week, yet data from population-based surveys consistently show that over 50% of the U.S. population is sedentary, with higher rates for those who are older, racial or ethnic minorities, female, less educated, overweight, and have a history of being physically inactive. Physical activity patterns of childhood and adolescence begin the lifetime patterns that promote health in adulthood, but unfortunately the evidence indicates that activity declines in adolescence, particularly for girls.

Lox, Martin, and Petruzzello (2006) summarize the epidemiological data on physical activity patterns around the world as follows:

- The number of people worldwide who exercise at even the minimal level to achieve physical benefits is low (conservatively estimated at 50%); at least 25% do not exercise at all.

- Participation in physical activity declines linearly across the life span and time spent in sedentary activities increases.

- Males are more likely to engage in vigorous activity, although women engage in as much moderate physical activity as men.

- Differences are small, but low-income groups and minority groups tend to participate in less physical activity than the overall population.

- The higher the education level, the greater the participation in physical activity.

Moreover, 50% of the adults who start to exercise in fitness programs drop out within 6 months, and as Buckworth and Dishman (2002) note, this high dropout rate has not changed over the past 20 years.

EXCESSIVE PARTICIPATION: EXERCISE DEPENDENCE

So far, we have focused on encouraging participation in physical activity. Indeed, that is the major concern for health promotion. However, excessive exercise may become health damaging. Athletes may train excessively (overtrain), resulting in negative mental health (e.g., depression, tension, fatigue, reduced energy) as well as poorer performance. As Raglin and Moger (1999) note, the switch to negative mood states is related to the training load and in extreme cases can result in clinical depression.

Exercise dependence syndrome is more often associated with participants who are not competitive athletes and whose excessive exercise is not associated with training to enhance performance. Hausenblas and Symons Downs (2002a, p. 90) define exercise dependence as "a craving for leisure-time physical activity, resulting in uncontrollable excessive exercise behavior, that manifests itself in physiological . . . and/or psychological . . . symptoms." As the definition indicates, it is not simply the amount or level of exercise, but the dependence (craving) and inability to control behavior that characterize the syndrome. In their review, Hausenblas and Symons Downs (2002a) further delineate the characteristics of exercise dependence as follows:

- **Tolerance:** An increased amount of exercise is needed to achieve the desired effect.

- **Withdrawal:** Withdrawal symptoms are felt when exercise is missed.

- **Intention effect:** Exercise lasts longer than was originally intended.

- **Loss of control:** Unsuccessful effort is made to control or cut back on the amount of exercise.

- **Time:** Lots of time is spent in activities needed to obtain exercise.

- **Conflict:** Important social or relationship activities are given up because of exercise.

- **Continuance:** Exercise is maintained in spite of knowing that it is problematic.

Hausenblas and Symons Downs' description brings some clarity to the literature. They have also developed and validated an exercise dependence scale based on clinical criteria for substance dependence (Hausenblas & Symons Downs, 2002b). Excessive exercise has been termed *compulsion, dependence,* and *obsession* but might also be characterized as *commitment* or a *healthy habit.* Early literature focused on running addiction, which Sachs (1981) defined as a psychological or physiological addiction to regular running that is characterized by withdrawal symptoms after 24 to 36 hours without running. Morgan (1979) suggested that addicted runners believe they need to exercise and cannot live without running daily; if deprived of exercise, they experience withdrawal symptoms including anxiety, restlessness, guilt, irritability, tension, and discomfort, as well as apathy,

Key Point

Excessive exercise participation, sometimes termed an *addiction, dependence,* or *commitment,* has been discussed as a problematic behavior. Some reports have also linked excessive exercise with eating disorders.

sluggishness, lack of appetite, sleeplessness, and headaches. Thompson and Blanton (1987) proposed a psychophysiological explanation, hypothesizing that exercise dependence is mediated by adaptive reductions in sympathetic output during exercise, which results from increased efficiency of energy use with exercise training.

Several studies suggest that many regular exercisers fit the addiction criteria. For example, Kagan and Squires (1985) found that college students who exercised regularly tended to fit an addictive personality, and Robbins and Joseph (1985) reported that over 50% of runners in a large sample experienced deprivation sensations when unable to run.

Not only has excessive exercise been discussed as a problem in itself, but some reports have linked excessive exercise with anorexia nervosa and bulimia. Yates, Leehey, and Shisslak (1983) interviewed 60 obligatory runners and suggested similarities to anorexia nervosa patients. Blumenthal, O'Toole, and Chang (1984), on the other hand, found that obligatory runners generally fell within the normal range of behavior whereas people with anorexia did not. In a follow-up article, Blumenthal, Rose, and Chang (1985) argued against a psychopathological or disease model of habitual running. Although most research does not link excessive exercise to clinical disorders, Pierce (1994) differentiated primary and secondary exercise dependence based on the exercise objective. In primary exercise dependence, exercise is an end in itself, whereas in secondary exercise dependence, exercise is a means to control body composition (i.e., weight or appearance). Excessive exercisers may well display unhealthy behaviors, particularly disordered eating, and professionals should be alert for signs of exercise dependence syndrome.

Application Point

As a kinesiology professional, you may well encounter students or clients who exercise excessively. If you suspected that your client at a performance training facility were developing exercise dependence syndrome, what signs or behaviors would you look for?

Whether considering those who engage in excessive exercise or the vast majority who do not participate in sufficient physical activity for health and well-being, we are dealing with human behavior. Sport and exercise psychology, which focuses on behavior in exercise and sport settings, can contribute to the development of effective programs and practices that promote healthy physical activity. The issue is behavior, and more precisely, motivation for starting and maintaining physical activity behaviors. Before moving to specific motivational strategies, the next section draws from motivational research and theories discussed in other chapters to provide an integrated model for professional practice.

PARTICIPATION MOTIVATION FOR LIFESTYLE PHYSICAL ACTIVITY

Much of the early research on participation motivation was descriptive and focused on identifying reasons young people engaged in physical activity. Research on participation motivation has extended to college-aged and adult participants, and the general pattern of factors and important reasons is similar. However, the area of exercise and health promotion has unique concerns. The current literature on exercise motivation relies more on theoretical models than on purely descriptive studies, and as noted earlier, it focuses on lifestyle physical activity and health promotion.

Duda and Tappe (1988, 1989) developed a measure that retains the wide range of options of participation-motivation measures (e.g., Gill, Gross, & Huddleston, 1983) but places them within the framework of personal investment theory with a focus on exercise activities and motives for a wide range of participants. Duda and Tappe's (1989) Personal Incentives for Exercise Questionnaire (PIEQ) has 10 subscales: appearance, competition, mental benefits, affiliation, social recognition, mastery, flexibility and agility, health benefits, weight management, and fitness. Gill, Dowd, Williams, Beaudoin, and Martin (1996) used the PIEQ with older and more diverse samples of adults in a running club, fitness club, and cardiac rehabilitation program, and they used a shorter version with senior games participants. All four groups were similar to each other and to previous samples, but they varied on specific motives. Females rated fitness, flexibility, affiliation, and appearance higher than males did. Generally, participants were diverse in motives and positive about participation.

THEORIES AND MODELS OF EXERCISE BEHAVIOR

Unlike the largely descriptive research on youth sport motivation, the work on participation motivation in health-related physical activity settings is largely theory based. Because behavior change and maintaining activity are the main concerns, the models draw heavily upon behavioral and social-cognitive models that have been applied to health behaviors. Bess Marcus, a major contributor to that work, and her colleagues (Marcus, Bock, Pinto, Napolitano, & Clark, 2002) reviewed theoretical models that have been applied to exercise behavior. The following section summarizes the main theoretical models and then provides applications of integrated models in physical activity interventions and health promotion programs.

Health Belief Model

The health belief model developed by Rosenstock (1974) includes four major components:

1. Perceived susceptibility, or the assessment of risk for the particular health threat
2. Perceived severity of the health threat
3. Perceived benefits of taking action to reduce the threat
4. Perceived barriers to or costs of the action

The health belief model has considerable support in relation to health behaviors and medical compliance but limited application to exercise and physical activity. The strongest support has been found for components related to other theories and for selected components with investigations following other models. Specifically, perceived barriers, which relates to self-efficacy, has stronger support than other components.

Decision Theory

Decision theory (Janis & Mann, 1977) entails the perception and evaluation of relative costs and benefits. In applied settings, participants might generate lists of short- and long-term consequences of an exercise program and then weigh them. Decision theory has been applied successfully with many health behaviors (e.g., Marlatt & Gordon, 1985), and these decision-balancing procedures have been used to increase awareness of benefits and promote participation in physical activity (Jordan, Nigg, Norman, Rossi, & Benisovich, 2002; Marcus, Rakowski, & Rossi, 1992; Nigg & Courneya, 1998; Wankel, 1984).

Theories of Reasoned Action and Planned Behavior

The attitude-based theories of reasoned action (TRA; Fishbein & Ajzen, 1974) and planned behavior (Ajzen, 1985) have received more attention in research on exercise behavior. Both propose that intentions are the main determinants of behavior. That is, to predict whether people will exercise, ask them whether they intend to exercise. Behavioral intentions, in turn, are determined by attitudes toward the behavior, along with social norms. The theory of planned behavior (TPB) moves beyond reasoned action by adding the notion of perceived behavioral control. Perceived behavioral control is similar to self-efficacy (as discussed in chapter 6) in that it involves perceptions that one has the ability to carry out the behavior.

Several sport and exercise psychologists have applied reasoned action or planned behavior to understand and predict exercise behavior (e.g., Brawley & Rodgers, 1992; Courneya, Estabrooks, & Nigg, 1997; Godin, 1993; McAuley & Courneya, 1993). Meta-analyses by Downs and Hausenblas (2005) and Hagger, Chatzisarantis, and Biddle (2002) support the TPB in finding that the most important predictor of physical activity is intention and that attitude and behavioral control predict intention. Subjective norm has not received consistent support, and Courneya, Plotnikoff, Hotz, and Birkett (2000) advocate substituting social support as the social influence predictor in TPB.

Social-Cognitive Theories

Social-cognitive theories (see chapter 9) have been applied to many health behaviors, including exercise behavior. On the basis of earlier work with other health behaviors (e.g., weight management, smoking cessation), Marcus, Selby, Niaura, and Rossi (1992) developed a five-item self-efficacy measure for exercise that includes the situational factors of negative affect, resisting relapse, and making time for exercise. As discussed in chapter 6, considerable literature supports the role of self-efficacy and social-cognitive theory in sport and exercise behavior. For example, Dzewaltowski (1989) and colleagues (Dzewaltowski, Noble, & Shaw, 1990) found that self-efficacy predicted exercise behavior in college undergraduates; McAuley (1992) demonstrated that self-efficacy predicted exercise adherence for middle-aged adults; and Sallis et al. (1986) reported relationships between efficacy and physical activity in a community sample.

Several researchers have applied social-cognitive models and found self-efficacy to be a strong predictor of physical activity in various populations, including obese people (Dallow & Anderson, 2003) and people with physical disabilities (Cardinal, Kosma, & McCubbin, 2004). McAuley, Jerome, Marquez,

Elavsky, and Blissmer (2003) confirmed the reciprocal efficacy–behavior relationships of social-cognitive theory in reporting that previous exercise behavior predicted efficacy and future exercise behavior in older adults. At the other end of the age range, Lubans and Sylva (2006) applied social-cognitive theory in a physical activity intervention with high school students. At the end of the program, the intervention group reported both more physical activity and greater self-efficacy for exercise than the control group.

Self-determination theory (SDT; Ryan & Deci, 2000) focuses on self-motivation and ways the social environment can optimize performance and well-being. Deci and Ryan's (1985) extensive research on cognitive evaluation theory and intrinsic motivation has often been applied in sport and exercise psychology. Oman and McAuley (1993) found that intrinsic motivation related to attendance in an 8-week fitness program, and others are investigating strategies to increase intrinsic motivation as participants move to maintenance stages of fitness programs. To date, SDT has seldom been used in exercise interventions, but programs that focus on promoting self-determination and intrinsic motivation are promising. Landry and Solmon (2002, 2004) applied SDT with adult African American women and reported that self-determination was related to stage of exercise behavior.

Application Point

As SDT suggests, self-determination and intrinsic motivation are related to exercise behavior. As an exercise instructor in a cardiac rehabilitation program, what could you do to promote self-determination and intrinsic motivation and thus enhance adherence among participants? Give specific examples.

Behavioral Approaches to Exercise Adherence

Although social-cognitive models dominate the literature on exercise adherence and physical activity motivation, behavioral approaches have a clear role in intervention programs. Martin and Dubbert (1984) provide a useful framework. First, they separate exercise behavior into two stages: acquisition of the exercise habit and exercise maintenance. Similar to Marcus, they suggest that different strategies are more effective at different stages. Specifically, during the acquisition phase, Martin and Dubbert suggest the following behavioral strategies:

- **Shaping.** This is an important strategy for establishing a long-term exercise habit. Establishing the exercise habit is more important than building training effects, and gradual progression with reinforcement for small steps is more effective than exercise goals that cannot be reached within a reasonable time.

- **Reinforcement control.** Frequent reinforcement is advocated during the acquisition phase. Social support and praise during sessions are effective, and tangible reinforcers, attention, and specific feedback may also be used.

- **Stimulus control.** Stimulus control, which involves the use of cues, is helpful in acquiring the exercise habit. Many morning exercisers put their gym bags out the night before as a prompt, and organized programs typically use cues in both their advertising and ongoing programs.

- **Behavioral contracts.** Creating specific contracts, often in writing, may be effective for some beginning exercisers. Contracts are a form of goal setting that can provide direction and incentive for exercise behavior.
- **Cognitive strategies.** Martin and Dubbert suggest several cognitive strategies such as goal setting, positive self-talk, and association–dissociation (distraction) as part of a cognitive-behavioral approach during the acquisition phase.

After an exerciser has developed the habit, behavioral strategies should change to match the needs of the exerciser and help the person move from a structured, organized program into the exercise maintenance phase.

- **Generalization training.** Generalization training involves gradual fading of the program as the person makes the difficult transition from a structured to an unstructured setting (that is, generalizing the exercise behavior to other settings or circumstances). Incorporating home exercise during a structured program might aid the transition, and generalization training might include family or friends.
- **Reinforcement fading.** Reinforcement gradually fades in frequency and intensity as the person transfers to natural reinforcers such as increased feelings of control and increased energy.
- **Self-control procedures.** As discussed earlier, a sense of control leads to intrinsic motivation, which is essential for exercise maintenance. Self-monitoring is the most common procedure and actually should begin in the earlier acquisition phase. Self-evaluation and rewards may also be included, often in a contract procedure.
- **Relapse-prevention training.** Most exercisers, even the most faithful, eventually relapse. Thus, most professionals advocate some type of relapse-prevention training, as described in the next section.

Relapse-Prevention Model

Regardless of how people start exercising, relapse is a problem, as it is for most health behaviors (Brownell, Marlatt, Lichtenstein, & Wilson, 1986). As noted earlier, about 50% of exercise program participants typically drop out within 6 months. Sallis et al. (1990) found that 40% of exercisers experienced relapse (stopped exercising for at least 3 months) and that 20% had three or more relapses. In relapse-prevention training, exercisers learn to view exercise as a continuum, to recognize and avoid risk situations, and sometimes to try a planned relapse. The principles of relapse prevention include identifying high-risk situations (e.g., a change in work hours) and then problem solving for those high-risk situations (e.g., when it starts to snow, walk inside the local mall).

When exercisers experience a relapse, they must deal with the abstinence violation effect (AVE), which is the belief that one slip means doom (e.g., one cookie ruins your diet, one missed exercise class and you're a couch potato). Brownell (1989) differentiates among a lapse (slip), relapse (string of lapses), and collapse (giving up and returning to past behaviors). Brownell advocates helping people become aware of AVE and the differences among lapses, relapses, and collapses in order to reduce recidivism. Marcus, Dubbert, and colleagues (2000) suggest that the relapse-prevention model can be a useful framework for understanding the lapse-to-collapse process in exercise behavior.

Many exercise programs and personal trainers adopt some of the behavioral strategies suggested by Martin and Dubbert, and most practitioners use both cognitive approaches and behavioral techniques that draw from multiple theories. Given the diversity of participants, multifaceted programs with varied strategies are most likely to meet participants' needs and preferences. Grodesky, Kosma, and Solmon (2006), focusing on older adults' physical activity behavior, specifically advocated the transtheoretical model as an overall guiding framework and incorporated elements of both the TPB and SDT within a comprehensive approach.

Integrated Approach: The Transtheoretical Model

Several researchers have advocated integration of the many available theoretical approaches. At this time, the most useful approach for practicing professionals is the transtheoretical model (TTM; Prochaska & DiClemente, 1983) applied to exercise behavior by Bess Marcus and colleagues (e.g., Marcus, Rossi, Selby, Niaura, & Abrams, 1992; Marcus & Forsyth, 2003). Generally, the TTM helps us understand the relationship between individual readiness and actual exercise behavior, and it provides guidance for intervention programs aimed at increasing physical activity. According to the model, people progress through certain stages of change:

> **Key Point**
>
> The TTM helps us understand the relationship between individual readiness and actual exercise behavior, and it provides guidance for intervention programs aimed at increasing physical activity.

1. Precontemplation
2. Contemplation
3. Preparation
4. Action
5. Maintenance

Precontemplators do not exercise and do not intend to do so within the next 6 months. Contemplators do not exercise but intend to start within 6 months. Preparers are exercising but not regularly (three or more times per week for 20 minutes or longer, or 30 accumulated minutes or more per day on 5 or more days per week). People at the action stage exercise regularly but have done so less than 6 months, whereas those at the maintenance stage have been exercising regularly for more than 6 months (Marcus, Rossi, Selby, Niaura, & Abrams, 1992).

Marcus also relates the decisional balance and self-efficacy constructs to stages of change. In relation to stages, the decisional balance typically favors the costs in the precontemplation and contemplation stages, crosses over in the preparation stage, and favors benefits over costs in the action and maintenance stages (Marcus, Rakowski, et al., 1992; Prochaska et al., 1994). Over several studies (Marcus, Eaton, Rossi, & Harlow, 1994; Marcus & Owen, 1992; Marcus, Pinto, Simkin, Audrain, & Taylor, 1994; Marcus, Selby, et al., 1992), Marcus and colleagues have found a positive relationship between enhanced self-efficacy and higher levels of readiness for change. Their work has been especially useful in promoting physical activity. At the end of this chapter, we will discuss specific applications that have been effective in the promotion of physical activity.

Social Ecological Models

Social ecological models move beyond the integration of social-cognitive and behavioral theories to emphasize the social environment and environmental interventions that can influence physical activity for the larger community. In particular, social ecological models often focus on the built environment, such as housing patterns, walkways, and trails, as well as public policies. Sallis, Bauman, and Pratt (1998) developed a social-ecological model for physical activity that suggests coordinating and planning efforts among agencies (e.g., transportation, urban planning, schools) in order to facilitate policies and practices that support physical activity. Although social ecological models are broad and offer few clear, testable predictions, they provide guidance for promoting physical activity and health at the community level. Specifically, such models suggest that physical activity levels can be increased by improving the availability of facilities and programs and supporting active transportation such as walking and biking.

Application Point

Kinesiology professionals can, and should, promote physical activity in their larger communities as well as in professional practice. A neighborhood group interested in promoting physical activity is meeting at the school where you are a physical education teacher and the group asks for your advice. What will you say? Consider social ecological models and suggest specific policy and environmental changes to promote physical activity in the community.

The CDC clearly advocates such approaches, and their Web site includes suggestions and resources for developing active environments that promote physical activity (www.cdc.gov). As noted on the Web site, interest in environmental and policy strategies to promote physical activity has grown over the last few years, as has the evidence that supports such approaches. Environmental and policy approaches are especially important because they can benefit everyone within the environment, including those at high risk for inactivity. Strategies include providing access to facilities and programs and supporting social environments that favor activity, such as walking and bicycle trails, public funding for facilities, zoning and land use that facilitates activity in neighborhoods, mall walking programs, and building construction that encourages physical activity. Such approaches hold particular promise and should be taken into account when designing community-based physical activity interventions. The CDC Web site also links to related sites that complement their efforts to create an active environment, such as the Robert Wood Johnson Foundation Active Living Web site (www.activelivingresearch.org). For example, Active Living by Design is a national program of the Robert Wood Johnson Foundation that establishes and evaluates innovative approaches to increase physical activity through community design, public policies, and communications strategies.

Evidence to support such broad-based programs is growing. The Robert Wood Johnson Foundation has sponsored several Active Living Research conferences. Papers from the 2005 conference, published in a special issue of *Journal of Physical Activity and Health* (Kraft, Sallis, Moudon, & Linton, 2006), attest to the efforts of researchers and public health professionals. Following are a few examples of these articles. Taylor, Carlos Postoin, Jones, and Kraft (2006) advocate environmental justice, referring to efforts to address disproportionate harmful environmental conditions experienced by low-income and racial and ethnic minority populations, and they provide evidence of the challenges faced in efforts to become active (e.g., crime, sidewalks, safe places, recreational facilities). Heath et al. (2006) identified two interventions that were effective in promoting physical activity: community-scale and street-scale urban design and land-use policies and practices. Cohen et al. (2006) found that distance to school was inversely related to moderate-vigorous physical activity in adolescent girls, with those more than 5 miles (8 kilometers) away the most adversely affected. That special issue of the *Journal of Physical Activity and Health* contains many more relevant articles that provide information for professional practice and guidance for further research. Clearly, physical activity promotion is a multifaceted concern, and we cannot ignore the profound influence of the social and physical environment.

Using Integrated Models: A Practical Guide

The TTM incorporates cognitive theories and behavioral strategies, emphasizes the need to individualize interventions, considers environmental barriers, and provides a useful guide for developing effective programs. Marcus and colleagues have gone beyond proposals to carry out interventions based on the TTM (see Marcus & Forsyth, 2003). In the Imagine Action campaign, 610 adults enrolled through work sites in response to community announcements, received a 6-week intervention consisting of stage-matched self-help materials, a resource manual, weekly fun walks, and activity nights. The manual for contemplators was called *What's In It for You,* which is the critical question at that stage. Similarly, the preparation manual was *Ready for Action,* and the manual for those in action was *Keeping It Going.* Following the intervention, 30% of those in contemplation and 61% of those in preparation progressed to action, and an additional 31% of those in contemplation progressed to preparation, whereas only 4% of those in preparation and 9% in action regressed. A subsequent controlled, randomized-design investigation of a stage-matched intervention at the workplace (Marcus, Emmons, et al., 1994) was also successful, with more subjects in the stage-matched group demonstrating stage progression at the 3-month follow-up; in contrast, more subjects in the standard-care group displayed stage stability or regression.

More recently, Marcus and Forsyth (2003) compiled research and theoretical work into a practical guide: *Motivating People to Be Physically Active.* The guide emphasizes stages of change as an individual difference variable and suggests behavioral and cognitive strategies, as well as social support and environmental approaches, to promote physical activity. Sources of information and guidelines for the general public, such as Corbin et al.'s (2008) fitness and wellness manual and the CDC Web site, reference Marcus and recommend a similar approach. Project Active (Dunn et al., 1999) has successfully applied the model in a community-based physical activity program.

Marcus and Forsyth (2003) use the stages of change model as framework for individualizing intervention strategies. As noted earlier, people are at different stages depending on their current level of physical activity. The main point for professionals is that intervention programs should match the stage of change; that is, programs and strategies should be tailored to the individual, situation, and context.

Processes of behavior change are strategies and techniques for modifying behaviors. Processes fall into two categories: cognitive and behavioral. Cognitive processes involve thinking and awareness and include increasing knowledge, being aware of risks, caring about consequences to others, comprehending benefits, and increasing healthy opportunities. Behavioral processes involve action and include substituting alternatives, enlisting social support, rewarding yourself, committing yourself, and reminding yourself.

Programs based on the model match interventions to the participant's stage of readiness. In general, cognitive strategies are more useful for people in the early stages (precontemplation, contemplation), whereas people at later stages (preparation, action, and maintenance) use mostly behavioral strategies. Within that general framework, Marcus and Forsyth provide more specific examples and suggestions for consultants or fitness professionals who want to help clients use these strategies in the process of behavior change. Many of the specific strategies draw upon the behavioral and cognitive strategies and psychological skills discussed in the previous sections of this chapter. Strategies that are appropriate for the current stage help the person take positive steps toward fitness while overcoming barriers and building confidence. The Marcus and Forsyth book is readable and practical, as well as based on current theory and empirical evidence. It is highly recommended as a guide for sport and exercise psychologists working with individual clients, groups, or community programs to promote healthy physical activity.

 ## Application Point

You are the activity director at a senior center. Two participants ask for your advice on how they can stick with their exercise programs. One is just beginning, and the other one has been walking regularly for several months. What specific strategies would you suggest for each person?

PUTTING IT INTO PRACTICE

Now you are ready to put the content of chapter 10 into practice. Read the chapter summary, discuss the case study, answer the review questions, and enhance your knowledge by researching the recommended readings.

Summary

This chapter focused on participation motivation for lifestyle physical activity and interventions in health promotion settings. Although lifestyle physical activity differs from the sport and exercise behaviors emphasized in other chapters, motivation models and research can be applied to enhance continuing participation in physical activity. Indeed, effective application of behavioral and cognitive strategies within a theoretical framework is essential for effective programs.

Several motivational theories have been applied to physical activity participation and maintenance, and integrated models that incorporate both cognitive and behavioral strategies are the most useful. The TTM, which integrates theoretical perspectives and combines cognitive and behavioral strategies, has been successfully used in interventions and community programs to help people move through beginning stages to physical activity maintenance. Social ecological models that focus on the social and physical environment have been especially useful in community and population-based promotion of physical activity. In health promotion programs, the overriding goal is maintaining activity rather than continually striving to achieve performance standards.

Interventions that help participants focus on lifestyle activity are likely to be effective. Behavioral strategies and social-cognitive approaches that focus on recognizing health and fitness benefits, overcoming barriers, and developing self-control and perceived competence in a supportive environment are particularly appropriate. Specific behavioral and cognitive strategies used within an integrative model that matches strategies to the individual can help participants overcome barriers, develop confidence, and gain greater health and wellness through fitness activities.

Case Study

This chapter brings together motivational theories and research to provide guidelines for promoting lifestyle physical activity in professional practice. For this case, use the chapter material and draw from other motivation chapters to develop a plan for promoting physical activity among overweight adolescents.

Your school is starting an after-school program for overweight middle school students with support from a community grant. The stated goals of the program are to reduce risk for cardiovascular disease and diabetes and to promote health and well-being through physical activity. The students in your urban, public school can participate at no cost, school facilities are available, and the grant will provide for a student intern to assist. Present your plan to the school officials and parent–teacher group. Include your overall approach, specific strategies and activities you would include, and a rationale.

Hints: Refer to motivational theories, particularly integrated models. Participants are likely to be in early stages of exercise, so focus on strategies to move from contemplation and preparation toward action and maintenance. Consider cognitive predictors and outcomes (e.g., self-efficacy, self-determination), tailor your program to individuals, and don't forget the larger social environment.

Review Questions

1. Describe the overall physical activity patterns in the United States. How do these patterns differ by age and gender?
2. What are some of the characteristics of exercise dependence? How can excessive exercise become a problem?
3. What are the main components of the TRA and TPB? How do these theories explain exercise behavior?
4. What behavioral strategies are recommended during the acquisition phase of an exercise habit?
5. List the five stages of change in the TTM. Explain how behavioral and cognitive processes can be matched to stages to help people progress through the stages.
6. What is the relapse-prevention model? How does it apply to exercise behavior?
7. Describe social ecological models of physical activity behavior and explain how they include the physical and social environment.

Recommended Reading

Marcus, B.H., Bock, B.C., Pinto, B.M., Napolitano, M.A., & Clark, M.M. (2002). Exercise initiation, adoption, and maintenance in adults: Theoretical models and empirical support. In J.L. Van Raalte & B.W. Brewer (Eds.), *Exploring sport and exercise psychology* (2nd ed., pp. 185-208). Washington, DC: APA.

Marcus, B.H., & Forsyth, L.H. (2003). *Motivating people to be physically active.* Champaign, IL: Human Kinetics.

> Bess Marcus and her colleagues have done considerable research on exercise motivation, applying the TTM to enhance exercise participation in various populations. The first reference provides an overview of that work and approaches for promoting physical activity. For those interested in more direct applications, read the Marcus and Forsyth book, which provides a guide to the basic principles and focuses on promoting physical activity with individuals, groups, community programs, and public health campaigns.

Kraft, M.K., Sallis, J.F., Moudon, A.V., & Linton, L.S. (2006). The second Active Living Research Conference: Signs of maturity. *Journal of Physical Activity and Health, 3* (Suppl. 1), S1-S5.

The Robert Wood Johnson Foundation *Active Living* Web site (www.activelivingresearch.org).

> In addition to applying integrated psychological models, physical activity and health, professionals are increasingly taking a broader view to promote active living among the wider population. For more information, check selected papers from the second Active Living conference and the Active Living Web site.

Part IV

Emotions, Stress, and Coping

In the ABCs of psychology, emotion is the *A*, or affect component, encompassing all the feelings and moods that are part of human behavior. Emotion has a long history in psychology, but in recent times, the field has devoted more attention to the *B* and *C* components—behavior and cognition—and left the messier emotions for the poets and philosophers. Emotion is pervasive and obvious in the real world, and it is prominent in sport and exercise psychology. To date, research and practice have focused on competitive anxiety, but it is expanding to include a wider range of emotions, physical activity settings, and participants. Chapter 11 covers the major theories and models of emotion as well as the research on competitive anxiety and exercise effects on emotion. Chapter 12 emphasizes using emotional control and stress management in physical activity settings.

Chapter 11

Emotion Models and Research

Chapter Objectives

After studying this chapter, you should be able to

◆ understand emotion as a concept and define related terms,

◆ explain the major theoretical perspectives on emotion from psychology,

◆ describe the models and measures of emotion used in sport and exercise psychology research,

◆ discuss the research on physical activity and emotions, and

◆ explain the anxiety–performance models used in sport and exercise psychology and discuss the research on the anxiety–performance relationship.

Emotion is everywhere. We recognize the thrill of victory and the agony of defeat in Olympic competitors and in 10-year-old soccer players. You might feel exhilarated after a daily run or embarrassed when looking in the mirror at the fitness center. Emotions in sport and exercise reflect all the complexities of psychology and behavior. They combine the biological, psychological, and social in a complex, dynamic mix that adds to life—but frustrates scientists.

Scholars cannot ignore such a pervasive and powerful aspect of behavior as emotion, and the psychology literature has considerable emotional content. William James discussed emotion more than 100 years ago, and since then psychologists have offered theories and empirical observations from varied perspectives. Anxiety and stress are the most prominent emotion topics in sport and exercise psychology, but research is expanding to a broader range of emotions and processes.

First, we will look at the broader area of emotions. Then we will focus on the sport and exercise psychology work, including exercise and emotions, competitive anxiety, and some exciting work on positive emotions in sport and exercise.

EMOTION CONCEPTS AND DEFINITIONS

Emotion is a messy research topic, and the related terminology matches. As Reeve (2005) noted in a recent text, everyone knows what emotion is, but the definition is problematic. Reeve defined emotion with a model that includes four aspects—bodily arousal, social expressive, sense of purpose, and feelings—and stated the following:

> *Emotions are short-lived, feeling-arousal-purposive-expressive phenomena that help us adapt to the opportunities and challenges we face during important life events. (p. 294)*

Plutchik (2003) listed several definitions, starting with James in 1884 and moving through the major conceptual works on emotion over the next 100 years. Most psychologists recognize both physiological and psychological components of emotion and consider emotion to be a process rather than a static state. However, psychologists differ greatly in the details of the process and the relative roles of physiological and social-cognitive processes. Concise definitions cannot capture the complexity of emotions. Kleinginna and Kleinginna's (1981) all-embracing definition reflects many of the emotion models:

> *Emotion is a complex set of interactions among subjective and objective factors, mediated by neural/hormonal systems, which can (a) give rise to affective experiences such as feelings of arousal, pleasure/displeasure; (b) generate cognitive processes; (c) activate widespread physiological adjustments to the arousing conditions; and (d) lead to behavior that is often, but not always, expressive, goal-directed, and adaptive. (p. 58)*

As Reeve, Plutchik, and the previous definition suggest, emotion is a complex phenomenon that cannot easily be defined. The literature identifies key aspects of emotion, as in Reeve's definition, that are reflected in the major theoretical work. Emotions are short-lived feeling states that occur in response to events. However, as Reeve notes, emotion is more than the sum of its parts. Before considering some models of emotion that provide frameworks for understanding emotion, we will consider related terms and constructs. The following are not formal definitions but clarifications of the terms used in sport and exercise psychology.

Key Point

Emotion is a complex phenomenon that cannot easily be defined. Simply, emotions are short-lived feeling states that occur in response to events, but most psychologists recognize both physiological and psychological components of emotion and consider emotion to be a process rather than a static state.

Key Point

Arousal is defined as a general state of activation ranging on a continuum from deep sleep to extreme excitement. *Anxiety* is defined as arousal with a negative (avoidance) direction.

Emotion Terms

Affect, the *A* of psychology's ABCs, is the general term for valenced (positive–negative) response. Emotions and moods are part of affect.

Mood differs from emotion in duration, antecedent, and action specificity. Moods are also feeling states or affect, but unlike emotions, moods are more enduring (duration), do not have identifiable causes or precipitating events, and do not prompt specific actions.

Arousal, another term associated with emotion, is prominent in competitive anxiety. As noted in part III, motivation includes both intensity and direction of behavior. Arousal, defined as a general state of activation ranging on a continuum from deep sleep to extreme excitement, is the intensity dimension of behavior. Arousal per se is neither positive nor negative; it increases as we look forward to exciting events as well as when we worry about threats. Arousal and the associated physiological activation are critical for emotion, but without direction and related cognition, arousal is not emotion. For example, anxiety, one of the most studied emotions, is typically defined as arousal with a negative (avoidance) direction—athletes might worry about making an error (and want to avoid it) as their heart races, their hands sweat, and they breathe heavily.

Anxiety, then, is a negative feeling state characterized by high arousal and cognitive worry.

Stress is commonly defined as the perceived imbalance between environmental demands and capabilities. However, stress is a complex process paralleling the broader emotional process that guides research and practice (e.g., Lazarus, 1991, 1993).

POSITIVE AND NEGATIVE EMOTIONS

As just noted, anxiety is an often-studied emotion, particularly in sport and exercise psychology. What are the other emotions? As with many questions in this text, there is no one correct answer. As noted by Reeve (2005), various scholars have identified 2 to 10 primary emotions, along with a host of other emotions. Fear, joy, sadness, and anger are on nearly every list, but given that psychology scholars have not agreed upon a list, we will not specify one here. Regardless of the number of primary emotions, many emotions exist.

All lists of emotions, including those in the sport and exercise psychology literature, are heavy with negative emotions—anxiety, anger, depression, and so on. Joy jumps in occasionally, but research and practice focus on negative affect. The positive psychology movement reminds us that positive emotions are as prevalent as negative and deserve equal attention in research and professional practice. Positive emotions are especially relevant to sport and exercise psychology because physical activity is promoted as a path to positive health and personal growth.

Fredrickson (2005) describes positive emotions as markers of optimal functioning and argues that cultivating positive emotions is a way to foster psychological growth and physical health. She suggests that positive emotions have been neglected in psychology because definitions and models of emotion were developed to fit the negative emotions. Positive emotions are more general and diffuse and less closely tied to specific action tendencies (e.g., fight or flight).

Fredrickson offers an alternative broaden-and-build theory of positive emotions. That is, positive emotions broaden people's momentary thought-action repertoires and build enduring personal resources. Negative emotions narrow options—to fight or flee. Positive emotions such as joy, interest, or contentment do not provoke a specific response; many actions are possible and appealing. The broadening tendency of positive emotions builds enduring resources. Fredrickson cites play as an example, noting that play builds physical resources, as we often argue in kinesiology, and also builds social resources (social bonds, attachments) and intellectual resources (creativity).

EMOTION MODELS

Emotion, with all its physiological and cognitive aspects, is a complex phenomenon. Accordingly, the explanations of emotion are multidimensional and complex. This section reviews the major historical perspectives on emotion and focuses on Lazarus' model, which is widely used and useful for sport and exercise psychology.

Early Models of Emotion and Stress

In his 1884 essay, "What Is an Emotion?", William James proposed, "My theory is that the bodily changes follow directly the perception of the exciting fact, and that our feeling of the same changes as they occur is the emotion" (p. 204). Danish scientist Lange (1885) presented similar views, and the theory is known as the James–Lange theory. Walter Cannon (1929) challenged this focus on physiology, but the most notable counter to the physiologically oriented

James–Lange theory is the cognitive approach of Schachter and Singer (1962), who emphasized the cognitive labeling of emotion. In their classic experiments, subjects received either injections of epinephrine that created physiological arousal or a placebo. Then, through manipulation of circumstances, some subjects found the emotions appropriate but others had no obvious label. Without a ready explanation, subjects used situational cues to label their emotion. Thus, Schachter and Singer proposed an interaction of cognitive factors with physiological state.

Psychologists continue to debate the roles of physiology and cognition, and models have become increasingly complex and typically add a social dimension. Richard Lazarus, a leading researcher in stress, emotion, and coping, provides an encompassing model that approaches emotion as a multidimensional, dynamic process rather than an easily identified state.

Lazarus' Model of Emotion

Lazarus' model provides a guiding framework for sport and exercise work on stress and emotion. In his early writing on stress (the precursor to his emotion model), Lazarus (1966) emphasized cognitive appraisal. That is, actual events, such as waiting for the serve in a close tennis match, pose a potential threat. But, only when we think about it—during cognitive appraisal—do we perceive a threat that then leads to an emotional response, such as anxiety. Lazarus has maintained this cognitive emphasis but has also expanded the model greatly. Lazarus (1991, 1993) describes emotion as including an appraisal, outcome tendencies, a psychological response, and a subjective experience, with all this translated into coping processes after the appraisal. It is not easy to illustrate the complex dynamics of the model, but Lazarus (1991, p. 210) listed five principles underlying his cognitive-relational theory of emotion:

- *System principle.* Emotion is an organized process with many interdependent variables.

- *Process principle.* The emotion process involves both flux (change) and structure with stable person–environment relationships, resulting in recurrent emotional patterns.

- *Developmental principle.* Biological and social variables influence emotional development and change.

- *Specificity principle.* The emotion process is distinct for each emotion.

- *Relational meaning principle.* Emotions are defined by unique relational meanings—core relational themes for each emotion. Emotional meaning is constructed by cognitive appraisal.

Over 30 years of stress and emotion research, Lazarus moved to a more social, dynamic model with emphasis on recursive relationships, dynamic process, and social context. The story of emotion in sport and exercise psychology began with simpler anxiety–performance models, progressed to cognitive approaches emphasizing perceptions (similar to appraisal in Lazarus' model), and has now moved to more dynamic multidimensional approaches that better fit the complexities of emotion.

The most useful models incorporate key features of Lazarus' model: They highlight cognitive appraisal in a multidimensional system of interrelated psychobiological variables, and the complexity of the model highlights the importance of individualizing applications. Given the almost limitless possibilities, the emotion process is different for everyone, even in the same situation. This is one of the most important practical implications of the research on stress and emotion. The complexity of the model makes universal principles or predictions virtually impossible. Stress is individual, coping is individual, and sport and exercise psychologists cannot apply universal strategies to all. The importance of individualizing training and intervention is a key element of stress management in addition to the cognitive-psychological skills covered in earlier chapters.

SPORT AND EXERCISE PSYCHOLOGY RESEARCH ON EMOTION

The large body of research on emotion in health psychology is influential in sport and exercise psychology. Many topics in health psychology (e.g., adherence, stress management, coping, and quality of life) have obvious connections to sport and exercise. Also, health psychology uses a multidimensional, biopsychosocial approach that is particularly appropriate for sport and exercise psychology. Considerable health psychology work involves the link between emotion and health; for example, research links stress with cardiovascular disease and immune function. Alternative approaches to medicine, which emphasize the mind–body connection and health psychology themes, are popular with the public and increasingly with the traditional medical community. Both health psychology and sport and exercise psychology researchers are actively exploring these questions and other links in the triad of emotion, health, and physical activity. Moreover, the medical and health community recognizes the role of physical activity and typically welcomes the contributions of kinesiology scholars.

Models and Measures of Emotion

If researchers are to investigate how physical activity fits into the health psychology models of stress and emotion, relevant models and measures are needed. Despite the consistently reported emotional benefits of exercise, the research is not at all consistent. Most research that supports benefits of exercise is narrowly focused on negative emotions, specifically anxiety. Gauvin and Brawley (1993) suggest more encompassing conceptual models. Russell's (1980) model represents affect along two dimensions: hedonic tone (pleasure–displeasure) and activation (arousal–sleepiness). On the affect grid (Russell, Weiss, & Mendelsohn, 1989) respondents mark a square on a 9-by-9 grid to indicate affect state along those dimensions.

The affect grid is seldom used in sport and exercise psychology, but researchers have followed a similar two-dimensional approach. Hardy and Rejeski (1989) used the Feeling Scale (Rejeski, Best, Griffith, & Kenney, 1987), a bipolar scale reflecting how good or bad one feels during exercise, and they also used the rating of perceived exertion (RPE), which might be considered similar to activation. Increased exercise intensities related to decreases on the Feeling Scale and increases in RPE. The Feeling Scale is among the few measures of emotion developed for exercise, and such measures are critical for extending our understanding of exercise and emotion.

The RPE, developed in the 1960s by Borg (1973, 1998), is widely used in exercise physiology research, but it was not designed as a measure of emotion or within any psychological framework. A comprehensive review (Robertson & Noble, 1997) indicates the use of several forms of RPE, most commonly the 15-category scale (from 6 = no exertion at all to 20 = maximal exertion). As a physiologist, Borg took a psychophysical perspective, and the RPE scales correspond to increases in heart rate with increases in exercise intensity.

Although most work with RPE is from a physiological base, some have examined psychological correlates. Morgan (1994) summarized research demonstrating that anxiety, depression, neuroticism, and extroversion influence RPE during exercise. Morgan's review focuses on one side of the emotion–exercise relationship: how emotion influences exercise and performance.

Most research on emotion and physical activity examines the reverse relationship, that is, how exercise influences emotion. Watson and Tellegen's (1985) two-factor model of affect and the related Positive and Negative Affect Schedule (PANAS; Watson, Clark, & Tellegen, 1988), which includes scales for positive affect and for negative affect, have been used in several studies in physical activity settings (e.g., Crocker, 1997; Crocker & Graham, 1995).

McAuley and Courneya (1994) suggested that the PANAS may be limited for exercise settings and pointed out that research on physical activity and affect is limited by the emphasis on negative emotions. For example, the most popular emotion measure, the POMS (McNair, Lorr, & Droppleman, 1971), assesses five negative moods (tension, depression, anger, fatigue, confusion) and only one positive mood (vigor). Most other studies have measured specific negative emotions such as depression or anxiety. As McAuley and Courneya note, psychological health includes both positive and negative emotion—psychological well-being (e.g., positive affect) and psychological distress (e.g., anxiety, depression, stress-related emotions).

McAuley and Courneya (1994) developed the Subjective Exercise Experiences Scale (SEES), with positive and negative factors corresponding to psychological well-being and psychological distress, as well as a third factor representing subjective indicants of fatigue. The initial work provided validity evidence, and the SEES is an easy-to-use and useful measure for investigating questions about emotion and physical activity.

Circumplex Model in Sport and Exercise Psychology

Ekkekakis and Petruzzello (1999, 2002) offer the most extensive conceptual work on emotion in sport and exercise psychology, and their circumplex model of affect is a useful base for research on physical activity and emotion. Like the Russell (1980) and Watson and Tellegen (1985) models, Ekkekakis and Petruzzello's circumplex model has two dimensions—an activation dimension and a valance dimension—that result in four quadrants (see figure 11.1):

- Pleasant–activated (energy, excitement)
- Pleasant–unactivated (relaxation, calm)
- Unpleasant–unactivated (boredom, fatigue)
- Unpleasant–activated (anxiety, tension)

Ekkekakis and Petruzzello (1999) have applied the model and related measures to research on exercise and emotion. Generally, moderate-intensity exercise results in greater positive-valenced affective states, such as energy

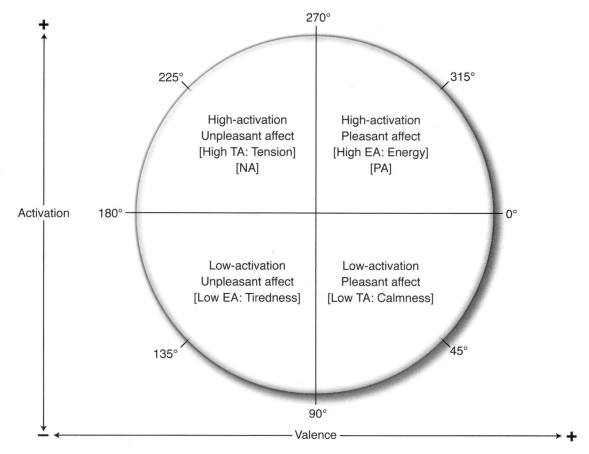

Figure 11.1
The circumplex model has two dimensions—an activation dimension and a valance dimension—that result in four quadrants.
Adapted from *Psychology of Sport and Exercise,* Vol. 3, P. Ekkakakis and S.J. Petruzzello, Analysis of the affect measurement conundrum in exercise psychology: IV. A conceptual case for the affect circumplex, pp. 35-63, Copyright 2002, with permission from Elsevier.

or vigor, but negative-valenced affect does not change. With high-intensity exercise, negative affect states may increase while positive decrease, especially with people who are less fit. The implications for exercise programs are clear—moderate-intensity exercise is likely to make people feel better and thus keep them coming back. On the other hand, if the trainer pushes high-intensity exercise, clients may feel worse and soon drop out.

 ## *Application Point*

Consider the models and research on exercise and emotions (both positive and negative). What are the implications for an exercise instructor in a community-based physical activity program with participants who are low fit and low active? Assuming you want participants to have a positive experience and stick with the program, what types of activities would you offer and how would you organize your program?

Research on Physical Activity and Emotions

Research on exercise and emotion is not new (for an early review, see Folkins & Sime, 1981). However, that work has emphasized negative emotion. In their review on the affective benefits of aerobic exercise, Tuson and Sinyor (1993) concluded that acute exercise may be associated with reduced anxiety but does not appear to influence other affective states. They also reported that although many explanations and mechanisms have been suggested, none has been supported.

That conclusion still holds, but the research has grown considerably. There is more evidence linking exercise and fitness to specific emotions, particularly anxiety and depression, and the research includes a wide range of participants in clinical and non-clinical settings. Overall, the growing research in this area confirms popular beliefs in the benefits of physical activity. Exercise relieves stress and makes people feel better. However, specific relationships have not been delineated, and we know little about the exact processes and the many variations.

Stress Responses

One research line involves physical activity as a mediator between stress and illness (or health). Do people who are more physically fit have less response to stress, and might that help prevent illness or injury? The simple answer is yes, but it is not that simple. Not all studies show benefits, and questions remain about processes, mechanisms, and variations.

Much research demonstrates benefits of physical activity and fitness. Crews and Landers' (1987) meta-analysis indicated that exercise leads to less stress reactivity and faster recovery from stress responses. In their meta-analysis, Long and van Stavel (1995) concluded that exercise training had low to moderate positive effects on anxiety reduction and that adults with more stressful lifestyles benefited more from exercise training. Holmes (1993) reviewed research on aerobic fitness and psychological stress, concluding that

- fitness is associated with lower cardiovascular arousal during and following stress,
- exercise training can reduce arousal during stress,
- exercise training can reduce depression following prolonged life stress,
- exercise training can improve cardiovascular and psychological functioning of cardiac patients, and
- fitness is associated with less physical illness following prolonged life stress.

An intriguing line of research on psychoneuroimmunology has demonstrated that stress affects immune function, and immune function may be the key link between stress and illness. Of relevance to sport and exercise psychology, Hong and Mills (2006) suggest that regular exercise may lead to adaptations that protect against stress-induced immune suppression.

Even if physical activity does not have a clear biological effect, it can serve as a coping mechanism in recovery and rehabilitation (e.g., physical activity programs with cancer or acquired immunodeficiency syndrome [AIDS] patients). In extensive research using exercise programs with human immunodeficiency virus (HIV) and AIDS patients, LaPerriere and colleagues (LaPerriere et al., 1990, 1991) reported that exercise reduced depression.

Following LaPerriere's lead, Lox, McAuley, and Tucker (1995) examined the influence of an exercise intervention on psychological well-being with an HIV-1 population: both aerobic and weight training exercise enhanced physical self-efficacy, positive and negative mood (assessed with PANAS), and life satisfaction. These research programs and related practical applications do not simply look at biological medical outcomes; instead, they consider the whole person. Psychological well-being is a key part of health and medical research, and many programs are examining connections between psychology and health in innovative ways.

Research on physical activity and stress continues, and generally it suggests exercise is beneficial, leading to less negative and more positive emotional responses for a variety of people in clinical and non-clinical settings. Latimer and Martin Ginis (2005), for example, found that people with spinal cord injury had reduced stress and less perceived pain with an exercise training program. Courneya and colleagues (Courneya, Friedenreich, Sela, et al., 2003; Courneya, Mackey, & Jones, 2000) have conducted extensive research with cancer patients and survivors demonstrating the benefits of physical activity.

> **Key Point**
>
> Research on physical activity and stress suggests that exercise is beneficial, leading to less negative stress responses and more positive emotional responses for people in clinical and non-clinical settings.

Anxiety and Depression

Much of the research on physical activity and emotion has focused on anxiety and depression, and the research has accumulated, allowing for stronger conclusions. A meta-analysis of exercise and depression literature (North, McCullagh, & Tran, 1990) indicated that exercise decreased depression and was as effective as traditional therapies. The evidence has continued to accumulate with both clinically depressed and non-clinical participants. Craft and Landers (1998) conducted a meta-analysis of training studies with clinically depressed participants and reported a larger effect size than did North and colleagues. Motl, Birnbaum, Kubik, and Dishman (2004) examined physical activity levels and change in relation to depression in adolescents in a large study over 2 years. They found that more active adolescents had less depression and that change in activity related to change in depression. Those who became more active had less depression, whereas lower activity related to higher depression levels.

Several studies have involved older adults and people with chronic illness or injury. Martin Ginis, Latimer, McKechnie, et al. (2003) used exercise training with people with spinal cord injury and found lower depression. Exercise has also been found to result in lower depression with older adults (Mobily et al., 1996), with chronic obstructive pulmonary disease (COPD) patients (Emery, Schein, Hauck, & MacIntyre, 1998) and with breast cancer survivors (Segar, Katch, Roth, et al., 1998). Heller, Hsieh, and Rimmer (2004) compared an experimental exercise program with a control condition for adults with Down syndrome and found that exercise led to increased life satisfaction and lower depression.

In their meta-analysis, Petruzzello, Landers, Hatfield, Kubitz, and Salazar (1991) confirmed that aerobic exercise is associated with reductions in anxiety. More specifically, acute exercise was associated with reduced state anxiety, and chronic exercise was related to lower trait anxiety. In a review, Landers and Petruzzello (1994) found that physically fit people have less anxiety than those who are unfit, and Goodwin (2003) found physical activity to be associated with a reduced chance of anxiety disorders, suggesting a preventive role for physical activity. As well as the Petruzzello et al. meta-analysis, several studies suggest that physical activity can be effective in treating anxiety disorders. Broocks et al. (1998) and Meyer et al. (1998) found that exercising led to improvements in panic disorder patients.

Other Mental Health Effects

In addition to specific effects on stress response, anxiety, and depression, researchers have found that physical activity relates to cognitive function and psychological well-being. Several meta-analyses have found a positive relationship between physical activity and cognitive function among older adults (Colcombe & Kramer, 2003; Etnier et al., 1997). Kramer and Hillman (2006) reviewed the research from a psychobiological perspective and suggested that exercise effects are the most beneficial for cognitive tasks that involve executive control, especially for the elderly.

Mechanisms and Explanations

Boutcher (1993) categorized explanations for the benefits of exercise into the physiological and psychological mechanisms listed in the box below and concluded that no proposed mechanism had convincing support. He suggested that several physiological and psychological factors might be involved and that the process may vary from person to person. Most people who exercise cite multiple reasons and benefits that fit into different categories. More recent reviews (e.g., Lox, Martin Ginis, & Petruzzello, 2006) offer slightly different lists but do not make many more conclusive statements about underlying mechanisms. Most scholars conclude that multiple mechanisms are involved and that different mechanisms and processes likely underlie different emotions (e.g., mechanisms for effects on depression may differ from mechanisms for effects on cognition). Continuing research may well lead to a complex mix of multidimensional processes rather than one mechanism. Integration of multiple physiological and cognitive processes matches the complexity of emotion and provides a better guide than simpler mechanistic explanations.

Benefits of Exercise: Physiological and Psychological Mechanisms

Physiological

Hyperthermic changes: Increases in body temperature lead to changes in the brain, particularly the hypothalamus, leading to relaxation and feeling better.

Visceral feedback: Rhythmic feedback from exercise may dampen brain activity, leading to relaxation and positive affect.

Neurotransmitter changes: Exercise increases neurotransmitters that are depleted with stress (norephinephrine, dopamine, serotonin), leading to greater psychological well-being.

Endorphins: Exercise increases levels of endorphins, which offset pain and induce euphoria, leading to a positive emotional state.

Autonomic rebound: Sympathetic activity dominates during exercise, but after stopping, homeostasis restores parasympathetic influence. The parasympathetic rebound is associated with relaxation and restoration.

Psychological

Self-esteem: As discussed in chapter 6, exercise typically leads to enhanced physical self-esteem.

Mastery: Successful completion of an activity or exercise bout increases the sense of mastery and related positive emotion.

Social factors: Developing and maintaining friendships and social contact enhances positive emotion.

Time-out: Exercise is a distraction or escape from stress-inducing activities.

Positive Emotions in Sport and Exercise

Thus far we have concentrated on negative emotion because of the research emphasis. But to understand emotion in kinesiology, we must give equal attention to positive emotion. We could even argue that positive emotion is more important in physical activity than stress and anxiety. In general, sport and exercise psychology researchers have neglected the role of physical activity in enhancing positive emotion and psychological well-being (McAuley & Courneya, 1994; Rejeski, Brawley, & Schumaker, 1996). Most people do not participate in exercise and sport to reduce stress but because they feel better and because physical activity is fun!

Within sport and exercise psychology, the most notable lines of research on positive emotions are the work of Tara Scanlan and colleagues (Scanlan & Simons, 1992) on enjoyment in sport and Csikszentmihalyi's (1975, 1990) long-term work on flow, which has inspired sport and exercise psychology researchers.

Enjoyment in Sport

Tara Scanlan is one of the few sport and exercise scholars to give equal attention to positive and negative aspects of emotion. Scanlan's work focuses on youth and development and includes extensive research on stress and anxiety, as well as equally extensive and more current work on sport enjoyment and commitment (Scanlan, Babkes, & Scanlan, 2005). In line with the emotion theme of this chapter, Scanlan and Simons (1992, p. 202) defined enjoyment as a positive affective response to the sport experience that reflects generalized feelings such as pleasure, liking, and fun.

As discussed earlier, the general models of emotion now include positive dimensions, but we do not have measures of positive affect to match the carefully developed and validated (and often sport-specific) measures of anxiety and stress. Several studies of enjoyment have used open-ended measures in a more qualitative approach (e.g., Scanlan, Stein, & Ravizza, 1989). Others have used simple measures developed for specific studies, and Wankel and Sefton (1989) simply asked, "How much fun did you have in the game today?" Kendzierski and DeCarlo (1991) developed an 18-item Physical Activity Enjoyment Scale (PACES) and provided some initial evidence for its reliability and validity with college students. Crocker, Bouffard, and Gessaroli (1995) subsequently failed to support the unidimensional structure of PACES and suggested that the scale may represent both antecedents and perceptions of enjoyment rather than one enjoyment construct.

Kimiecik and Harris (1996) attempted to provide a framework for positive emotions in physical activity. They defined enjoyment with an adaptation of Csikszentmihalyi's flow definition as "an optimal psychological state that leads to performing an activity primarily for its own sake and is associated with positive feeling states" (p. 256).

In their development of the sport commitment model, Scanlan, Simons, Carpenter, Schmidt, and Keeler (1993) developed and validated a four-item measure of enjoyment that has been used by others in sport and exercise psychology research. In reviewing the literature on sport enjoyment, Scanlan et al. (2005) classified the sources of enjoyment as intrapersonal, situational, and significant others. Intrapersonal sources include perceived ability, mastery, motivational goal orientation, personal movement experiences, and personal coping and emotional release through sport. Specifically, research indicates that enjoyment is associated with perceived high ability, mastery experiences, higher task orientation, movement sensations, and emotional release.

Situational sources include competitive outcomes, achievement process, recognition, and opportunities. Not surprisingly, winning is associated with enjoyment, but the relationship is not as strong or absolute as one might assume. Several studies in Scanlan and colleagues' review showed that post-game stress was related to enjoyment regardless of win–loss outcomes. Being engaged in competition (playing) was associated with enjoyment, as were social recognition and opportunities to travel.

Finally, significant-other sources of enjoyment involve positive perceptions of interactions and feedback from coaches, parents, and peers. Many sources of enjoyment have parallel sources of stress, and those are also classified into the same three categories in the Scanlan et al. review. As Scanlan and colleagues conclude, the diverse sources of enjoyment make it easy to tap a number of them to maintain motivation and activity. Notably, the researchers emphasized enjoyment rather than stress in their conclusions. In line with positive psychology, we might emphasize positive emotion in professional practice to promote physical activity and health for all participants.

Flow in Sport

Not only has Csikszentmihalyi's flow construct contributed to work on enjoyment and intrinsic motivation, but several researchers have more specifically explored flow states with sport and exercise participants. Flow occurs when the performer is totally connected to the performance in a situation in which skills equal challenges (Csikszentmihalyi, 1975, 1990). Csikszentmihalyi used innovative experience sampling and in-depth methods to develop his conceptualization of the optimal flow experience and its antecedents. In the original flow model, flow occurs when perceived challenges are in balance with perceived skills; when challenges are too high, anxiety results, and when they are too low, boredom results. The current model (Nakamura & Csikszentmihalyi, 2005) expands to include a wider range of emotions (see figure 11.2). Flow is experienced when perceived challenges and perceived skills are both above average, and apathy is experienced when both are below average. More intense reactions occur as challenge and skill move further from average levels, as represented in concen-

Figure 11.2

Current model of flow state. Flow is experienced when perceived challenges and skills are above the actor's average levels; when they are below, apathy is experienced. Intensity of experience increases with distance from the actor's average levels of challenge and skill, as shown by the concentric rings.

Adapted from M. Csikszentimihalyi, 1997, *Finding flow* (New York, NY: Basic Books), 31, by permission of *BASIC BOOKS*, a member of Perseus Books group.

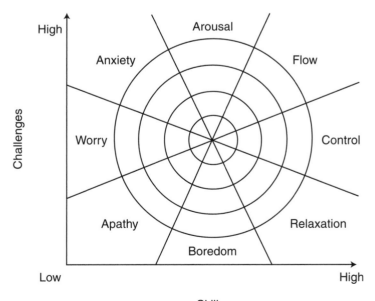

tric circles in the model. Flow is clearly a positive emotional state—perhaps the ultimate positive state.

Most participants at any level in any physical activity can relate to flow. Athletes may recall a peak experience—a time when everything came together and they were totally immersed in the activity. Sue Jackson started from Csikszentmihalyi's model and used in-depth interviews along with more typical survey approaches to identify characteristics and antecedents of flow with athletes (Jackson, 1995; Jackson & Marsh, 1996). Jackson and Marsh (1996) used qualitative and quantitative analyses to develop the Flow State Scale (FSS). The nine scales of the 36-item FSS represent the dimensions of flow identified by Csikszentmihalyi, and Jackson and Marsh provided good psychometric evidence for the scales and the FSS. These are the nine dimensions of flow, from both Csikszentmihalyi's work and Jackson's work with athletes:

- *Challenge–skill balance:* The person perceives a balance between the challenges of a situation and the person's skills, with both at a high level.

- *Action–awareness merging:* Involvement is so deep that it becomes spontaneous or automatic.

- *Clear goals:* Clearly defined goals give the person a strong sense of knowing what to do.

- *Unambiguous feedback:* The person receives immediate and clear feedback, usually from the activity itself.

- *Concentration on task at hand:* Total concentration on the task occurs.

- *Sense of control:* The person experiences a sense of exercising control but without actively trying to exert control.

- *Loss of self-consciousness:* Concern for the self disappears as the person becomes one with the activity.

- *Transformation of time:* Time alters perceptibly, either slowing down or speeding up.

- *Autotelic experience:* An autotelic experience is intrinsically rewarding, done for its own sake.

> **Key Point**
>
> Flow occurs when the performer is totally connected to the performance in a situation where skills equal challenges and both perceived challenges and perceived skills are above average. Flow is perhaps the ultimate positive emotional state.

The work of Scanlan, Jackson, and others provides direction and measures for the continuing exploration of flow and enjoyment, as well as for moving toward more positive emotions in sport and exercise psychology.

Physical Activity and Quality of Life

A significant body of research indicates that physical activity promotes quality of life (e.g., McAuley & Elavsky, 2005; Rejeski, Brawley, & Shumaker, 1996; Stewart & King, 1991). In their seminal review, Rejeski et al. (1996) noted that quality of life (QoL), a key concern in health-related research and practice, has not been clearly conceptualized and measured. Instead, studies have used various measures, typically focusing on negative emotions. Rejeski and colleagues conceptualize health-related quality of life (HRQoL) along six dimensions, including global HRQoL and subdomains of physical function, physical symptoms and states, emotional function, social function, and cognitive function. Emotional function, the main concern in this chapter, includes both positive and negative aspects. Rejeski et al. conclude that physical activity is associated with improved HRQoL but that the research largely deals with anxiety, depression, and negative aspects of HRQoL.

Since then, the distinction between HRQoL and QoL has blurred, and the evidence that physical activity promotes QoL, particularly with older adults and in clinical settings, has continued to accumulate. Schechtman and Ory (2001), who conducted a meta-analysis on the effects of exercise on older adults, found a modest improvement in QoL. Schmitz, Kruse, and Kugler (2004) found higher levels of physical activity were associated with higher health-related QoL in a German cross-sectional survey of people with mental disorders.

Additionally, Lee and Russell (2003), who investigated physical activity and mental health with a large sample of Australian women, found that higher levels of physical activity were associated with higher scores on all mental health variables. Further, women who had made a transition from some physical activity to none showed negative changes in emotional well-being, whereas those who maintained or adopted physical activity had better outcomes. Stathi, Fox, and MacKenna (2002) used a qualitative approach to identify dimensions of subjective well-being in older adults and ways in which they might be influenced by physical activity. They concluded that physical activity contributes to the mental health of older adults through maintenance of a busy and active life, mental alertness, a positive attitude toward life, and avoidance of stress, negative function, and isolation.

Despite the seemingly consistent results, the approaches to QoL are not at all consistent. Each of the studies just cited used a different measure, and there are no guiding theoretical frameworks for QoL and physical activity. QoL measures range from subjective well-being, such as Diener's (1984; Diener et al., 1985) widely used Satisfaction with Life Scale to aggregate measures of separate components of QoL such as physical function and social well-being, and extend to related constructs (e.g., depression) as markers of QoL. The most commonly used QoL measures, such as the SF-36 (Ware, 2000), were designed for clinical purposes and did not emerge from a conceptual base. To advance sport and exercise psychology research, stronger conceptual frameworks and common assessments are needed.

Quality of Life Model for Sport and Exercise Psychology

Both QoL and HRQoL have been defined in varied and often overlapping ways; the distinction is not clear. O'Connor (2004, p. 9) cites a number of definitions of QoL and HRQoL, all of which are similar, and his summary description—patients' subjective experience of their overall health state—reflects the typical approach to QoL. The WHO (1948) definition of health is the basis for most QoL definitions and measures: "Health is a state of complete physical, mental, and social well-being, and not merely the absence of disease or infirmity." The introduction to the 1998 WHOQOL User Manual defines Quality of Life as

> *individuals' perceptions of their position in life in the context of the culture and value systems in which they live and in relation to their goals, expectations, standards and concerns. (http://www.who.int/mental_health/evidence/ who_qol_user_manual_98.pdf) So defined, QoL is a broad-ranging concept incorporating the person's physical health, psychological state, personal beliefs, social relationships and their relationship to salient features of the environment.*

Given such a far-reaching definition, it is not surprising that measures and approaches are varied, but that variation makes it difficult to draw conclu-

Key Point

QoL reflects positive health and may be defined as a broad, integrative construct that includes the person's perceived physical, social, and psychological well-being. In Gill et al.'s (2006) hierarchical model, subdomains of physical, social, and psychological well-being contribute to an integrative subjective well-being.

sions on the role of physical activity in QoL. For sport and exercise psychology research on physical activity and QoL, a broad integrative model of QoL that reflects positive health and well-being is desirable. In line with the WHO model, the definition of QoL in this text is as follows: QoL is a broad, integrative construct, comprising the person's perceived physical, social, and psychological well-being. In our lab (e.g., Gill et al., 2006), we developed a working conceptual model for QoL assessment. Specifically, we propose a hierarchical model, with subdomains of physical, social, and psychological well-being contributing to an integrative subjective well-being (see figure 11.3).

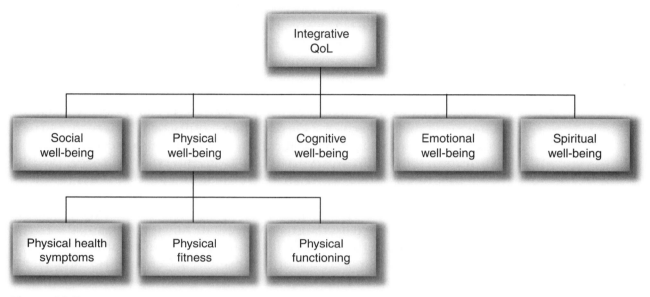

Figure 11.3
Conceptual model of QoL. The model reflects our definition of QoL as a broad, integrative construct composed of the person's perceived physical, social, and psychological well-being.

Application Point

As an exercise therapist in a clinical rehabilitation setting, your clients will be concerned about QoL as well as their physical recovery. Using the QoL model, which specific aspects of QoL might be enhanced through the exercise program?

COMPETITIVE ANXIETY

Anxiety, and specifically, competitive anxiety, is the emotion that has received the most attention in sport and exercise psychology. Until recently, research on anxiety and athletic performance did not incorporate cognitive appraisal or fit with the emotion models discussed in the previous section. Instead, anxiety was typically conceptualized and measured more narrowly, as arousal.

As defined earlier, arousal is intensity—the general state of activation. Hans Selye (1956) referred to bodily reactions to stress as the *general adaptation syndrome*—the fight-or-flight response of the autonomic nervous system that we all experience in stressful situations. You know you are anxious when you breathe rapidly, your heart pounds, your hands sweat, your stomach does flips, your knees turn to jelly, and your mouth tastes like cotton. Arousal by itself, without the context and cognitive appraisal, is not emotion. A softball player experiencing physiological arousal may also think about the mistakes made last game, worry about everyone watching, and be aware of feeling anxious. Competitive anxiety is a multidimensional emotional state with both physiological and cognitive components.

The cognitive component of anxiety typically involves worrying about performance evaluation or possible failure. Much physical activity involves competition, but even noncompetitive activities may create arousal and worry. A child in an elementary physical education class wants to please the teacher and not be the last one through the obstacle course; an adult in a corporate fitness program does not want to appear out of shape in front of colleagues. That combination of physiological arousal and cognitive worry is called *state anxiety*.

Competitive anxiety has been measured with physiological measures (e.g., heart rate, respiration rate, galvanic skin response) and behavioral observations, but most often with self-report measures, such as the state anxiety inventory of the STAI (Spielberger, Gorsuch, & Lushene, 1970). Some self-report anxiety scales assess physiological (somatic) anxiety and cognitive worry on separate dimensions, such as the Worry-Emotionality Inventory (WEI; Morris, Davis, & Hutchings, 1981), a state anxiety scale. Martens and his colleagues (Martens, Vealey, & Burton, 1990) built upon their work with competitive trait anxiety (discussed in chapter 4) to develop a sport-specific, multidimensional measure of competitive state anxiety, the Competitive State Anxiety Inventory-2 (CSAI-2), which assesses cognitive worry and somatic anxiety on separate scales. The CSAI-2 has been widely used in sport and exercise psychology research on the anxiety–performance relationship.

ANXIETY–PERFORMANCE MODELS AND RESEARCH

The anxiety–performance relationship is a prominent research and practical concern for sport participants. Pregame rituals and pep talks to get players psyched up are assumed to enhance performance, but do they work? Most of us can recall times when a pep talk helped or when an athlete responded to the big game with the best performance of the season. The Olympic Games certainly induce high arousal, and the pressure and excitement of the Games seem to elicit a large share of record-breaking performances and personal bests.

However, you can probably recall other times when performers have choked under pressure. I once coached a team of seventh-grade girls who demonstrated modest basketball skills in practices and intramural games. When faced with competition against a team from another school, those same players completely missed the basket on shots, dribbled off their feet, threw passes into the bleachers, and managed to go through the game without scoring a basket. Clearly, a "psych-up" speech would have only made the situation worse.

Coaches who hold the image of a stirring Knute Rockne pep talk as the key to mental preparation might be surprised to learn what Rockne actually said about such tactics. In December 1924, Coleman Griffith wrote to Rockne to ask about his motivational tactics. Rockne replied as follows.

Letter from Knute Rockne

Dear Mr. Griffith:

I feel very grateful to you for having written me, although I do not know a great deal about psychology. I do try to pick men who like the game of football and who get a lot of fun out of playing. I never try to make football hard work. I do think our team plays good football because they like to play and I do not make any effort to key them up, except on rare, exceptional occasions. I keyed them up for the Nebraska game this year, which was a mistake, as we had a reaction the following Saturday against Northwestern. I try to make our boys take the game less seriously than, I presume, some others do, and we try to make the spirit of the game one of exhilaration and we never allow hatred to enter into it, no matter whom we are playing.

Thanking you for your kindness, I am

Yours cordially,

Knute Rockne

From the Coleman Griffith Collection, University Archives, University of Illinois at Urbana-Champaign.

People have done strange things in the cause of psyching up athletes even though such tactics often psych them out. Many beginning coaches turn to these approaches at the very times they are least likely to help—when the situation has already raised arousal beyond optimal levels. How can such contrary psych-up and psych-out results be explained? In psychology, the dominant early models were drive theory, which holds that increased arousal increases performance of the dominant response, and the inverted-U hypothesis, which predicts that performance is best at a moderate optimal level and progressively worsens with either increases or decreases in arousal.

Drive Theory

Drive theory, as developed by Hull (1943) and modified by Spence (1956), is complex, but we'll consider a simple version as $P = f(H \times D)$. Performance (P) is a function of habit (H) times drive (D). Drive is essentially arousal, and habit refers to learned responses. The more a response has been reinforced, the greater its habit strength and the more likely it will occur. Essentially, this theory proposes that as drive increases (as when facing competition), learned responses are more likely to occur. The basic relationship is linear: As arousal increases, performance increases. But drive theory is not that simple. Overall performance does not necessarily improve; instead, performance of the person's dominant response improves. Performance improves only if the dominant and most likely response is correct performance. Until athletes become proficient at a skill and have automatic expert responses, they are more likely to make mistakes than to do everything right.

For example, for the perfect golf swing the golfer must have proper body alignment; shift weight correctly; keep the body and club in proper alignment throughout the swing; and perform the backswing, forward swing, and follow-through with the correct length, in the correct plane, and at an optimal speed. Unless you are an accomplished golfer with a grooved swing, your dominant response is not likely to be the correct swing. As arousal increases, such as in a club match, you are likely to revert to your dominant, error-ridden swing even more than usual; perhaps you will swing too fast, swing out too much, and slice more than usual. In contrast, a professional golfer has performed each shot so often that the correct swing is the automatic, dominant response and thus increased arousal improves performance. Drive theory predictions for motor performance can be summarized as follows:

- Increased arousal or drive increases the likelihood that the dominant response will occur.

- If a skill is relatively simple or is well learned, the dominant response is the correct response, and increased arousal will improve performance.

- If a skill is complex (as most motor skills are) and not well learned, the dominant response is an incorrect response and thus increased arousal will impair performance.

Inverted-U Theory

The inverted-U theory is a popular alternative explanation of the arousal–performance relationship. The inverted-U (figure 11.4) proposes that performance is optimal at a moderate level of arousal and it declines as arousal increases or decreases from that optimal level. The inverted-U model makes sense and fits our observations. People need some arousal to perform at their best; those who are too mellow give subpar performances. However, with too much arousal, performers are tense and prone to errors.

Although the inverted-U theory makes intuitive sense, controlled tests of the curvilinear relationship are difficult and empirical support is limited. The original inverted-U research of Yerkes and Dodson (1908) involved lab-based, experimental animal research. Martens and Landers (1970) tested the inverted-U theory by having junior high school boys perform a tracking task

Figure 11.4
The arousal–performance relationship according to the inverted-U hypothesis.

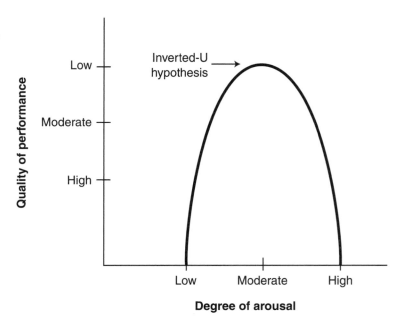

Key Point

Drive theory pro-
poses that as drive
increases (as when
facing competition),
learned responses are
more likely to occur.
The basic relationship
is linear: As arousal
increases, performance
increases. The inverted-
U theory proposes that
performance is optimal
at a moderate level of
arousal and it declines
as arousal increases or
decreases from that
optimal level.

under low-, moderate-, and high-stress conditions. The resulting performance scores formed an inverted-U pattern, with best performances in the moderate stress condition.

Sonstroem and Bernardo (1982) confirmed the inverted-U pattern in a field study with female university basketball players; the best performances were associated with moderate state anxiety and the poorest performances with high state anxiety. Sonstroem and Bernardo also found that the inverted-U was more pronounced for high competitive, trait anxious athletes, illustrating individual differences. Given the same situation, such as a club tennis match, one player might be below optimal arousal and need to psych up a bit, whereas another player might need to calm down to play in top form.

As well as differing from person to person, optimal levels may vary across tasks and skills. For example, putting in golf has a low optimal arousal level; golfers perform best with low arousal, and even slight increases may disrupt their concentration and performance. Weightlifting has a higher optimal arousal level.

However, as Landers (1978) noted, most sport tasks involve multiple skills, such as a sprinter who must use strength and speed to get out of the blocks and also focus to avoid distraction. Performance is optimal at a moderate level of arousal, but optimal levels vary across tasks and people; we cannot predict precise optimal arousal levels for each performer in each task. Practically, we might better direct our efforts at helping performers recognize their own optimal states in varying situations.

Sport and exercise psychologists have tested and debated drive versus inverted-U. The inverted-U has intuitive appeal, and drive theory is cited in some work (e.g., audience effects on performance). However, neither is prominent in current research and both miss one key element—cognitive appraisal.

Hanin's Zones of Optimal Functioning

Yuri Hanin (1989, 1995) proposed an alternative that relates to the inverted-U model but emphasizes individual differences. Hanin proposes that athletes have a zone of optimal functioning (ZOF) that is unique to the individual and can be identified through retrospective analyses and systematic multiple observations of athletes' state anxiety and performance levels. Hanin developed his model in the former Soviet system with its emphasis on applied work with elite athletes. Thus, the ZOF model has practical appeal as well as some empirical support. Hanin and Syrja (1996) extended the ZOF model beyond anxiety to patterns of emotions, moving closer to current emotion models.

Application Point

Consider the drive and inverted-U models of arousal–performance as well as Hanin's ZOF. Would you use psych-up or calm-down approaches if you were coaching a high school volleyball team? How would your approaches differ with an experienced senior team favored to win their state championship compared with an inexperienced fresh-man team?

ANXIETY PATTERNS AND PERFORMANCE

Psychologist and parachutist Walter Fenz (1975, 1988) added important insights with his innovative studies of arousal patterns of parachute jumpers. Fenz went out into the field, or into the air, rather, and recorded anxiety changes and patterns over time. Over several years of research the findings were consistent. Good performers and experienced jumpers did not differ from poorly skilled or novice jumpers in absolute arousal levels. Instead, they differed in anxiety patterns (figure 11.5).

Figure 11.5

Recordings of heart rate during a jump sequence of parachutists with good and poor performance.

Reprinted from *Journal of Psychosomatic Research*, vol. 18, W.D. Fenz and G.B. Jones, "Cardiac conditioning in a reaction time task and heart rate control during real life stress," p. 201, copyright 1974, with permission from Elsevier.

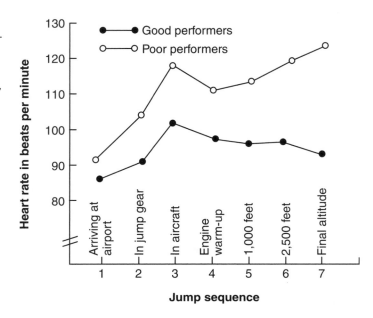

As the figure shows, arousal levels of poor performers (here measured by heart rate) increase from arrival at the airport to the time of the jump. Good performers increase in arousal at first, but peak earlier and gradually decrease in arousal so that they are at moderate levels at the time of the jump. Fenz's work suggests that the difference between better and poorer performers is not a difference in absolute levels but a difference in the ability to control emotion. Good performers seem to bring anxiety under control so that they are experiencing moderate levels at the time of performance.

Additional studies suggest that anxiety control can be disrupted even in experienced, skilled performers. Fenz (1975) reported that one experienced jumper broke an ankle on a jump. Upon returning, this jumper reverted to the novice's pattern of continual increases in arousal until the jump. Athletes in other sports returning to competition after injury might well exhibit similar patterns. In another study, an experienced jumper was told his chute could malfunction during any of the next 10 jumps. Although the jumper had an emergency chute and knew emergency procedures, the perceived threat (cognitive appraisal) of malfunction led to arousal patterns for those 10 jumps that were similar to those of novices, with continual increases to a peak at the time of the jump.

In one particularly encouraging training study, Fenz (1988) taught anxiety-control techniques (such as those described in the next chapter) to novice jumpers before their first jump. Even in their first jumps, the trained group demonstrated the controlled arousal pattern of the experienced jumpers. Fenz reported that the experimental jumpers had more fun during their training, and several eventually became experienced skydivers, suggesting that emotional-control training may benefit even novice athletes.

As part of their study of Olympic qualifiers and nonqualifiers, Mahoney and Avener (1977) examined anxiety patterns over time. Retrospective reports revealed that the qualifiers' anxiety levels were just as high as or higher than those of nonqualifiers before performance; but qualifiers reported lower anxiety than nonqualifiers during performance. As with the parachutists, the better performers seemed to bring anxiety under control at the right time.

Mahoney (1979) suggested that differences in cognitive patterns, specifically precompetition thoughts, accompany the reported differences in anxiety patterns. The qualifiers seemed to approach competition with a task orientation and to focus their energy and attention on the task. In contrast, nonqualifiers worried more about being anxious. One Olympic qualifier described high anxiety, but then shifted his thoughts from the worry to the performance:

> *I get out there and they're waiting for me and all I can think is how scared I am. Twelve years I've worked to lay my life on the line for 30 seconds. Then I try to concentrate—"O.K., this is it; it's now or never. Let's pay attention to your tuck, stay strong on the press-out, and be ready for that dismount." I just start coaching myself. (Mahoney, 1979, p. 436)*

Individual differences in competitive anxiety and the ability to control anxiety are major concerns in competitive sport programs, and indeed, in all physical activity settings. Many consultants spend considerable time helping participants learn to control anxiety.

Key Point

In general, the early anxiety–performance literature suggests that performance is best at a moderate level of arousal, although the precise optimal level varies among individuals, tasks, and situations. The ability to control anxiety is a key factor that separates better and poorer performers.

CURRENT ANXIETY–PERFORMANCE MODELS

Multidimensional models and measures dominate current sport and exercise psychology work on competitive anxiety. Research during the development of the CSAI-2, as well as considerable subsequent work, suggests that cognitive worry and somatic anxiety show different patterns of change over time. In two studies with gymnasts and wrestlers, Martens et al. (1990) found that cognitive anxiety and self-confidence remained relatively stable before competition whereas somatic anxiety rapidly increased as time to competition neared. Gould, Petlichkoff, and Weinberg (1984) substantiated these trends with high school volleyball players who completed the CSAI-2 starting 1 week, 48 hours, 24 hours, 2 hours, and 20 minutes before competition. As predicted, only somatic anxiety increased over time. These results add to Fenz's (1975) work on arousal patterns, and multidimensional anxiety measures permit further advances in our understanding of anxiety–performance patterns over time.

Multidimensional Anxiety and Performance

On the basis of multidimensional anxiety theory, Martens et al. (1990) predicted that cognitive anxiety and self-confidence would be stronger predictors of performance than would somatic anxiety because such anxiety dissipates at the onset of competition. However, in their study with golfers, CSAI-2 scores did not predict performance. Later, Burton (1988) used the CSAI-2 and more precise performance measures with intercollegiate swimmers over a season. Burton predicted an inverted-U relationship between somatic anxiety and performance but a negative linear relationship between cognitive anxiety and performance (and a positive linear relationship between self-confidence and performance). The results confirmed those predictions and supported the application of multidimensional anxiety theory to competitive sport.

Gould, Petlichkoff, Simons, and Vevera (1987) used a similar intraindividual approach to compare CSAI-2 scores and shooting performance at a police training institute. The results supported the inverted-U relationship of somatic anxiety and performance but did not show a relationship between cognitive anxiety and performance. As Martens et al. (1990) noted in their review of the CSAI-2 research, other studies failed to find anxiety–performance relationships, and we cannot draw definitive conclusions. This inconsistency has prompted consideration of other multidimensional approaches and more elaborate models of the anxiety–performance relationship.

Rather than consider multiple dimensions separately, the most recent models have addressed interactions. As an example of one simple interaction, if cognitive anxiety is positive (e.g., confidence, no worry), then somatic anxiety or physiological arousal is positively related to performance. On the other hand, if cognitive anxiety is negative (e.g., high worry), then somatic anxiety and performance are negatively related. Although this is not a theory, reversal theory as proposed by Kerr (1990) is similar.

Reversal Theory

Reversal theory, first advanced as a general framework for arousal and emotional affect (Apter, 1984), holds that the relationship between arousal and affect depends on one's cognitive interpretation of arousal (again, cognitive appraisal is the key). High arousal may be interpreted in positive terms as excitement, or in negative terms as anxiety. Similarly, low arousal may be interpreted as relaxation (positive) or boredom (negative). Both arousal and interpretive affect vary on a continuum, and reversal theory also adds that a person may switch from one curve to the other—a reversal. Kerr (1985, 1990) has adapted reversal theory to competitive anxiety with arousal and stress (cognitive) dimensions that yield four quadrants: overstimulation (anxiety), understimulation (boredom or fatigue), sleep, and excitement. Perhaps the most important guidelines from reversal theory are that arousal may be either positive or negative and that cognitive interpretation makes all the difference in the anxiety–performance relationship.

Catastrophe Model of Anxiety

Catastrophe theory has been applied to competitive anxiety by several sport psychologists, particularly Lew Hardy (1990, 1996). The catastrophe model includes an interaction similar to the example, but it is more complex, with three-dimensional, nonlinear relationships. In addition to incorporating an interaction of cognitive anxiety and arousal, the catastrophe model clearly defines physiological arousal as one key dimension. Performance changes depend on the interaction of physiological arousal and cognitive anxiety.

Catastrophe theory suggests that as arousal increases, performance increases up to a point (as in the inverted-U), but as arousal goes beyond the optimal

Key Point

Catastrophe theory suggests that as arousal increases, performance increases up to a point (as in the inverted-U), but as arousal moves beyond the optimal level, performance drops abruptly as the athlete goes over the edge—a catastrophe. Moreover, athletes who have gone over the edge and tried to regain control cannot simply go back on the same path. Instead, they must go back to much lower anxiety levels in order to get on track and then gradually build arousal again.

level, performance drops abruptly as the athlete goes over the edge—in other words, a catastrophe. Moreover, athletes who have gone over the edge and tried to return to an optimal level cannot simply go back on the same path. Instead, they must go back to much lower anxiety levels in order to get on track and then gradually build arousal again. These statements seem reasonable, but showing the process on the model and demonstrating it empirically are a challenge, to say the least. The mathematics is complex, and testing the relationships requires multiple, precise, consistent, and valid measures of both anxiety and performance, which is easier said than done.

Hardy (1996) clarified the catastrophe model, offered methodological suggestions for testing its predictions, and discussed more practical applications. Hardy's interpretation, informed by his extensive research with the model and with competitive anxiety, provides a helpful guide for researchers who wish to apply catastrophe theory. The following key predictions provide guidance in understanding the catastrophe model (Hardy, 1996).

- **Interactive effects**—First, the model describes combined, interactive effects of cognitive anxiety and physiological arousal on performance. The model proposes that high cognitive anxiety will lead to enhanced performance when physiological arousal is low (e.g., days before competition), but it will lead to impaired performance when physiological arousal is high (e.g., on game day). Edwards and Hardy (1996) provided some support for interactive effects in a study of netball players using a modified CSAI-2 with a directional scale assessing the facilitative or debilitative interpretation of anxiety. They found the predicted interaction; the combination of low physiological arousal and high cognitive anxiety led to better performance than low physiological arousal and low cognitive anxiety. However, the combination of high physiological arousal and high cognitive anxiety led to worse performance than that of high physiological arousal and low cognitive anxiety.

- **Facilitative versus debilitative effects**—In contrast to most views that cognitive worry is always debilitating, Hardy emphasizes that cognitive anxiety can sometimes enhance performance. Specifically, the model predicts that performers' best performances should be better and their worst performances worse when they perform under high cognitive anxiety than under low cognitive anxiety. Edwards and Hardy did not find any directional facilitative effects in their study, but earlier work (Hardy & Parfitt, 1991; Hardy, Parfitt, & Pates, 1994) supported this hypothesis.

- **Hysteresis effects**—The third feature, hysteresis, is particularly intriguing. *Hysteresis* is a mathematical term, and in the model it implies that the graph of performance against physiological arousal follows a different path when arousal is increasing than when arousal is decreasing. Performance increases linearly as arousal increases until arousal peaks and performance suddenly drops off sharply. As the athlete tries to gain control and decrease arousal, performance does not jump back up but stays low and only begins to rise gradually as arousal returns to much lower levels. Hysteresis explains the sudden drop-off or choking phenomenon, and the differing paths have implications for practical questions related to control and recovery.

In discussing practical applications of the catastrophe model, Hardy (1996) highlights the notion that cognitive anxiety is not necessarily detrimental to performance. Hardy suggests that cognitive anxiety is most likely to be beneficial when performers have low physiological arousal and interpret their anxiety as beneficial; in the real world, those conditions may be difficult to achieve. Second, Hardy notes that if cognitively anxious performers become too physiologically aroused, they will reach a choke point and performance will drop suddenly and dramatically. Recovery will be faster if cognitive anxiety and physiological arousal are addressed simultaneously. Hardy proposes a multimodal stress management approach, advising coaches and sport psychologists to use psyching-up strategies with great caution. Although cognitive anxiety and physiological arousal can be beneficial, there's a fine line between peak performance and disaster.

PUTTING IT INTO PRACTICE

Now you are ready to put the content of chapter 11 into practice. Read the chapter summary, discuss the case study, answer the review questions, and enhance your knowledge by researching the recommended readings.

Summary

Emotion pervades all physical activities, and explanations of sport and exercise behavior that omit the emotional component are incomplete and rather dull. Emotion is a complex biopsychosocial process that challenges researchers. Sport and exercise psychology research focuses on negative emotions, particularly anxiety. The expanding research on physical activity and emotion consistently confirms the benefits of physical activity, but that work is just beginning to address the relationship of physical activity to positive emotions. People might respond to physical activity with hope, anger, or sadness or find themselves in a flow state. If we consider the broader possibilities of emotional response within a dynamic system of interrelationships, we may better understand sport and exercise behavior. More encompassing approaches such as Lazarus' (1991) model provide guidance.

Competitive anxiety is one of the most prevalent topics in sport and exercise psychology. Early work suggested that performance is best at an optimal level of arousal, but optimal levels vary with the individual, activity, and situation. Research examining anxiety patterns over time reveals that the ability to control anxiety is crucial in separating better and poorer performers. Sport-specific work with multidimensional approaches has moved closer to the emotion models, and it may progress beyond the focus on anxiety by considering multiple emotional processes in physical activity.

Case Study

You are the director of an exercise program for breast cancer survivors at a cancer center. Your exercise program includes yoga and tai chi as well as more typical aerobic and anaerobic exercises. No doubt the participants are concerned about quality of life as well as physical health. Consider the research on physical activity and emotion, as well as quality of life models. How will you organize your program for optimal health benefits, both physical and mental? Consider exercise types and levels, as well as alternative activities, and discuss how you might address various aspects of quality of life in your program.

Review Questions

1. Define *emotion,* and explain how it is related to and different from arousal, affect, and mood.

2. Explain the major historical perspectives on emotion, including the James–Lange theory, Schachter and Singer's cognitive approach, and Lazarus' model of emotion.

3. Discuss the sport and exercise psychology research on physical activity and emotion, including the effects of exercise on mental health.

4. Define *flow.* Describe Csikszentmihalyi's model and Jackson's work on flow with athletes.

5. Compare and contrast drive theory and the inverted-U hypothesis as explanations of the anxiety–performance relationship.

6. Explain how Fenz's (1975, 1988) work with parachute jumpers supports the idea that anxiety-control training may benefit athletes.

7. Describe the current multidimensional anxiety–performance models used in sport and exercise psychology, including reversal theory and the catastrophe model.

Recommended Reading

Csikszentmihalyi, M. (1990). *Flow: The psychology of optimal experience.* New York: Harper & Row.

> Csikszentmihalyi is widely cited for his innovative work on flow state. Many sport and exercise psychology students are drawn to his work, with good reason—they find new ideas and directions. Perhaps you will get caught up in the flow as you read his work.

Hardy, L. (1996). Testing the predictions of the cusp catastrophe model of anxiety and performance. *The Sport Psychologist, 10,* 140-156.

> Hardy is a leader in applying catastrophe theory to anxiety and sport performance. Although catastrophe theory is mathematically and theoretically complex, this article is one of the most readable and understandable presentations. If you are interested in anxiety and performance, you would do well to read this article, even if you do not specifically test catastrophe theory.

Lazarus, R.S. (1993). From psychological stress to the emotions: A history of changing outlooks. *Annual Review of Psychology, 44,* 1-21.

> Lazarus has been a leading scholar on stress and coping since the 1960s. His most recent work emphasized the broader complexities of emotion. This review presents some of his many insights in moving from stress to emotions.

Martens, R., Vealey, R.S., & Burton, D. (1990). *Competitive anxiety in sport.* Champaign, IL: Human Kinetics.

> Martens and colleagues began the move toward sport-specific constructs and measures with the development of the SCAT and followed with the

development of a multidimensional sport-specific state anxiety measure. This book presents the background literature and information on the SCAT and CSAI-2 measures.

Scanlan, T.K., Babkes, M.L., & Scanlan, L.A. (2005). Participation in sport: A developmental glimpse at emotion. In J.L. Mahoney, R.W. Larson, & J.S. Eccles (Eds.), *Organized activities as contexts of development* (pp. 275-309). Mahwah, NJ: Erlbaum.

Scanlan is one of the few sport and exercise psychology scholars to devote attention to both positive (enjoyment) and negative (stress and anxiety) emotions. Much of her research is with young people, and this chapter summarizes the developmental research on stress and emotion in sport.

Chapter 12

Emotional Control and Stress Management

Chapter Objectives

After studying this chapter, you should be able to

◆ identify several stress models and discuss their use in sport and exercise psychology;

◆ describe several stress management techniques, including meditation and progressive relaxation; and

◆ explain several cognitive-behavioral approaches to stress management.

Emotions and stress are common and powerful in physical activity. Both participants and the professionals who work with them can use emotional control and stress management to enhance the physical activity experience. The emotion models and related research discussed in chapter 11 provide some guidance. Emotion is a complex process and competitive anxiety has both physiological and cognitive components. Stress management or emotional-control strategies may address either or both components at any stage of the process. Because optimal emotional states vary across people, tasks, and situations, the key factor for both good performance and positive experiences is the ability to control emotion. Many of the cognitive interventions discussed in chapter 5 apply to emotional control. Other techniques zero in on the physiological aspect of stress and emotion, and more comprehensive intervention programs combine cognitive strategies with physiological relaxation techniques.

Research on emotional control and stress management does not allow us to say with certainty which stress management techniques are most effective for specific people in specific situations or to identify the best way to develop emotional control. However, the growing literature combined with information from sport and exercise psychology consultants provides guidance and a place to start.

IMPORTANCE OF EMOTIONAL CONTROL AND STRESS MANAGEMENT

The first step is to make the case for why it is important for participants to develop emotional-control skills. As discussed in chapter 11, some level of physiological arousal is necessary to mobilize energy and perform physical activities. A person who is below an optimal arousal level during a practice session, a repetitive workout, or a match against a weaker opponent might want to increase arousal. More often, however, participants want to lower arousal, and that is not easy. Competition or any performance evaluation increases anxiety, and typical warm-up activities increase physiological activity. When arousal increases beyond the optimal level, emotional control is needed. Most strategies for stress management involve relaxation.

In competitive anxiety, physiological arousal typically is accompanied by cognitive worry, and increased cognitive worry is associated with lower self-confidence and poorer performance. Tactics for increasing arousal may be useful in non-stressful teaching and practice situations, but those strategies need not have anxiety-provoking connotations that increase cognitive worry. Even with physiological arousal, the benefits are limited. No research has demonstrated that arousal-increasing techniques enhance performance. The autonomic stress responses (e.g., increased heart rate, palmar sweating) have no functional value for most physical activities and can actually be detrimental. Stressing the cardiovascular system more than necessary can induce early fatigue and decrease endurance, and increased muscle tension creates problems.

In a unique early investigation of anxiety effects on motor performance, Weinberg (1977) used electromyographic recordings to examine muscular activity of high- and low-anxious participants (identified with the SCAT). High-anxious performers exhibited more unnecessary muscular activity and wasted energy before, during, and after the movement. Further, they exhibited simultaneous contraction of the agonist and antagonist muscles, which interferes with coordinated muscle action and creates the feelings of paralysis that most performers can identify. Low-anxious individuals exhibited the more efficient sequential pattern—one muscle contracting as the opposing muscle relaxes.

As the emotion models indicate, physiological arousal interacts with cognition. If you notice your heart beating faster, you may become more worried. Arousal can be distracting; if you're thinking about your rapid breathing or upset stomach, you can't be thinking about an upcoming performance. As described in chapter 5, high arousal and narrowed attention can create problems for activities such as leading the play in soccer or being the quarterback in American football. Conversely, tasks requiring more concentrated attention, such as weightlifting, can be performed effectively with higher arousal and narrower attention. Nideffer's attentional control training (1993; see chapter 5) uses relaxation and arousal control because of the relationship between arousal and attention.

In addition to the detrimental effects of overarousal that have already been noted, initial increases in either physiological arousal or cognitive worry can quickly create a negative thought–anxiety cycle (see figure 12.1), as described by Ziegler (1978). In a stressful situation such as competition, evaluation in physical education, or the presence of spectators in an exercise class, an initial increase in cognitive anxiety occurs along with the physiological changes associated with the stress response. Even slight changes, such as increased muscle tension, can interfere with coordination. Perhaps you are playing shortstop in baseball and bobble the first ball hit to you because you are thinking about the last time this batter hit one by you. Making that error increases cognitive worry and further heightens physiological arousal, decreasing your concentration and increasing the probability of more errors. Unless you can break out of the negative cycle by controlling your worry and physiological arousal, you're in for a long afternoon. Effective stress management skills are the key to breaking the negative cycle.

Figure 12.1
Worry and increases in arousal create a negative cycle that decreases performance.

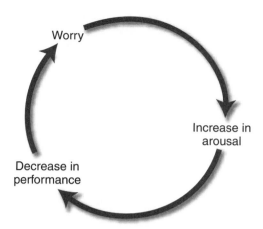

In sport and exercise psychology, research on emotional control and stress management focuses on athletes and performance enhancement. However, emotional control can also enhance performance in physical education classes, recreational sport, and exercise programs. Moreover, many people engage in physical activity to help relieve stress. Teaching emotional control in exercise or youth programs can not only enhance the activity experience but also build emotional-control skills for life enhancement.

Application Point

You are coaching a high school basketball team. How could emotional-control skills be helpful to you and the players on the team? List as many ways as you can and give specific examples.

Emotional intelligence, a popular topic in the media, also relates to positive psychology and promotion of positive health and development. *Emotional intelligence* refers to the ability to process emotion-laden information competently and to use it to guide cognitive activities such as problem solving and to focus energy on required behaviors (Salovey, Mayer, & Caruso, 2005). Salovey et al. (2005) refer to Mayer and Salovey's (1997) model of emotional intelligence, which includes four branches:

- *Emotional perceptions and expression* (ability to identify and express emotion in oneself and others)

- *Emotional facilitation of thought* (ability to use emotional intelligence to solve problems, redirect thought, or facilitate memory and creativity)

- *Emotional understanding* (ability to understand causes, consequences, and relationships among emotions)

- *Emotional management* (ability to monitor and manage emotions)

Emotional intelligence encompasses the specific emotional-control skills covered in the following sections. Clearly, fostering those skills can benefit participants by enhancing the physical activity experience and contributing to personal growth. The emotion models provide guidance, and several sport and exercise psychology researchers and consultants have adapted those models to the physical activity context.

STRESS MODELS IN SPORT AND EXERCISE PSYCHOLOGY

Several sport and exercise psychology researchers have developed models that incorporate the key elements of the Lazarus emotion model, which was discussed in chapter 11. The models are multidimensional, include physiological and cognitive components, start with a situation or stressor, highlight cognitive appraisal, and include recursive relationships in a dynamic process. Most of the widely used models stem from stress models and highlight coping processes that provide guidance for emotional-control and stress management training.

Smith's Mediational Model of Stress

Key Point

Smith (1980) developed a stress management program with an integrated coping response involving both cognitive and behavioral strategies. With an integrated set of coping skills and possible strategies, people can tailor coping responses to the situation and their personal preferences.

One of the earliest and most influential models is Ron Smith's (1980) cognitive stress model. The basic model (figure 12.2) highlights cognitive appraisal, includes multiple interrelated variables, and involves a process that changes over time. External events, specifically demands and resources in the situation, may trigger stress, but appraisal is the key to the person's response. The response has physiological, psychological, and behavioral correlates and consequences. Cognitive appraisal of the situation and coping ability interact with physiological responses within the central stress appraisal process, which then results in certain behaviors, particularly task and coping behaviors. Smith's model provides the basis for many stress management techniques used in sport and exercise psychology.

Figure 12.2
Mediational model of stress underlying the cognitive-affective stress management program along with the major intervention techniques used in development of an integrated coping response.

Reprinted, by permission, from R.E. Smith, 1980, A cognitive-affective approach to stress management training for athletes. In *Psychology of motor behavior and sport-1979*, edited by C.H. Nadeau et al. (Champaign, IL: Human Kinetics), 56.

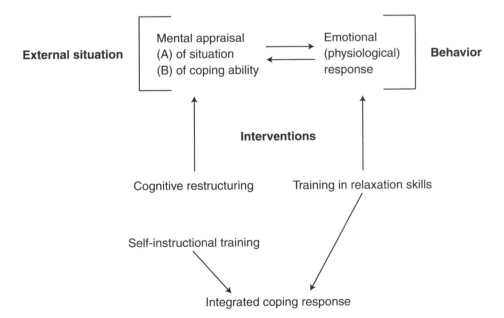

Stress and Burnout

In addition to providing a framework for stress management, Smith's model has been adapted for burnout and injury in sport. Smith's (1986) burnout model parallels the stress model; indeed, burnout is a form of stress. Smith's burnout model, as well as most related work in sport and exercise psychology, follows Maslach and Jackson (1986), who developed the most widely used model and measure of burnout. Burnout is a consequence of prolonged stress that may result in

- emotional exhaustion,
- depersonalization (distancing oneself from others), and
- reduced sense of meaning or personal accomplishments.

Maslach and Jackson's (1986) Burnout Inventory assesses these three dimensions. As in the Lazarus and Smith models, the burnout process begins with a stressful situation. As the person perceives overload, helplessness, or lack of accomplishments, the appraisal interacts with physical symptoms, including tension, depression, or fatigue, which results in the multidimensional burnout syndrome.

Vealey, Udry, Zimmerman, and Soliday (1992) used Smith's model as a framework and supported the mediating role of cognitive appraisal in coach burnout. Kelly and Gill (1993) also supported the main relationships of the model. Specifically, satisfaction with social support, low experience, and gender (being female) were related to stress appraisal and perceived stress, which in turn predicted burnout. Kelly (1994) extended that work to examine the influence of social support, hardiness, gender, and win or loss on stress appraisal and burnout.

Other research on health and stress suggests that social support is an important social factor and that hardiness, a multidimensional personality construct consisting of control, commitment, and challenge (Kobasa, 1988; Kobasa, Maddi, & Courington, 1981), is an important individual variable in the stress process. Kelly (1994) found some support in that both male and female coaches who were lower in hardiness had greater perceived stress, as did male coaches who were lower in social support. Again, stress appraisal predicted all burnout components.

Raedke and Smith (2004) used Smith's stress and burnout model as a guide to investigate the role of coping resources and social support in the stress–burnout relationship with age-group swimmers. They found that perceived stress, general coping behaviors, and social support satisfaction were related to burnout. As the models suggest, coping resources and social support mediated the stress–burnout relationship.

Stress and Injury

The psychology of injury has become a popular research and applied area within sport and exercise psychology, and the work is guided by emotion and stress models. Mark Anderson and Jean Williams (Anderson & Williams, 1988) first adapted the stress model to sport injuries and rehabilitation. They have continued their work, models have been updated, and researchers from both sports medicine and psychology have investigated psychological aspects of injury. Williams and Anderson's (1998) updated model and the expanded model of Wiese-Bjornstal, Smith, Shaffer, and Morrey (1998) both have guided considerable research and practice.

The models (see figures 12.3 and 12.4) reflect the key aspects of Lazarus' emotion model and Smith's stress management model. Again, the process begins with a potentially stressful situation, but the key to the stress process (and injury) is the interaction of the cognitive appraisal and physiological processes. As with the stress and burnout models, the stress response is influenced by personal (e.g., hardiness, trait anxiety) and situational (e.g., history of stressors, social support) factors. The models provide a guide for examining antecedents of injury, which may aid in prevention and guide interventions for rehabilitation and recovery.

Much of the research on injury prevention stems from the research on stress and health. As noted in the last chapter, stress influences immune function and relates to health and illness. Similarly, stress is related to injury risk. Bramwell, Masuda, Wagner, and Holmes (1975) modified the Holmes and Rahe (1967) life events scale for athletes and demonstrated that American football players with greater life stress were more likely to sustain injuries. Several subsequent studies supported that relationship, although the mechanisms are not clear and the relationship may be mediated by several factors, including attentional deficits, muscle tension, and low coping resources (see Udry & Anderson, 2002, for review).

As the models suggest, coping resources are a key factor in the appraisal process and subsequent response. Coping responses, which are positive psychology characteristics, are most commonly classified using Lazarus and Folkman's (1984) distinction between emotion-focused coping and problem-focused coping. Emotion-focused coping includes emotional-control strategies, as well as less formal strategies such as denial or seeking emotional support. Problem-focused coping involves strategies such as weighing alternatives and developing action plans. Several measures of coping strategies are available

Key Point

In stress models, coping resources are a key factor in the appraisal process and subsequent response. Coping responses are commonly classified as emotion focused or problem focused. Emotion-focused coping includes emotional-control strategies, as well as less formal strategies such as denial or seeking emotional support. Problem-focused coping involves strategies such as weighing alternatives and developing action plans.

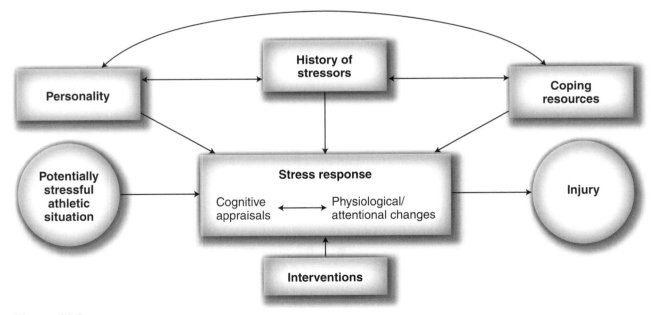

Figure 12.3
Williams and Anderson's (1998) model of injury antecedents.

Reprinted from J. Williams and M. Anderson, 1998, "Psychological antecedents of sport injury: Review and critique of the stress-injury model," *Journal of Applied Sport Psychology* 10(1): 5-25, by permission of Taylor & Francis. www.informaworld.com

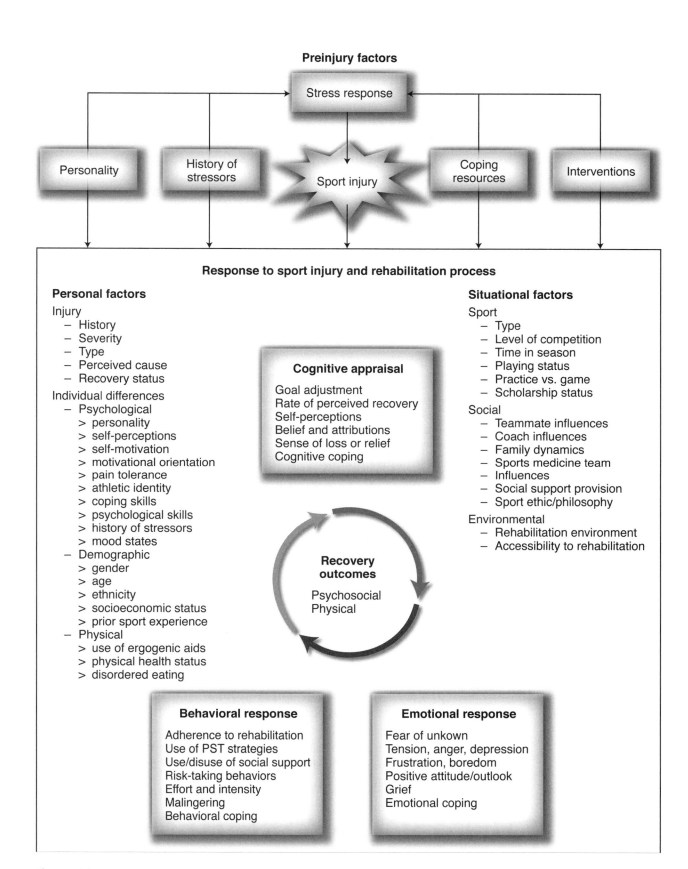

Preinjury factors

Stress response

Personality History of stressors Sport injury Coping resources Interventions

Response to sport injury and rehabilitation process

Personal factors

Injury
- History
- Severity
- Type
- Perceived cause
- Recovery status

Individual differences
- Psychological
  > personality
  > self-perceptions
  > self-motivation
  > motivational orientation
  > pain tolerance
  > athletic identity
  > coping skills
  > psychological skills
  > history of stressors
  > mood states
- Demographic
  > gender
  > age
  > ethnicity
  > socioeconomic status
  > prior sport experience
- Physical
  > use of ergogenic aids
  > physical health status
  > disordered eating

Situational factors

Sport
- Type
- Level of competition
- Time in season
- Playing status
- Practice vs. game
- Scholarship status

Social
- Teammate influences
- Coach influences
- Family dynamics
- Sports medicine team
- Influences
- Social support provision
- Sport ethic/philosophy

Environmental
- Rehabilitation environment
- Accessibility to rehabilitation

Cognitive appraisal

Goal adjustment
Rate of perceived recovery
Self-perceptions
Belief and attributions
Sense of loss or relief
Cognitive coping

Recovery outcomes

Psychosocial
Physical

Behavioral response

Adherence to rehabilitation
Use of PST strategies
Use/disuse of social support
Risk-taking behaviors
Effort and intensity
Malingering
Behavioral coping

Emotional response

Fear of unkown
Tension, anger, depression
Frustration, boredom
Positive attitude/outlook
Grief
Emotional coping

Figure 12.4

Wiese-Bjornstal, Smith, Shaffer, and Morrey's (1998) model of injury response.

Reprinted from D.M. Wiese-Bjornstal et al., 1998, "An integrated model of response to sport injury: Psychological and sociological dynamics," *Journal of Applied Sport Psychology* 10(1): 46-69, by permission of Taylor & Francis. www.informaworld.com

and have been used with physical activity participants, including the Ways of Coping (WOC) scale (Lazarus & Folkman, 1985) and the Coping Orientations to Problems Experienced (COPE) scale (Carver, Scheier, & Weintraub, 1989).

Udry (1997) used the stress model with its emphasis on cognitive appraisal to investigate the role of coping and support in athletic injury and recovery after knee surgery. During recovery athletes most frequently used instrumental coping, which is problem focused and uses activities to alleviate stress, and instrumental coping predicted adherence to the rehabilitation program. Udry's initial information suggests that stress and emotion models offer a framework for research and practice regarding sport injury and rehabilitation.

Application Point

As an athletic trainer, you would be likely to encounter athletes coping with injuries in many ways. List examples of both emotion-focused and problem-focused coping strategies that injured athletes might use. Be specific and include both effective strategies and strategies that are less likely to be effective.

EDUCATIONAL STRESS MANAGEMENT TECHNIQUES

One simple but effective stress management technique is learning about anxiety and its impact on performance. Many performers mistakenly believe that high arousal is necessary and that they should prepare by psyching up. However, the optimal state for most sport and exercise activities is one of relaxed concentration. Carl Lewis, who demonstrated peak performance under pressure when he won four gold medals at the 1984 Olympics, described his running as follows: "When I run like Carl Lewis, relaxed, smooth, easy, I can run races that seem effortless to me and to those watching" (Callahan, 1984, p. 52).

Of course, Carl Lewis put in tremendous effort and worked hard to develop his skills. But at the time of competition, he reduced his physiological arousal to achieve a relaxed state. Athletes and exercisers must be alert and attentive, but they should also be free of excess muscle tension and worry. In short, they should be in control. Most stress management techniques aim to achieve this controlled, relaxed state.

Sometimes simply telling people about the importance of relaxation and control is enough to eliminate ineffective approaches. For example, a baseball player may try to deal with a batting slump by increasing tension and arousal, or a well-intentioned coach might put extra pressure on the athlete, thereby aggravating a negative thought–anxiety cycle. Information about negative effects of muscle tension and overarousal and about the importance of relaxed concentration may make participants aware of the desired psychological state and encourage alternative tactics.

Key Point

Many performers mistakenly believe that high arousal is necessary, but the optimal state for most sport and exercise activities is one of relaxed concentration.

COGNITIVE STRESS MANAGEMENT TECHNIQUES

Simple cognitive techniques often are effective in managing stress. Mahoney (1979) and Fenz (1975, 1988) both reported that successful performers who were able to control anxiety were more task oriented. Helping athletes shift their focus from negative thoughts to specific actions might well enhance performance. Many of the cognitive interventions discussed in chapter 5, such as thought stopping, can be applied to control anxiety. When recognizing a negative thought such as "My feet are rooted to the floor," the person might stop the negative thought and substitute a positive statement, such as "I'm relaxed and ready to move."

Similarly, attentional control strategies might help an anxious person direct attention away from worry and onto something else. For example, a basketball substitute waiting to enter the game might focus on the movement of an opposing forward along the baseline. As discussed in chapter 5, many athletes use imagery to mentally practice moves or routines, and imagery can also serve as a relaxation technique. Simply imagining a calm, peaceful scene may allow a person to mentally transcend a stressful situation and gain control. As in the process of counterconditioning, in which one response is substituted for another, it is impossible to be both relaxed and anxious at the same time. Pictures, audiotapes, or videotapes may be helpful in prompting relaxing imagery.

RELAXATION EXERCISES

The most widely recognized stress management techniques work directly on physiological arousal. Relaxation techniques include simple breathing exercises, progressive relaxation, meditation, and variations of these.

Breathing Exercises

One of the simplest but most effective relaxation techniques is slow, deep breathing. Increased respiration rate is part of the autonomic stress response, and respiration is one of the physiological responses most easy to control; controlling heart rate or body temperature is much more difficult. In his work with parachute jumpers, Fenz (1975) reported that respiration rate tended to come under control earlier in the jump sequence, whereas other physiological responses, including heart rate and palmar sweating, remained at high levels longer. This suggests that controlling breathing might be an effective way to initiate relaxation.

Breathing techniques emphasize slow, deep breathing. One technique is to breathe in slowly and deeply while counting to four, hold the breath for four counts, and then exhale slowly for four counts. A consultant might help by starting the exercise and counting aloud. Many other relaxation techniques incorporate similar breathing. Both progressive relaxation and meditation include attention to slow, deep breathing.

Application Point

Participants in an exercise class often bring worries and muscle tension with them to class. As an exercise instructor, how could you incorporate breathing exercises into your exercise class? Provide guidelines to help participants use these techniques in class and in their daily lives.

Progressive Relaxation

Progressive relaxation, originally developed by Jacobson (1938), is one of the most popular relaxation techniques used today. Although relatively simple, it requires practice. The technique involves the progressive tensing and relaxing of various muscle groups. An example is included in appendix C.

Sport and exercise psychology consultants use progressive relaxation extensively when helping clients develop psychological skills. Typically a consultant conducts several sessions, giving cues to tense and then relax specific muscle groups. The first sessions may take 45 minutes to an hour, but as clients become more proficient, sessions become shorter as muscle groups are combined and as the tension phase is gradually reduced and finally omitted. The goal is for the person to learn to recognize subtle levels of muscle tension and to relax those muscles at will. For example, the exerciser in a spinning class who notices tightness in the neck and shoulders can then focus attention on those muscles, relax them, and refocus on the task.

People can learn progressive relaxation with the aid of instructions, handouts, or tapes. Many athletes and exercisers already use versions of progressive relaxation. The 10K runner who shakes out his muscles just before the event and the basketball player who tightens her shoulders and lets them drop while preparing for a free throw are using a form of progressive relaxation. Readers who wish to know more about progressive relaxation might refer to Bernstein and Borkovec's (1973) *Progressive Relaxation: A Manual for the Helping Professions,* an excellent source of background information and practical advice, or to more current applied sport psychology sources (e.g., Williams & Harris, 2006).

Meditation

As a stress management technique, progressive relaxation involves relaxing the muscles and letting the mind follow. Meditation techniques work the other way, relaxing the mind and letting the body follow. Meditation generally involves a relaxed, passive focusing of attention and an avoidance of tension and strain. Often the person who is meditating simply focuses on breathing with no analytic thought or special effort.

Benson's (1976) relaxation response is an easy and popular technique. To use the Benson method, practitioners first find a quiet setting without distractions and then attend to their breathing. Benson suggests silently repeating the word *one* or any other nonstimulating word with each exhalation to help maintain attention. Williams and Harris (2006) note that the word *one* often is stimulating to achievement-oriented athletes, suggesting that *calm* or *warm* might be better choices. Meditation involves passive attention. Neither the mind nor the body is active; you simply attend to breathing, and when attention wanders, bring the focus back to breathing without straining or worrying about it. Williams and Harris (2006, p. 297) offer these directions for a meditation exercise:

> **Key Point**
>
> As a stress management technique, progressive relaxation involves relaxing the muscles and letting the mind follow. Meditation techniques work the other way, relaxing the mind and letting the body follow.

1. Sit quietly in a comfortable position.

2. Close your eyes.

3. Deeply relax all your muscles, beginning at your feet and progressing to the top of your head (or progress from head to feet if you prefer). Keep the muscles relaxed.

4. Breathe through your nose. Concentrate on your breathing. As you breathe out, silently say the word *calm* or some other word or nonsense sound. For example, breathe in, out, and silently say "Calm," and so forth. Breathe easily and naturally.

5. You may open your eyes to check the time, but do not use an alarm. When you finish, sit quietly for several minutes, at first with your eyes closed and later with your eyes open. Wait a few minutes before standing up.

Do the exercise for about 5 minutes at first and build to 15 to 20 minutes with practice. Don't worry about whether you are successful in achieving a deep level of relaxation—just remain passive and let relaxation happen. Practice the technique once or twice daily, but wait at least an hour after any meal because digestive processes seem to interfere with the relaxation response.

Autogenic Training

Autogenic training, developed in the 1930s by Johannes Schultz in Germany (Williams & Harris, 2006), is similar to meditation and is a form of autohypnosis, or self-hypnosis. As in meditation, attention is passive and one lets the feelings happen. However, autogenic training takes several months and proceeds through six stages as the person tries to induce sensations of warmth and heaviness.

Given the extensive time demands of autogenic training and its lack of direct connection to sport and exercise, it has not been the relaxation technique of choice. It is more popular in Europe, and for people who like the idea of hypnosis, autogenic training with its focus on physical sensations may be particularly appealing.

COGNITIVE-BEHAVIORAL STRESS MANAGEMENT

The cognitive and relaxation techniques covered so far are all relatively simple techniques that require no special training. More elaborate and comprehensive stress management may be appropriate, especially when a consultant works with a person over a longer time frame. Some athletes have used hypnosis or biofeedback for stress management; these both require special training and extended time to be effective. The most popular stress management programs in educational and clinical psychology work are cognitive-behavioral programs combining relaxation exercises with cognitive interventions.

Suinn's Visuomotor Behavioral Rehearsal Technique

Richard Suinn (1976, 1983, 1993) uses a combination of progressive relaxation and imagery in his visuomotor behavioral rehearsal (VMBR) technique. As described by Suinn (1976, 1993), VMBR is a covert activity whereby a person experiences sensory-motor sensations that reintegrate reality experiences and that include neuromuscular, physiological, and emotional involvement. It involves two steps: relaxation training and imagery rehearsal. In VMBR, unlike mental practice, relaxation is an essential step that always precedes imagery. Practitioners use all senses to re-experience an event and actually feel as though they are in the situation, performing the activity. In VMBR, the images that are produced and the actions that occur are subject to control.

In his 1993 review, Suinn cites several case examples and research studies illustrating the effectiveness of VMBR with athletes. He notes that VMBR is a training tool that must be applied in accordance with known principles of skill acquisition, skill building, and skill enhancement. Suinn's use of VMBR with Olympic skiers was among the first and most widely cited psychological skills programs. The combination of relaxation and cognitive intervention as used by Suinn is still the dominant model for psychological skills training.

Smith's Cognitive-Affective Stress Management Model

As discussed earlier, Smith's (1980) stress model provides a guide for stress management programs in sport and exercise. Recall that in the model, the stress process begins with an external situation and individual characteristics and then adds cognitive appraisal and physiological components that interact to influence responses and behavior. Stress management may work in any part of the model, including the initial conditions. For example, youth sport programs that provide behavioral guidelines for parents or even ban spectators aim to reduce situational stressors. Similarly, exercise classes designed for specific groups, such as older adults, single-sex groups, or overweight adolescents, may reduce stress for participants.

Specific cognitive interventions, such as thought stopping or imagery, work on the cognitive component, whereas relaxation techniques focus on the physiological component. Cognitive-behavioral programs, such as VMBR and Smith's cognitive-affective stress management program, include both cognitive and relaxation skills in more comprehensive programs. Smith's program incorporates progressive relaxation, emphasizes breathing cues as a relaxation technique, and uses either cognitive restructuring or self-talk as the cognitive component. The key skill in Smith's program is the integrated coping response, which combines relaxation with cognitive restructuring. Smith's stress management program is based on earlier work, particularly Meichenbaum's (1977) stress inoculation training.

Smith's cognitive-affective stress management training follows Meichenbaum's stress inoculation model with some variations, and Smith (1980) has specifically applied the model with athletes. However, the model fits anyone developing stress management skills. Smith's program typically follows these steps:

1. *Pretreatment assessment.* Before any training, the first step is to assess the situation and individual characteristics. For example, what specific situations bring out excessive anxiety? What physiological symptoms dominate? Some of the measures discussed in chapter 11 (e.g., CSAI-2, SAS) might be used, as might reports or observations.

2. *Treatment rationale.* The consultant and client develop a plan, and the consultant presents the rationale. This is the education phase, giving the client information and an explanation for the training. Most sport and exercise psychology consultants emphasize that the client must believe in the training and commit to it if the training is to be effective.

3. *Skill acquisition.* During skill acquisition, which continues over several sessions, the client learns the integrated coping response. Specifically, the person learns relaxation and cognitive coping techniques and combines them into the integrated coping response. Smith uses progressive relaxation exercises, and similar to Meichenbaum, emphasizes breathing as a relaxation cue. Cognitive coping emphasizes cognitive restructuring and includes self-statements similar to those used in stress inoculation training. Smith notes that for some people, particularly young athletes, simple self-instruction

statements may be more effective than cognitive restructuring, and cognitive skills might involve either of those strategies.

4. *Skill rehearsal.* As with the application-training step of stress inoculation, the person practices coping skills in stressful situations. However, here Smith departs from the stress inoculation model in advocating practice in situations that are more stressful than the problem situation. Smith aims to induce affect (hence the term *cognitive-affective*) that is greater than the person will deal with in actuality. For example, the person might image the worst possible scenario, develop all the affect (worry and physiological arousal) that accompanies that situation, and then use the integrated coping skills to control the affect. Training as a clinical psychologist is essential for these procedures. A typical educational sport psychology consultant would not attempt to induce extreme anxiety and affect.

5. *Evaluation.* No effective program stops at training, and Smith recognizes the role of evaluation in applied work. Evaluation is important in order for the client to determine whether training is effective, to make modifications and adjustments, and to maintain skills. Evaluation is also important for the sport and exercise psychologist to develop and refine skills and programs, as well as for the field of sport and exercise psychology to build the knowledge base and provide guidance for others.

Emotional Control for Anger and Aggression

Larry Lauer (2005) has extended emotional-control strategies that have been applied to anxiety control and performance enhancement in ice hockey. Specifically Lauer has used cognitive-behavioral approaches to help youth hockey players control emotion and subsequently reduce aggressive behavior in order to play tough and clean hockey.

Lauer's tough-and-clean hockey program focuses on the three Rs—react, relax, and refocus. Players working on emotional toughness first react—they recognize the negative emotion, feel it, but don't let it control their reaction. Then they relax or calm down by using simple techniques such as those just reviewed—deep breathing, self-talk, or visualizing responding positively. As the third *R,* players refocus to return to play immediately. They might have a cue word or phrase (e.g., "Focus on hockey," "Play my game") to help get back into the game, visualize, or otherwise redirect emotion into positive actions.

Lauer used the three Rs in an extensive case study of six participants who were identified as players who could benefit from the program. Self-reports of the participants, along with extensive observations, indicated that the program was successful. All participants indicated that the program was effective; they learned the skills and were able to use them on the ice. All showed some improvement in some areas. The emotions that the players experienced did not change much, again suggesting that control is the key. Aggressive behavior showed some change, particularly for the player who was the most aggressive.

 Application Point

As the director of an after-school youth development program, how could you adapt Lauer's three Rs to help your participants develop emotional control? Include specific guidelines and suggestions for each *R.*

Lauer's skill development program with youth hockey players is a great example of using emotional control for positive development. Not only might emotional-control skills relieve stress and anxiety to enhance performance, but such skills can help physical activity participants develop positive characteristics and behaviors. As the positive psychology literature suggests, promoting positive characteristics such as resiliency, joy, and commitment is at least as important as dealing with psychological problems. Physical activity settings are particularly appropriate for using emotional-control skills to enhance positive psychological development.

PUTTING IT INTO PRACTICE

Now you are ready to put the content of chapter 12 into practice. Read the chapter summary, discuss the case study, answer the review questions, and enhance your knowledge by researching the recommended readings.

Summary

Stress and emotion are everywhere in sport and exercise. Stress management techniques are key psychological skills in many interventions, and emotional-control skills can enhance the physical activity experience and help any participant develop life skills. Stress has cognitive and physiological components, and stress management encompasses both cognitive and physical relaxation techniques. Cognitive interventions discussed in chapter 5, such as imagery and cognitive restructuring, are effective techniques. Physical relaxation techniques include breathing exercises, progressive relaxation, and meditation.

Sport and exercise psychology consultants working with participants often use more comprehensive stress management programs, such as Smith's cognitive-affective stress management training. These cognitive-behavioral programs typically include both cognitive and relaxation techniques within a training program that progresses from initial assessment and education through skill development and practice sessions, application of the skills in sport and exercise settings, and evaluation of the stress management program.

Case Study

Following are two opportunities in which to apply your understanding of emotion, stress, and coping. Here are your cases.

Case 1

You are working at a camp for talented junior tennis players. One promising young player has emotional ups and downs, with play to match. He easily gets upset at calls, errors, and opponent moves, and even when things go well in a match, he's always on edge. He rarely plays up to his potential, especially in the final rounds of tournaments when the competition is toughest. What might you do to help this athlete in terms of emotional control?

Case 2

You are working as a personal trainer with a number of clients. One of your clients is a financial manager who works long hours in a position with high responsibility. She often remarks that the training sessions help her relieve the stress of the office as well as get in shape. How could you incorporate stress management or emotional control in your work with this client?

Review Questions

1. Identify several reasons why emotional control is beneficial in exercise and sport.

2. Define *burnout* and explain the role of cognitive appraisal in burnout models and stress and injury models.

3. Compare educational stress management techniques, cognitive stress management techniques, and relaxation exercises.

4. Describe progressive relaxation, meditation, and breathing exercises as stress management techniques, and explain how they could be used for emotional control in sport and exercise settings.

5. Describe the elements of Suinn's VMBR technique and Smith's cognitive-affective stress management model (1980) that qualify them as cognitive-behavioral programs.

Recommended Reading

Smith, R.E. (1980). A cognitive-affective approach to stress management training for athletes. In C.H. Nadeau, W.R. Halliwell, K.M. Newell, & G.C. Roberts (Eds.), *Psychology of motor behavior and sport—1979* (pp. 54-72). Champaign, IL: Human Kinetics.

This article is more than 25 years old, but its presentation of Smith's cognitive-affective stress management model and his approach to professional practice is still a model for sport and exercise psychologists who want to be effective practitioners.

Udry, E., & Anderson, M.B. (2002). Athletic injury and sport behavior. In T.S. Horn (Ed.), *Advances in sport psychology* (2nd ed., pp. 529-553). Champaign, IL: Human Kinetics.

This chapter reviews the rapidly growing research on psychology and injury. Much of that work applies stress and emotion models to psychological aspects of injury prevention, rehabilitation, and recovery, as well as to interventions.

Williams, J.M., & Harris, D.V. (2006). Relaxation and energizing techniques for regulation of arousal. In J.M. Williams (Ed.), *Applied sport psychology: Personal growth to peak performance* (5th ed., pp. 285-305). Boston: McGraw-Hill.

This chapter provides a good overview of stress management techniques that can be used in many sport and exercise settings, including several muscle-to-mind and mind-to-muscle techniques.

Part V

Social Processes

Earlier chapters focused on the individual and cognitive-behavioral influences on the individual's behavior in sport and exercise settings. In part V, we'll look at the bigger picture and view the individual in relation to others. Specifically, we will consider how others such as coaches, family, and friends, as well as the larger social context, influence individual behavior, interpersonal interactions, and group processes.

Chapter 13 covers the broad topic of social influence, including the influence of others as spectators, instructors, and models. Chapter 14 takes a more developmental view to consider social development with a focus on aggression and moral behavior in physical activity settings. The last two chapters move even further from the individual to the social context. Chapter 15 addresses group dynamics and interpersonal processes, including social support and team building, in sport and exercise psychology. The final chapter considers social diversity, emphasizing gender relations and extending to wider cultural diversity concerns.

Chapter 13

Social Influence

Chapter Objectives

After studying this chapter, you should be able to

◆ identify ways in which the presence of others can influence sport and exercise performance, and

◆ understand the concept of modeling and how significant others can affect sport and exercise behavior.

Social influence, central in the research of the 1960s and 1970s, remains prominent because virtually all sport and exercise activity is social. Much sport activity involves competition, which is social by definition. Noncompetitive activities such as physical education classes, fitness programs, recreational sport, and rehabilitation settings usually involve social interaction. Similarly, exercise instructors and sport leaders exert social influence when they give directions, watch us perform, and tell us how we are doing. We often win or lose in front of family, friends, and the general public. Classmates see whether we can perform a handstand, and colleagues in the aerobic exercise group notice if we're out of shape. Additionally, we learn by watching others. How many times have you learned a new skill by watching someone else perform it?

In this chapter, we will consider the major types of social influence that sport and exercise psychology research has addressed. We will focus on social facilitation (the influence of the presence of others on performance), the more active influence of social reinforcement (evaluative comments and actions), competition, and modeling (learning through observation). Our focus here is both the specific processes of social influence that dominated early research and the modern approaches that address modeling effects.

SOCIAL FACILITATION

Social facilitation is the influence of the presence of others on performance, including audience (i.e., spectators simply observing) and coaction (i.e., people doing the same thing at the same time) effects. Social facilitation is one of the oldest research topics in social psychology. Triplett (1898) found that paced times were faster (by about 35 seconds per mile) than unpaced times and that competitive times were fastest of all. He also found that children winding a fishing reel were faster when they worked in pairs than alone. Triplett proposed the principle of dynamogeny, asserting that the presence of others arouses competitive drive, releases energy, and increases speed of performance.

Expanding on Triplett's work, Allport (1924) coined the term *social facilitation* to refer to performance improvements due to the presence of others. Allport found that the presence of others did not always improve performance; sometimes the presence of others hindered performance (see the review by Landers & McCullagh, 1976, for more information)

Zajonc (1965) proposed that drive theory (discussed in chapter 11) explained these apparent contradictory findings. He posited that

- the presence of others, either as an audience or as coactors, creates arousal or drive;

- increased arousal increases the likelihood that the person's dominant response will occur;

- if the skill is simple or well learned, the dominant response is the correct response and performance improves (facilitation); and

- if the skill is complex and not well learned, the dominant response is an incorrect response and performance is impaired.

Subsequent research (e.g., Martens, 1969) confirmed Zajonc's predictions: The presence of an audience creates arousal, which impairs learning but facilitates performance after the task is well learned. Subsequent sport and exercise psychology studies added further support. Furthermore, coactors elicited better performance on well-learned or simple tasks (e.g., Obermeier, Landers, & Ester, 1977) but worsened performance on more complex tasks (e.g., Martens & Landers, 1972).

According to Zajonc (1965), the mere presence of others creates arousal that affects performance. Since then, several researchers (e.g., Baron, Moore, & Sanders, 1978; Cottrell, 1968; Landers, 1980) challenged this, arguing that other factors such as evaluation apprehension, distraction, and attentional conflict caused the heighten arousal or changes in performance. Thirty years ago, Geen and Gange (1977) concluded that drive theory was the best explanation for social facilitation but argued for more attention to cognitive processes. Even though neither drive theory nor evaluation apprehension has stirred much interest in the last 30 years, sport and exercise psychologists have turned to more cognitive approaches, such as self-presentation (see chapter 6), and to a wider investigation of social interaction processes.

Key Point

Social facilitation is the influence of the presence of others on performance, including audience and coaction effects.

AUDIENCE EFFECTS IN THE REAL WORLD

Perhaps the main reason sport and exercise psychologists abandoned social facilitation research was the failure to demonstrate any effects in the real world. Many of the experiments were trivial, finding that laboratory experiments supporting Zajonc's predictions were not generalized to actual sport settings and that the research had limited practical value (e.g., Martens, 1979). However, one interesting and practical phenomena related to social facilitation, the home advantage, lingers today.

Schwartz and Barsky (1977) documented the home advantage with professional and collegiate men's team sport. Teams won games more often at home than away for all sports, and the home advantage was greatest for the indoor sports (hockey and basketball). The home advantage held for offensive play (e.g., hits, goals, shots, points), but defensive statistics (e.g., errors, saves, fouls) did not differ for home and away games. Varca (1980) observed that home and away basketball teams did not differ on field-goal percentage, free-throw percentage, or turnovers. Instead, the home team demonstrated more functionally aggressive behavior (e.g., steals, blocked shots, rebounds), whereas the away team demonstrated more dysfunctionally aggressive behavior (e.g., fouls). Courneya and Carron (1992) reviewed more than 30 studies, concluding that the likelihood of home teams winning ranged from 55% (effect size = .07) for baseball to 69% (effect size = .38) for soccer. They noted that these largely descriptive studies did not address possible reasons for a home advantage.

Carron and his colleagues (Carron, Loughhead, & Bray, 2005) forwarded a revised conceptual framework highlighting and organizing features of the home advantage. They suggested that the location of the game affects teams differently, which in turn affects the psychological, physiological, and behavioral states of players and coaches, thus affecting performance outcomes. In their review, they concluded that location factors such as spectators (e.g., crowd density), degree of unfamiliarity the visiting team has with playing conditions (e.g., artificial versus natural turf), and inconvenience associated with traveling (e.g., travel distance) contribute to the home advantage. Research findings on key psychological states and behaviors of players and coaches since 1992 have been modest at best, and no conclusive statements can be made. Carron and his colleagues urge future researchers in this area to use theory as a guide when identifying the key psychological states and behaviors that should be affected by location factors.

Research of the last 30 years indicates that the home advantage exists, but there is also evidence that playing in front of the supportive home crowd is sometimes a disadvantage. Baumeister (1984; Baumeister & Steinhilber, 1984) argued that directing attention internally, or increased self-consciousness, can disrupt the performance of well-learned, automatic skills. They reasoned that the opportunity to win a championship in front of the home crowd and thus redefine themselves from contender to champion would increase self-consciousness and disrupt skilled performance. Data from World Series baseball and professional basketball confirmed Baumeister's views; home teams tended to choke in the final, decisive game.

Based on suggested improvement to Baumeister and Steinhilber's methodology, Voyer, Kinch, and Wright (2006) set out to test Baumeister's redefinition hypothesis. They argued that support for the redefinition hypothesis would be found if fewer home teams won critical than noncritical games, but only for first-time winners in the championships. Using archival National Football League (NFL) data and assessing only win percentage, championship round, type of winner, and game criticality, their results do put into question the veracity of the redefinition hypothesis. However, in light of the methodological weakness associated with this study and the paucity of research in this area, the jury on the final-game choke is still out.

Application Point

The two top teams from the district are playing: the Hawks and the Eagles. They have similar season records against the same teams and are 1–1 against each other. Your friends are convinced the Hawks will win because they will have the home advantage. How do you respond when they ask you if you think the home advantage will help the Hawks win?

SOCIAL REINFORCEMENT AND MOTOR PERFORMANCE

Similar to social facilitation, social reinforcement was prominent in the early research. The work on social reinforcement followed the same designs as, and is a variation of, the research on social influence and motor performance. Social facilitation involves a passive audience, but in social reinforcement, audience members play an active (although limited) role. Social reinforcement consists of positive and negative evaluative comments and actions, such as verbal praise, criticism, and body language (smiles, frowns, gestures). Most audiences in sport and exercise settings—including home and away audiences and most instructors and coparticipants—provide social reinforcement, so it was logical to extend social influence to include this evaluative component.

Early social reinforcement using novel complex motor tasks failed to find social reinforcement effects (e.g., Martens, 1972). Martens suggested that performers received better and more specific information from the task itself than from social reinforcement, which provided redundant information that did not help improve performance. Harney and Parker (1972) proposed that social reinforcement must be frequent and intense to affect performance. When they administered positive and negative social reinforcement enthusiastically after every trial, performance was better than in a control condition.

Most sport and exercise tasks, and even the motor tasks of these experiments, already have a clear goal and intrinsic interest. Most people want to perform well, and unless they have been doing the task to the point of boredom, social reinforcement will not add much to an already high level of intrinsic motivation. Thus, in some cases social reinforcement may provide motivational effects. Gill and Martens (1975) created four conditions:

1. Social reinforcement with praise for good scores and negative comments for poor scores
2. Knowledge of results with precise error scores
3. Social reinforcement combined with knowledge of results
4. Control with neither social reinforcement nor knowledge of results

Both social reinforcement and knowledge of results improved performance, and the group receiving both performed best. Surprisingly, the group with only social reinforcement performed better than the group with only knowledge of results, suggesting that social reinforcement was sufficient for performance improvement and possibly had a motivational effect.

Overall, the above studies suggest that social reinforcement may have an informational effect when other information sources are absent and may have a motivational effect when the activity is not intrinsically motivating. However, no observed effects were dramatic, and most experimental situations were quite artificial. Most performers have information that is clearer and more precise than social reinforcement. Thus, the social reinforcement effects on motor performance are limited at best.

The limited extent of this influence does not imply that social reinforcement is undesirable, though. None of these studies showed detrimental effects on performance, and social reinforcement has other beneficial effects. It is a key component of teaching and coaching behavior and of communication and interpersonal style. The work on coaching behaviors, discussed in chapter 7, indicates that the use of positive, reinforcing behaviors versus punitive behaviors strongly influences players' attitudes toward the coach and the activity.

Communication styles and social reinforcement are part of the current work on social support. Sport and exercise psychology has moved well past the controlled lab experiments of the early research to real sport and exercise settings and more complex social interactions. The current work on social support moves from isolated effects on performance to more complex processes.

COMPETITION AND MOTOR PERFORMANCE

Competition involves the presence of others, but similar to social reinforcement, it involves more. Competition entails a more direct social evaluation than the standard audience situation. Because social evaluation is so clear and intense, competition should increase arousal and affect performance just as the presence of others does—or even more so. Although research on competition is more limited than research on audience effects, the findings show parallels.

> **Key Point**
>
> Generally, competition improves performance of simple or well-learned skills and of speed, strength, and endurance tasks.

Gross and Gill's (1982) results suggest that the influence of competition is complex. They varied instructions on a dart-throwing task across five conditions ranging from complete emphasis on speed to equal emphasis on speed and accuracy to complete emphasis on accuracy. Competition improved speed, but only when the instructions emphasized speed. When the instructions emphasized accuracy, performers were slower in competition. However, competition did not affect accuracy, even when the instructions emphasized accuracy.

Competition and Arousal

Starkes and Allard (1983) investigated competition effects using a signal-detection paradigm to see how quickly and accurately participants could detect a volleyball in slides flashed rapidly on a screen. Volleyball players and nonplayers attempted the task under competitive and noncompetitive conditions. Overall, players were faster than nonplayers, but the more important finding was that competition increased arousal (assessed as increases in heart rate) and elicited faster times in both players and nonplayers, with a much greater increase in speed for players. Competition also decreased accuracy on the detection task, but Starkes and Allard asserted that the increased speed was more striking than the decreased accuracy and that volleyball players may purposely choose to sacrifice a small degree of accuracy for a fast response. The results from Starkes and Allard and Gross and Gill (1982) imply that performers can adopt varying speed and accuracy strategies depending on the task demands and that competition may further modify the speed and accuracy of performance.

Competition and Winning or Losing

The social influence of competition on performance may be complex, and to complicate matters even further, we must consider winning and losing, or success and failure. Success or failure affects competitors' emotions, satisfaction, and perceived ability (e.g., Gill, 1977) and likely affects performance in competition. In a controlled experiment, Martens and White (1975) systematically varied the win–loss ratio and reported that people performed better when the ratio was

50–50 than when it was higher or lower. This finding fits with the achievement motivation literature discussed in chapter 8; achievement situations with a 50% chance of success represent maximum challenge and elicit the strongest achievement efforts.

Cooperation Within Competition

In sport and exercise psychology, we often assume that competition is the model and that cooperation is a different world. However, a moment's reflection should counter that view. Most sport and exercise activity, even highly competitive athletics, involves considerable cooperation. Within the classic reward definition framework (Deutsch, 1949), competition is a zero-sum game: What one wins, the other loses. In a cooperative situation, everyone works for the same goal and shares in the rewards. We can also add the typical third situation—the individual structure—in which what one person achieves has no effect on anyone else.

Triplett's (1898) early research set the stage for the common assumption that competition leads to better performance than cooperation or individual structures. Despite the firmly held belief in competition, though, considerable evidence indicates that cooperation leads to greater achievement as well as greater social and psychological benefits in most areas of society, including sport and exercise. Cooperation even aids in bicycle racing. Albert (1991) used ethnographic and interview approaches to investigate the subculture of bicycle racing, and his data counter the conventional view of unambiguous conflict or competition among racers. Instead, cooperative efforts between opponents were central to the social order, with strong sanctions for noncompliance. Albert further noted that media coverage, which ignores cooperative efforts, creates and perpetuates erroneous stereotypes.

Several educational psychologists have researched cooperative learning environments (for reviews of research on cooperative groups, see Hertz-Lazarowitz & Miller, 1992), and the conclusions are uniform—cooperative learning environments lead to achievement, learning, and social and psychological development. Johnson and Johnson (1992), who have extended this work to sport and exercise, have summarized their own research (more than 80 studies over 20 years) as well as more than 500 other studies comparing cooperative, competitive, and individualistic structures. In terms of achievement or productivity, cooperation was most effective, with an advantage over both competitive (effect size = .67) and individualistic (effect size = .66) structures.

Stanne's (1993) dissertation at the University of Minnesota (Johnson and Johnson's institution) was a meta-analysis of social interdependence (cooperation) and motor performance—the particular interest of sport and exercise psychology. Stanne found similar cooperative advantages over competition (effect size = .82) and individualist structures (effect size = .66). In their review, Johnson and Johnson (1992) offered three general conclusions:

1. Under a broad range of conditions, cooperative efforts resulted in higher achievements and greater productivity than did competitive or individualistic efforts.

2. Generally, cooperative efforts resulted in greater interpersonal attraction and more social support than did competitive or individualistic efforts.

3. Generally, cooperative efforts resulted in higher self-esteem and greater psychological health than did competitive or individualistic efforts.

The evidence is convincing. But we should not view sport as a contest between competition and cooperation. Competition is a social process, and even competitive sport activities typically involve cooperation or social interdependence. Researchers and practitioners would do a great service if we devoted more attention to developing and maintaining effective social interdependence in sport and exercise settings, whether we work with intercollegiate athletes, children in a community sport program, or adults in a cardiac rehabilitation clinic.

Application Point

The belief that competition is the best way to get performance gains is a common belief in sport and exercise contexts. In light of what you have read thus far, what is the role of competition and cooperation in physical activity and rehabilitation settings?

SOCIAL LEARNING THEORY

Social facilitation and the home advantage help explain the emergence of behavior in different social settings and are consistent with Bandura (1977, 1986), who was interested in the process by which people learn social behavior. According to his social learning theory, the situation in which people find themselves affects their behavior. For example, you may behave differently in the classroom than you do in the gym or with your parents than you do with your friends. Variations in the environment that change the way people view the situation can influence behavior. For example, shooting a free throw early in the game is typically different than shooting a free throw with the scored tied with no time remaining in the game. Behavior, though, is not merely a function of situation and the person in that situation. Rather, behavior, the person, and the situation constantly influence each other. A change in one has meaning to the others.

With a specific focus on social behavior, Bandura posited that we learn social behavior through direct reinforcement and observational learning. With a detailed discussion of reinforcement in chapter 7, we will turn our attention to observational learning and modeling.

MODELING: THE DEMONSTRATION PROCESS

Key Point

The first two processes of modeling, attention and retention, relate to learning or acquisition of a skill. The motor-reproduction and motivation processes determine actual performance of the acquired skill.

People learn by observing others. Observational learning via modeling is most prominent in sport and exercise. Instructors teach by modeling and instruct students to "watch how I do it." The pervasiveness of observational learning raises many questions. Does modeling provide information or motivation to change motor performance? When and how often should skills be demonstrated? Who should demonstrate skills? Should parts of complex skills and common errors be demonstrated or only complete, correct skills? Sport and exercise psychologists and other motor-behavior researchers continue to search for the answers. According to Bandura's (1986) social-cognitive theory, when we observe others we form a cognitive representation of the action that serves as a reference of correctness. Specifically, modeling affects behaviors through the four-component process illustrated in figure 13.1. The first two processes, attention and retention, relate to learning or acquisition of the skill. The motor-reproduction and motivation processes determine actual performance of the skill.

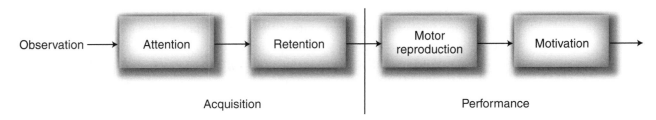

Figure 13.1
Component processes in Bandura's social learning analysis of observational learning.
BANDURA, ALBERT, SOCIAL LEARNING THEORY, 1st, © 1977. Electronically reproduced by permission of Pearson Education, Inc., Upper Saddle River, NJ.

ATTENTIONAL PROCESSES

To learn any skill through modeling, people must first pay attention to the model. Specifically, they must attend to and accurately perceive the significant features of the modeled behavior. If your tennis instructor demonstrates a backhand return but you are watching the ball instead, you may not pick up the key elements of the stance, swing, and follow-through. Many factors, including characteristics of the model, the observer, and the skill, can affect attentional processes. For instance, young athletes attend to and imitate their favorite professional players. They not only imitate effective techniques but also may pick up an awkward stance or learn to yell at umpires. Models usually present more information than an observer, especially a beginner, can process effectively, so observational learning can be enhanced by channeling attention to critical features of the demonstrated skill (Minas, 1980). Generally, athletes are attentive because they like their instructors, trust their instructors' knowledge, and want to improve their skills. Thus, the instructor may use cues or techniques to direct the learner's attention to key elements of the skill.

RETENTION PROCESSES

People must not only attend to the model, they must remember the modeled behavior. Retention involves developing symbolic representations of the skill that serve as internal models for later action. Activities that aid retention, particularly imagery and verbal or symbolic coding, can improve observational learning (Bandura & Jeffery, 1973). For example, mentally rehearsing the tennis serve immediately after a demonstration may strengthen the performer's image of the skill. Good instructors are masters at giving just the right cues or phrases to help performers code the skill in memory. For example, dance students usually remember steps with phrases such as "step-together-step."

Motor-Reproduction Processes

After attending to and retaining a modeled skill, performers must match their actions to the internal representation of correct performance, which is not easy. Most people can watch Michael Jordan slam-dunk a basketball and retain a clear image of how to perform that skill but will never do a slam dunk. Of course, we usually do not demonstrate skills unless we believe observers can do them. On the other hand, even a capable student does not immediately imitate a complex golf swing or complicated gymnastics move. After modeling sets up an internal image of the skill, performers self-correct and practice with an instructor's feedback in order to gradually match actual performance to that image. Physical capabilities, the ability to retain appropriate responses, and accurate feedback are important considerations in the motor-reproduction phase.

Motivational Processes

The final component in Bandura's model is motivation. We do not imitate everything we learn through observation. External reinforcement (reinforcement to the performer), vicarious reinforcement (reinforcement to the model), and self-reinforcement all help determine which behaviors we will imitate. When you see a teammate elude a defender with a particular dribbling move, you have incentive to imitate that move. Likewise, if your instructor praises you for getting the idea of the demonstrated serve, you will probably keep trying to do it.

MODELING AND MOTOR PERFORMANCE

Generally, the quality of a motor skill is determined by the movement form and outcome, and both of these aspects can be influenced by modeling (McCullagh & Weiss, 2001). Earlier research showed that modeling provides information about how to perform motor skills (Feltz, 1982; Feltz & Landers, 1977; Gould, 1978; Martens, Burwitz, & Zuckerman, 1976). For example, Gould (1978) compared the effectiveness of modeling across several motor tasks and reported that modeling was more helpful for a complex task with several steps than for relatively simple tasks.

Research by Weiss and colleagues (McCullagh, Stiehl, & Weiss, 1990; Weiss, 1983; Weiss & Klint, 1987) suggests that age or developmental level also influences the effectiveness of modeling. For example, older children (aged 7-8) performed equally well after observing either a silent or a verbal model, but younger children (aged 4-5) improved only after observing the verbal model (Weiss, 1983). Interestingly, Weiss and Klint (1987) found no age differences; children ranging in age from 5 to 10 years all experienced the performance-enhancing effects of verbal rehearsal. In a subsequent study, McCullagh and colleagues (1990) discovered that the effectiveness of the model partly depended on whether the performance outcome or movement form was assessed. Viewing a model resulted in higher form scores regardless of verbal rehearsal. Interestingly, people who received verbal instructions with no modeling were better able to recall the order of tasks. Collectively, these results suggest that it is necessary to consider developmental factors, particularly verbal-cognitive abilities, when examining the observational learning process.

The characteristics of the model may also have motivational effects. In their review, McCullagh and Weiss (2001) suggest the following:

- Although it is intuitive to assume that skilled models would be the best type of model to use because they would provide the most accurate cognitive representation of the skill, research has not consistently supported this assumption. Learning by watching someone else learn a skill (i.e., a learning

model) and receiving corrective feedback has been shown to be an effective tool for enhancing motor performance.

• Coping models can be effective for teaching skills to people for whom the performance is accompanied by apprehension or fear. Coping models verbalize their increasing confidence regarding their ability to complete the task, improve, and overcome their fear as they are improving. Weiss, McCullagh, Smith, and Berlant (1998) found that children fearful of swimming improved in swimming equally as well with coping models as with mastery models (similar to skilled models).

• Although Bandura (1986) suggested that models with higher status would be more effective than those with lower status, research has produced equivocal findings. It was thought that higher-status models would command more attention from the learner, thus resulting in greater learning, but research by McCullagh (1987) brings into question whether model characteristics affect attention.

Perceived similarity of the model may explain why it has been difficult to discern which model characteristics influence performance. That is, learners may perform better when they perceive the model to be like them. For example, Gould and Weiss (1981) found that among female sport participants, a similar model (athletic female) resulted in greater endurance performance than dissimilar model (unathletic male).

MODELING OF NONPERFORMANCE BEHAVIORS

Although the influence of modeling on performance is our main concern, models also influence nonperformance behaviors. As discussed in chapter 6, vicarious experiences are a major source of self-efficacy. Modeling can enhance self-efficacy and reduce anxiety on fear-provoking sport tasks as well as facilitate performance (Feltz, Landers, & Raeder, 1979; McAuley, 1985). Lirgg and Feltz (1991) found that people who watched a skilled model were more efficacious than those viewing either no model or unskilled models.

One of the most notable roles of modeling is in the development of aggressive and prosocial behaviors. Bandura is widely recognized for his Bobo doll experiments demonstrating the influence of models on the learning and performance of aggressive behaviors (see chapter 14). As we will discuss in more detail in chapter 14, modeling probably plays a major role in violent and aggressive behaviors in sport. Research (Bryan & Walbek, 1970) implies that our actions speak louder than our words when communicating social behaviors.

Bryan (1969) compared the relative importance of words and deeds on the generosity behaviors of elementary school children. After playing a miniature bowling game, the children received certificates that they could either redeem for prizes or donate to the poor. The model in the study either acted generously and donated the certificates or acted greedily and kept them. At the same time, the model either preached generosity by extolling the values of charity or preached greed by pointing out that the certificates were earned and need not be donated.

Bryan's findings confirmed that actions spoke louder than words. Children did as the model did regardless of what the model said. Children were just as generous when the model preached greed but donated the certificates as when the model both preached and practiced generosity, and the findings were analogous when the model kept the certificates. Bryan did suggest that words might provoke thoughts and have long-term effects on behavior even if they did not affect immediate actions. Nevertheless, his findings imply that out-of-shape instructors advocating fitness exercises and coaches who talk about being a good sport while storming up and down the sidelines may be wasting their breath.

Application Point
There is an old adage: Actions speak louder than words. Does the research support this saying? If so, how so? If not, what questions need to be answered to determine this?

MODELS: THE SELF AND SIGNIFICANT OTHERS

The previous sections provided evidence for modeling effects. But, just who are these models? Research has primarily focused on parents, peers, and coaches, the primary socializing agents who can influence cognitions, affect, behaviors, and overall self-concept throughout life. Recent research has also shown that we can learn from ourselves. In this final section of this chapter, we will discuss both the self and others. We begin with the self because the research is limited to modeling effects and move on to discuss significant others as social influences.

Self-Observation

Although we often think of observing others, technological advances provide us with greater opportunity to observe ourselves. Summarizing the work of Dorrick (1999), McCullagh and Weiss (2002) identify three methods of self-observation. Using videotape feedback, people can watch themselves execute skills and behaviors and then self-critique and improve performances. In self-modeling, participants watch themselves perform a correct or adaptive behavior of which they are capable. This often requires editing the videotape. Using feed-forward techniques, people watch themselves performing behaviors beyond their capabilities.

Self-observation is thought to be especially effective because research in the physical domain has highlighted the importance of model similarity on performance and psychological responses. McCullagh and Weiss (2001) report on the efficacy of self-observation in the physical domain and cite research indicating that self-modeling may be more effective than peer modeling relative to learning, self-efficacy, and anxiety effects (Starek & McCullagh, 1999). However, two studies have provided evidence that self-modeling does not enhance self-efficacy or performance (Ram & McCullagh, 2003; Winfrey & Weeks, 1993). Certainly, more research needs to be done in the area of self-observation.

Significant Others as Social Influences

As we move on to the significant others, remember that modeling is just one way that significant others influence cognitions, affect, and behavior. Significant others are also just one aspect of a person's environment, but an important one. According to Eccles (2004; Eccles, Wigfield, & Schiefele, 1998), significant others can affect people's self-perceptions, attitudes, values, beliefs, and behaviors. Further, the relationship is thought to be reciprocal; people can also affect the attitudes, values, beliefs, and behaviors of their significant others.

Most of the sport and exercise psychology research on significant others has focused on parents, peers, and coaches. Parental influence is particularly strong in childhood, with peers and coaches becoming more influential as children approach adolescence (Coakley, 1993; Greendorfer, 1977; Greendorfer, Lewko, & Rosengren, 1996; Horn & Weiss, 1991; Weiss & Frazer, 1995). Most research involves coaches, but we are gaining knowledge on the role of parents and beginning to consider the role of peers and siblings. Despite the complexity of social relations with and between social groups (Ullrich-French & Smith, 2006), in this section we will examine the literature dealing with parents, peers, and coaches separately.

> **Key Point**
>
> Three socializing agents can influence physical activity–related cognitions, affect, and behaviors, as well as overall self-concept throughout life: parents, peers, and coaches.

Parents

Horn and Horn (2007) explain that parents' belief and value systems (e.g., their attitudes, values, and beliefs) determine the parents' behaviors toward their child. The behaviors (e.g., modeling, providing opportunities, emotional support) then influence the child's belief and value systems, which determine the child's behavior (see figure 13.2).

Values can be evaluated in four ways (Fredricks & Eccles, 2004). First, parents can assess the *utility value* of physical activity (e.g., sport, exercise, rehabilitation) in terms of how useful it is to the child's current and future goals. *Intrinsic value* is assessed in terms of enjoyment the child may experience. *Attainment value* is assessed in terms of how important it is for the child to do well in the activity. Finally, *cost* is assessed in terms of the negative consequences (e.g., financial, psychological, emotional, social) of participation. Further, parents

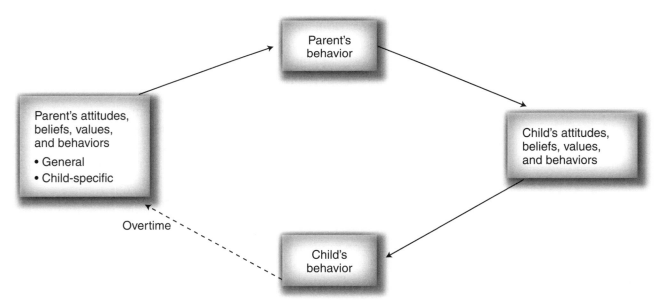

Figure 13.2
Parental behaviors such as modeling, providing opportunities, and emotional support affect a child's belief and value systems, which ultimately determine the child's behavior.

hold two types of belief systems: general beliefs about physical activity and beliefs that are specific to their child (Fredricks & Eccles, 2004). For example, a father could value sport and believe that his daughter is better suited for softball than volleyball.

Horn and Horn's (2007) review indicates that parents' general belief systems do relate to children's belief systems and their behavior. For example, the more children perceive that their parents value sport participation the more likely they are to perceive themselves as competent, value their own sport participation more, and actually participate (Eccles & Harold, 1991; Fredrick & Eccles, 2005). Stuart's (2003) qualitative research suggests that parents' beliefs and values, particularly utility values, about sport participation affected children's own values about their sport participation.

Research examining parents' belief and value systems specific to their child also supports the social influence of the parent. Eccles and Harrold (1991) suggest that parental influence is expressed in two ways. First, parents who value a given activity and hold high expectations are more likely to seek out that type of activity for their child. Second, parents help their children interpret information about their ability. Parental influence gives children reason to want to do well and to believe they can do well (Brustad, 1993, 1996; Dempsey, Kimiecik, & Horn, 1996; Fredricks & Eccles, 2002; Kimiecik & Horn, 1998; Kimiecik, Horn, & Shurin, 1996; Xiang, McBride, & Bruene, 2003).

Brustad (1988) has focused on the child's psychological outcomes and argued that we must start with an understanding of parents' expectancies and values and then explore how these influence children's psychosocial development, including attraction to physical activity. Brustad (1993, 1996) found that fourth-graders were more attracted to physical activity when they perceived themselves to be more competent, and those who perceived themselves as more competent had parents who encouraged them to participate. These encouraging parents enjoyed physical activity more than parents who were less encouraging. Boys reported receiving more encouragement from their parents than girls, and boys also viewed themselves as more competent than girls—further supporting the relationship between encouragement and perceived competence. Perhaps if parents encouraged their daughters as much as their sons, girls would perceive themselves as more competent and in turn be more attracted to physical activity.

The work of several researchers (Dempsey et al., 1996; Fredricks & Eccles, 2002; Kimiecik & Horn, 1998; Kimiecik et al., 1996; Xiang et al., 2003) examining parental beliefs associated with children's self-perceptions and participation in physical activity has provided several interesting findings. Their research demonstrates that (a) parents who value physical activity are more likely to have children who are effortful and better performers; (b) parents who perceive their children to be competent in physical activity are more likely to have children who perceive themselves to be competent and who are attracted to physical activity; (c) fathers' perceptions of their child's ability is more strongly related to the child's own perceptions of ability than the mothers' perceptions; and (d) children who believe they are competent in physical activity are more likely to engage in it. That is, children are more likely to be physically active, effortful in their physical activity, and perform well when they believe they are capable, and they are more likely to believe this if their parents do. Further research is needed to clarify the relationships among these elements.

As noted by Horn and Horn (2007), the children of parents who perceive them as competent and have high expectations are advantaged, but it is also possible to hold expectations that are too high. Unrealistic parental expectations have been linked with anxiety, stress, burnout, and injury. Despite the need for further research on socializing effects of parents, it is evident that parents play a big role in shaping children's sport and exercise behaviors. Children's peers also play a role in shaping attitudes, cognitions, and behaviors relative to physical activity.

Peers

Peer influence in sport and physical activity is well documented (e.g., Gill, Gross, & Huddleston, 1983). As discussed in chapter 8, children indicate that being with friends is an important reason for their sport participation, and peer comparison is an important source of competence information (e.g., Weiss, Ebbeck, & Horn, 1997). Research has also shown that conflict resolution via dialogue with peers can positively influence children's moral development (e.g., Romance, Weiss, & Bockoven, 1986).

Although peers are important, particularly in youth sport, the systematic study of peer groups, relations, or interactions in sport is in its infancy. Relying heavily on developmental psychology, Weiss and colleagues (Smith, 1999; Weiss & Smith, 2002; Weiss, Smith, & Theeboom, 1996) began an in-depth investigation into peer relationships. Current research on peer relationships focuses on friendship and peer acceptance. Friendship involves having a close, mutual, dyadic relationship, whereas peer acceptance (Smith, 2003) involves status (worthiness) and popularity (likability) within a group.

Smith, Weiss, and their colleagues (Smith, 1999; Weiss & Smith, 1999, 2002; Weiss et al., 1996) examined the nature of friendship and the relationships among peers, as well as various psychosocial and motivational variables. One of the earliest studies in this line of research began with the investigation of the nature of friendship in physical activity. Based on interviews with 38 athletes aged 8 to 16 years, Weiss and colleagues (1996) found both positive and negative dimensions of friendship. Children reported that they liked the companionship, having fun while playing, the acceptance and respect of friends (self-esteem enhancement), the help they received, the nice things their best friends did for them (prosocial behavior), the mutual trust and understanding (intimacy), the common interests, and the mutual emotional support of friendship.

Several aspects of friendship were also discussed in both positive and negative terms. For instance, children liked their best friends but recognized their faults. Participants liked the loyalty when their best friends stuck up for them and not surprisingly did not like to be betrayed. Betrayal included such things as when a best friend "pays more attention to another friend" (Weiss et al., 1996, p. 371). Lastly, participants did not like conflict with their best friends, but they did note that conflict was rare and easy to resolve. From these findings, the Sport Friendship Quality Scale (SFQS) was developed (Weiss & Smith, 1999), which has been used in much of the research on peer relationships.

Continued investigations of peer relationships have demonstrated that peer acceptance and friendship quality are potentially meaningful constructs in physical activity and human movement. For example, Smith (1999) examined the influence of peer relationships on motivation and affective responses associated with physical activity among 418 middle school students. Smith found that adolescents who have close personal friendships within physical activity are more apt to like the activity, to be more motivated to achieve through hard work, and to be active participants. Additionally, those who reported greater self-worth were also more apt to have a sense of pride and confidence in physical activity endeavors.

Positive peer relationships are associated with higher perceived competence, more self-determined motivation, higher enjoyment, stronger feelings of self-esteem, and greater sport commitment (McDonough & Crocker, 2005; Ullrich-French & Smith, 2006; Weiss & Smith, 2002). Further, it is thought a close friendship or high peer acceptance may buffer the negative effects of lacking one or the other. For example, acceptance by one's peers may buffer the negative effects of not having a close friendship. Smith and colleagues (Smith, Ullrich-French, Walker, & Hurley, 2006) examined the motivational profile of 10- to 14-year-old boys and girls. Not surprisingly, participants with positive friendship quality and peer acceptance had the most adaptive profile and participants with poor friendship quality and lack of peer acceptance had the worse. However, it doesn't appear that the nature of friendship quality makes an overall difference when peer acceptance is low. For example, participants who perceived low peer acceptance scored lower on perceived competence and sport enjoyment and scored higher on self-presentational concerns and anxiety than the more adaptive groups.

In a recent review, Weiss and Stuntz (2004) remind us that peer acceptance is linked with athletic ability. Generally, good athletes are accepted by their peers, particularly those participating in activities perceived as gender appropriate. Popularity rates were highest among females who participated in traditionally feminine sports such as volleyball and among males who participated in traditionally male sports such as football (e.g., Holland & Andre, 1994). Highly skilled athletes are also granted leadership opportunities. For example, the highly skilled participants (a sample of boys) were the team captains, selected team members, and decided who would play and where (Evans & Roberts, 1987), and girls who were viewed by their teammates as physically skilled, confident, and expressive were rated the most favorably. The types of leadership opportunities provided by physical prowess and peer acceptance result in opportunities for further development both physically and socially. This may contribute to the reason why young people with higher perceived peer acceptance are also more apt to have high physical self-worth (Smith, 1999).

Although still young, initial research on peer relationship indicates that peers are indeed a powerful socializing agent, but coaches, who structure the sporting environment, are also highly influential. In the next section, we will briefly summarize what we know about coaches as socializing agents.

Coaches

Early research focused on coaches' leadership behavior and the influence of feedback patterns on athlete cognitions, affect, and behavior. For example, Chelladurai's (1993) multidimensional model of leadership and related research, discussed in chapter 15, suggests that the more the leader's actual behaviors match the preferences of the group members and the situation requirements, the better the group's performance and the greater the group members' satisfaction.

Research using Chelladurai's (1993) model and Smith and Smoll's (1997) work on coaching effectiveness, discussed in chapter 7, indicates that athletes seem to be satisfied with the leadership of coaches who emphasize training and instruction and positive feedback contingent on good performance.

Social Influence in Exercise Settings

In a meta-analysis on social influence and exercise, Carron, Hausenblas, and Mack (1996) defined social influence as including family, important others, class leaders, and group cohesion, as well as more traditional social facilitation (coexercisers). They concluded that social influence has a small to moderate positive effect (effect size from .20 to .50) on exercise behaviors, cognitions, and affect. However, the larger effects did not involve traditional audience influences. Moderate to large effects were found for family support and attitudes, task cohesion and adherence, important others and attitudes, and family support and compliance behavior.

Similarly, several studies (e.g., Bray, Gyurcsik, Martin Ginis, & Culos-Reed, 2004; Turner, Rejeski, & Brawley, 1997) investigated the influence of exercise leaders who engaged in either bland or socially enriched interactions. In the socially enriched environment, exercise leaders followed a positive approach similar to Smith and Smoll's positive coaching model (discussed in chapter 7), provided encouragement and reinforcement, showed interest in individuals, and engaged participants in general conversation. Lox, Martin Ginis, and Petruzzello (2006) concluded that socially supportive instructors have the following positive effects in a single exercise class:

- Greater exercise self-efficacy
- More energy and enthusiasm
- Less postexercise fatigue
- Less concern about embarrassing themselves and trying new things
- More enjoyment
- Greater confidence in the instructor's capabilities
- Stronger intentions to join future exercise classes

Although research on specific exercise behaviors and adherence is lacking, Lox et al. (2006) further note that preliminary findings suggest positive effects. Bray, Gyurcsik, Culos-Reed, et al. (2001) found that when participants were more confident in their fitness instructor, they attended more classes.

These studies reflect the current work on social influence in the real world. Early social influence work with drive models and isolated variables focused on limited performance responses rather than the full range of cognitions, feelings, and behaviors. The current research emphasizes social support and represents the complexities of interpersonal relationships and group dynamics in sport and exercise, as discussed in more detail in chapter 15.

PUTTING IT INTO PRACTICE

Now you are ready to put the content of chapter 13 into practice. Read the chapter summary, discuss the case study, answer the review questions, and enhance your knowledge by researching the recommended readings.

Summary

Social influence is prominent in sport and exercise, but we have abandoned the limited approaches of the early research on social facilitation and moved to more process-oriented and multifaceted approaches. Audiences and instructors are not passive evaluators or simply providers of reinforcement. Competition is not a simple stimulus but an interactive process involving cooperative behavior. Effective social influence can enhance physical activity for all participants. Through modeling, people learn social behaviors for sport and exercise participation. Most commonly, people learn through reinforcement and observation. We tend to act in a way we will be rewarded for, and we imitate those we wish to learn from. Parents, peers, and coaches and exercise leaders are the primary significant others in physical activity settings.

Case Study

This chapter brings together theories and research of social influence. For this case, use the chapter material to develop a plan that uses a variety of social influence strategies to enhance physical activity performance and attitudes.

The local park and recreation department is planning their annual campaign to increase the membership. This year they are particularly interested in targeting family memberships, and the director wants to ensure that worthwhile programs are available to families. As the exercise and fitness specialist, you've been asked to develop the Families Together and Active program. The primary goals of your program are to improve participants' performance and to foster positive attitudes toward physical activity. Present your program to the director. Include a brief description of the program and explain how the program is designed to meet its goals.

Hints: Refer to the theories of social influence that guide your program. Identify elements of the program that should lead to enhanced performance and attitudes, explain why this is so, and refer to research that supports the effectiveness of the program.

Review Questions

1. Define *social facilitation*.
2. Explain the relationship between drive theory and social facilitation.
3. Trace the research documenting evidence of the home advantage.
4. Contrast social facilitation and social reinforcement.
5. Describe the effect of competition on performance.
6. Explain how modeling affects behavior by relating the concepts of attention processes, retention processes, motor-reproduction processes, and motivation processes.
7. Describe performance and nonperformance modeling effects.
8. Identify the four types of models discussed in this chapter and explain how they can influence physical activity–related cognitions and behaviors in young athletes.
9. Explain the role of social support and positive social interaction in the exercise setting.

Recommended Reading

Carron, A.V., Hausenblas, H.A., & Mack, D. (1996). Social influence: A meta-analysis. *Journal of Sport & Exercise Psychology, 18,* 1-16.

This article presents a meta-analysis of the literature on social influence. The authors summarize a long-time research topic and provide interpretations that may help take research in more productive directions.

Carron, A.V., Loughhead, T.M., & Bray, S.R. (2005). The home advantage in sport competitions: Courneya and Carron's (1992) conceptual framework a decade later. *Journal of Sports Sciences, 23,* 395-407.

This article presents a revised conceptual framework of the home advantage. The framework presented may re-ignite research in this area and take it in more productive directions.

Smith, A.L. (2003). Peer relationships in physical activity contexts: A road less traveled in youth sport and exercise psychology research. *Psychology of Sport and Exercise, 4,* 25-39.

This article provides a rationale for pursuing research on peer relationships. The author overviews the existing literature, emphasizes the relevance of peers to a variety of psychosocial and motivational variables, and discusses future research directions.

Chapter 14

Aggression and Character Development

Chapter Objectives

After studying this chapter, you should be able to

◆ explain several concepts and theories of aggression,

◆ understand the effects of aggression on performance, and

◆ understand the concept of character development and how it can be encouraged in sport and exercise.

Aggressive behavior is obvious in sport and physical activity. We often see basketball players fight for rebounds or runners throw elbows and jostle for position in a race. At the more extreme end of the spectrum, you may have read about the Tennessee Titan defensive tackle who kicked the helmetless Dallas Cowboys center in the head twice ("Notebook: Cowboys C. Gurode needs stitches after being kicked," 2006, October); the father who beat his son's ice hockey coach to death following an altercation about practice (Butterfield, 2003, July); or the South American soccer player who was killed when he tried to calm rival fans who invaded the field at halftime ("Argentine footballer shot in riot," 2005, August). Of course, not all aggressive sport behavior is violent or as egregious as these examples. Many forms of aggressive behavior are accepted and even promoted as part of the game.

Using the term *aggression* to refer to such a wide range of behaviors can cause confusion. We label violent outbursts in sport as aggression but also talk about the aggressive player who takes chances in a close contest. Value judgments and emotional connotations further cloud our understanding. We encourage certain aggressive behaviors and praise people who use so-called good aggressive tactics, but we consider bad aggressive acts to be shocking. Most aggressive behaviors in physical activity are neither clearly desirable nor clearly undesirable. Instead, they are usually viewed as distasteful by some and as justifiable by others. Although not all researchers will agree (see Mummendey & Mummendey, 1983), we can explain aggression more easily if we do not think of aggression as totally positive or negative but simply as behavior that we want to understand.

In this chapter we will consider concepts and theories of aggression and then look more closely at aggression in sport, including its antecedents and its effects on performance. We will then give some attention to the other side of the coin—the development of character in sport.

DEFINING AGGRESSION

Before we discuss explanations of aggression, we need to clarify terms. We can all agree that some behaviors constitute aggression. When Nolan Ryan put a headlock on Robin Ventura and pummeled him with six punches (Wulf, 1993), that was clearly an act of aggression. Take a minute and write down a definition that you think clearly delineates behaviors that you consider aggressive.

Now, let's see how well your definition works as you watch the play-off game between two youth ice hockey teams, the Blue Bombers and the Red Barons.

1. Mark, one of the Bombers' top players, slams Jeff, a Baron forward, into the boards to keep him away from the puck (a perfectly legal move).

2. Jeff retaliates by swinging his stick and smashing Mark in the ribs (not a perfectly legal move).

3. When the same thing occurs later in the game, Jeff again tries to retaliate by swinging his stick at Mark, but Mark skates away and Jeff misses.

4. Tim, Mark's younger brother and the least skilled Bomber player, gets into the game for his required ice time in the final minute. Tim is defending the goal as Baron forward Marcia skates toward it to take a shot that could tie the game. Tim tries to take the puck away from Marcia, catches his stick on her skate, and accidentally trips her.

5. Missing her chance to make the tying goal and become the first girl to score a hat trick in a play-off game, Marcia jumps up and yells at Tim that he's a wimp who "should stick to figure skating and eating quiche."

6. Gary, Marcia's father and the Barons' assistant coach, sees his team's championship hopes end as the time runs out and smashes his clipboard over the bench.

How many of those incidents do you consider to be aggression? Does your definition clearly demarcate aggressive from nonaggressive incidents? Do you define legal tactics as aggression? What about accidental injuries? What if someone tries to hit you but misses? Can aggression be verbal? Is throwing a golf club aggression? Not everyone will agree on the answers to all of these questions. However, most agree that aggression involves the intent to injure. That is, when Jeff swings his stick at Mark and misses, it is aggression, but Tim's accidental tripping of Marcia is not. Most definitions of aggression include this notion of the intent to harm. In *Human Aggression,* Baron and Richardson (1994) offer the following representative definition:

Aggression is any form of behavior directed toward the goal of harming or injuring another living being who is motivated to avoid such treatment. (p. 7)

This definition raises several key points. First, aggression is behavior. It is not an attitude, emotion, or motive. Wanting to hurt someone is not aggression. Anger and thoughts might play a role in aggressive behavior, but they are not defining characteristics. Unlike violence, aggression includes verbal and nonverbal acts. *Violence* refers to extreme physical aggression (Widmeyer, Dorsch, Bray, & McGuire, 2002). Second, aggression is directed or intentional behavior. Accidental harm is not aggression, but acts that are intended to injure are, whether successful or not. Third, aggression involves harm or injury. Aggressive acts are intended to cause physical or psychological harm or to deprive a person of something, as when destroying a teammate's equipment. Purposeful, goal-directed behavior performed with no intent to harm is referred to as *assertion*. Fourth, aggression involves living beings. According to Baron and Richardson (1994), kicking your dog is aggression, but kicking a bench is not. Finally, Baron and Richardson limit aggression to incidents in which the victim is motivated to avoid such treatment, eliminating sadomasochistic and suicidal acts from the definition.

Aggression is not accidental. Aggression can be categorized by the end goal of the act and the presence of anger (Bushman & Anderson, 2001). Behavior performed for the sole purpose of causing harm and done with anger is referred to as *hostile aggression*. Here both the intent and the end goal are to cause harm, and the behavior is often impulsive. Intentionally harmful behavior performed as a means to achieve a nonaggressive goal is referred to as *instrumental aggression*. A vicious tackle to get the star player out of the game is instrumental aggression. Here the behavior is intentional, but causing harm is the means to the end goal. Instrumental aggression is typically premeditated.

Application Point

You call it—violence, assertion, aggression, or an accident? These examples are designed to help you become more familiar with the concepts. Do not worry if you run into a classmate with a different answer than yours. The key here is to be able to defend your call knowledgeably.

1. Worried about a patient's slow recovery, a physical therapist tells her client, "Your failure to do home therapy and your lack of effort for the exercises you do at the clinic are the cause of your slow recovery. You must work much, much harder if you are going to achieve your goal of walking independently in 2 months."
2. A basketball coach breaks a chair in protesting a disputed call.
3. After a bad practice, the football coach calls his players stupid.
4. A pitcher throws a fastball that gets away from her and hits the batter.
5. Behind by two strokes on the 18th hole, a golfer deliberately coughs as her opponent tees off in hopes of throwing her off her game.
6. A race-car driver spins out of control around a curve and hits the car of a competitor, paralyzing him for life.
7. A boxer knocks out his opponent with a crushing blow to the head.
8. Disagreeing with the linesman, a player questions the call by pointing to the mark made by the ball on the clay court so the linesperson will see her error and change her call.
9. An umpire is taken to the emergency room with possible brain damage after a coach attacked him from behind with a bat.

THEORIES OF AGGRESSION

The aggression literature is rich in theory. Because of its prevalence and social implications, people want to know why aggression occurs, what characteristics predispose a person to aggression, what environmental and social factors elicit it, and whether it can be directed or controlled. Explanations of aggression fall into three major categories: instinct theories, drive theories, and social learning theories.

Instinct Theories

Instinct theories propose that aggressiveness is an innate characteristic: We are born with an instinct that makes aggressive behavior inevitable. This ethological approach to aggression was made most familiar through the work of Konrad Lorenz (1966) and others who assert that aggression is an innate fighting instinct developed through evolution. Much of the ethological literature draws comparisons between humans and other species. Ardrey (1966), for example, discusses the tendency of animals to defend their territory with aggressive behaviors and notes that humans do the same thing. For example, do you consider it an invasion if another person bypasses all the empty tables in the library to sit right next to you?

According to Lorenz, the fighting instinct spontaneously generates aggressive energy that builds up, like steam in a boiler, until it is released through an aggressive act. The more built-up energy there is, the more easily the aggressive behavior is triggered and the more potentially destructive the outburst is. Lorenz suggests that because aggressive energy always accumulates, the best way to prevent destructive violence is to ensure that people release aggressive energy in less destructive ways. Ethologists strongly advocate competitive sport as one of the best ways for people to let off steam. Lorenz asserted that the greatest value of sport is its provision of an outlet for aggressive energy, and Storr (1968) presented the following view:

> It is obvious that the encouragement of competition in all possible fields is likely to diminish the kind of hostility which leads to war rather than to increase it . . . . Rivalry between nations in sport can do nothing but good. (p. 132)

Although many coaches and teachers are attracted to these aspects of the instinct theory, most researchers do not accept the psychoanalytic or ethological explanations of aggressive behavior. Instinct theories predict that all people and cultures have the same innate urges, generate similar levels of aggressive energy, and exhibit similar levels of aggressive behavior. Cross-cultural comparisons, however, suggest that this is not the case. Instinct theories also imply that the cultures with the greatest number of nondestructive outlets for aggression, or the most aggressive games, will be the least warlike. Again, anthropological evidence suggests otherwise. Are athletes who participate in the most aggressive competitive sports the calmest and least aggressive people off the field? Perhaps some are, but this generalization would probably not hold across many comparisons. Most psychologists do not accept instinct theories but believe instead that reasoning plays a critical role.

Drive Theories

Drive theory, the second major theoretical perspective on aggression, has more credibility among psychologists. The most notable drive approach is the frustration–aggression hypothesis of Dollard, Doob, Miller, Mowrer, and Sears (1939). The hypothesis holds that frustration always leads to some form of aggression, and aggression always stems from frustration. Frustration does not cause aggression directly; instead, it induces an aggressive drive, which in turn facilitates aggressive behavior.

The proposition that frustration always leads to aggression fits with many of our personal experiences in sport, but it is not widely advocated today. Retain-

Key Point

The most notable drive approach is the frustration–aggression hypothesis, which holds that frustration always leads to some form of aggression, and aggression always stems from frustration.

ing some elements of the theory, Leonard Berkowitz (1962, 1993) proposes that frustration creates a readiness for aggressive behavior. Frustration is not a sufficient cause for aggression, however, and readiness for aggression is not a drive that must be released. Instead, learning and situational cues determine whether aggressive behavior actually occurs.

Berkowitz is one of the most productive researchers in aggression. In a typical experiment, a subject was angered or not angered and then given the opportunity to commit aggression against a victim, usually by administering shocks. Within that framework, Berkowitz examined several cues and situational factors. In general, anger arousal influenced aggressive behavior; subjects who were angered usually gave more shocks. However, situational cues exerted an even greater influence. Watching an aggressive film, the presence of aggressive weapons, and characteristics of the victim that were associated with aggression (such as being a boxer and having the same name as an aggressive character in a film) all increased aggressive behavior.

Social Learning Theories

Proponents of the social learning perspective, most notably Albert Bandura (1973), assert that aggression is a learned social behavior and as such is acquired, elicited, and maintained in the same manner as other behaviors. According to Bandura, we learn or acquire aggressive behaviors through direct reinforcement and observational learning. Clearly, many aggressive behaviors are reinforced in sport. For example, fans cheer when a hockey player slams an opponent into the boards, and giving an opponent a hard elbow may keep that opponent off the player's back for the rest of a basketball game. Similarly, when a runner takes out the shortstop on the slide into second base, that runner interferes with the throw and allows the batter to reach first base safely.

Sometimes the reinforcement is more subtle. Although youth soccer coach and league rules punish aggressive acts, when Alan gets home his parents tell him he did a great job intimidating the opposing forward with his tough, aggressive play. Perhaps another coach formally abides by the rules against aggressive play but cheers when a player pushes an opponent to get to the ball.

Key Point

Proponents of the social learning perspective assert that aggression is a learned social behavior and as such is acquired, elicited, and maintained in the same manner as other behaviors. According to Bandura (1973), we learn or acquire aggressive behaviors through direct reinforcement and observational learning

In Bandura's Bobo doll studies on the modeling of aggressive behavior (Bandura, 1965; Bandura, Ross, & Ross, 1963a, 1963b), children watched a model playing with various toys. In one condition, the model threw and punched the Bobo doll while making statements such as "Sock him in the nose" and "Hit him down," whereas another model did not demonstrate aggressive behaviors. Observing an aggressive model, whether live or on film, invariably increased the children's aggressive behavior. Seeing an aggressive model receive a reward or praise especially elicited aggressive behavior, whereas children who saw an aggressive model punished did not display as much aggressive behavior. When those same children were offered rewards for imitating the aggressive model, however, they displayed just as much aggressive behavior as those who had seen the aggressive model rewarded. The vicarious rewards and punishments .to the model influenced the children's actual display of aggressive behaviors, but apparently all of the children learned the behaviors.

Unlike instinct and drive theories, social learning theory does not propose any constant drive toward aggression. Instead, people learn aggression through reinforcement and modeling, and they commit aggression only under facilitating conditions. Social learning theory is the most optimistic approach to aggression and violence. If people can learn aggressive responses to certain situations and cues, they can also learn nonaggressive responses to those situations. Whereas instinct and drive theories see aggression as inevitable, social learning theory suggests that aggression is learned and can be controlled.

Application Point

Think of someone who is aggressive in sport. Use social learning theory to explain how that person may have learned to be aggressive.

AGGRESSION AND SPORT

Sport and exercise psychology research on aggression has taken three main routes. Some have approached aggression in sport as a catharsis that releases aggressive impulses and reduces aggressive behavior in nonsport settings. Others have examined the antecedents and consequences of aggression in sport, and still others have focused on how aggressive behavior affects sport performance.

Sport as a Catharsis for Aggression

Although many contend that sport acts as a catharsis for aggressive behavior, the evidence does not support such claims. As noted earlier, instinct theories support sport as a catharsis, and the original frustration–aggression hypothesis implies that sport acts as a catharsis by releasing the aggressive drive. Those theories are not major forces in today's aggression literature, however, and neither social learning theory nor the revised frustration–aggression hypothesis provides support for the catharsis phenomenon. Both Bandura (1986) and Berkowitz (1993) argue that learning and reinforcement of aggressive behavior should increase rather than decrease the probability of later aggressive behavior. Indirect support for this comes from Koss and Gaines (1993), who found that participation in sport, particularly revenue-generating sport, was associated with sexual aggression whereas fraternity membership was not.

People may debate whether engaging in aggressive behavior reduces the tendency to engage in subsequent aggressive behavior, but the evidence indicates that merely observing aggressive behavior has no cathartic effect. Berkowitz (1970) concludes:

> A decade of laboratory research has virtually demolished the contention that people will lessen their aggressive tendencies by watching other persons beat each other up. (p. 2)

Just as laboratory research refutes the cathartic value of observing aggression, field studies demonstrate that watching aggressive sport increases rather than decreases hostility. In a unique field study, Goldstein and Arms (1971) questioned spectators at a football game and at a gymnastics meet. Spectators at the American football game experienced increased feelings of hostility after the game, whereas spectators at the gymnastics meet did not. In a more extensive and controlled replication, people who watched aggressive sport contests (wrestling and ice hockey) experienced increased feelings of hostility, but those who watched a swimming meet did not (Arms, Russell, & Sandilands, 1979). The aggression research allows us to conclude that if anything, observing aggressive sport increases the probability of aggressive behavior.

Even though observing aggression has no cathartic value, participating in vigorous, aggressive activity often seems to help when we are angry. Perhaps performing an aggressive act, even a relatively noninjurious one, lowers arousal and reduces the probability of further aggressive actions. But few studies (e.g., Konecni, 1975) indicate that committing aggression directly against the person who annoyed you may reduce aggressive behavior. For example, if you give an extra elbow to an opposing player who has been on your back during most of a game, that act may reduce your anger and make you less likely to commit other aggressive acts. Other studies, however (e.g., Geen, Stonner, & Shope, 1975), contradict these findings, indicating that even if you do not hit anyone else during that game, the reinforcement may increase the chances that you will commit similar aggressive acts in future games.

The few existing studies on catharsis and physical activity indicate that vigorous activity is not cathartic. Following the Berkowitz paradigm (1962), Ryan (1970) compared the aggressive behaviors of people in a control condition to behaviors of those who engaged in vigorous physical activity (pounding a mallet), won in competition, or lost in competition. Ryan found no support for a cathartic effect; the pounding activity did not reduce aggressive behavior.

In another test of the cathartic effect of physical exercise, Zillmann, Katcher, and Milavsky (1972) compared people who were provoked and then performed exercise on a bicycle ergometer with people who were provoked and then performed a nonarousing task. Not only did the results fail to support catharsis, but the people who exercised behaved more aggressively than those who performed the nonarousing activity. These findings suggest that the arousal created by exercise could actually facilitate aggressive behavior.

A subsequent experiment (Zillmann, Johnson, & Day, 1974) revealed that exercise-induced arousal did not increase aggressive behavior if people knew that their increased arousal was due to exercise. Zillmann and colleagues reasoned that when heightened arousal clearly stems from exercise, competition, noise, or other sources unrelated to aggression, people do not become more aggressive. But when the source of arousal is not easily identified—as when time has elapsed after exercise—the arousal may be labeled as anger and may increase aggressive behavior. Considering all the catharsis research, aggressive acts sometimes reduce arousal, but even when they do, they may not reduce the probability of later aggression (Barron & Richardson, 1994).

Application Point

A know-it-all friend explains to you that American football is such a violent game because players build up a lot of anxieties in the off-season because they have no outlets for them. In other words, football provides a way for players to blow off the excess energy that builds up in them. Explain to your friend in a brief yet convincing way how this is faulty thinking.

Antecedents of Aggression in Sport

Factors associated with aggression can be categorized into environmental, intergroup-intragroup, intrapersonal, and interpersonal factors (see Kirker, Tenenbaum, & Mattson, 2000). In their review, Kirker and colleagues separate environmental and intergroup-intragroup factors, but collectively these can be considered the socializing environment, which include things such as the competitive environment, game importance, importance of events within a game, fan reaction, and moral atmosphere of the team. For example, aggression is more likely when people perceive their teammates to be supportive of aggression (Stephens, 2001, 2004; Stephens & Kavanagh, 2003). The more players perceived their teammates as likely to injure opponents, the more likely they are to indicate aggressive tendencies against an opponent. At the youth sport level, the more willing players are to injure for their coach, the more apt they are to report a willingness to aggress.

Michael Smith has written extensively about aggression in sport, particularly the causes of violence in youth ice hockey. Smith (Morra & Smith, 1996; Smith, 1988) discounts the instinct and drive theory arguments that speed, contact, intensity, frustration, or a need for catharsis account for the violence in hockey. Referring specifically to youth hockey, Smith takes a social learning perspective and argues that violence is caused by the influence of the professional game. First, the hockey system encourages aggressive behavior as a way to advance to higher levels. Smith reports that the majority of young hockey players agree with the statement, "If you want personal recognition in hockey, it helps to play rough." Additionally, significant others (parents, coaches, teammates) accept and praise aggressive acts. Moreover, the media reward such behavior by focusing on violent incidents. Thus young hockey players learn aggressive behaviors through reinforcement and modeling, just as Bandura would predict. This work suggests that situational reinforcements and modeling play key roles in sport aggression, but Smith's data are limited, and few controlled studies have examined sources of aggression in sport.

Intrapersonal factors, which we have referred to as *individual-difference factors* in this book, include such variables as personal expectancies, perceptions and judgments of opponents, personal attitudes toward aggression, achievement motivation, and emotions. For example, players express less guilt for aggressive behavior in sport than in other contexts, implying its greater acceptability in sport. Ryan and colleagues (Ryan, Williams, & Wimer, 1990) examined perceived legitimacy of aggressive behaviors, behavioral intentions to commit aggression, and actual aggressive behaviors of female basketball players. Players who accepted aggressive actions as legitimate engaged in a greater number of aggressive behaviors. Further, highly anxious low achievers scored higher on aggression than other low achievers and high achievers (Watson, 1986). Task orientation was linked with more positive prosocial attitudes and aggression (Duda, Olson, & Templin, 1991; Stephens, 2004), whereas predominantly ego-oriented athletes were more likely to view injuring an opponent as a legitimate behavior than athletes who were predominantly task oriented (Duda et al., 1991).

Gender is another individual factor that relates to aggression. Though there is disagreement as to whether males are more aggressive than females, Bjorkqvist, Osterman, and Kaukiainen (1992) suggest that females are more likely to use indirect (e.g., gossiping, spreading rumors, writing nasty notes) and verbal (e.g., insults, name calling, threats) aggression. In sport and exercise, aggression has been defined in terms of physical behavior, which is a common form of aggression for males. If males and females prefer these different forms of aggression, it is not surprising that in the sport setting males tend to be more physically aggressive than females (Bredemeier, 1994; Duda et al., 1991; Silva, 1983). Examination of table 14.1 indicates that both high school and college male and female

Table 14.1   Average Frequency (Standard Deviation) of Wanting to Harm Opponents at Least Once per Game

	Physically	Psychologically
Female	28.71 (18.82)	57.01 (7.78)
Male	47.41 (20.48)	78.00 (11.54)

athletes are more apt to report the use of more psychological aggression than physical aggression, but males still hold the lead in the overall self-reporting of aggression (Widmeyer et al., 2002). Among youth sport participants, boys also report being more physically and nonphysically aggressive (Bredemeier, Weiss, Shields, & Cooper, 1986; Widmeyer et al., 2002)

Application Point

Why are males reporting that they want to aggress against their opponents more than females? Use the information in this chapter and all the logic you can muster to explain this.

Consequences of Aggression

Not much has changed since Diane Gill's (1986) review on the relationship between aggression and performance. Although many athletes and coaches still believe that aggression on the field leads to better performance, research does not bear this out. To the contrary, hostile aggression may create anger and arousal that interfere with performance. Results also suggest that the consequences of both hostile and instrumental aggression may extend beyond immediate performance effects.

Larry Lauer (2005) argues that the negative effects of aggression far exceed the positive. He cites injury as the most significant consequence, with aggression accounting for 50% of all injuries in ice hockey (cf. Lorentzen, Werden, & Pietila, 1988). Checking from behind resulted in 40% of the spinal cord injuries in Canadian minor and junior ice hockey (cf. Tator, Carson, and Cushman, 2000). These statistics may not be surprising, particularly considering that 77.7% of high school male ice hockey players and 77.1% of football players report wanting to physically injure opponents.

Intimidation is another negative consequence of aggression. Lauer argues that the psychological harm that is created when players send an aggressive message to their opponent may cause some players to withdraw from the game. Although players seldom admit to being intimidated and often like aggression, intimidation is hard to measure; however, we do know that athletes use intimidation in a variety of sports. Widmeyer et al. (2002) report that 89.5% of high school male football players report wanting to psychologically harm their opponent once per game, with university male basketball players at a close second (88.8%). Only 44.4% of university female basketball players and 47.9% of high school female volleyball players reported wanting to psychologically harm their opponent at least once per game.

Two concerns regarding the use of aggression, whether it be psychological or physical, are that athletes are learning to be aggressive, and they may transfer aggressive tendencies off the playing field. Currently, we do not know the degree

Key Point

Although many athletes and coaches still believe that aggression on the field leads to better performance, research does not support this belief. To the contrary, hostile aggression may create anger and arousal that interfere with performance, and Lauer (2005) argues that the negative effects of aggression far exceed the positive.

to which children with aggressive tendencies select certain sports versus the degree to which children learn to be aggressive in sport. We do know, however, that physical activity environments can have an impact on what participants think and how they behave. We have already discussed one theory that can have a powerful impact on participants' behavior: social learning theory. Later in the chapter we will discuss a couple of social development interventions in the physical domain that use social learning principles. First, though, we are going to explore why people do what they do.

Structural Development Approach and Aggression in Sport

Bredemeier and Shields (1995) conceptualize aggression as a moral issue. They contend that aggression is a social interaction, not simply a behavioral response, and they take a structural development approach to the study of aggression and other character-related concerns. Structural development approaches focus on reasoning processes underlying behavior. They are aptly named because as people reason about why they act as they do, the structure of their judgments cognitively matures (Weiss & Smith, 2002). This development in reasoning typically moves from self-concern to other-concern to principled social welfare.

Through their work in the contextual morality of aggression in sport, Bredemeier and her colleagues advocate Haan's (1991) interactional model of moral processing. According to Haan, morality in everyday life involves three components: mutually acknowledged moral balance, moral dialogue, and concern for the needs and interests of self and others (Bredemeier & Shields, 1986a). However, the context of sport may promote a morality different from that of everyday life. First, sport is separated from everyday life by specific spatial and temporal boundaries. Second, much of the decision-making power is held by coaches and officials, giving athletes the opportunity to negate moral responsibility and accountability for their actions. Third, game rules reduce and often inhibit constructive dialogue between teams and opponents. Finally, shared yet unspoken moral agreements among athletes encourage a morality distinct from that of everyday life: Athletes realize that each player is out for herself and that aggression is often necessary in the pursuit of victory. In these ways, sport releases athletes from the moral requirement of thinking of others. Sport appears to have its own self-centered or egocentric morality referred to as *game reasoning* (Bredemeier & Shields, 1986b).

This is not to say that sport is free from moral confines. Although bracketed from everyday life, sport does take place under conditions in which moral imbalance can occur. In sport, moral balance is disrupted when the game turns personal and the athlete's goal is to harm rather than defeat. For example, it is okay for a linebacker to take out the quarterback to win the game, but this is unacceptable if the linebacker is acting out a personal vendetta unrelated to game play. Athletes also view unfair play, such as when opponents get away with cheating or take cheap shots, as upsetting the moral balance (Bredemeier & Shields, 1986b).

Moral Reasoning and Athletic Aggression

As mentioned, research suggests that athletes bracket the morality of sport separately from everyday life and use game reasoning. When Bredemeier and

Shields (1984a, 1986a) asked high school and collegiate basketball players, swimmers, and nonathletes to respond to hypothetical dilemmas in sport and daily life, they found that the athletes used lower levels of moral reasoning in sport. Interestingly, in sport the moral reasoning used by females was more mature than that used by males, but there were no gender differences in the context of daily life. The authors suggest that females may emphasize human connection over individuation and may not develop egocentric sport reasoning and that gender role socialization combined with less experience in competitive sport may explain why females' sport reasoning was higher than that of males.

Hypothetical dilemmas have also been used with young children (aged 9-13) to examine moral reasoning and athletic aggression (e.g., Bredemeier, 1994; Bredemeier et al., 1986). They found that assertive behaviors were associated with more mature levels of moral reasoning and that aggressive behaviors were associated with less mature moral reasoning in both sport and daily life. One reason for these results may be that the males participated in activities that allowed for more contact and therefore possibly more opportunity to reason at lower levels and aggress more than the females.

In the research just discussed, aggression was measured with a self-report measure of aggressive tendencies. Bredemeier and Shields (1984b) provide an example of research in which the aggression was measured by coaches' evaluation of their players' aggressiveness. Consistent with previous findings, female and male intercollegiate basketball athletes with less mature moral reasoning were described by their coaches as more likely to engage in aggressive behaviors than were athletes who were more mature in their moral reasoning.

Collectively, the research on moral reasoning and aggression sport reveals these general findings:

1. The higher the moral reasoning, the less apt one is to aggress.
2. Males are more apt to aggress both physically and psychologically than females.
3. Females tend to use higher levels of moral reasoning than males in sport contexts.
4. The use of various levels of moral reasoning depends on the situation.

This research indicates that people reason differently in sport than in daily life. Whether they learn to be aggressive through sport or not remains unanswered. Fortunately, that is not the critical question because we know physical activity environments can affect what participants think and how they behave. Whether sport helps to create people with honesty and integrity or people who hurt others and engage in other questionable behaviors depends on the character of its leaders and the environment in which the athletes play. In the next section, we focus on interventions for character development.

 ## *Application Point*

The local recreation center is having a meeting to debate whether young people participating in combative sports can learn to be good people off the field while learning to hit each other on the field. You will be speaking at the meeting. What will you say?

INTERVENTIONS FOR CHARACTER DEVELOPMENT THROUGH PHYSICAL ACTIVITY

Social learning and structural developmental theories are two useful approaches to interventions for character development. Together, these theories inform us that by identifying and being appropriate role models, reinforcing desirable behaviors, and providing opportunities to discuss different perspectives, we can foster positive personal outcomes. Two examples of interventions that promote character development are Fair Play for Kids, a curriculum developed jointly by the Commission for Fair Play and Sport Canada, and Don Hellison's (1995) personal-social responsibility model.

Fair Play for Kids incorporates fair play principles (including respect for rules and others, and self-control) into all classroom settings. The curriculum emphasizes respect for rules, officials, and opponents; the right of all participants to play; and the importance of self-control. Gibbons and colleagues (Gibbons Ebbeck, & Weiss, 1995) investigated the effects of Fair Play for Kids on the moral judgment, reasoning, intention, and behavior of fourth and sixth graders. They assigned groups as control classes, Fair Play for Kids curriculum in physical education classes only, and Fair Play for Kids curriculum in all classes. After 7 months, both treatment groups scored higher than the control groups on moral judgment, reasoning, intention, and behavior.

In a follow-up study, Gibson and Ebbeck (1997) compared social learning with structural developmental strategies. They found that both groups were higher in judgment, intention, and behavior in only 4 months and that the structural developmental group scored higher on reasoning than did the social learning group or the control group. Overall, these results confirm that sport and physical activity can have a positive impact on moral growth and that the structural developmental strategies have the biggest impact on moral reasoning when designed to do so.

The second character development intervention arose from the desire to help at-risk children. Today, not only inner-city children and adolescents are at risk for social ills such as child neglect and abuse, homelessness, gang violence, and delinquency, but according to Hellison (1995), 50% of affluent suburban families living in the Chicago area are dysfunctional.

On the basis of his experience and his commitment to help students, Hellison (1995) developed a teaching model based on responsibility called the *personal-social responsibility model*. The model is grounded in the beliefs that

- the teaching of life skills must be integrated with the teaching of physical activity;

- lessons learned on the playing field must be taught in a way that kids can apply to other aspects of life;

- teaching strategies must gradually shift responsibility from the program leader to the participants; and

- the program leader must respect the capacity and ability of the participants to make decisions (Hellison & Walsh, 2002).

The model gives students opportunities to feel empowered, purposeful, and connected to others as well as to experience responsible behavior, persevere, and acknowledge activities that impinge upon others' rights (Hellison & Templin,

1991). Responsibility is defined via goals or levels; being responsible outside the gymnasium is the ultimate, level V goal.

In Hellison's cumulative approach, each higher level encompasses all lower levels. People can, and often do, function at multiple levels. For example, a student may engage in self-directed play and cooperate with others one minute and shout at and blame another player the next minute. Figure 14.1 describes Hellison's levels. In Hellison's (1995) gym, lessons usually begin with awareness talks in which students learn about the importance of the levels. During the lesson, students experience the levels in action. For example, students may play an inclusion game to stress the notion that everyone has a right to participate. Opportunities for individual decision making, such as choosing activities, are built into instruction. Group meetings provide opportunities to share ideas, opinions, and feelings about the program and to practice group decision making. Individual and group decision-making strategies typically come into play in response to a particular incident. The lessons always close with reflection time in which students discuss the degree to which they have been respectful of others, involved in the program, self-directed, and helpful to others.

Level V, Outside the gym

Students at Level V are able to play Level Zero to Level IV in life outside the gymnasium.

Level IV, Caring

Students at Level IV, in addition to respecting others, participating, and being self-directed, are motivated to extend their sense of responsibility beyond themselves by cooperating, giving support, showing concern, and helping.

Level III, Self-direction

Students at Level III not only show respect and participation, but also are able to work without direct supervision. They can identify their own needs and begin to plan and carry out their physical education programs.

Level II, Participation

Students at Level II not only show at least minimal respect for others but also willingly play, accept challenges, practice motor skills, and train for fitness under the teachers' supervision.

Level I, Respect

Students at Level I may not participate in the day's activities or show much mastery or improvement; but they are able to control their behavior enough so that they don't interfere with the other students' right to learn or the teacher's right to teach. They do this without much prompting by the teacher and without constant supervision.

Level Zero, Irresponsibility

Students at Level Zero make excuses and blame others for what they do or fail to do.

Figure 14.1

Hellison's levels presented as a cumulative progression.

Adapted, by permission, from D.R. Hellison, 2003, *Teaching responsibility through physical activity*, 2nd ed. (Champaign, IL: Human Kinetics), 28.

Research on Hellison's responsibility model has been encouraging (e.g., DeBusk & Hellison, 1989; Martinek, Schilling, & Johnson, 2001; Schilling, 2001). For example, after conducting interviews before and after a 6-week responsibility intervention with 10 fourth-grade boys identified as having behavioral problems, DeBusk and Hellison (1989) concluded that the intervention helped the students become more aware of self-responsibility concepts and incorporate some of these concepts into their lives. None of the changes was dramatic, and the responsibility lessons did not transfer outside the gym. Research by Martinek and colleagues (2001), however, did show that participants showed elements of self-control and respect for others in the classroom.

In a recent review of 26 programs, including 6 theory- or research-based peer-reviewed journal articles, Hellison & Walsh (2002) concluded that participants in programs grounded in the social-responsibility model demonstrated greater respect and feelings for others, were willing to try hard and work together, and were more self-directed in the physical activity setting. They also concluded that self-control, effort, self-esteem, and other positive social and personal characteristics outside of the physical activity setting are possible. They caution, however, that the personal-social responsibility model must be faithfully implemented and that the results of their review provide greater evidence that the program is worth doing than it does that the program is working. More control and generalizable research are needed before such a conclusion can be made.

Application Point

As the director of the local recreation center, you have been charged with creating a youth sport program designed to foster character development. What will your program look like? What positive character traits do you think are important to foster? What approach (social learning, structural developmental, or a combination of both) will you use to foster those traits?

PUTTING IT INTO PRACTICE

Now you are ready to put the content of chapter 14 into practice. Read the chapter summary, discuss the case study, answer the review questions, and enhance your knowledge by researching the recommended readings.

Summary

Many have written about aggression in sport, but few have conducted systematic research on the topic. Aggression is defined as an intentional act designed to inflict harm to other living beings. The strongest theoretical work suggests that aggression is learned through the modeling and reinforcement of aggressive behaviors. Research does not support the popular notion that sport acts as a catharsis to release aggressive urges. Instead, it is likely that the modeling and reinforcement of aggression in sport increase the probability of aggressive behaviors in both sport and nonsport settings. Work by structural developmental theorists links aggression to moral reasoning. Both research and practical sport programs have demonstrated that character development in sport and physical activity is possible when the programs are designed for that purpose.

Case Study

This chapter brings together theories of aggression, moral development, and research to provide guidelines for promoting character development. For this case, use the chapter material, to develop a plan for promoting character development.

In response to an increase in violence by students after school, the principal has decided to start an after-school program so students will have something to do before their parents come home from work. You have been hired by the principal to create the program. Your mandate is to create a physical activity program that builds character. The principal wants to see more positive sporting behavior when playing and less in-school fighting. Present your program to the principal. Include your overall approach, specific strategies, and a rationale. Be sure to state whether your program is for elementary, middle, or high school students.

Hints: Refer to the theories that guide your program, identify specific strategies you will use that will affect character development both on and off the playing field, and refer to research that supports the effectiveness of your program.

Review Questions

1. Define *aggression* as the term is used in this text.
2. Compare and contrast instrumental aggression, hostile aggression, and assertive behavior.
3. Describe the characteristics of instinct theories of aggression.
4. Describe drive theories of aggression, as well as Berkowitz's related theory.
5. Describe social learning theories of aggression.
6. Contrast instinct, drive, and social learning theories of aggression.
7. Explain what researchers have found regarding the idea that sport can act as a catharsis for aggression.
8. Using youth ice hockey as an example, explain how situational cues can contribute to the prevalence of violence in a particular sport setting.
9. Explain the effects of aggression on sport performance.
10. Identify and contrast the components of morality in everyday life versus within a sport context.
11. Describe the relationship between moral reasoning and athletic aggression.
12. Explain two sport-oriented programs designed for character development.

Recommended Reading

Berkowitz, L. (1993). *Aggression: Its causes, consequences, and control.* Philadelphia: Temple University Press.

> Berkowitz has been a leading scholar on aggression throughout his distinguished career, and his research and ideas have shaped our view on aggression.

Gibbons, S.L., & Ebbeck, V. (1997). The effect of different teaching strategies on moral development of physical education students. *Journal of Teaching Physical Education, 17,* 85-98.

Anyone interested in learning more about strategies for building character in sport will be interested in this source. Gibbons and Ebbeck's work complements their earlier work with Maureen Weiss (Gibbons, Ebbeck, & Weiss, 1995) who found that the Fair Play for Kids sport program promoted character building in fourth through sixth graders both in physical education and academic classes.

Weiss, M.R., & Smith, A.L. (2002). Moral development in sport and physical activity. In T.S. Horn (Ed.), *Advances in sport psychology* (pp. 243-280). Champaign, IL: Human Kinetics.

Weiss and Smith provide a comprehensive overview of theories of moral development and a review of theory- and practice-based literature. Those interested in learning more about moral development will want to look at this book chapter.

Chapter 15

Group Dynamics and Interpersonal Relationships

Chapter Objectives

After studying this chapter, you should be able to

◆ understand group dynamics concepts and models as they relate to sport and exercise settings,

◆ explain the relationship of individual capabilities and motivational processes to group performance,

◆ explain several leadership models used in sport and exercise psychology,

◆ identify types of social support and describe the influence of social support on behavior and health outcomes in sport and exercise,

◆ understand the relationship between group cohesion and group performance, and

◆ explain team-building models and research related to sport and exercise settings.

Physical activities are social activities that usually involve groups. People play on volleyball teams, learn motor skills in physical education classes, join racquetball clubs, and participate in exercise groups. Sport and exercise psychologists might pose many questions about interpersonal relationships and group processes. How does turnover of team members affect performance? Does social support increase adherence to exercise programs? Answers to these types of questions are few. The traditional social psychology literature on groups typically ignores physical activity, and the organizational models are far removed from the unique relationships of sport teams and exercise groups. Groups by definition involve interaction, and the dynamic nature of group processes makes it difficult to draw clear conclusions. Still, the sport and exercise psychology literature on interpersonal relationships and group dynamics provides guidelines for enhancing the experience for participants in sport and exercise groups.

GROUP DYNAMICS CONCEPTS AND MODELS

First, we should define *group*. Certainly a professional basketball team, a youth soccer team, and the noon exercise club are groups. What about several people jogging on the same route or the crowd at a football game? Most people who have written about groups agree that a collection of individuals does not make a group—interaction is the defining feature. Group members must be aware of each other, relate to each other in some way, and be able to interact with each other through group processes. As McGrath (1984, p. 7) states, "Groups are those social aggregates that involve mutual awareness and potential interaction." When you jog, you may meet and exchange greetings with walkers, in-line skaters, and joggers, but you do not interact and are not a group. McGrath also excludes crowds; groups must be small enough to allow interdependence and continuity over time.

Sport and exercise psychology research on groups adopts similar definitions and models. In an excellent chapter on sport teams and groups, Eys, Burke, Carron, and Dennis (2006) also focus on dynamic mutual interdependence, and Carron, Hausenblas, and Eys (2005, p. 13) define a sport group as

> *a collection of two or more individuals who possess a common identity, have common goals and objectives, share a common fate, exhibit structured patterns of interaction and modes of communication, hold common percep- tions about group structure, are personally and instrumentally interdepen- dent, reciprocate interpersonal attraction, and consider themselves to be a group.*

For our purposes, most sport teams, exercise groups, and physical skill classes meet these criteria, and application of a group dynamics framework may help us understand sport and exercise groups.

McGrath's Conceptual Framework for Groups

Key Point

According to McGrath's conceptual framework for groups, individual character- istics influence group structures and pat- terns, environmental properties affect the group task and situa- tion, and those factors collectively influence the behavioral setting under which group interaction takes place. Group interaction is influenced by all those components, as well as by forces within the interaction process itself.

McGrath's (1984) conceptual framework provides the framework for most of the psychology literature on group dynamics. Interaction, the defining characteristic of a group, is the central element of the model. The rest of the model specifies factors and relationships that both influence and are influenced by those inter- active processes. Individual characteristics influence group structures and pat- terns, environmental properties affect the group task and situation, and those factors collectively influence the behavioral setting in which group interaction takes place. Group interaction is influenced by all those components, as well as by forces within the interaction process itself. Furthermore, the interaction process may in turn influence the group members, the environment, and the relationships in the group.

For example, consider a soccer team. Players have varying individual char- acteristics, including physical characteristics, specific soccer skills, goals and motivational orientation, cognitive skills, competitive experience, and so on. Those individual characteristics affect group structures and patterns, such as starting positions, leadership roles, and offensive and defensive plays. Also, the environment, such as the opponent, field conditions, and weather, might influence positioning and strategies. The ongoing interaction and game progress may then change the environment, individuals, and relationships. For example, the player who is having a great day may get the ball more often and play with enhanced confidence.

Group Dynamics Models

Widmeyer, Brawley, and Carron (2002) offer a linear model that has guided much of the sport and exercise psychology research on group dynamics. Like McGrath, Widmeyer and colleagues include individual attributes and the environment as starting input components. These influence group structure, which influences group cohesion, which then influences group processes. Finally, group processes influence group and individual outputs. Group cohesion stands out in this framework, reflecting the prominence of group cohesion in the sport and exercise psychology literature. In current work on team building, discussed later in the chapter, Carron and colleagues have moved cohesion to the output side of the model, reflecting the mutual relationships and dynamic nature of group processes.

GROUP PERFORMANCE IN SPORT AND EXERCISE

Group performance is a pressing practical concern in sport and exercise psychology. Those professionals who work with sport teams focus on maximizing group performance. Perhaps the maxim most accepted by researchers and practitioners is that the best players make the best team. In general, this rule undoubtedly holds; five intercollegiate basketball players will consistently defeat five intramural players. However, the relationship between individual abilities and group performance is far from perfect. You probably can recall instances when teams with all the talent to win the championship did not or times when teams without individual stars performed exceptionally well as a group. Simply summing the abilities of individual group members does not accurately describe group performance; we must also consider the group process—interaction.

Steiner's Model of Individual–Group Performance

Steiner (1972) proposed a theoretical model of the individual–group performance relationship, which is expressed in this equation:

Actual productivity = potential productivity – losses due to faulty process.

Potential productivity, which is the group's best possible performance, depends on the following:

- Resources
- Task demands

The group's resources are composed of all the relevant knowledge and skills of individual members, including the overall level and distribution of talents. Individual ability, demonstrated by individual performance, is the most important resource of most sport groups. Greater resources increase potential productivity. As in the maxim, the best players make the best team, but Steiner's model goes beyond the maxim. To contribute to potential performance, resources must be relevant to the task. Height is a relevant resource for volleyball, but not for track. Task demands—the rules and requirements of the task—determine which resources are relevant to performance. When a group effectively uses its available resources to meet task demands, its actual productivity approaches its potential.

In Steiner's model, a group's actual performance falls short of its potential (we're never perfect) because of faulty process. The process includes all individual and interactive actions by which a group transforms its resources into a collective product or performance—putting it all together. Process losses fall into two categories:

- Coordination losses occur when poor timing or ineffective strategies detract from the group's potential, such as when a basketball team fails to get the ball to the top scorer.
- Motivational losses occur when group members slack off or give less than their best effort.

These process losses are critical considerations in work with sport and exercise groups. Coaches have some influence on group resources when they recruit individual talent or provide instruction to improve individual skills, but resources and task demands are relatively stable. The main task of a coach is to reduce process losses by developing organizational strategies that reduce coordination losses and by maintaining optimal motivation levels.

Application Point

You are coaching the jump-rope team at your middle school. The team will perform at regional, state, and national events. Keeping in mind the resources and task demands, identify some possible coordination losses and motivational losses that might affect the jump-rope team's performance over the season. Be specific. Also, think of some strategies you might try to reduce those process losses.

Process losses and the strategies for reducing them vary with the task. Activities requiring considerable interaction or cooperation, such as basketball, are more susceptible to coordination losses than are activities demanding less interaction, such as softball or swimming. Consequently, the basketball coach emphasizes strategies and drills to achieve precise timing and team movement patterns. The softball coach spends some time on interactive skills, such as double plays, but emphasizes individual batting and fielding skills. And the swimming coach may try to develop efficient transitions among relay members but spends little time on interactive skills.

Research on Individual–Group Motor Performance

Early lab-based research (Wiest, Porter, & Ghiselli, 1961) and comparison of team and individual statistics in professional sport teams (Jones, 1974) confirmed that group effectiveness was positively related to individual effectiveness. However, it also suggested that interaction requirements may reduce the individual–group performance relationship.

In a controlled experiment (Gill, 1979) with two-person teams performing a motor maze task, average ability was the primary predictor, but ability discrepancy (a large difference between partners) negatively affected cooperative group performance. A second experiment within that study indicated that individual performance was not reliable from session to session and was almost totally unreliable from trial to trial. Sport team performance, which is subject to numerous influences that were controlled in the lab, is likely even less reliable. For example, a baseball batter often goes 3 for 4 in one game and 1 for 4 in the next. Individual abilities relate to group performance, but in light of the variability of both individual and group performance, more than a moderate prediction of team performance is unrealistic.

Some research has gone beyond individual–group performance by incorporating group processes and motivation to provide more useful information for sport and exercise groups, as we'll see in the following sections.

Ringelmann Effect

Research on the role of group process originates in an obscure, unpublished study of individual and group performance on a rope-pulling task. More than 100 years ago, Ringelmann observed individuals and groups of various sizes pulling on a rope (cited in Ingham, Levinger, Graves, & Peckham, 1974; Kravitz & Martin, 1986). Groups pulled with more force than individuals, but not with as much force as would be predicted by adding individual scores. Eight-person groups pulled only four times as hard as individuals. The average individual force exerted by members of 2-person groups was 93% of the average individual force in solo performance, that for 3-person groups was 85%, and that for 8-person groups was 49%. This phenomenon of average individual performance decreasing with increases in group size is called the *Ringelmann effect.*

No one actually demonstrated the Ringelmann effect until Ingham and colleagues (1974) resurrected the original Ringelmann paradigm with updated controls. Ingham et al. first replicated Ringelmann's work using individuals and groups of 2, 3, 4, 5, and 6 people. Experiment 1 partially replicated the Ringelmann effect; the average performance of individuals in 2-person groups was 91% of the average solo performance, and that for three-person groups was 83%. Groups of 4, 5, and 6 did not exhibit further decreases but leveled off, with the average performance in 6-person groups at 78% of the average solo performance. (See figure 15.1 for a comparison of the Ingham et al. and Ringelmann findings.)

Ingham et al. then eliminated the coordination requirements of the group task, to see whether the Ringelmann effect was attributable to coordination losses or motivation losses. In experiment 2, only one subject actually pulled on the rope, but through use of blindfolds and trained confederates who pretended to pull, subjects were led to believe they were performing in groups of 1 to 6

Figure 15.1

Individual rope-pulling scores as a function of group size.

Reprinted from *Journal of Experimental Social Psychology,* Vol. 10, A. Ingham, G. Levinger, J. Graves, and V. Peckham, The Ringelmann effect: Studies of group size and group performance, p. 377, Copyright 1974, with permission from Elsevier.

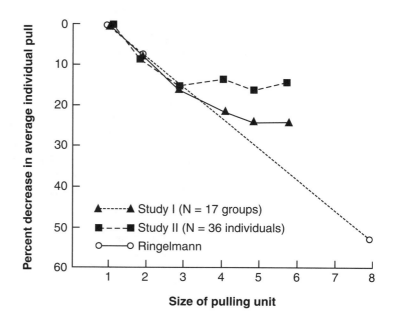

members. The results were virtually identical to those of experiment 1. The researchers concluded that the decreases in average performance were due to motivational losses within groups, which led to further research on motivation and performance in groups.

Social Loafing in Groups

In the 1970s, Latane and colleagues undertook a systematic investigation of group performance, and in light of the Ingham et al. (1974) findings dubbed the motivational losses in groups as *social loafing.* Their first study (Latane, Williams, & Harkins, 1979), which used clapping and shouting as group tasks, confirmed the Ringelmann effect: The average sound produced per person decreased to 71% of solo performance in 2-person groups, 51% in 4-person groups, and 40% in 6-person groups. In a second experiment, instructions and background noise played through earphones led subjects to believe they were clapping or shouting in groups when in fact they were performing alone (pseudogroups). Actual groups replicated the results of the first experiment, and pseudogroups also exhibited social loafing, with the average sound dropping to 82% in 2-person groups and 74% in 6-person groups. Because coordination losses (e.g., interfering sound waves) were eliminated, Latane and colleagues concluded that the performance drop was due to motivation losses—social loafing. The greater performance drop for actual groups represented a combination of coordination losses and motivation losses.

After confirming the motivation losses, Latane and colleagues pursued explanations and proposed that identifiability of individual performance is critical (Williams, Harkins, & Latane, 1981). When individual efforts are lost in the crowd, performance decreases. In two experiments, Williams et al. demonstrated that when group members believed their individual outputs were identifiable (i.e., known to others), social loafing was eliminated.

Key Point

The phenomenon of average individual performance decreasing with increases in group size is called the *Ringelmann effect.* Latane and colleagues called such motivational losses in groups *social loafing.*

Social Incentives in Sport Groups

If monitoring individual performance can eliminate social loafing, perhaps other tactics can provide social incentives to increase individual efforts in groups. Sport teams certainly seem to provide social incentives. Latane and colleagues (Williams, Nida, Baca, & Latane, 1989) noted the common belief that athletes perform better in a relay or group than alone, and they examined social loafing and identifiability in a sport setting.

They first checked individual and relay times at the 1977 Big Ten intercollegiate swim meet and found no social loafing. Instead, relay times were faster than individual times. Faster starts in relays could account for the difference, so they designed an experiment to test their observations (Williams, Nida, Baca, & Latane, 1989). In an experimental competition, 16 members of an intercollegiate team swam both as individuals and as one member of a relay team. Starts were standardized to the faster relay starts and identifiability was manipulated by announcing or not announcing swimmers' lap times. Results revealed an interaction between identifiability and individual-relay conditions. Under low identifiability, individual times (61.34 seconds) were faster than relay times (61.66), implying social loafing. Under high identifiability, individual times (60.95) were slower than relay times (60.18). Not only was social loafing eliminated, but the group seemed to provide a social incentive. Time differences were small; however, such small differences often determine places in competitive events.

Research on social loafing has continued, and Karau and Williams (1995) reviewed more than 80 studies on social loafing, which they formally defined as "a reduction in motivation and effort when individuals work collectively compared to when they work individually or coactively." (p. 134) Their meta-analysis yielded a moderate effect size of 0.44, and they found social loafing consistently across a wide variety of tasks and populations. Karau and Williams proposed an integrated model incorporating four theories that have guided most research on social loafing:

- **Social impact theory** suggests that when individuals work collectively, social influence is diffused across group members, and each additional group member has less influence as group size increases.

- **Arousal reduction** follows a drive model, which suggests that working collectively reduces arousal, thereby reducing performance on simple tasks but enhancing performance on complex tasks.

- **Evaluation approaches** suggest that evaluation may eliminate social loafing if the participants' inputs are identifiable and if there is a standard with which these inputs can be compared.

- **Dispensability of effort** suggests that working collectively reduces effort because people feel their input is not essential to a quality group product.

> **Key Point**
>
> Karau and Williams' (1993) CEM combines traditional expectancy-value models of effort with self-evaluation processes in groups. The CEM proposes that individuals will exert effort on a collective task only to the degree that they expect their efforts to help them obtain valued outcomes that are important, meaningful, or intrinsically satisfying.

As an integrative framework, Karau and Williams (1993) offer the collective effort model (CEM), which combines traditional expectancy-value models of effort with self-evaluation processes in groups. The CEM proposes that individuals will exert effort on a collective task only to the degree that they expect their efforts to help them obtain valued outcomes that are important, meaningful, or intrinsically satisfying. For people to work hard on a collective task, (1) individual effort must relate to individual performance; (2) individual performance in turn must relate to group performance; (3) group performance must lead to a favorable group outcome, which is related to a favorable individual outcome; and (4) the individual must attach personal value to this outcome.

Karau and Williams (1995) suggest that social loafing is reduced in the following situations:

- *When individuals believe that others can evaluate their collective performance.* Coaches, instructors, and exercise leaders might make special effort to evaluate group outcomes.

- *When people work in smaller groups.* Use small-group activities (or partners) rather than one large group in practice, instruction, or recreational settings.

- *When people perceive their contributions to the collective product as unique.* Coaches and instructors can explicitly recognize individual contributions. Such recognition is especially important with team or group activities that obscure individuals. Latane, Harkins, & Williams (1980) noted that effective football coaches used several techniques to increase the identifiability and recognition of individual linemen.

- *When people have a standard with which to compare their group's performance.* Standards typically are clear with team sports, but clarifying group standards for an elementary activity class or exercise group could be a greater challenge. Still, if group outcomes (performance or nonperformance) are valued, standards are important.

- *When people work on tasks that are intrinsically interesting, meaningful, important to others, or high in personal involvement.* Although physical activities usually are intrinsically interesting to participants, this may not hold for all sport and exercise settings. Even highly competitive athletes who thrive on their sport may find practice or training activities less than thrilling and thus loaf.

- *When individuals work with people they respect or in a situation that activates a salient group identity.* Sport teams typically have a salient identity, but the mix of people is constantly changing, posing challenges. Group identity is unlikely to be present in most exercise settings without special effort, but the effort is worthwhile if it's important for the group to work together.

- *When individuals expect their coworkers to perform poorly.* If group members want to do well and believe others will have difficulty, they may put in extra effort to compensate.

- *When people have a dispositional tendency to view favorable collective outcomes as valuable and important.* Some people are more team players than others. Interestingly, Karau and Williams (1993, 1995) found social loafing effects were smaller for women than for men and for participants from Eastern cultures than for those from Western cultures.

We have far to go to fully understand social loafing and collective efforts in groups. Most studies do not reflect groups in the real world and do not involve physical activity. Moreover, in focusing on social loafing, the research is one-sided; social incentives have been ignored. Recent initiatives related to team building and the expanding literature on social support, discussed later in the chapter, may help us move in that direction.

Even with the apparently straightforward relationship of individual abilities to group performance, we must consider the social context and interpersonal relationships within group interaction processes. Even those who work with highly competitive, task-oriented teams often engage in team-building activities to improve group communication or cohesion. Professionals in physical education, recreational activities, and exercise programs may be more concerned with interpersonal relationships than with performance outcomes. The following sections focus on interpersonal relationships in sport and exercise groups, including leadership, social support, and cohesion.

LEADERSHIP IN SPORT AND EXERCISE GROUPS

Leadership is a traditional topic in group dynamics, and sport and exercise psychology has adapted some of that work. Although we often think of the team coach, class instructor, or exercise director as the leader, leadership is not simply a characteristic of a single person. Instead, leadership is a complex social relationship, defined by Barrow (1977) as "the behavioral process of influencing individuals and groups toward set goals" (p. 232). Thus defined, leadership involves the situation and all group members as well as an identified leader.

Early research on leadership emphasized common characteristics of great leaders, or the great-man theory of leadership (indeed it was a theory of great men—no women were included). Similar to early trait personality research, the leadership trait work yielded few conclusive findings. Gradually leadership research shifted to an interactive model considering leadership styles and behaviors in varying group situations.

Early Models

Fiedler's (1967) contingency model of leadership effectiveness, which guided much of the early work, classifies leaders as task oriented (primarily focused on performance) or person oriented (primarily concerned with interpersonal relationships) and proposes that leader effectiveness depends on situation favorableness. The situation is most favorable with positive leader–member relations, a clearly defined task structure, and strong position power. According to Fiedler, task-oriented leaders are more effective in both the most favorable and least favorable situations, whereas person-oriented leaders are more effective in moderately favorable situations. Fielder's model was the leader in the 1970s, but the variables are difficult to assess and findings were inconclusive. More important, its appropriateness for sport and exercise groups is questionable.

In 1963, Grusky applied a model of group structure and organizational leadership to professional baseball and proposed that players in more central playing positions perform more dependent, coordinative tasks and interact more with players in other positions. Those high interactors then develop leadership skills and become managers more often than low interactors. The high interactors in baseball are infielders and catchers, whereas pitchers and outfielders are low interactors. Grusky's examination of baseball records confirmed his theory: Catchers and infielders become managers more often than pitchers and outfielders did.

Subsequent studies supported Grusky's model (for a review see Loy, Curtis, & Sage, 1979), but related research did not extend far beyond Grusky's original propositions. Approaches that consider both individual characteristics and situational factors offer more promise for understanding leadership in sport and exercise.

Chelladurai's Multidimensional Model of Leadership

Chelladurai and colleagues conducted one of the few systematic investigations of leadership in sport and exercise with several studies over several years (see Chelladurai, 1984; Chelladurai & Turner, 2006). Chelladurai's (1984) model considers the influence of situational, leader, and member characteristics on leader behaviors and the subsequent influence of leader behaviors on group performance and satisfaction. The major proposition is that the degree of congruence among the three components of leadership behavior is positively related to performance and satisfaction. In other words, the more the leader's actual behaviors match the preferences of group members and situation requirements, the better the group's performance and the greater the group members' satisfaction.

As an initial step, Chelladurai and Saleh (1980) developed the Leadership Scale for Sports (LSS). Psychometric testing revealed good reliability and factor analysis yielded five dimensions of leader behaviors in sport: training and instruction, democratic, autocratic, social support, and positive feedback behaviors. In a test of the congruence prediction, Chelladurai (1984) reported that the discrepancy between preferred and actual leader behavior was related to satisfaction. Athletes in wrestling, basketball, and track and field preferred an emphasis on training and instruction, and the more the coach matched those preferences, the greater the athletes' satisfaction was. Basketball players were more satisfied when positive feedback met or exceeded their preferences, but athletes in wrestling and track were not.

Chelladurai's Research on Coaches' Decision-Making Styles

More recently, Chelladurai (e.g., Chelladurai & Turner, 2006) has adapted the leader behavior dimensions of the LSS to investigate decision-making styles of coaches. With the LSS dimensions, training and instruction and positive feedback relate to task and performance, social support relates to athletes' personal needs, and autocratic and democratic behavior refer to decision making.

Earlier leadership research suggested that an autocratic style was incompatible with social support, but Chelladurai and Turner (2006) note that athletes' preferences for autocratic styles do not negate their desire for social support.

Democratic styles imply participative decision making. As Chelladurai and Turner (2006) point out, participatory decision making has advantages: More information is available; members feel decisions are their own, increasing acceptance; and participation contributes to personal growth. On the other hand, participative decision making is time consuming, less effective for complex problems, and heavily dependent on the degree of group integration. Moreover, the situation may constrain participation.

Chelladurai and Haggerty (1978) proposed a normative model of decision-making style that specifies three decision styles:

- **Autocratic style.** The coach makes the decision. In later research, this style was divided into an autocratic style in which the coach simply makes the decision with available information (autocratic I), and a second autocratic style in which the coach makes the decision but has obtained information from players (autocratic II).

- **Participative style.** The coach is a member of the group, and the group makes the decision. This has sometimes been labeled a group style.

- **Delegative style.** The coach delegates decision making to one or more team members and does not participate in the decision.

With further research, the decision-making styles have been modified to represent actual coaching style variations and player preferences. Most notably, a consultative style has been singled out. In this style, the coach consults with players and then makes the decision. In consultative I the coach consults with individuals, and in consultative II the coach consults with the group as a whole.

In early studies the delegative style was rejected and eliminated and subsequent studies (e.g., Chelladurai, Haggerty, & Baxter, 1989) used five decision-making styles (autocratic I and II, consultative I and II, and group) to examine coaches' styles and athletes' preferences. Although the style choices varied among groups and across situations, overall preferences were consistent. Autocratic styles were the first choice, with preference for the coach making the decision alone. The second choice was the consultative style on a group basis; the participative group style was chosen less than 20% of the time by all groups.

Chelladurai and Turner (2006) noted that choices varied with the problem situation, suggesting that it would be appropriate to refer to the situation as democratic or autocratic rather than labeling coaches as democratic or autocratic. Notably, the autocratic choice was quite acceptable, despite its reputation as a tool of dictators. The authors stressed that contrasting decision styles do

Key Point

Chelladurai and Turner (2006) suggested that coaches and other leaders need to select a decision style appropriate to the situation. With coaching decisions, more time-consuming participative styles might be ineffective and frustrating. In typical exercise groups, on the other hand, participative styles may well be more effective and preferred by participants.

not concern values—an autocratic style can reflect humanism and concern for team members' welfare. They also suggested that coaches and other leaders need to select a decision style appropriate to the situation rather than assume that participatory decisions are always best.

Chelladurai's model dominates the sport and exercise psychology literature on leadership, and most studies focus on the coach as leader. With coaching decisions, more time-consuming participative styles might be ineffective and frustrating. In typical exercise groups or less competitive sport settings, participative styles may well be more effective and preferred by participants.

Leadership Development

A few studies have considered leadership development within sport teams. Glenn and Horn (1993) investigated leadership within female high school soccer teams. Coaches suggested that leadership was associated with soccer skill, whereas peers identified several psychological characteristics, including self-esteem, psychological androgyny, and lower trait anxiety, in addition to soccer competence.

Wright and Cote (2003) interviewed male collegiate leader-athletes to investigate leadership development and identified four central components: high skill, strong work ethic, enriched cognitive sport knowledge, and good rapport with people. The leader-athletes also reported that feedback, acknowledgment, support, cognitive engagement, mature conversations with adults, and encounters with older peers were important in developing the leadership components.

Within the wider range of physical activity contexts, leadership per se has seldom been examined. However, an expanding body of research has addressed interpersonal relationships, particularly social support, within exercise settings.

SOCIAL SUPPORT

Social support, a prominent topic in psychology, and specifically in health psychology, is related to the early social influence work discussed in chapter 13. Here we focus on social support as an ongoing social interaction process, drawing on the extensive research on the health benefits of social support.

Social Support Defined

Social support is a familiar term, referring to the support of others, but more specific definitions are needed for research and practice. Researchers have often operationally defined social support as the number of friends, relatives, or social involvements and conceptually as denoting a vague sense of belongingness or acceptance. With advances in research and conceptual models, social support is viewed as multidimensional, and the quality of support is more important than quantity of social contacts. Here, we'll use Shumaker and Brownell's (1984) definition of social support as "an exchange of resources between at least two individuals perceived by the provider or the recipient to be intended to enhance the well-being of the recipient" (p. 13).

Model of the Social Support Process

Shumaker and Brownell's definition, which is consistent with current research and theory, suggests that social support is a process with both provider and recipient. Rosenfeld and Richman's (1997) model depicts that process and includes the commonly accepted dimensions of social support (see figure 15.2).

The figure shows three broad types of social support:

- Tangible (e.g., assisting someone with a task)
- Informational (e.g., telling team members they have mutual responsibilities)
- Emotional (e.g., comforting someone)

Providers communicate these types of support through behaviors, and behaviors constitute social support when the recipient perceives them as enhancing well-being. Sarason, Sarason, and Pierce (1990) argue that more than actual received support, perceived social support is the key contributor to health and well-being.

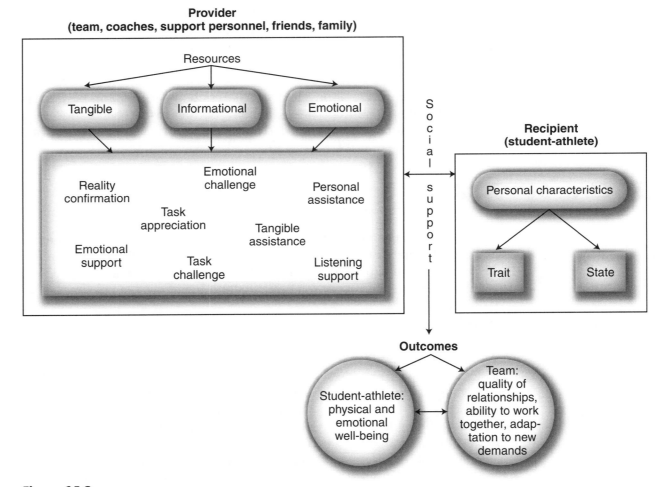

Figure 15.2

Model of the social support process.

Reprinted from L.B. Rosenfeld and J.R. Richman, 1997, "Developing effective social support: Team building and the social support process," *Journal of Applied Sport Psychology* 9: 133-153, by permission of Taylor & Francis. www.informaworld.com

The perceived communicated behaviors take eight forms in the Rosenfeld and Richman (1997) model:

- **Listening support:** Others listen to you without giving advice or being judgmental.

- **Emotional support:** Others comfort and care for you and indicate they are on your side.

- **Emotional challenge:** Others challenge you to evaluate your attitudes, values, and feelings.

- **Task appreciation:** Others acknowledge your efforts and express appreciation for the work you do.

- **Task challenge:** Others challenge your way of thinking about your work in order to stretch you, motivate you, and lead you to greater creativity, excitement, and involvement.

- **Reality confirmation:** Others are similar to you, see things the way you do, and help you confirm your perception of the world.

- **Tangible assistance:** Others provide you with financial assistance, products, or gifts.

- **Personal assistance:** Others provide services or help, such as running errands or offering expertise, to help you accomplish your tasks.

Other investigators have listed different dimensions of social support, but all suggest similar main dimensions. Specifically, most scholars agree that social support involves direct assistance (tangible support), advice (informational support), or encouragement (emotional support).

Social Support Measures

Measures of social support reflect similar dimensions. Commonly used measures include the Social Support Questionnaire (SSQ; Sarason, Levine, Basham, & Sarason, 1983), the Social Provisions Scale (SPS; Cutrona & Russell, 1987), and the Social Support Survey (SSS; Richman, Rosenfeld, & Hardy, 1993). The SSQ, which assesses the number of others who provide support and the degree of satisfaction with that support, is widely used and has psychometric strength, but it is one-dimensional and seems to best reflect emotional support.

Several social support measures have been used or adapted for research in sport and exercise settings. Duncan and McAuley (1993) used the SPS to investigate social support, self-efficacy, and exercise behaviors with sedentary, middle-aged men and women. Social support did not directly influence exercise behavior but had an indirect effect through self-efficacy. The results suggest that social support may help promote self-efficacy for exercise and thus health-related exercise behavior. Duncan and McAuley cautioned that in practice, exercise leaders or others in support positions may have difficulty matching support to needs, and it is important to monitor perceived support in relation to intentions and program goals. Also, with the mediating role of self-efficacy, supportive interventions should try to foster self-reliance and avoid dependency.

Sarason et al. (1990) summarized much social support research using the SSQ, and Kelley and Gill (1993) used the SSQ to investigate the role of social support in stress and burnout with collegiate coaches. Using Smith's (1986) stress and burnout model as a framework, they found that satisfaction with social support was related to perceived stress and that perceived stress in turn predicted burnout. Rosenfeld, Richman, and Hardy (1989) found that student-athletes' social support networks consisted of coaches and teammates who provided mostly task challenge support, friends who provided mostly listening support, and parents who provided mostly task appreciation support.

Social support is particularly applicable to sport injury and rehabilitation (Hardy & Crace, 1993). Health psychology research (e.g., Cohen, 2004; Shumaker & Brownell, 1984) indicates that social support plays a role in stress reduction and health promotion. Several sport and exercise psychologists suggest that social support may play a similar role in sport injury and rehabilitation (e.g., Shaffer & Wiese-Bjornstal, 1999; Wiese & Weiss, 1987).

Providing Social Support to Injured Athletes

On the basis of the literature, Hardy and Crace (1993) offer guidelines to sport psychology consultants and other sports medicine professionals for providing social support to injured athletes.

Providing Emotional Support

- **Listen carefully.** Be an active listener. Use supportive and confirming behaviors while listening, and be patient.
- **Know thyself.** Be aware of your needs as well as your reactions to others.
- **Switch hats occasionally.** Be ready to use various forms of support, and find a form that is natural for you.
- **Involve the natural helping network.** Have regular informal contact with coaches, teammates, trainers, family, and important others.
- **Create an open environment.** Create an open and accepting environment.

Providing Informational Support

- **Develop your injury knowledge base.** You must have content expertise in order to provide task support.
- **Deliver effective instructional feedback.** Feedback should affirm task mastery and effort and should be sincere.
- **Use technical modalities.** Use physiological, biomechanical, or psychological tools as appropriate. Modern technology has much to offer.
- **Don't be afraid to challenge and confront.** Deal with injured athletes in a straightforward, honest manner.
- **Provide reality touchstones.** This might involve meetings with other injured athletes or support groups.

Providing Tangible Support

- **Beware of boundaries.** Consider National Collegiate Athletic Association (NCAA) regulations, and check with coaches, administrators, or trainers.
- **Define your boundaries.** Develop your philosophy in relation to regulations, your qualifications, and options. Communicate your boundaries to athletes.
- **Deliver on time.** Tangible support is best received at the time it is requested. But although timeliness is important, some injured athletes may require long-term tangible support and a supportive network can help avoid depletion of resources or burnout.
- **Offer interest-free tangible support.** Do not put the recipient in a state of indebtedness to you, especially psychologically. Give support freely and unconditionally.

Application Point

Assume you are an athletic trainer or therapist working with an injured athlete. How could you provide tangible, informational, and emotional support in your clinic or training room? Give specific examples.

Hardy and Crace (1993) also offer general advice for effectively supporting injured athletes. Athletes should list potential supporters and describe what they would like these people to do. Then athletes should develop a plan, listing steps for requesting support, a time frame, and some alternative plans. Athletes should maintain regular contact with their support network and monitor the support process. They need to find ways to show that the support provider is appreciated and valued. Also, athletes must realize that they can use their own resources as a support system for themselves and others. As with most psychological skills and strategies, the goal is self-control, mastery, and the development of self-support.

At this time, sport and exercise psychologists have incorporated social support primarily in relation to injuries and rehabilitation. This work is promising not only for sport injury but also for wider application. Social support has obvious ties to such group dynamics topics as communication and cohesion, and Rosenfeld and Richman (1997) offer a social support perspective on team building.

COHESION IN SPORT AND EXERCISE GROUPS

Cohesion is the most popular group dynamics topic in sport and exercise psychology. Most of the research is on the cohesion–performance relationship in sport, with some more recent research on cohesion in exercise groups. Despite more than 35 years of research on the relationship between cohesion and sport team performance, the evidence does not consistently support the intuitive assumption that cohesive teams win more games. Research does suggest that cohesion benefits the group and group members, but relationships vary with individual and group characteristics and ever-changing group processes.

Cohesion Defined

Before discussing the research, let's clarify the terms *cohesion* and *cohesiveness*, which are used interchangeably in the literature. Within the group dynamics literature, most articles cite the classic definition of cohesiveness as "the total field of forces which act on members to remain in a group" (Festinger, Schachter, & Back, 1950, p. 164) or variations such as "resultant forces," "fields of forces," "attraction to group," or "sense of we-ness." Unfortunately, these characterizations are nearly impossible to operationalize, and they emphasize individuals rather than group cohesion.

Within sport and exercise psychology, the most systematic research has been conducted by the Canadian trio of Bert Carron, Larry Brawley, and Neil Widmeyer. Carron, Brawley, and Widmeyer (1998) laid the groundwork by developing a conceptual framework and defining cohesion as "a dynamic process which is reflected in the tendency for a group to stick together and remain united in the pursuit of its instrumental objectives and/or the satisfaction of member affective needs" (p. 213). Carron's definition provides a starting point and incorporates some features particularly relevant to sport and exercise psychology.

First, cohesion is multidimensional, resulting from many factors that may differ across groups. Second, cohesion is dynamic, changing over time through the dynamic group processes. Third, cohesion is instrumental; group members cohere for reasons, whether to be part of a university basketball team or to maintain an exercise program. Fourth, cohesion has an affective dimension; even in highly task-oriented groups such as sport teams, social cohesion generally develops through interactions and communications. Finally, cohesion is perceived differently by different groups and members. Carron and colleagues (e.g., Carron et al., 2005; Widmeyer et al., 2002) proposed a multidimensional model that is the basis for most current sport and exercise psychology work on cohesion.

Carron's Model of Cohesion

Carron's model, which is illustrated in figure 15.3, includes environmental, personal, leadership, and team factors that contribute to and are influenced by multidimensional cohesion. These cohesion sources parallel the environmental, individual, and group factors of the group dynamics models presented earlier.

Environmental factors include physical proximity; people who are physically close to each other tend to bond together, as do team members who live near each other or travel together. Distinctiveness from other groups also increases feelings of unity. Special privileges, club T-shirts, or group rituals might all enhance distinctiveness. Widmeyer, Brawley, and Carron (1990) suggest an inverted-U relationship between group size and social cohesion in intramural basketball, with moderate-sized groups showing greatest cohesiveness. However, Williams and Widmeyer (1991) found no relationship between group size and social cohesion with golf teams, and we cannot draw strong conclusions about size and cohesion.

Personal factors reflect individual abilities, attitudes, and commitment. Eys et al. (2006) suggest that the most important personal factor is satisfaction; other personal sources of cohesion include similarity of group members, competitive state anxiety, degree to which members engage in social loafing, and commitment to the team. Leadership factors reflect relationships with the coach. Generally, a more democratic decision style is better for cohesiveness than an autocratic style, and compatibility between coaches and athletes and among group members is also related to cohesiveness.

Team factors relate to the group structure (roles, norms), group processes (goals, communication), and group outcomes. Group roles are behaviors expected of people who occupy specific positions. For example, a coach has a clear position and expectations, such as planning strategies and instructing athletes. Roles may be formal (e.g., team captain, exercise leader) or informal (e.g., team enforcer, class clown). Research suggests that when people understand their roles (role clarity), accept their roles (role acceptance), and carry out their roles (role performance), groups are more effective, and as Eys et al. (2006) note, more cohesive. Group norms, which are standards or expectations, are also related to cohesion (Gammage, Carron, & Estabrooks, 2001). Eys et al. (2006) note that establishing group goals promotes cohesion, and they suggest that coaches emphasize group goals and downplay individual rewards.

Key Point

Research suggests that when people understand their roles (role clarity), accept their roles (role acceptance), and carry out their roles (role performance), groups are more effective and more cohesive.

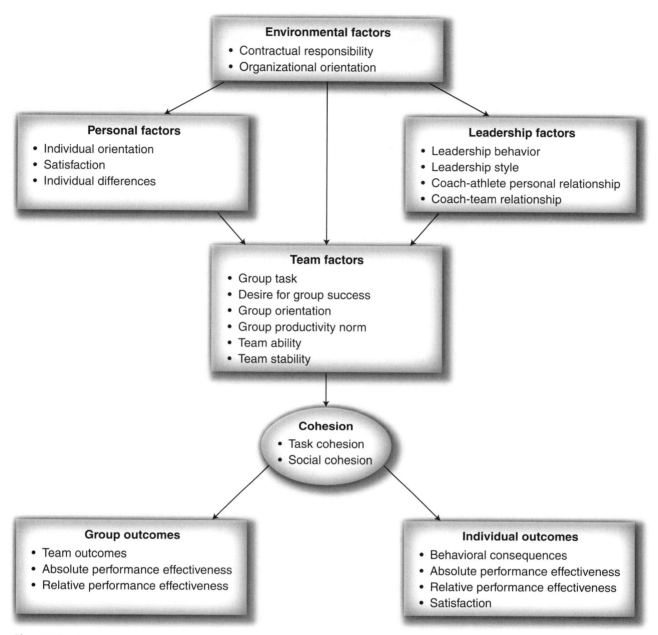

Figure 15.3

Framework for examining correlates of cohesion in sport teams.

Reprinted, by permission, from A.V. Carron, 1982, "Cohesiveness in sport groups: Interpretations and considerations," *Journal of Sport Psychology* 4: 131.

Communication is associated with cohesiveness in a circular way: Increased communication on task and social issues increases cohesion, and more cohesive groups have increased communication. Finally, performance success increases cohesion (Eys et al., 2006), as will be discussed in more detail when reviewing the research.

Measures of Cohesion

Most definitions and measures of cohesion are multidimensional. They are usually divided into interpersonal attraction (assessed in individual terms with friendship choices or other sociometric items) and a more direct attraction-to-group dimension (assessed with group-related items). Most early work used simple measures, with attraction-to-group the most common measure.

The first instrument developed to measure cohesiveness in sport was the Sport Cohesiveness Questionnaire (SCQ; Martens, Landers, & Loy, 1972). Items assess attraction among group members, attraction to the whole group, and perception of the entire group. The SCQ was the only sport-specific measure before 1984, but researchers have questioned its validity and it is seldom used today.

Carron's (1982) conceptual model prompted two sport-specific instruments. The Multidimensional Sport Cohesion Instrument (MSCI; Yukelson, Weinberg, & Jackson, 1984) assesses both task and social aspects of group cohesiveness, but it was not developed from a conceptual model, and items are specific to basketball. Reliability and validity have not been established, and the MSCI has not been used subsequently.

Brawley, Carron, and Widmeyer worked together to develop the most widely used cohesion measure in sport and exercise psychology. Using Carron's (1982) definition, they developed a model with two general categories: Group integration, or perceptions of the group as a whole, and individual attractions to the group (figure 15.4; for detailed discussion, see Carron, Brawley, & Widmeyer, 2002, or Widmeyer et al., 2002). Each category has task and social aspects, and the resulting model includes four related dimensions of cohesion:

- Group integration–Task
- Group integration–Social
- Individual attractions to the group–Task
- Individual attractions to the group–Social

To measure the four dimensions, the authors developed the Group Environment Questionnaire (GEQ; Brawley, Carron, & Widmeyer, 1987; Carron, Brawley, & Widmeyer, 2002; Carron, Widmeyer, & Brawley, 1985). This 18-item, four-scale measure has good internal consistency and is applicable to a variety of sport and exercise groups.

Subsequently, Estabrooks and Carron (2000) adapted the GEQ to develop a cohesion measure more appropriate for exercise groups, the Physical Activity GEQ (PAGEQ), which has the same four subscales.

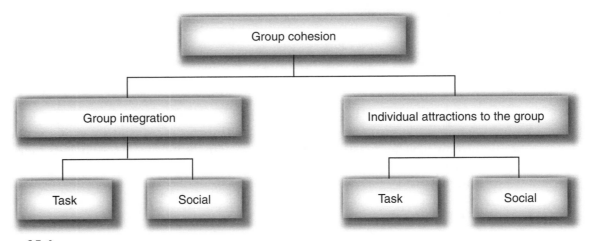

Figure 15.4
Conceptual model of group cohesion.
Reprinted, by permission, from A.V. Carron, W.N. Widmeyer, and L.R. Brawley, 1985, "The measurement of cohesion in sport teams," *Journal of Sport Psychology* 3(7): 244-264.

RESEARCH ON THE COHESION–PERFORMANCE RELATIONSHIP

Martens and Peterson's studies involving more than 1,200 male intramural basketball players on 144 teams are an early benchmark, providing some of the strongest support for a positive relationship between cohesiveness and performance. The first study (Martens & Peterson, 1971), which examined preseason cohesiveness as a determinant of team success, showed that high-cohesive teams won more games than low-cohesive teams. The second study (Peterson & Martens, 1972), which investigated the influence of team success on postseason cohesiveness, showed that successful teams were more cohesive than less successful teams.

Several studies (e.g., Landers, Wilkinson, Hatfield, & Barber, 1982) confirmed the positive relationship between cohesion and success with basketball teams. Others found similar positive relationships for several other sports (e.g., Bird, 1977; Carron & Ball, 1977; Ruder & Gill, 1982; Williams & Hacker, 1982; Williams & Widmeyer, 1991).

These studies seem to make a strong case, but several studies found either no relationship (e.g., Melnick & Chemers, 1974) or negative relationships (e.g., Landers & Lueschen, 1974). Some of the inconsistent research results reflect questionable measures, poor sampling procedures, and inappropriate analyses, but methodological deficiencies are not confined to studies with negative relationships and do not account for the equivocal findings. With updated models and measures, researchers have examined moderators, mediators, and causality to shed more light on the cohesion–performance relationship.

Causality in the Cohesion–Performance Relationship

Causality is a key consideration: Does cohesion predict success, or does success predict cohesion? A common way of inferring causality is to examine how preseason cohesion relates to subsequent team performance (usually win–loss ratio). Generally, research on the reverse relationship (i.e., how season performance relates to postseason cohesion) has yielded stronger and more consistent positive relationships.

Key Point

The research on cohesion and performance suggests that causality flows from performance success to cohesion; evidence in the other direction is weaker. However, Carron, Colman, et al. (2002) found similar relationships in both directions in their meta-analysis.

Bakeman and Helmreich (1975) used a cross-lagged panel design assessing both cohesion and performance at two separate times with aquanaut teams. Results indicated that first-segment performance was highly related to second-segment cohesiveness, whereas first-segment cohesiveness was not related to second-segment performance. Carron and Ball (1977) applied the cross-lagged panel design with ice hockey teams and also found a positive correlation between midseason performance and postseason cohesion—but no support for the influence of cohesion on later performance success.

These findings do not necessarily imply that cohesion does not influence performance. Preseason cohesiveness that is assessed before members have interacted as a group is likely to be unreliable. With postseason measures, the team members have had an opportunity to interact and develop cohesiveness, but retrospective postseason measures may reflect the glow of success. Continuing research using stronger designs and measures indicates that the cohesion–performance relationship is more dynamic and complex than observations and the early research findings suggest. Several studies, as well as Mullen and Copper's (1994) review, confirm a stronger relationship from performance success to cohesion than from cohesion to success. However, Carron, Colman, Wheeler, and Stevens (2002) found similar relationships in both directions in their meta-analysis.

Moderators of the Cohesion–Performance Relationship

Widmeyer et al. (2002) identified several moderating and mediating variables that may have an impact on cohesion and performance, and task characteristics are particularly important. Landers (1974) noted that positive relationships had generally been reported for divisible or interactive tasks (e.g., basketball, hockey), whereas negative relationships had generally been observed with unitary tasks (e.g., bowling, rowing). However, subsequent reviews (Carron, Colman, et al., 2002; Mullen & Copper, 1994) suggest similar positive cohesion–performance relationships across both interactive and coactive tasks.

Zander (1971) suggested that cohesiveness leads to greater motivation and commitment to team goals, which implies that cohesion should have a positive influence on team goals and performance. However, if team goals detract from individual goals, cohesion may negatively influence individual performance. When individual performance is critical and team members do not interact (e.g., wrestling, golf, swimming), individual goals should be emphasized. Support and encouragement from teammates may help, but such support can be directed toward individual performance. If cohesion enhances commitment to team goals, and if team goals emphasize important individual contributions, then cohesiveness should enhance performance for noninteractive as well as interactive sports. Indeed, a study with golf teams (Williams & Widmeyer, 1991) supports a positive relationship between team task cohesion and performance.

Another moderating variable, *group norms,* received more attention in the early social psychology literature. In a classic lab experiment, Schachter, Ellerton, McBride, and Gregory (1951) observed that members of high-cohesive groups complied with the group norm whether the norm was for greater or lesser productivity. Subsequent studies confirmed that highly cohesive groups outperformed less cohesive groups only if the group norms called for better performance.

A sport team adhering to a group norm that contradicts performance success is difficult to imagine, but sport and exercise groups may well have unique norms. Sport teams are highly task-oriented groups, and cohesion is more likely related to commitment to team task goals, agreement on task roles and strategies, and other task-related team norms than to interpersonal attraction.

Cohesion and Exercise Groups

Investigations of cohesion in physical activity settings other than sport teams are rare but expanding. The initial research on cohesion in exercise settings suggests that cohesion facilitates exercise adherence. Studies with university classes indicate that participants who report higher cohesion attend more classes and are less likely to drop out (Carron, Widmeyer, & Brawley, 1988; Spink & Carron, 1992, 1993). Task cohesion was the key dimension in university classes, but with a private health club, social cohesion was more important in predicting dropout rates (Spink & Carron, 1994). In their meta-analysis of social influence and exercise, Carron, Hausenblas, and Mack (1996) suggested that cohesion, especially task cohesion, influences exercise adherence.

Summary of the Cohesion–Performance Research

The sport and exercise psychology literature indicates that cohesion, defined and measured as a multidimensional construct, is positively related to sport team performance. Although some studies and reviews suggest success is more likely to lead to cohesion than vice versa, the relationship seems cyclic. In their meta-analysis of the sport research, Carron, Colman, et al. (2002) concluded that the moderate positive relationship held for both task and social cohesion, across sport type and levels of competition, and in both directions. Mediators and moderators influence the relationship, which is complex and dynamic. However, the practical value of team cohesion is clear. Teamwork is one potential consequence of cohesion, which may affect teams and individuals beyond performance. Sport and exercise psychologists could investigate the influence of cohesion on interpersonal and cooperative skills. Regardless of performance, cohesion could influence group members' satisfaction with the experience, liking for the activity, and later participation in physical activity.

We know little about how cohesion is developed and maintained in sport and exercise groups. The key likely lies in the complexities of group process. The recent work on team building may help us move to a fuller understanding of cohesion and the dynamics of sport and exercise groups.

PUTTING GROUP DYNAMICS INTO PRACTICE: TEAM BUILDING

Team building puts group dynamics models and research into practice. That team-building approach moves beyond the limited focus of the earlier work on cohesion and performance to a more encompassing group dynamics framework. Also, researchers and consultants have applied the team-building approach in both sport and exercise settings.

Team Building Defined

Key Point

Team building can be characterized as team enhancement for both task and social purposes.

Team building is popular in organizational psychology research and application. That work is quite adaptable to physical activity settings, and coaches and other kinesiology professionals often use team building. Brawley and Paskevich (1997) summarized the organizational development definitions and concluded that team building is a method of helping the group to increase effectiveness, satisfy the needs of its members, or improve work conditions. In a more concise statement, Carron et al. (2005) stated that team building can be characterized as "team enhancement for both task and social purposes" (p. 327).

Team-Building Models

Team-building models are similar to the Widmeyer et al. (2002) group dynamics model. Hardy and Crace (1997) noted that most models focus on enhancing team effectiveness by improving team processes. Team performance is often the output of interest, but in Carron and Spink's (1993) team-building framework (figure 15.5), cohesion is the target output. Here, inputs include group environment (distinctiveness) and group structure (i.e., group norms and positions). Throughput is the

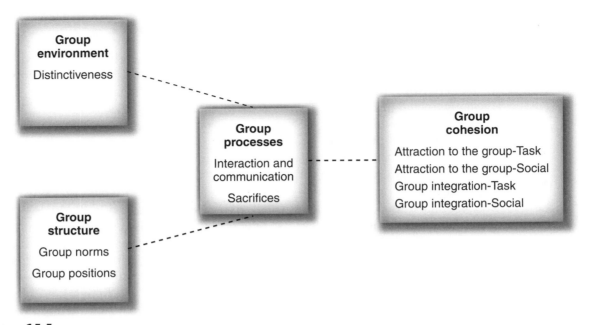

Figure 15.5
Conceptual framework of a team-building program for fitness classes.
Adapted, by permission, from A.V. Carron and K.S. Spink, 1993, "Team building in an exercise setting," *The Sport Psychologist* 7(1): 11.

group process—interaction, communication, and sacrifices. Cohesion, the output component, is typically measured as the four dimensions of the GEQ.

Team-Building Interventions

According to Carron and colleagues (Carron & Spink, 1993; Carron, Spink, & Prapavessis, 1997), the aim of team-building interventions is to increase group effectiveness by enhancing group cohesiveness. Team-building work in sport and exercise settings differs from work in organizational settings in that the team-building interventions are more indirect (Carron et al., 1997)—most interventions are filtered through a coach or leader. Thus, Carron and colleagues work with the coach or leader a great deal. Others who have used team building, such as Yukelson (1997), have worked more directly with team members.

The guiding model for the team-building efforts of Carron and colleagues involves four stages. The first three stages typically occur in a workshop with coaches or leaders; in the fourth stage, the coach or leader applies team-building strategies with the team members. The introductory stage and the conceptual stage give the coach or leader an overview of the benefits of cohesion and a frame of reference. The conceptual model identifies factors within each category that contribute to the development of cohesiveness. In the practical stage, coaches or leaders brainstorm to identify specific strategies to use for team building with their group. Finally, in the intervention stage, the coaches or leaders introduce and maintain the team-building protocols in the group setting.

Carron and colleagues (Carron & Spink, 1993; Carron et al., 1997) have used their intervention successfully with fitness classes and sport teams. With university aerobics classes (Carron & Spink, 1993), specific interventions addressed group environment, group structure, and group processes. Distinctiveness, the target of the group-environment intervention, included such strategies as group names and T-shirts. Group structure included both individual position (e.g., pick spots) and group norm (e.g., establish partner goals) interventions. Group process interventions included sacrifices (regulars helping new people) and interaction and communication (taking turns in partner activities). The 8-week intervention increased group task cohesion, which was consistent with the goal of the intervention. Continuing research and team-building interventions with other sport and exercise groups are providing promising results (see Eys et al., 2006, or Carron et al., 2005, for more detailed reviews).

In their team-building interventions, Crace and Hardy (1997) take a values-based approach and emphasize awareness of individual and team values, identification of interfering factors, and development of interventions to improve mutual respect and cohesion. Yukelson (1997) focuses on developing an effective team culture with open communication and offers the following suggestions:

- Get to know your athletes as unique individuals (find out something special about each athlete).
- Develop pride in group membership and a sense of team identity (goal boards, team covenants).
- Develop team goals and team commitment (comprehensive goal-setting program).
- Provide for goal evaluations (chart progress, ongoing evaluation, and feedback).
- Make roles clear (clarify role expectations, build mutual understanding).
- Have periodic team meetings to discuss how things are progressing (designated time to talk openly).
- Use player counsel (Yukelson has used player counsel through regularly scheduled meetings with team leaders or representatives).

Eys et al. (2006, p. 169) provide a list of team-building strategies based on the existing research, along with examples for both sport and exercise groups. Following are examples from the five categories of distinctiveness, individual positions, group norms, individual sacrifices, and interaction and communication:

- Distinctiveness
  - Sport: Provide unique identifiers such as T-shirts, logos, or mottoes.
  - Exercise: Provide neon headbands or shoelaces; hang posters for class.
- Individual positions
  - Sport: Create team structure with clearly differentiated roles.
  - Exercise: Provide specific positions for high-, moderate-, and low-impact exercisers.
- Group norms
  - Sport: Point out individual contributions to the team's success.
  - Exercise: Encourage members to become fitness friends.
- Individual sacrifices
  - Sport: Ask veterans to sit out to give novices playing time.
  - Exercise: Ask regulars to help new people.
- Interaction and communication
  - Sport: Have players write down what they want from fellow teammates.
  - Exercise: Use partner work; take turns showing moves.

Application Point

You are coaching a regional softball team made up of players from several different teams that will go on to play in a state tournament. Thus, the players have not all been together on the same team before. Refer to the suggestions of Yukelson (1997) and Eys et al. (2006) and identify team-building strategies you might use with this team in your practice sessions and during the tournament.

PUTTING IT INTO PRACTICE

Now you are ready to put the content of chapter 15 into practice. Read the chapter summary, discuss the case study, answer the review questions, and enhance your knowledge by researching the recommended readings.

Summary

Interpersonal relationships and ongoing processes are keys to understanding group dynamics. At the same time, the complex dynamics of these interrelationships and processes make it difficult to draw firm conclusions and offer specific guidelines. First, the group dynamics literature confirms the common belief that the best players make the best team. Selecting the best players is not easy; group performance may require interactive skills not evident in individual performances. Coaches, instructors, and leaders might direct efforts toward developing interactive skills as well as performance skills in order to reduce coordination losses and enhance group performance.

The research on social loafing suggests strategies to reduce motivational losses; specifically, social loafing is reduced and individual effort enhanced when individual contributions to the group are clearly identified and recognized. Research on leadership suggests that the effectiveness of a specific style varies with the situation. Participatory styles are often promoted, but they may be ineffective and are seldom preferred by coaches and athletes on competitive teams. On the other hand, participatory styles might enhance cohesion and adherence in an exercise program.

Social support has many potential applications, especially in relation to exercise adherence and rehabilitation with injured athletes, and positive interpersonal relationships can enhance physical activity for all participants. Research indicates that cohesion is positively related to team success, but many mediators and moderators influence the cohesion–performance relationship.

To understand group dynamics, we must consider multidimensional relationships and dynamic processes. The team-building work clearly fits this approach and offers suggestions for developing cohesion and enhancing effectiveness of sport and exercise groups.

Case Study

The sport and exercise psychology literature reviewed in this chapter provides guidelines for using group dynamics research in professional practice. Several examples involve using team building to develop cohesion in sport teams and ways to use social support to promote rehabilitation with injured athletes. Group dynamics and interpersonal relationships are just as integral to other areas of kinesiology practice, including physical education and exercise programs. For each case, apply the chapter material to first determine why you might use social influence strategies (e.g., to enhance group performance or promote individual development) and then list specific strategies you might use.

Case 1

You are teaching middle school physical education and want to try team building with your seventh grade class. The students are a diverse group of boys and girls with varying skill levels and interests. First, why use team building? Second, what team-building strategies will you use? Refer to the examples in the chapter, but consider the unique characteristics of your class (e.g., individuals, structure, environment) and be creative.

Case 2

You are the instructor for the older adults exercise program at the senior center. Participants are in good health and come to the center three times a week for a 1-hour session that includes individual exercises (weights, machines, stretching) as well as group instruction. As the chapter indicates, social support has positive effects in exercise settings. First, why use social support? Second, what specific strategies will you use to provide social support as the instructor and to foster social support among group members?

Review Questions

1. Define *group* as the term is used in sport and exercise psychology.
2. Compare McGrath's (1984) conceptual framework for groups and Widmeyer et al.'s (2002) model.
3. Discuss Steiner's (1972) model of individual–group performance.
4. Define the *Ringelmann effect* and its related term, *social loafing*.
5. Explain Karau and Williams' (1995) collective effort model, and identify strategies for reducing social loafing.
6. Define *social support*. Identify the three main types of social support, and give an example of each in sport and exercise settings.
7. Describe Carron's (Carron et al., 2005) conceptual model of cohesion.
8. Describe Carron and Spink's (1993) team-building framework.
9. Identify guidelines and suggestions for team-building interventions in sport and exercise settings.

Recommended Reading

Carron, A.V., Spink, K.S., & Prapavessis, H. (1997). Team building and cohesiveness in the sport and exercise setting: Use of indirect interventions. *Journal of Applied Sport Psychology, 9,* 61-72.

> Team building is particularly relevant to sport and exercise psychology practice. In this article the authors present their model of team building and sport group cohesion, and they offer suggestions for both research and intervention.

Eys, M.A., Burke, S.M., Carron, A.V., & Dennis, P.W. (2006). The sport team as an effective group. In J.M. Williams, *Applied sport psychology: Personal growth to peak performance* (5th ed., pp. 157-173). Boston: McGraw-Hill.

This chapter provides an overview of the sport team as an effective group, including models of group processes, the role of cohesion, leadership, and team building in effective groups.

Karau, S.J., & Williams, K.D. (1995). Social loafing: Research findings, implications, and future directions. *Psychological Science, 4*(5), 134-139.

Social loafing refers to individuals giving less effort in groups, and Karau and Williams provide an excellent overview of that research and its implications.

Chapter 16

Gender, Diversity, and Cultural Competence

Chapter Objectives

After studying this chapter, you should be able to

♦ understand what is meant by *multicultural psychology;*

♦ identify ways in which a person's sport and exercise experience can be affected by gender, race, and cultural stereotypes and discrimination; and

♦ discuss the role of cultural competence in professional practice.

Gender and cultural diversity are ever present and powerful in sport and exercise. Participants are diverse, and physical activity takes place in a culturally diverse world. People cannot be separated from their gender and cultural context. Gender makes a difference, and race matters (to borrow the title of Cornel West's 1993 book).

This chapter takes an encompassing multicultural perspective, covers gender and multicultural scholarship, and offers directions for enhancing multicultural competencies in professional practice. It should help you understand the critical role of cultural context and the many ways in which the sport and exercise experience is shaped by gender and culture.

MULTICULTURAL FRAMEWORK

The growing multicultural psychology scholarship, along with the feminist and sport studies literature, converge on common themes that form the multicultural framework for this chapter. All emphasize multiple, intersecting cultural identities; highlight power relations; and call for social action and advocacy.

• *Multiple, intersecting cultural identities.* We all have gender, race and ethnicity, and other intersecting identities, with the mix varying across individuals, time, and contexts.

• *Power relations.* Gender and culture relations involve power and privilege: Who makes the rules? Who is left out?

• *Action and advocacy.* Multicultural perspectives demand action for social justice. Psychology and kinesiology professionals develop multicultural competencies and advance sport and exercise psychology in the public interest.

Multicultural psychology may be defined as the "systematic study of behavior, cognition and affect in many cultures" (Mio, Barker-Hackett, & Tumambing, 2006,

p. 3). Culture, however, is complex and not easily defined. Narrow definitions emphasize ethnicity, but multicultural psychologists typically broaden the definition to shared values, beliefs, and practices of an identifiable group of people. Thus, culture includes race and ethnicity, language, spirituality, sexuality, and of particular relevance for sport and exercise psychology, physicality (physical abilities and characteristics). Multicultural psychology further emphasizes intersections of identities and the totality of experiences and contexts.

Feminist and sport studies scholarship also emphasizes intersecting cultural relations and calls for moving from scholarship to social action. For example, bell hooks' definition of feminism as "a movement to end sexism, sexist exploitation, and oppression" (2000, p. viii) is inclusive rather than exclusive and focuses on action to end oppression.

Sport studies scholar M. Ann Hall (1996) also emphasizes multiple, intersecting identities and calls for moving from theory into real-world action. Feminism and multiculturalism demand professional and social action. Specifically, culturally competent kinesiology professionals must take action to ensure that physical activity is inclusive and empowering for all participants.

Psychology has moved beyond its decidedly nonmulticultural past, described in Robert Guthrie's (1998) aptly titled book, *Even the Rat Was White*. Multicultural scholars have expanded scholarly research and professional practice and have challenged the foundations of psychology. For example, Trickett, Watts, and Birman (1994) advocate moving from the dominant psychology emphasis on biology, isolating basic processes, rigorous experimental designs, and a critical-realist philosophy of science to an emphasis on people in context. By definition, psychology focuses on individual behavior, thoughts, and feelings, but we cannot fully understand the individual without considering the larger world.

Derald Wing Sue (2004), who has written extensively on multiculturalism in psychology, argues that psychology must make the invisible visible—recognize white privilege and the culture-bound nature of our scholarship and practice—to advance its mission and enhance the health and well-being of all people. But moving beyond cultural boundaries and traditional approaches is no easy task. The sport and exercise context has clear cultural boundaries, and we must consider people in that context in order to understand their behavior. Multicultural psychologists call for attention to power relations and social context but also retain concern for the individual. The combined focus on the individual and cultural relations may seem paradoxical, but that combination is the essence of a useful multicultural sport and exercise psychology. The goal is to apply our understanding to help people in the real world—to promote inclusive and empowering physical activity for all.

CULTURAL CONTEXT OF SPORT AND EXERCISE

Before reviewing the literature on gender and cultural diversity, let's identify the cultural context of sport and exercise. As a warm-up, consider how gender and culture might affect your thoughts, feelings, and behaviors in the following cases:

- A 10-year-old soccer player who lacks control and is prone to angry outbursts on the field explains this behavior by stating, "I really get into the game, and sometimes I just lose it."

• A student in high school physical education is withdrawn and reluctant to get into the action despite good physical skills and your encouragement.

• An athletic trainer suspects that a figure skater may have an eating disorder, but the skater claims to be working to make it to nationals and get endorsements.

Imagine each case with a female and then with a male. Does gender influence your response to these cases? Do you think a teacher, coach, trainer, or parent would behave the same with a female versus a male? What about culture—would your responses vary if the participants were immigrants from a non-Western cultural tradition? If you try to eliminate all considerations of gender and ethnicity and treat everyone the same, you will have difficulty. Again, gender makes a difference and race matters. Trying to treat everyone in the same manner does a disservice to the participants.

Application Point

Assume that you are an exercise instructor in a community recreation center. Identify various ways participants in your exercise classes might differ from you (consider gender, age, race and ethnicity, physical characteristics, and so on). Then identify ways participants are likely to differ from each other. No doubt you will have a long list. Participants are diverse, and that diversity affects behaviors and relationships.

Gender in Sport and Exercise

Our world is shaped by gender and culture; the influence is so pervasive that it's impossible to pinpoint. Gender influence is particularly powerful in sport and exercise and has some unique features.

Physical activity participants are diverse, but not as diverse as the broader population. Until the 1970s, when an identifiable sport and exercise psychology emerged, *athlete* meant male athlete, and male athletes were not culturally diverse. School physical education and community youth programs may come close to reflecting community diversity, but elite sport and exercise programs reflect cultural restrictions, particularly gender relations.

The physical education roots of sport and exercise psychology provide a unique gender context. Strong women leaders developed women's physical education as an alternative to men's physical education programs and provided a female-oriented environment long before the women's movement of the 1970s. At a 1923 conference, physical education leaders set guidelines that included putting athletes first, preventing exploitation, downplaying competition while emphasizing enjoyment and good sporting behavior, promoting activity for all rather than an elite few, and developing women as sport leaders. A related clarifying statement (National Amateur Athletic Federation [NAAF], 1930, p. 41) concluded with the classic statement, "A game for every girl and every girl in a game." The 1972 passage of Title IX of the Education Amendments, the U.S. law that prohibits sex discrimination against students and employees of educational institutions, marked the beginning of a move away from the early women's physical education model toward the competitive women's sport programs of today.

Female athletic participation has exploded in the last generation. Still, the numbers of female and male participants are not equal. More important, female athletes are not the same as male athletes—gender makes a difference. To understand gender concerns, we must look beyond biological sex and simple dichotomous sex differences to the social context.

Citius, Altius, Fortius—the Olympic motto—translates as "swifter, higher, stronger," underscoring the physical but also implying that sport is competitive and hierarchical. The average male may be taller, faster, and stronger than the average female, but biological sex is only part of the gender mix. All the meanings, social roles, and expectations, as well as the standards of behavior, beauty, and power, are constructed in the sport and exercise culture. Sport does not have to be higher, faster, and stronger; instead, it might consist of fun, flair, and friendship. (I disclose my biases: I am not high, fast, strong, or competitive.)

Cultural Diversity in Sport and Exercise

In considering cultural diversity, it is important to go beyond participation numbers to consider power and privilege, or who makes the rules. Sue (2004) illustrates the power differential in noting that although white males make up just 33% of the U.S. population, they hold 80% of tenured faculty positions, 92% of *Forbes* 400 CEO-level positions, 80% of House of Representatives seats and 84% of Senate seats, and of special interest here, they make up 99% of athletic team owners. Most readers of this chapter are in privileged positions, but as Sue noted, we seldom recognize our own privilege. So-called color blindness often denies opportunity to others.

Richard Lapchick has been monitoring gender and racial diversity in sport for several years, and his *Racial and Gender Report Card* shows racial and gender inequities with little progress. The 2004 report card (Lapchick, 2005) indicates that African Americans are 24.6% of the male athletes and 14.8% of the female athletes in Division I, a higher percentage than in the overall U.S. population. Latino athletes are around 3% for both males and females, far less than their population percentage, with Asian American and Native American athletes at even lower percentages. Interestingly, nonresident aliens make up a higher percentage (around 4.5%) than any racial or ethnic minority group other than African Americans.

When we consider positions of power, diversity is nonexistent. Before Title IX (1972), more than 90% of women's athletic teams were coached by women and had a woman athletic director. Today less than half of women's teams are coached by women, and less than 20% have a woman director (Carpenter & Acosta, 2006). White men dominate coaching, even of women's teams. The 2004 racial report card indicated that African American men coach 7.2% of men's teams and 3.4% of women's teams, but African American women coach only 1.6% of women's teams. Coaches of other racial and ethnic identities hardly can be counted, and administration remains solidly white male. Clearly, elite sport is elite and not culturally diverse.

What about exercise? The typical exerciser in research and in the fitness club is a young, white, fit, middle-class male. *Physical activity,* a more inclusive term, suggests diversity, but census data and public health reports indicate otherwise: Physical activity is limited by gender, race, class, and especially by physical attributes. Physical activity decreases across the adult life span, with men more active than women, racial and ethnic minorities less active across all age groups, and young adult women (particularly African American women) one of the most inactive populations in the United States (Kimm et al., 2002; Pratt, Macera, & Blanton, 1999; U.S. Department of Health and Human Services [USDHHS], 2000).

In one of the few studies to specifically look at social class with a national database, Crespo, Ainsworth, Keteyian, Heath, and Smit (1999) found inactivity to be more common in less privileged social classes and females to be more inactive in all class groups. Crespo (2005) outlines the cultural barriers and calls for professionals to consider unique needs and cultural constraints when giving advice on exercise. Physical activity professionals can use resources such as the Robert Wood Johnson report on the Active Living Diversity Project (www.rwjf.org/publications).

Cultural Diversity in Sport and Exercise Psychology

Despite the diversity of participants and need for cultural competence in professional practice, sport and exercise psychology has not adopted multicultural perspectives. Research does not address diversity, professional practice focuses on elite sport, educational programs do not incorporate multicultural competencies, and sport and exercise psychology does not serve the public interest.

Duda and Allison (1990) first identified the lack of research on race and ethnicity, reporting that only 1 of 13 published theoretical papers and 7 of 186 empirical papers (less than 4%) considered race or ethnicity, and most of those were sample descriptions. Ram, Starek, and Johnson (2004) reviewed articles in sport and exercise psychology journals between 1987 and 2000 for both race and ethnicity and sexual orientation content, and they confirmed the persistent void in the scholarly literature. They found that only 20% of the articles made reference to race or ethnicity and 1.2% to sexual orientation. More important, those few articles provided little analysis or insights. Ram et al. concluded that there is no systematic attempt to include the experiences of marginalized groups. Further, Cindra Kamphoff and colleagues (Kamphoff, Araki, & Gill, 2004) surveyed AASP conference programs from the first conference in 1986 to 2003 and found little attention to multicultural concerns. Those few abstracts that examined diversity focused on sample comparisons and gender differences. Clearly, multicultural perspectives are missing and cultural diversity is marginalized in sport and exercise psychology.

Sport and exercise settings, educational programs, and professional practice are culturally elite. Sport and exercise psychology could play a unique role by applying its expertise to promote physical activity for all so that the health and well-being benefits are not limited to the elite. To do that, sport and exercise psychology must expand the research base on gender and cultural diversity and adopt multicultural competencies for professional practice. Although sport and exercise psychology does not yet have a multicultural scholarly base, we can draw from related gender and multicultural psychology scholarship.

GENDER SCHOLARSHIP IN SPORT AND EXERCISE PSYCHOLOGY

Gender scholarship in sport and exercise psychology largely follows gender scholarship within psychology, which has shifted from sex differences to gender role as personality to social context and processes. As Basow and Rubin (1999) explain, *gender* refers to the meaning attached to being female or male in a particular culture, and gender-role expectations vary with ethnicity, social class, and sexual orientation. This section highlights the gender scholarship that has most influenced sport and exercise psychology (see Gill, 2002, for extended discussion).

Sex Differences

Maccoby and Jacklin's (1974) classic review exemplifies the research on sex differences. Their main finding, which often is ignored, was that few conclusions could be drawn from the diverse literature on sex differences. Similarly, Ashmore (1990) later concluded that sex differences are relatively large for certain physical abilities (i.e., throwing velocity) and body use and posturing, are more modest for other abilities and social behaviors (e.g., math, aggression), and are negligible for all other domains. Average differences are elusive, and the evidence does not support biological dichotomous sex-linked connections. Hyde (2005) recently reviewed 46 meta-analyses of the extensive literature on sex differences and concluded that results support the gender similarities hypothesis: Males and females are more alike than different on psychological variables, and overstated claims of gender differences cause harm and limit opportunities.

Personality and Gender-Role Orientation

Psychologists interested in gender emphasize personality, following Bem's (1978) lead and using the Bem Sex Role Inventory (BSRI). Both males and females can have masculine or feminine personalities, and indeed, androgyny (high levels of both) is desirable. More recently, the masculine and feminine categories and measures have fallen out of favor, and even Bem (1993) has progressed to a more encompassing gender perspective. Still, most sport and exercise psychology gender research is based on that early work.

Spence and Helmreich (1978) reported that most female collegiate athletes were either androgynous or masculine, in contrast to nonathlete college females who were most often classified as feminine. Several studies yielded similar findings (e.g., Harris & Jennings, 1977), but that extensive research provides little insight into gender and physical activity. One recent study (Koca & Asci, 2005) expands our cultural perspective by surveying a large Turkish sample of female elite athletes and nonathletes. As with Western samples, Turkish female athletes scored higher on masculinity and were more likely to be classified as androgynous, whereas nonathletes were most often classified as feminine. Koca and Asci cited Choi (2000) in acknowledging that athletics, like other male-dominated occupations, is highly competitive and individual, and both females and males must be competitive, assertive, independent, and willing to take risks—all characteristics classified as masculine.

Overall, this research suggests that female athletes possess more masculine personality characteristics than do female nonathletes, but this is not particularly enlightening. The higher masculine scores of female athletes probably reflect an overlap with competitiveness, which can be measured directly (e.g., Gill & Deeter, 1988).

SOCIAL PERSPECTIVES IN GENDER RESEARCH

The social aspect of gender is more than perceptions and stereotypes; it's part of the larger social context. In *The Female World,* Jesse Bernard (1981) proposed that the social worlds for females and males are different even when they appear similar. In earlier times we created separate worlds with segregated physical education and sport programs. Although most activities are coed, the social worlds are different for female and male university basketball players, joggers, and youth soccer players.

Gender Stereotypes

Today, most psychologists look beyond the male–female and masculine–feminine dichotomies to developmental and social-cognitive models. That is, how people *think* males and females differ is more important than how they actually differ. Although actual differences between females and males are small and inconsistent, gender stereotypes are pervasive (e.g., Deaux, 1984; Deaux & Kite, 1993).

Gender stereotypes certainly exist within sport and exercise. In her classic analysis, Eleanor Metheny (1965) identified gender stereotypes and concluded that it is not socially appropriate for women to engage in contests in which

- the resistance of the opponent is overcome by bodily contact,
- the resistance of a heavy object is overcome by direct application of bodily force, or
- the body is projected into or through space over long distances or for extended amounts of time.

Gender stereotypes did not fade away with the implementation of Title IX. Kane and Snyder (1989) confirmed gender stereotyping of sports and more explicitly identified physicality with emphasis on physical muscularity, strength, and power as the key feature.

Stereotypes are a concern because we act on them, exaggerating minimal gender differences and restricting opportunities for everyone. Both girls and boys can participate in youth gymnastics or baseball, and at early ages physical capabilities are similar. Yet children see female gymnasts and male baseball players as role models, peers gravitate to sex-segregated activities, and most parents, teachers, and coaches support gender-appropriate activities of children. This cycle reflects the feminist position that gender is socially constructed, and it highlights cultural context.

Gender Bias in the Media

One prominent source of differential treatment is the media. Research (e.g., Kane, 1989; Kane & Parks, 1992; Messner, Duncan, & Jensen, 1993) shows that female athletes receive much less coverage than males. Moreover, females and males receive different coverage, with the emphasis on athletic ability and accomplishments for men and on femininity and physical attractiveness for women.

In a study of NCAA basketball tournaments and U.S. Open tennis coverage, Messner et al. (1993) noted less stereotyping than in earlier studies. However, they still found considerable gender marking (e.g., Women's Final Four, but Final Four for men) and gendered hierarchy of naming (e.g., females referred to as *girls, young ladies,* or *women;* men never referred to as *boys*).

Gender marking may be appropriate when symmetrical, as it was for most of the tennis coverage, but dissimilar marking labels females as other. Gendered language was also apparent in comments about strength and weakness (e.g., comments were clearly about strength for men; emotional reasons for failure were cited more often for women). Messner et al. (1993), noting that dominants in society are typically referred to by last names and subordinates by first names, found first names used more than 50% of the time to refer to females but only 10% of the time for males. Also, the few male athletes referred to by first names were black male basketball players. Current observations suggest less stereotyping, but institutional change is slow, and gendered beliefs persist.

Application Point

Select a newspaper, television news sport report, sport magazine, or sport Web site that covers a wide range of men's and women's sports, and review the coverage of men's and women's athletics. Note the proportion of the coverage of men compared with women and the type of coverage (e.g., references to accomplishments, personal lives, and gender marking). Did you find gender bias in this media coverage?

Gender and Competitive Achievement Orientation

Research on competitive achievement illustrates the shift from sex differences and gender roles to more complex social models. The early achievement research (McClelland, Atkinson, Clark, & Lowell, 1953) took male behavior as the norm until Horner (1972) focused attention on gender and fear of success. Horner's work faded quickly, and McElroy and Willis (1979) concluded that no evidence supports a fear of success in female athletes.

In our work with the Sport Orientation Questionnaire (SOQ; Gill & Deeter, 1988), competitiveness has been the primary discriminator between athletes and nonathletes (Gill, 1993). With international and university athletes and nonathletes from Taiwan (Kang, Gill, Acevedo, & Deeter, 1990), we found strong differences between athletes and nonathletes but minimal gender differences. One unique sample of ultramarathoners had low win orientations but very high goal orientations with no gender differences (Gill, 1993).

Other researchers report similar findings. When McNally and Orlick (1975) introduced a cooperative broomball game to children in urban Canada and in the northern territories, they found girls were more receptive than boys, and they also noted cultural differences in that northern children were more receptive. Duda (1986) reported similar gender and cultural influences with Anglo and Navajo children in the southwestern United States; male Anglo children were the most win oriented and placed the most emphasis on athletic ability. Weinberg (U.S.) and colleagues in Australia and New Zealand (Weinberg et al., 2000) found similar gender differences across the three cultures, with males higher on competitive, extrinsic, and social recognition motives and females higher on fitness, fun, and teamwork motives.

The competitiveness research helps put gender differences into perspective. Generally, males are more competitive than females, but overlap and similarity are the rule. Moreover, differences between athletes and nonathletes are stronger than gender differences. Overall, gender differences in competitiveness are limited and seem to reflect opportunity and experience in competitive sport—the context.

Physical Activity and Self-Perceptions

Gender and culture are prominent in the continuing research of Eccles and colleagues (e.g., Eccles, 1985; Eccles et al., 1999). Eccles and Harold (1991) confirmed that the model holds for sport achievement, that gender influences children's sport achievement perceptions and behaviors at a young age, and that these gender differences seem to be the product of gender-role socialization. Eccles consistently finds larger gender differences in sport competence than in other domains. Moreover, even in sport, the gender differences in perceptions are much larger than the gender differences in actual sport-related skills.

Fredericks and Eccles' (2004) review of the literature on parental influence and youth sport involvement revealed that parents held gender-stereotyped beliefs about athletics and were gender-typed in their behaviors, providing more opportunities and encouragement to sons than to daughters. Fredericks and Eccles (2005) tested these hypotheses and found that mothers and fathers were gender stereotyped in beliefs and practices. In addition, the parents' perception of the child's ability had the strongest relationship to the child's beliefs and participation. Their results confirmed that boys had higher perceived competence, value, and participation, despite the absence of gender differences in motor proficiency.

Considering the gender concerns in perceived sport competence and body image, physical activity has a tremendous potential to enhance girls' and women's sense of competence and control. Some research (Brown & Harrison, 1986; Choi, 2000; Holloway, Beuter, & Duda, 1988; Krane et al., 2004) confirms that exercise programs enhance the self-perception of female participants. Tiggemann and Williamson (2000), in one of the few studies including both women and men and a wide age range (16-60 years), found a negative relationship between exercise and self-perception for younger women but a positive relationship for mature women and both young and mature men. The results suggest that developmental changes and also different social processes are operating for young women.

Body Image

Body perceptions are particularly relevant to sport and exercise psychology. Most women recognize and strive for the societal ideal, which is much less than ideal in terms of physical and mental health. Boys and men also have concerns about body image, but the literature indicates that girls and women are much more negative and concerns are gender related. Girls are particularly concerned with physical beauty and maintaining the ideal thin shape, whereas boys are more concerned with size, strength, and power. Sanchez and Crocker (2005) found a negative relationship between investment in gender ideal and well-being with a culturally diverse sample of women and men. Those who buy into the unrealistic gender ideal pay the price in health and well-being.

Research on body image and gender in sport and exercise psychology focuses on gender ideals and unhealthy eating behaviors of female participants. Some researchers find positive relationships between participation in physical activity and body perceptions (Hausenblas & Mack, 1999), but others find negative relationships (Davis, 1992). Justine Reel and colleagues examined body image, eating disorders, and unique pressures in cheerleading and dance, activities likely to emphasize body issues. Reel and Gill (1996) found strong relationships between body dissatisfaction and eating disorders in high school and college cheerleaders. Reel and colleagues (Reel, SooHoo, Jamieson, & Gill, 2005) found that social physique anxiety and eating disorder scores were moderate, but college female dancers overwhelmingly reported pressure to lose weight due to mirrors, performance advantages, and landing roles.

Krane, Waldron, Michalenok, and Stiles-Shipley (2001) found that athletes reported positive affect and body image when considering themselves in the athletic context, but they reported more negative body image and maladaptive behaviors (disordered eating) in other social contexts. Cox and Thompson (2000) similarly reported that elite female soccer players were confident in their athletic bodies yet experienced dissatisfaction and anxiety related to their bodies. Greenleaf (2002) found that competitive female athletes recognized conflict between their athletic bodies and social ideals, but the incongruence did not seem problematic.

Fewer studies have examined self-perceptions and body image with the wider range of physical activity settings, but research suggests that exercise is associated with stronger self-perceptions (Caruso & Gill, 1992; McAuley, Bane, & Mihalko, 1995). Hausenblas and Fallon (2002) found that exercise behavior was the strongest predictor of body satisfaction for men, but it was not a predictor for females. Berman, DeSouza, and Kerr (2005) extended that line with recreational exercisers and found that although all women cited numerous benefits of physical activity, weight and appearance were the key motivators for exercise. They further explored the direction of the relationship and reported that concerns about weight and appearance prompted physical activity, with no evidence for reverse effects. Daubenmier (2005) found that yoga participants had more positive self-perceptions, higher body satisfaction, and less disordered eating than participants in aerobics and other activities.

Conception and Ebbeck (2005) explored the role of physical activity with survivors of domestic abuse, women who clearly can benefit from programs that foster empowerment and competence. The participants reported that physical activity provided a sense of accomplishment, enhanced mental and physical states, and a sense of normality. Although the study was limited in scope, it offers promising directions for using physical activity to enhance the well-being of women in a particular cultural context.

Overall, research on body perceptions and physical activity suggests that body image concerns are powerful and gender related, and that relationships vary with the activity and cultural context. Sport and exercise psychologists and kinesiology professionals who understand the role of gender and culture in body perceptions can better promote healthy sport and exercise behaviors.

Physical Activity and Social Development

Several researchers and community service professionals have promoted sport and physical activity programs for youth development (as discussed in chapter 14). Research supports benefits for both girls and boys, with gender and cultural variations.

Miller, Sabo, Farrell, Barnes, and Melnick (1999) used data from the CDC 1995 Youth Risk Behavior Survey of culturally diverse high school students to explore gender and sexuality in the sport context and to address the practical question, does sport reduce the risk of teen pregnancy? Girls who participated in sport were indeed at less risk for teen pregnancy, reporting lower rates of sexual experience, fewer partners, later age of first intercourse, higher rates of contraception use, and lower rates of past pregnancies. Boys in sport also reported higher contraceptive use, but on other measures they reported more sexual experience. Miller and colleagues suggested that athletic participation for girls leads to less adherence to conventional cultural scripts and more social and personal resources in sexual bargaining. Sport for boys provides similar resources but strengthens their commitment to traditional masculine scripts.

Notably, Miller and colleagues included a racially and ethnically diverse sample of both males and females. In addition to the main results on sport and sexual behaviors, Miller et al. (1999) reported that males had higher sport participation rates than did females, and whites had the highest participation of the three race and ethnic groups, with Hispanic youth reporting the lowest rates. To date, few studies within sport and exercise psychology have incorporated such diverse samples, but the growing work on adolescent development, which often focuses on underserved youth, necessarily brings that perspective and offers insights into the role of physical activity (e.g., Danish, Fazio, Nellen, & Owens, 2002; Hellison et al., 2000).

Erkut, Fields, Sing, and Marx (1996) describe experiences (including sport experiences) that influence urban girls from across the United States representing five ethnic backgrounds (Native American, African American, Anglo-European American, Asian Pacific Islander, and Latina). When asked, "What activities make you feel good about yourself?", athletics was the most common response, mentioned by nearly half (46%) of the girls. When asked what about the activity made them feel good, the most common response was mastery or competence (e.g., "I'm good at it"), followed by enjoyment. Erkut and colleagues' large, diverse sample and the many variations in findings highlight the importance of cultural contexts in the lives of these girls and suggest exciting directions for sport and exercise psychology.

As the research just reviewed indicates, gender affects men as well as women, and it interacts with other cultural identities. Sport is not only male but white, young, middle class, and heterosexual. Still, sport and exercise psychology has seldom addressed multicultural diversity.

GENDER AND SEXUALITY

Sexuality and sexual orientation are clearly linked with gender and are discussed in the following section. Then the chapter moves to the emerging multicultural scholarship and intersections of race and ethnicity, social class, and gender.

Sexual Prejudice, Heterosexism, and Homophobia

Before reviewing the scholarship related to sexuality and sexual orientation, some clarification of terminology is in order. Discrimination and prejudice on the basis of sexual orientation is often described as *homophobia,* but Herek (2000), a leading psychology scholar on lesbian, gay, and bisexual (LGB) issues, prefers *sexual prejudice.* As Herek notes, sexual prejudice is an attitude (evaluation) that is directed at a social group and involves hostility or dislike. *Homophobia* is typically understood as an irrational fear, and the term implies individual psychopathology. *Heterosexism* refers to a social ideology and institutionalized oppression of nonheterosexual people. *Sexual prejudice* is the more appropriate term for this chapter, but related scholarship, particularly in sociocultural sport studies, often refers to *homophobia* and *heterosexism.*

Messner (1992), a sport studies scholar, describes sport as a powerful socializing force and argues that homophobia leads all boys and men (gay or straight) to conform to a narrow definition of masculinity. Real men compete and avoid anything feminine that might lead them to be branded a sissy. Messner (1992) also links homophobia with misogyny; sport bonds men together as superior to women. We expect to see men dominate women, and we are uncomfortable with bigger, stronger women who take active, dominant roles expected of athletes.

Homophobia in sport has been discussed most often in relation to women's athletics. Despite the visibility of a few prominent lesbian athletes, most remain closeted, and many female athletes go out of the way to avoid any appearance of lesbianism. Most people stereotypically assume that sport attracts lesbians, but there is no inherent relationship between sexual orientation and sport (no gay gene will turn someone into a softball player or figure skater). No doubt, homophobia has kept more heterosexual women than lesbians out of sport, and homophobia restricts the behavior of all women in sport. Moreover, as Messner (1992) suggests, homophobia probably restricts men in sport even more than it restricts women.

Pat Griffin (1998) has written extensively on homophobia in sport and physical education, focusing on connections among sexism, heterosexism, and sport, and Vikki Krane (2001; Krane & Barber, 2003) has addressed sexuality and heterosexism in sport and exercise psychology. Krane and colleagues draw connections among gender, sexism, and heterosexism, and they have applied social identity as a theoretical framework for their work (e.g., Krane & Barber, 2003). Barber and Krane (2005) have taken the feminist and multicultural approach of moving to social action and offer suggestions for considering gender and sexuality in sport psychology practice.

Sexual Prejudice in Sport and Physical Activity

Most sport and exercise psychology scholarship on sexual orientation focuses on competitive athletics, with few scholars examining sexual prejudice in wider physical activity settings. Considerable psychological research confirms that LGB individuals face persistent sexual prejudice and hostile climates (e.g., Herek, 2000; Rivers & D'Augelli, 2001). Although research is limited, national reports from the National Gay and Lesbian Task Force Policy Institute (Rankin, 2003) and Human Rights Watch (2001), as well as observations and anecdotal evidence, suggest that organized sport is a particularly hostile environment for LGB youths, and fitness clubs, sports medicine facilities, and recreational physical activity programs do not welcome gay men and lesbians.

In one of the few empirical studies, Morrow and Gill (2003) reported that both physical education teachers and students witnessed high levels of homophobic and heterosexist behaviors in public schools, but teachers failed to confront those behaviors. More than 60% of the teachers and students see homophobia, and more than 50% of gay and lesbian youths experience homophobia. The good news is that more than 75% of the teachers say that they want safe, inclusive physical education; the bad news is that more than 50% of those teachers report that they never confront homophobia.

In subsequent research, we examined attitudes and the climate for cultural minority groups, focusing on sexual prejudice. The initial study (Gill, Morrow, Collins, Lucey, & Schultz, 2006) examined attitudes toward racial and ethnic minorities, older adults, people with disabilities, and sexual minorities. Overall, attitudes of our preprofessional students toward gay men and lesbians were similar to attitudes reported in other samples, reflecting the sexual prejudice in society. Attitudes were markedly more negative for both gay men and lesbians than for other minority groups, with males especially negative toward gay men. Interestingly, on our demographic page, many students went out of their way to indicate that they were exclusively heterosexual, further confirming the stigma of gay or lesbian identity and social acceptance of sexual prejudice.

Sexual Harassment

Sexual harassment has clear gender connotations, and considerable psychological research (e.g., Koss, 1990) and public attention demonstrate the prevalence of sexual harassment. Sport studies scholars have addressed these concerns, but the sport and exercise psychology literature has been silent on this topic. Lenskyj (1992) linked sexual harassment to power relations and ideology of male sport and noted unique concerns for female athletes. Sport (as a nonfeminine activity) may elicit derisive comments, clothes are revealing, male coaches are often fit and conventionally attractive, female athletes spend much time training and less in general social activity, coaches are authoritarian, and for some sports, merit is equated with heterosexual attractiveness.

Interestingly, sexual harassment and abuse are receiving attention at the international level. At the 2001 ISSP Congress, Kari Fasting of Norway and Celia Brackenridge of the United Kingdom (2001) organized a symposium with colleagues from around the world. The collective works of these scholars from varying perspectives and countries indicate that the sport climate fosters sexual harassment and abuse; that young, elite female athletes are particularly vulnerable; that neither athletes nor coaches have education or training about the issues; and that both research and professional development are needed in sport and exercise psychology to address the issues (Brackenridge, 1997; Bringer, Brackenridge, & Johnston, 2001; Kirby & Wintrup, 2001; Leahy, Pretty, & Tenenbaum, 2001; Volkwein, 2001).

Sexual harassment and assault probably occur much more often in sport and exercise settings than we recognize. Professionals who are aware of gender and cultural dynamics might be quicker to recognize such problems and help athletes and exercisers deal with them. Both women and men must be aware of the issues, and administrators should be enlisted to support educational efforts and promote social action.

Gender and sexuality are particularly salient in the ever-changing cultural context of sport and exercise settings. Race and ethnicity is just as salient in practice but largely ignored in the sport and exercise psychology literature.

RACE, ETHNICITY, AND SOCIAL CLASS

As noted earlier, Ram and colleagues (2004) confirmed that the striking void in sport and exercise psychology on race and ethnicity persists despite the increased multicultural diversity in society and in sport. Social class often is conflated with race and ethnicity, but it is qualitatively different. Class operates within all racial and ethnic groups and also interacts with gender; however, there is little research on social class in psychology and none within sport and exercise psychology. Thus, most of the limited research covered in this section focuses on race and ethnicity and comes from psychology and sport studies.

Sport Studies Scholarship on Race and Ethnicity

Key Point

Sport studies scholars note that a significant number of athletes are not white and middle class, yet power remains solidly white and middle and upper class. The media and some scholars have discussed such practices as stacking and the white male dominance of coaching and management positions.

Sport studies scholars note that significant numbers of athletes are not white and middle class, yet power remains solidly white and middle and upper class. The popular media and some scholars have discussed such practices as stacking (i.e., assigning African Americans to certain positions such as American football running back or baseball outfield but not in central quarterback or pitching roles) and the white male dominance of coaching and management positions.

Most of that research focuses on professional male sport and confirms that white players tend to hold central, controlling positions whereas African Americans tend to hold peripheral positions (reflecting Grusky's leadership model discussed in chapter 15). Smith and Henderson (2000) argued that stacking reflects social isolation, marginalization, and systematic discrimination against African Americans. Jamieson, Reel, and Gill (2002) extended the stacking research to women's collegiate softball, finding different patterns from those in professional male sport. White women, as in previous studies, predominated in the most central position of catcher. As expected, African American women were stacked in the peripheral outfield positions, and so were Asian American women, in contrast to typical stereotypes. However, Latina players were stacked in the central positions of pitcher and infield, challenging the notion that all minority players are stacked in noncentral positions and calling for more complex cultural analyses.

In Brooks and Althouse's (2000) edited volume on racism in college athletics, Smith (2000) notes that community-based educational and sport structures have been the dominant support networks for African American female athletes, and the tradition of athleticism for women comes out of social acceptance of physicality and recognition of the inner strength of women. Corbett and Johnson (2000) similarly focus on the cultural context, calling attention to the overlooked heroines and continuing nonrepresentative media coverage. They cited the 1997 *Racial Report Card,* noting that black women held 2.1% of the Division I head coaching positions for women's collegiate teams (compared with 40.3% for white women and 52.1% for white men), and only 1% of college athletic director positions (compared with 6.3% for white women and 82.2% for white men). In the more recent 2004 *Racial Report Card* (Lapchick, 2005), the numbers have dropped to only 1.6% of the women's head coaching positions and no African American women in athlete director positions. Corbett and Johnson noted that the black community and networks of professionals provide a supportive environment. However, barriers persist and the cultural context in sport continues to exclude women of color.

Psychology Scholarship on Race and Ethnicity and Social Class

The psychology scholarship on race and ethnicity is beginning to take a multicultural perspective. Much of that work addresses health disparities, which are well documented (USDHHS, 2003) and particularly relevant for sport and exercise psychology. Adler and colleagues (1994) called attention to the role of social class in health risk, health behaviors, and health care, and Contrada et al. (2000) summarized research indicating that racial and ethnic minorities face stress based on discrimination, stereotypes, and conformity pressures and that these stresses affect health and well-being. As Yali and Revenson (2004) suggest, with the changing population demographics, socioeconomic disparities are likely to have an even greater effect on health in the near future. Health disparities are relevant to sport and exercise psychology in that physical activity is a key health behavior, and kinesiology professionals are in a position to promote physical activity for health and well-being.

Steele (1997) has done extensive research on gender, racial and ethnic stereotypes, and stereotype threat, or the influence of negative stereotypes on performance (Steele, Spencer, & Aronson, 2002). Steele's research indicates that stereotypes affect everyone, but the most devastating effects are on those minority group members who have abilities and are motivated to succeed. Steele's research also suggests that even simple manipulations that take away the stereotype threat (e.g., telling students the test does not show race differences) negate the stereotype effects. Stereotype threat has been widely researched and extended to sport. Beilock and McConnell (2004) reviewed that literature, concluding that negative stereotypes are common in sport and lead to performance decrements, especially when the performers are capable and motivated.

The prevalence of negative stereotypes for racial and ethnic minorities, particularly African American athletes, is well documented. Devine and Baker (1991) found that the terms *unintelligent* and *ostentatious* were associated with the category *black athlete,* and Krueger (1996) found that both black and white participants perceived black men to be more athletic than white men. Johnson, Hallinan, and Westerfield (1999) used photos of black, white, Hispanic, and composite male athletes and asked participants to rate attributes of success. Results conformed to stereotype; success for the black athlete was attributed to innate abilities, whereas it was attributed to hard work and leadership ability for the white athlete. Interestingly, no stereotyping was evident for the Hispanic athlete. This non-result may reflect the lower visibility of Hispanics in sport, and there is little research on racial and ethnic minorities other than African Americans; views seem limited to blacks and whites. Both Harris (2000) and Sailes (2000) document persistent stereotypes and report that African American athletes are more likely than white athletes to have higher aspirations for professional sport and to see sport as a route to social mobility. These views may reflect stereotypes or barriers in other areas, but they certainly suggest cultural influences and power relations within sport.

More important, stereotypes affect performance and relationships. Stone, Perry, and Darley (1997) had people listen to a college basketball game and evaluate players after being told that the player they were evaluating was black or white. Both white and black students rated black players as more athletic and white players as having more basketball intelligence. After confirming those stereotypes, Stone, Lynch, Sjomeling, and Darley (1999) had African Americans and

Caucasians perform a golf task framed as a test of sport intelligence or natural ability. Stereotype threat was confirmed; black participants performed worse when told the test was of sport intelligence, and white participants performed worse when told the test was of natural ability. Stone (2002) continued his line of research with a study demonstrating that white athletes faced with stereotype threat were prompted to use self-handicapping behaviors.

Beilock and McConnell (2004) linked stereotype threat to attention and cognitive strategies (as discussed in chapter 5), suggesting that stereotype threat both fills working memory and entices the performer to pay more attention to step-by-step control. They further suggested that positive stereotypes might enhance performance by increasing self-efficacy and attention to relevant tasks. Beilock and McConnell also pointed out that people belong to multiple groups, and how they think about their group membership is critical. Different aspects of cultural identity may be more or less salient to different people, and salience is a critical mediator of the effects of stereotype threat. As Beilock and McConnell conclude, we know less about stereotype threat in physical domains than in cognitive areas; clearly this is a relevant concern for sport and exercise psychology.

In one of the few studies to look at race and ethnicity, physical activity, and aging, Heesch, Brown, and Blanton (2000) examined exercise barriers with a large sample of adult women over age 40, including African American, Hispanic, Native American, and white women. They found several common barriers across racial and ethnic groups. For example, being tired was a barrier for all precontemplators, and lack of time was a barrier for most contemplators. However, they also reported variations by racial and ethnic group, and they cautioned that their results and specific community needs preclude definitive guidelines for interventions.

Key Point

Steele and colleagues have done extensive research on stereotype threat (Steele, 1997; Steele, Spencer, & Aronson, 2002). Stone and colleagues (1999) had African Americans and Caucasians perform a golf task framed as a test of sport intelligence or natural ability. Stereotype threat was confirmed when black participants performed worse when told the test was of sport intelligence and white participants performed worse when told the test was of natural ability.

Physicality and Cultural Diversity

Kinesiology professionals deal with physical activities, and thus physical abilities and characteristics are prominent. Moreover, opportunity is limited by physical abilities, physical skills, physical size, physical fitness, and physical appearance—collectively referred to here as *physicality*. The increasing public attention on obesity has created a negative culture for people who are overweight or obese, and people with disabilities certainly are among those who are left out in sport and exercise. Indeed, exclusion on the basis of physicality is nearly universal in sport and exercise, and this exclusion is a public health problem.

Physical activity professionals address physical disabilities with adapted activities, but they seldom address physicality as a cultural diversity issue. In discussing the role of physical activity in the health and well-being of those with disabilities, Rimmer (2005) notes that people with physical disabilities are one of the most inactive segments of the population. Rimmer cites the physical barriers but argues that organizational policies, discrimination, and social attitudes are the real barriers.

As part of a larger study on sexual prejudice, we (Gill, Morrow, Collins, Lucey, & Schultz, 2005) examined the climate for minority groups (racial and ethnic minorities, LGB people, older adults, and people with disabilities) in organized sport, exercise settings, and recreational settings. Notably, the climate was rated as most exclusionary for people with disabilities, indicating that these preprofessional students recognize the exclusion of minority groups, particularly those with disabilities, in exercise and sport.

Olkin and Pledger (2003) call for disability studies paralleling the critical studies of gender and race and ethnicity in order to emphasize empowerment and social context for disability. Several sport studies scholars have addressed disability from a cultural relations perspective (e.g., DePauw, 1997; Henderson & Bedini, 1995). Blinde and McCallister (1999) found that women aged 19 to 54 who had various physical disabilities participated in more fitness than sport activities, participated to maintain functional capabilities, valued intrinsic gains (e.g., perceived competence, enhanced body image, control), and perceived differences in the activity experiences of men and women with disabilities.

Physical diversity is more than ability or disability, and physicality is particularly relevant to sport and exercise psychology. Physical skill, strength, and fitness are key sources of restrictions and stereotyping. Physical appearance influences sport outcomes and behaviors, and physical size, particularly obesity, is a prominent source of social stigma and oppression in sport and exercise. With the current emphasis on the so-called obesity epidemic, stereotypes related to physical size are a particular concern for kinesiology professionals. Psychology research has documented the prevalence of negative stereotypes and bias against obese children and adults. In a review, Puhl and Brownell (2001) documented clear and consistent stigmatization and discrimination in employment, education, and health care.

Kinesiology professionals who typically profess concern about obesity are just as likely as others to hold negative stereotypes and biases. Greenleaf and Weiller (2005) found that physical education teachers held moderate antifat bias and strong personal weight-control beliefs (obese people are responsible for their obesity). They also held higher expectations for young people of normal weights, and as discussed earlier, expectations are strong determinants of behaviors and outcomes. Similarly, Chambliss, Finley, and Blair (2004) found a strong antifat bias with implicit measures among exercise science students (see the application point to test your own implicit attitudes). They concluded that antifat bias and weight discrimination among professionals have important implications for health promotion and may actually contribute to unhealthy behaviors and lower quality of life. Research confirms that obese people are targets for teasing, are more likely to engage in unhealthy eating behaviors, and are less likely to engage in physical activity (Faith, Leone, Ayers, Heo, & Pietrobelli, 2002; Puhl & Wharton, 2007; Storch et al., 2007).

 ### Application Point

Go to the Project Implicit Web site (https://implicit.harvard.edu/implicit/) and take the implicit association test on weight to assess your attitudes about obesity. Most likely you will find that you have some implicit bias, and you may become more aware of how such cultural biases may affect behaviors and interactions in sport and exercise settings. Think about how you might counter that implicit bias to make an exercise program more welcoming for people who are obese. Check the Project Implicit site and Puhl and Wharton's (2007) article for ideas.

Intersections and Relationships

Most reviews and theoretical works, as well as several studies, emphasize intersections of cultural identities and contexts. That is a key consideration easily overlooked in reviews of separate gender and race and ethnicity literature.

Within sport and exercise psychology, the person who has most eloquently addressed the intersections of gender, race, and sexuality is Ruth Hall, who brings a feminist and multicultural perspective whether drawing on her clinical experiences to discuss the role of exercise in therapy with African American women (Hall, 1998) or more explicitly trying to shake the foundation of sport and exercise psychology in discussing the marginalization of women of color in sport (Hall, 2001). Hall reminds us of key themes in this chapter—multiple intersecting identities, power and privilege, and social action. Keep those in mind as you try to understand and use gender and cultural diversity in sport and exercise psychology.

CULTURAL COMPETENCE IN SPORT AND EXERCISE PSYCHOLOGY

Cultural competence takes multicultural diversity directly into professional practice. Not only must sport and exercise research address multicultural relationships, but culturally competent professionals must act to empower participants and challenge restrictive social structures. Indeed, cultural competence is a professional competency required in psychology and many health professions. In 2004, an Institute of Medicine (IOM) report addressed the need to diversify the health care workforce and presented several recommendations. The Joint Commission on Health Education and Promotion Terminology (2002) defined cultural competence as:

> The ability of an individual to understand and respect values, attitudes, beliefs, and mores that differ across cultures, and to consider and respond appropriately to these differences in planning, implementing, and evaluating health education and promotion programs and interventions. (p. 5)

That definition recognizes the need for action and implies that cultural competence requires commitment to a continuing process. Psychology has been particularly active in promoting multicultural competencies, providing a model for sport and exercise psychology.

Multicultural Competencies

Key Point

Multicultural competence refers to the ability to work effectively with people who are of a different culture. These competencies are essential for anyone working with others, and certainly in all professional kinesiology roles.

Multicultural competence refers to the ability to work effectively with people who are of a different culture. Multicultural competencies are essential for anyone working with others, and certainly in all professional kinesiology roles. Multicultural competencies include three general areas: awareness of one's own cultural values and biases, understanding of the client's worldviews, and development of culturally appropriate intervention strategies (Mio et al., 2006). Multicultural competency is about applying multicultural knowledge and understanding in life, work, and interactions. For professionals, multicultural competencies increase effectiveness and lead to mutually enriching interactions.

The APA has recognized the key role of multicultural competencies in fulfilling the mission of psychology to promote health and well-being, and APA guidelines call for action for social justice. Sport and exercise psychology and kinesiology can move toward the goal of physical activity for the health and well-being of all by following those guidelines:

APA Multicultural Guidelines (2003)

• Guideline 1: Psychologists are encouraged to recognize that, as cultural beings, they may hold attitudes and beliefs that can detrimentally influence their perceptions of and interactions with individuals who are ethnically and racially different from themselves.

• Guideline 2: Psychologists are encouraged to recognize the importance of multicultural sensitivity and responsiveness, knowledge, and understanding about ethnically and racially different individuals.

• Guideline 3: As educators, psychologists are encouraged to employ the constructs of multiculturalism and diversity in psychological education.

• Guideline 4: Culturally sensitive psychological researchers are encouraged to recognize the importance of conducting cultural-centered and ethical psychological research among persons from ethnic, linguistic, and racial minority backgrounds.

• Guideline 5: Psychologists strive to apply culturally appropriate skills in clinical and other applied psychological practices.

• Guideline 6: Psychologists are encouraged to use organizational change processes to support culturally informed organizational (policy) development and practices.

William Parham (2005), a leader in APA multicultural programming as well as an active member of the sport and exercise psychology community, overviews the legacy of psychology with respect to culturally, ethnically, and racially diverse people, and he offers useful guidelines based on his professional practice. Parham's first guiding premise, that context is everything, is key when providing consultation services to diverse athletes. When working with diverse people (and that includes all people), history, economics, family, and social context are all relevant. Parham's second premise, that culture, race, and ethnicity as separate constructs do little to inform us, reminds us that cultural groups are not homogeneous and everyone has a unique cultural identity. Parham's third guiding premise underscores the importance of using paradigms that reflect differing worldviews. People from culturally diverse backgrounds may have developed resiliency and strength in dealing with power relations. The Western worldview is culturally limited, typically emphasizing independence, competitiveness, and individual striving. Emphasis on connectedness rather than separation, deference to higher power, mind–body interrelatedness rather than control, and a sense of spirit-driven energy may be more prominent in another's worldview.

Similar to Parham, Michael D'Andrea has been involved with APA multicultural programs for some time. Recently, D'Andrea and Daniels (2004) applied his multidimensional, multicultural competency model to sport and exercise psychology. They noted that multicultural psychology has expanded beyond the early focus on nonwhite racial groups in the United States to include other marginalized and devalued cultural groups. Their model of respectful sport psychology includes 10 factors to think about in dealing with people whose psychological development, athletic performance, and team membership are affected by cultural and contextual variables that have been previously underestimated or ignored in professional practice (figure 16.1).

In discussing fair treatment in sport, Krane (2004) argues that sport psychologists are in an ideal position to challenge unfair treatment and promote sport

Figure 16.1
RESPECTFUL sport psychology: A multidimensional, multicultural competency model.

R—Religious and spiritual identity
E—Economic class identity
S—Sexual identity
P—Psychological maturity
E—Ethnic and racial identity
C—Chronological challenges
T—Trauma and threats to well-being (injury, abuse)
F—Family history
U—Unique physical characteristics
L—Language, location of residence

practices that encourage social justice. Unfair treatment may be challenged at the societal level, as in the APA's recent stand against Native American mascots for athletic teams or lobbying for boycotts of sporting goods companies with exploitive practices. Sport and exercise psychologists and kinesiology professionals can challenge unfair practices in athletic and exercise programs, as well as in our educational and training programs.

Cultural Competence for Physical Activity Professionals

Given the role of physical activity in health, cultural competence is necessary for physical activity professionals. Cultural competence is integral to quality programs and effective practice, yet few kinesiology professional programs include multicultural competencies. Sport and exercise psychology specialists can play an important role in helping all kinesiology professionals develop cultural competence.

As part of a project to develop more inclusive physical activity programs, my colleagues and I (Gill, Jamieson, & Kamphoff, 2005) focused on the climate and cultural competencies of professionals in physical activity settings. Survey and focus group data were collected from professionals (physical education teachers, community program leaders) and pre-professionals and also from adolescent girls in community programs to assess the climate for diverse groups and the cultural competencies of professionals in physical activity settings.

Both professionals and participants rated the climate as inclusive, particularly for African American youths followed by other racial and ethnic minorities. Young people with physical and mental disabilities were most often excluded, followed by young gays and lesbians. Survey and focus-group responses from adolescent girls, however, suggested that programs are not very diverse and cater to boys and the physically skilled. Survey responses from pre-professionals and professionals indicated that they were confident about their multicultural competencies, rated their ability to deal with students of other cultural backgrounds as good, and recognized the importance of cultural competence. However, they also recognized exclusion in physical activity settings, seldom took any proactive steps to promote inclusion, and noted the lack of training and resources.

These preliminary results suggest that professionals and participants see the need for cultural competence resources and programs, but the work has barely begun. Following are sample resources from our project, including the cultural competence concept, cultural competence continuum, and selected resources.

Concept of Cultural Competence

Cultural competence has been defined many ways (e.g., Cross et al., 1999; Luquis & Perez, 2003). For physical education and recreation professionals, cultural competence must be applied to all levels, including teacher instruction, curriculum development, hiring practices, and organizational policies and procedures.

For our project, we used the following definition:

> *Cultural competence is the ability of physical activity professionals and their agencies to develop, implement, and evaluate physical activity programs that reflect, value, and promote varied culturally relevant forms of physical activity. Key to this comprehensive capacity is the ability to evaluate and understand the cultural values for physical activity held by one's self, one's agency, and one's clients.*

Locating Agency and Self on a Continuum of Cultural Competence

Cultural competence is a developmental process; there are no quick fixes. Cross et al. (1999) list six points on a continuum of cultural competence:

1. **Cultural destructiveness**—Characterized by policies, actions, and beliefs that are damaging to cultures.

2. **Cultural incapacity**—There is no intention to be culturally destructive, but there is a lack of ability to respond effectively to diverse people (e.g., bias in hiring practices, lowered expectations).

3. **Cultural blindness**—Philosophy of being unbiased and that all people are the same (e.g., encouraging assimilation, not valuing cross-cultural training, blaming people for not fitting in).

4. **Cultural precompetence**—Desire exists, but there is no clear plan to achieve cultural competence.

5. **Cultural competence**—Respect and recognition for diversity exists, as well as genuine understanding of cultural differences (e.g., seeking training and knowledge to prevent biases from affecting work, collaborating with diverse communities, willingness to make adaptations, continued training and commitment to work effectively with diverse groups).

6. **Cultural proficiency**—Culture is held in high esteem and is understood to be an integral part of who we are (e.g., conducting research to add to the knowledge base, disseminating information on proven practices and interventions, engaging in advocacy with diverse groups that support the culturally competent system).

Cross, Bazron, Dennis, and Isaacs (1999) describe several conditions to move along this continuum:

1. Diversity is valued.
2. One's own cultural biases are understood and acknowledged.
3. An unbiased consciousness of the dynamics when cultures interact is sought.
4. Development of cultural knowledge occurs.
5. The ability to adapt is cultivated.

Online Resources

National Center for Cultural Competence (www.georgetown.edu/research/gucdc/nccc/)

The National Center for Cultural Competence at the Georgetown University Center for Child and Human Development offers many online resources on cultural and linguistic competence.

Anti-Defamation League (www.adl.org)

The ADL's A World of Difference Institute is the leading provider of diversity and antibias training and resources. One great resource available online is Close the Book on Hate, a joint effort of Barnes and Noble and ADL that is designed to use education to help break the cycle of prejudice and hatred.

Center for Effective Collaboration and Practice (www.air.org/cecp/cultural/default.htm)

Offers definitions, research reports, strategies, and additional links.

Office of Minority Health (www.omhrc.gov)

Information on various initiatives, programs, health statistics, and resources relevant to minority health in the United States. Includes a section on cultural competency.

Bureau of Health Professions (http://bhpr.hrsa.gov/diversity/default.htm)

This site is sponsored by the USDHHS and aims at professional training programs for underrepresented groups.

Many of these resources are from health professions, which are far ahead of kinesiology in recognizing the essential role of multicultural competencies. Luquis, Perez, and Young (2006) surveyed health education programs in professional preparation programs, and they found that although fewer than one-third required specific courses, most were addressing cultural competence content in their curriculum. The resources and guidance from these health sources and from multicultural psychology are starting points. Many resources exist to help you develop your own multicultural competencies and to make your kinesiology practice inclusive and empowering for participants.

PUTTING IT INTO PRACTICE

Now you are ready to put the content of chapter 16 into practice. Read the chapter summary, discuss the case study, answer the review questions, and enhance your knowledge by researching the recommended readings.

Summary

Gender makes a difference, race matters, and human diversity characterizes all of us in all that we do. Gender is a pervasive force that is particularly ingrained in sport and exercise structure and practice. We cannot simply treat everyone the same. However, we also cannot assume that males and females are dichotomous opposites and treat all males one way and all females another way. Gender and culture are dynamic, social influences best understood within a multicultural framework that recognizes multiple, intersecting identities; power relations; and the need for social action.

Sport and exercise psychology has begun to address multicultural concerns. To date, most scholarship focuses on gender, with few truly multicultural frameworks. Multicultural perspectives are especially needed for sport and exercise psychology in the real world. To advance sport and exercise psychology and kinesiology in the public interest, we must develop our multicultural competencies, expand our reach to those who are marginalized, and promote physical activity for the health and well-being of all.

Case Study

Select one of the following professional settings: an exercise and fitness center, an athletic training facility, or physical education in a public school. As a professional in that setting, you want to promote the health and well-being of your students or clients. To do that, you must be a culturally competent professional and your program must be inclusive and empowering. Most likely you did not get any multicultural training in your professional preparation and your professional organizations do not have guidelines or resources. You are on your own (but you do have the information, resources, and examples from this chapter).

First, how would you develop your own multicultural competencies? What resources might you go to, what specific actions would you take, and how might you move up the cultural competence continuum? Next, describe how your agency (school, facility, or program) could be more culturally competent. How could you work with the other professionals to ensure that your program is inclusive and empowering for participants? (You might consider staff guidelines, program materials, available resources, and interpersonal relationships.)

Review Questions

1. Explain the emphasis on people in context in multicultural psychology.
2. Discuss the impact of Title IX on girls' and women's sport participation rates and on the prevalence of women in coaching and administration positions.
3. Discuss the shift in gender scholarship from sex differences to gender-role orientation to social perspectives.
4. Identify several forms of gender bias in media coverage of female and male athletes.
5. Discuss sexual prejudice, heterosexism, and homophobia in sport and exercise.
6. Define *stereotype threat,* and explain how it might operate in physical activity settings.
7. Describe the research on stereotypes and biases related to obesity, and discuss implications for physical activity programs.
8. Define *multicultural competence* and identify the three general areas of multicultural competencies.

Recommended Reading

American Psychological Association (APA). (2003). Guidelines on multicultural education, training, research, practice, and organizational change for psychologists. *American Psychologist, 58,* 377-402.

This document is also available online at www.apa.org/pi under Multicultural Guidelines.

Gill, D.L. (2007). Gender and cultural diversity. In G. Tenenbaum & R. Eklund (Eds.), *Handbook on research on sport and exercise psychology* (3rd ed., pp. 823-844). Hoboken, NJ: Wiley.

> This recent chapter includes more detail on gender and cultural diversity issues and research.

Parham, W.D. (2005). Raising the bar: Developing an understanding of athletes from racially, culturally, and ethnically diverse backgrounds. In M.B. Anderson (Ed.), *Sport psychology in practice* (pp. 201-215). Champaign, IL: Human Kinetics.

> Parham is a practicing clinical psychologist with considerable experience working with athletes. In this chapter, he offers insights and helpful suggestions for working with diverse athletes.

Web Sites

Institute for Diversity and Ethics in Sport (www.bus.ucf.edu/sport).

> The institute, directed by Richard Lapchick, serves as a comprehensive resource for questions related to gender and race in amateur, collegiate, and professional sport. Lapchick continues to monitor collegiate and professional sport and updates the *Racial and Gender Report Card* each year at the Web site.

Project Implicit (www.projectimplicit.net; https://implicit.harvard.edu/implicit).

> This Web site includes information from the research on implicit attitudes as well as demonstration tests of implicit attitudes. The first site is for general information and the other has demonstration tests.

Epilogue

We now conclude our discussion of sport and exercise psychology. Most likely you have read this text for a course, and you have discussed the material in class or with colleagues. Perhaps you focused on a specific topic, gathered further material, and developed a review paper or research study. Perhaps you used the guidelines to develop training interventions for psychological skills or to control your own mental game in your daily activities. We hope you will continue to use sport and exercise psychology to enhance your own physical activity experiences and in your professional practice.

We have covered a lot of material, including personality, self-perceptions, motivation, emotions, stress management, social development, group dynamics, and cultural diversity. Moreover, nearly every topic is multifaceted and can be addressed from several perspectives. Human behavior in sport and exercise is complex and dynamic, and answers to our many questions are also complex and dynamic. If you return to the questions posed in chapter 1 or to your own questions about behavior in sport and exercise, you may find that you can now answer them easily with your sport and exercise psychology knowledge. But, you have also developed new insights into the complexities of behavior, and as you reflect, you will likely find that the answers are not so simple.

Answering the questions in chapter 1 or on a course exam is not the true test of your understanding of sport and exercise psychology. The true test will come in your professional practice as you draw upon the knowledge and practical theories of sport and exercise psychology and integrate that knowledge with your professional insights. Perhaps you will use sport and exercise psychology when you are teaching a middle school dance class, coaching a youth soccer team, consulting with an intercollegiate athlete, developing a program for a cardiac rehabilitation client, organizing a community physical activity program, or trying to maintain a healthy lifestyle in your hectic daily schedule. Perhaps you will think about intrinsic motivation as you consider the rewards in your soccer program or use your knowledge to help a client develop stress management skills. We hope you will remember the many interacting influences, including social diversity, the environment, and individual differences, as you work with people in complex, changing settings. Guidelines and practical theories will help, but the mix is different for each person in each situation.

In writing this book, we have shared our knowledge and views of sport and exercise psychology. We now invite you to do the same. We would like to hear your reactions to the book—tell us what you found useful; what sections might be deleted, added, or revised; and any suggestions you might have for the next edition. Sport and exercise psychology continues to expand in new directions, and you can help advance our understanding of sport and exercise behavior.

Appendix A

Sport Competition Anxiety Test for Adults

Directions: Following are some statements about how people feel when they compete in sports and games. Read each statement and decide if you hardly ever, sometimes, or often feel this way when you compete in sports and games. If your choice is *hardly ever,* blacken the square labeled *A;* if your choice is *sometimes,* blacken the square labeled *B;* and if your choice is *often,* blacken the square labeled *C.* There is no right or wrong answer. Do not spend too much time on any one question. Remember to choose the word that describes how you *usually* feel when competing in sports and games.

	Hardly ever	Sometimes	Often
1. Competing against others is socially enjoyable.	A ☐	B ☐	C ☐
2. Before I compete, I feel uneasy.	A ☐	B ☐	C ☐
3. Before I compete, I worry about not performing well.	A ☐	B ☐	C ☐
4. I show good sporting behavior when I compete.	A ☐	B ☐	C ☐
5. When I compete, I worry about making mistakes.	A ☐	B ☐	C ☐
6. Before I compete, I am calm.	A ☐	B ☐	C ☐
7. Setting a goal is important when competing.	A ☐	B ☐	C ☐
8. Before I compete, I get a queasy feeling in my stomach.	A ☐	B ☐	C ☐
9. Just before competing, I notice my heart beats faster than usual.	A ☐	B ☐	C ☐
10. I like to compete in games that demand considerable physical energy.	A ☐	B ☐	C ☐
11. Before I compete, I feel relaxed.	A ☐	B ☐	C ☐
12. Before I compete, I am nervous.	A ☐	B ☐	C ☐
13. Team sports are more exciting than individual sports.	A ☐	B ☐	C ☐
14. I get nervous wanting to start the game.	A ☐	B ☐	C ☐
15. Before I compete, I usually get uptight.	A ☐	B ☐	C ☐

INSTRUCTIONS FOR SCORING THE SCAT FOR ADULTS

For each item, three responses are possible: (a) hardly ever, (b) sometimes, and (c) often. The 10 test items are 2, 3, 5, 6, 8, 9, 11, 12, 14, and 15. The spurious items (1, 4, 7, 10, and 13) are *not* scored. Items 2, 3, 5, 8, 9, 12, 14, and 15 are worded so that they are scored according to the following key:

1 = Hardly ever

2 = Sometimes

3 = Often

Items 6 and 11 are scored according to the following key:

1 = Often

2 = Sometimes

3 = Hardly ever

The range of scores is from 10 (low competitive A-trait) to 30 (high competitive A-trait).

If a person deletes 1 of the 10 test items, a prorated full-scale score can be obtained by computing the mean score for the 9 items answered, multiplying this value by 10, and rounding the product to the next whole number. When two or more items are omitted, the respondent's questionnaire should be invalidated.

Select raw scores and corresponding percentile norms for college-aged adults are included in the following section. A more detailed discussion of SCAT scores and additional norms are included in Martens' (1977) SCAT monograph.

SCAT-A Norms for Normal College-Aged Adults

Raw score	Male percentile	Female percentile
30	99	99
28	97	88
26	89	75
24	82	59
22	74	47
20	61	35
18	40	22
16	24	10
14	14	6
12	7	3
10	1	1

Note. Instructions and norms modified from Sport Competition Anxiety Test (pp. 91 & 99). By R. Martens, 1977, Champaign, IL: Human Kinetics. Copyright 1977 by Rainer Martens. Reprinted by permission.

REFERENCES

Martens, R. (1977). *Sport Competition Anxiety Test.* Champaign, IL: Human Kinetics

Appendix B

Participation Motivation Questionnaire

Following are some reasons that people give for participating in sport. Read each item carefully and decide if that item describes a reason why you participate in your sport. Mark an *X* to indicate if that reason is very important, somewhat important, or not at all important for you.

	Very important	Somewhat important	Not at all important
1. I want to improve my skills.	☐	☐	☐
2. I want to be with my friends.	☐	☐	☐
3. I like to win.	☐	☐	☐
4. I want to get rid of energy.	☐	☐	☐
5. I like to travel.	☐	☐	☐
6. I want to stay in shape.	☐	☐	☐
7. I like the excitement.	☐	☐	☐
8. I like the teamwork.	☐	☐	☐
9. My parents or close friends want me to play.	☐	☐	☐
10. I want to learn new skills.	☐	☐	☐
11. I like to meet new friends.	☐	☐	☐
12. I like to do something I'm good at.	☐	☐	☐
13. I want to release tension.	☐	☐	☐
14. I like the rewards.	☐	☐	☐
15. I like to get exercise.	☐	☐	☐
16. I like to have something to do.	☐	☐	☐
17. I like the action.	☐	☐	☐
18. I like the team spirit.	☐	☐	☐
19. I like to get out of the house.	☐	☐	☐
20. I like to compete.	☐	☐	☐
21. I like to feel important.	☐	☐	☐
22. I like being on a team.	☐	☐	☐
23. I want to go to a higher level.	☐	☐	☐
24. I want to be physically fit.	☐	☐	☐
25. I want to be popular.	☐	☐	☐
26. I like the challenge.	☐	☐	☐
27. I like the coaches or instructors.	☐	☐	☐
28. I want to gain status or recognition.	☐	☐	☐
29. I like to have fun.	☐	☐	☐
30. I like to use the equipment or facilities.	☐	☐	☐

REFERENCES

The Participation Motivation Questionnaire was developed and used as described in the following:

Gill, D.L., Gross, J.B., & Huddleston, S. (1983). Participation motivation in youth sports. *International Journal of Sport Psychology, 14,* 1-14.

Dwyer, J.M.J. (1992). Internal structure of Participation Motivation Questionnaire completed by undergraduates. *Psychological Reports, 70,* 283-290.

SCORING AND PSYCHOMETRICS

There is no scoring system for the original PMQ, and the authors did not continue with further psychometric analyses. Factor analysis was used in the original article and has been used by several researchers who have used the measure. The Dwyer (1992) article provides added information on psychometric structure.

Appendix C

Progressive Relaxation Exercise

This exercise is adapted from *Progressive Relaxation: A Manual for the Helping Professions* by D.A. Bernstein and T.D. Borkovec, 1973, Champaign, IL: Research Press. Copyright 1973 by the authors. Reprinted by permission.

INTRODUCTION

As the name implies, progressive relaxation involves the progressive tensing and relaxing of various muscle groups. Although it is a relaxation technique, we start with tension because most people find it easier to go from a tensed state to a relaxed state than to simply relax muscles. Progressing from a tensed state to relaxation also helps develop the ability to recognize the feelings of tension and relaxation in the muscles. The first session of progressive relaxation training might take 30 to 45 minutes. As training continues, however, the sessions become shorter because muscle groups can be combined and the tension phase can be omitted. The goal of progressive relaxation training is self-control. With practice, people can learn to recognize subtle levels of muscle tension and immediately relax those muscles.

GENERAL INSTRUCTIONS

As we proceed through this exercise, various muscle groups will be tensed for a short time and then relaxed on the following cues: *now* for tension and *relax* for relaxation. On the word *now,* you should tense the muscles and hold the tension until the word *relax,* and then you should let all the tension go at once, not gradually.

As we go through tension and relaxation, I will ask you to pay attention to the feelings of tension and relaxation. This is in part a concentration exercise; try to focus attention on the feelings in your muscles. Today, try to remain awake and pay attention to the feelings in your muscles. Later you can also use this exercise as a sleep aid.

Once a muscle group has been relaxed, try not to move it except to be comfortable. Try to tense only the particular muscle group that we are working on. Do not talk during the exercise, ignore distracting sounds and activities, and keep your attention on the feelings in your muscles.

We will go through each of 16 muscle groups twice. Each time I will remind you about the tension methods, give you the signal to tense (the word *now),* and then the signal to relax (the word *relax).* We will go through the tension and relaxation a second time, and then we will go on to the next muscle group.

The 16 muscle groups that we will go through and the general instructions for tensing those muscles are as follows:

1.   Dominant hand (right) and lower arm: Make a fist.

2. Dominant biceps and upper arm: Push elbow down and pull back without moving the lower arm.

3. Nondominant (left) hand and lower arm: Same as 1.

4. Nondominant biceps and upper arm: Same as 2.

5. Forehead (upper face): Lift eyebrows as high as possible and wrinkle forehead.

6. Central face: Squint and wrinkle nose.

7. Lower face and jaw: Clench teeth and pull back corners of mouth.

8. Neck: Pull chin forward and neck back.

9. Chest, back, and shoulders: Pull shoulder blades together and take a deep breath; continue to take a deep breath while tensing and release with slow, easy breathing as you relax.

10. Abdomen: Make abdominal muscles hard.

11. Dominant (right) upper leg: Contract both top and bottom thigh muscles at the same time.

12. Dominant calf and lower leg: Pull toes toward head.

13. Dominant foot: Curl toes and foot inward (do not hold too long so as to avoid foot cramps).

14. Nondominant upper leg: Same as 11.

15. Nondominant calf and lower leg: Same as 12.

16. Nondominant foot: Same as 13.

For a shorter session, the muscle groups may be combined as follows:

1. Dominant hand and arm (hand, lower arm, upper arm)

2. Nondominant hand and arm

3. Face (upper, central, and lower face muscles)

4. Neck

5. Trunk area (chest, back, shoulders, abdomen)

6. Dominant leg and foot (upper leg, lower leg, foot)

7. Nondominant leg and foot

Specific Instructions

Make yourself comfortable and remove any constraining items that might get in your way such as watches, glasses, or shoes. Close your eyes and take three deep, relaxed breaths. Breathe in slowly and completely, and breathe out slowly and relaxed.

Focus your attention on the muscles of your dominant (right) lower arm and hand. When I give the signal, make a fist and tense the muscles of your dominant lower arm and hand. Ready . . . *now.*

Tension Talk

Feel the tension . . . focus on the tension . . . feel the muscles pull . . . notice the tightness . . . hold the tension . . . put tension in the muscle . . . hold it (5-7 seconds) . . . and *relax.*

Relaxation Talk

Let all the tension go . . . let the muscles get more and more relaxed . . . let go . . . notice how you feel as relaxation takes place . . . notice the feelings of relaxation . . . relax deeper and deeper . . . just let the muscles go . . . more and more completely . . . notice the pleasant feelings of relaxation . . . continue letting the muscles relax . . . keep relaxing . . . let yourself relax . . . feel the relaxation through the muscles . . . continue letting go . . . let the muscles keep relaxing . . . nothing to do but let the muscles relax . . . feel the relaxation come into the muscles . . . pay attention to the feelings of relaxation as the muscles relax more and more . . . more and more completely . . . deeply relaxed . . . let the muscles loosen up and smooth out . . . relax . . . notice how you feel as the muscles relax . . . let the tension go away . . . feel calm, peaceful relaxation . . . let the tension go as you breathe slow and easy . . . feel calm, rested . . . with each breath the muscles relax more and more . . . notice the difference between tension and relaxation . . . see if the muscles of the arm feel as relaxed as those of the hand . . . just let the muscles continue to relax . . . relax . . . relax (30-40 seconds).

We're going to repeat the tension and relaxation sequence again for the dominant hand and lower arm. All right, I'd like you to again make a fist and tense the muscles of the dominant hand and lower arm. Ready, *now.* (Repeat tension phase, 5-7 seconds.) And *relax.* (Repeat relaxation phase, 45-60 seconds.)

All right, now I'd like you to shift your attention to the muscles of the upper arm and biceps of your dominant arm. Ignore the lower arm and focus only on the upper arm throughout the exercise. (Go through each of the 16 muscle groups twice, following the same tension and relaxation phases as for the dominant hand and lower arm.)

General Relaxation Talk

Notice the relaxation in all the muscles . . . complete and deep relaxation . . . check the muscles in your dominant hand; let those muscles keep relaxing . . . check your other muscles . . . if you notice tension, just let the muscle keep relaxing . . . let the tension go . . . let the face muscles relax . . . let your shoulders relax . . . breathe slowly and easily . . . with each breath, the muscles relax more and more . . . enjoy the feelings of relaxation (45-60 seconds).

End of Exercise

In a moment I will count backward from four to one. On the count of four, you should move your legs and feet; on three, move your arms and hands; on two, move your head and neck; and on one you can open your eyes and get up slowly. All right. *Four:* Move your legs and feet; stretch out. *Three:* Move your hands and arms. *Two:* Move your head and neck. *One:* Open your eyes, get up, and move around when you're ready. You may feel a little dizzy, so move slowly as you become more alert.

References

Chapter 1 The Scope of Sport and Exercise Psychology

Haywood, K.M., & Getchell, N. (2005). *Life span motor development* (4th ed.). Champaign, IL: Human Kinetics.

Lewin, K. (1935). *A dynamic theory of personality.* New York: McGraw-Hill.

Magill, R.A. (2007). *Motor learning: Concepts and applications* (7th ed.). Boston: McGraw-Hill.

Schmidt, R.A., & Wrisberg, C.A. (2004). *Motor learning and performance* (3rd ed.). Champaign, IL: Human Kinetics.

Seligman, M.E.P., & Csikszentmihalyi, M. (2000). Positive psychology: An introduction. *American Psychologist, 55,* 5-14.

Snyder, C.R., & Lopez, S.J. (Eds.). (2005). *Handbook of positive psychology.* New York: Oxford University Press.

Chapter 2 History of Sport and Exercise Psychology

Cratty, B.J. (1967). *Psychology and physical activity.* Englewood Cliffs, NJ: Prentice Hall.

Fitz, G.W. (1895). A local reaction. *Psychological Review, 2,* 37-42.

Gill, D.L. (1986). *Psychological dynamics of sport.* Champaign, IL: Human Kinetics.

Gill, D.L. (1997). Measurement, statistics and research design issues in sport and exercise psychology. *Measurement in Physical Education and Exercise Science, 1,* 39-53.

Gould, D., & Pick, S. (1995). Sport psychology: The Griffith era, 1920-1940. *The Sport Psychologist, 9,* 391-405.

Griffith, C.R. (1926). *Psychology of coaching.* New York: Scribners.

Griffith, C.R. (1928). *Psychology and athletics.* New York: Scribners.

Griffith, C.R. (1930). A laboratory for research in athletics. *The Research Quarterly, 1*(3), 34-40.

Hall, G.S. (1908). Physical education in colleges. *Report of the National Education Association.* Chicago: University of Chicago Press.

Harris, D.V., & Harris, B.L. (1984). *The athlete's guide to sports psychology: Mental skills for physical people.* New York: Leisure Press.

Johnson, W.R. (1949). A study of emotion revealed in two types of athletic sport contests. *Research Quarterly, 20,* 72-79.

Kenyon, G.S., & Grogg, T.M. (1970). *Contemporary psychology of sport.* Chicago: Athletic Institute.

Kroll, W., & Lewis, G. (1970). America's first sport psychologist. *Quest, 13,* 1-4.

Loy, J.W. (1974). A brief history of the North American Society for the Psychology of Sport and Physical Activity. In M.G. Wade & R. Martens (Eds.), *Psychology of motor behavior and sport* (pp. 2-11). Champaign, IL: Human Kinetics.

Martens, R. (1975). *Social psychology and physical activity.* New York: Harper & Row.

Martens, R. (1987a). *Coaches guide to sport psychology.* Champaign, IL: Human Kinetics.

Martens, R. (1987b). Science, knowledge and sport psychology. *The Sport Psychologist, 1,* 29-55.

McCloy, C.H. (1930). Character building through physical education. *Research Quarterly, 1,* 41-61.

Miles, W.R. (1928). Studies in physical exertion: I. A multiple chronograph for measuring groups of men. *American Physical Education Review, 33,* 361-366.

Miles, W.R. (1931). Studies in physical exertion: II. Individual and group reaction time in football charging. *Research Quarterly, 2,* 14-31.

Nideffer, R.M. (1976). *The inner athlete.* New York: Crowell.

Nideffer, R.M. (1985). *Athlete's guide to mental training.* Champaign, IL: Human Kinetics.

Ogilvie, B.C., & Tutko, T.A. (1966). *Problem athletes and how to handle them.* London: Pelham Books.

Orlick, T. (1980). *In pursuit of excellence.* Champaign, IL: Human Kinetics.

Patrick, G.T.W. (1903). The psychology of football. *American Journal of Psychology, 14,* 104-117.

Ryan, E.D. (1981). The emergence of psychological research as related to performance in physical activity. In G. Brooks (Ed.), *Perspective on the academic discipline of physical education* (pp. 327-341). Champaign, IL: Human Kinetics.

Singer, R.N. (1968). *Motor learning and human performance.* New York: Macmillan.

Triplett, N. (1898). The dynamogenic factors in pacemaking and competition. *American Journal of Psychology, 9,* 507-553.

Vanek, M. (1985, Summer). A message from the president of ISSP: Prof. Dr. Miroslav Vanek. *ISSP Newsletter, 1* (1), 1-2.

Vanek, M. (1993). On the inception, development and perspectives of ISSP's image and self-image. In S. Serpa, J. Alves, V. Ferreira, & A. Paula-Brito (Eds.), *Proceedings VIII World Congress of Sport Psychology* (pp. 154-158). Lisbon, Portugal: International Society of Sport Psychology.

Wade, M.G., & Martens, R. (1974). *Psychology of motor behavior and sport.* Urbana, IL: Human Kinetics.

Weiss, M.R., & Gill, D.L. (2005). What goes around comes around: Re-emerging themes in sport and exercise psychology. *Research Quarterly for Exercise and Sport, 76,* S71-S87.

Wiggins, D.K. (1984). The history of sport psychology in North America. In J.M. Silva & R.S. Weinberg (Eds.), *Psychological foundations of sport* (pp.9-22). Champaign, IL: Human Kinetics.

Williams, J.M. (Ed.) (1986). *Applied sport psychology: Personal growth to peak performance.* Mountain View, CA: Mayfield.

Chapter 3 Understanding and Using Sport and Exercise Psychology

APA Presidential Task Force on Evidence-Based Practice. (2006). Evidence-based practice in psychology. *American Psychologist, 61,* 271-285.

Boyer, E.L. (1990). *Scholarship reconsidered.* Princeton, NJ: The Carnegie Foundation for the Advancement of Teaching.

Brustad, R. (2002). A critical analysis of knowledge construction in sport psychology. In T.S. Horn (Ed.), *Advances in sport psychology* (2nd ed., pp. 21-37). Champaign, IL: Human Kinetics.

Carroll, L. (1992). *Alice's adventures in wonderland and through the looking glass.* New York: Dell Books.

Dewar, A., & Horn, T.S. (1992). A critical analysis of knowledge construction in sport psychology (pp. 13-22). In T.S. Horn (Ed.), *Advances in sport psychology.* Champaign, IL: Human Kinetics.

Dzewaltowski, D.A. (1997). The ecology of physical activity and sport: Merging science and practice. *Journal of Applied Sport Psychology, 9* (2), 254-276.

Forscher, B.K. (1963). Chaos in the brickyard. *Science,* 142, 3590.

Gill, D.L. (1997). Sport and exercise psychology. In J. Massengale & R. Swanson (Eds.), *History of exercise and sport science* (pp. 293-320). Champaign, IL: Human Kinetics.

Landers, D.M. (1983). Whatever happened to theory testing in sport psychology? *Journal of Sport Psychology, 5,* 135-151.

Lewin, K. (1935). *A dynamic theory of personality.* New York: McGraw-Hill.

Lewin, K. (1948). *Resolving social conflicts.* New York: Harper & Row.

Lewin, K. (1951). *Field theory in social science.* New York: Harper & Brothers.

Mahoney, M.J. (1991). *Human change processes: The scientific foundations of psychotherapy.* New York: Basic Books.

Mahoney, M. J. (2005). Constructivism and positive psychology. In C.R. Snyder & S.J. Lopez (Eds.), *Handbook of positive psychology,* (pp. 745-750). New York: Oxford University Press.

Martens, R. (1979). From smocks to jocks. *Journal of Sport Psychology, 1,* 94-99.

Martens, R. (1987). Science, knowledge and sport psychology. *The Sport Psychologist,* 1, 29-55.

Thomas, Nelson, and Silverman 2005

Whelan, J.P., Meyers, A.W., & Elkin, T.D. (2002). In J.L. Van Raalte and B.W. Brewer (Eds.), *Exploring sport and exercise psychology* (2nd ed., pp. 503-524). Washington, DC: APA.

Zizzi, S., Zaichowski, L., & Perna, F. (2002). In J.L. Van Raalte and B.W. Brewer (Eds.), *Exploring sport and exercise psychology* (2nd ed., pp. 459-478). Washington, DC: APA.

Chapter 4 Personality

Araki, K. (2004). *Development and validation of the Sport Perfectionism Scale.* Doctoral dissertation, University of North Carolina at Greensboro.

Bandura, A. (1977). *Social learning theory.* Englewood Cliffs, NJ: Prentice-Hall.

Butler, R.J., & Hardy, L. (1992). The performance profile: Theory and application. *The Sport Psychologist, 6,* 253-264.

Carver, C.S., & Scheier, M.F. (2005). Optimism. In C.R. Snyder & S.J. Lopez (Eds.), *Handbook of positive psychology* (pp. 231-243). New York: Oxford University Press.

Chartrand, J., Jowdy, D.P., & Danish, S.J. (1992). The Psychological Skills Inventory for Sports: Psychometric characteristics and applied implications. *Journal of Sport & Exercise Psychology, 14,* 405-413.

Costa, P.T. Jr., & McCrae, R.R. (1985). *The NEO Personality Inventory manual.* Odessa, FL: Psychological Assessment Resources.

Dishman, R.K. (1982). Contemporary sport psychology. In R.L. Terjung (Ed.), *Exercise and Sport Sciences Reviews* (Vol. 10, pp. 120-159). Philadelphia: Franklin Institute Press.

Dishman, R.K. (1984). Motivation and exercise adherence. In J.M. Silva & R.S. Weinberg (Eds.), *Psychological foundations of sport* (pp. 420-434). Champaign, IL: Human Kinetics.

Dishman, R.K., & Ickes, W.J. (1981). Self-motivation and adherence to therapeutic exercise. *Journal of Behavioral Medicine, 4,* 421-438.

Dunn, J.G.H., Causgrove Dunn, J., & Syrotuik, D.G. (2002). Relationships between multidimensional perfectionism and goal orientations in sport. *Journal of Sport & Exercise Psychology, 24,* 376-395.

Eysenck, H.J. (1991). Dimensions of personality: 16, 5, or 3?—Criteria for a taxonomic paradigm. *Personality and Individual Differences, 12,* 773-790.

Fisher, A.C., Ryan, E.D., & Martens, R. (1976). Current status and future directions of personality research related to motor behavior and sport: Three panelists' views. In A.C.

Fisher (Ed.), *Psychology of sport* (pp. 400-431). Palo Alto, CA: Mayfield.

Flett, G.L., & Hewitt, P.L. (2005). The perils of perfectionism in sports and exercise. *Current Directions in Psychological Science, 14,* 14-18.

Friedman, H.S., & Schustack, M.W. (2003). *Personality: Classic theories and modern research* (2nd ed.). Boston: Allyn & Bacon.

Galton, F. (1883). *Inquiries into human faculty and its development.* London: Macmillan.

Gould, D., Weiss, M., & Weinberg, R. (1981). Psychological characteristics of successful and nonsuccessful Big Ten wrestlers. *Journal of Sport Psychology, 3,* 69-81.

Griffith, C.R. (1926). *Psychology of coaching.* New York: Scribners.

Griffith, C.R. (1928). *Psychology and athletics.* New York: Scribners.

Hewitt, P.L., & Flett, G.L. (1991). Perfectionism in the self and social contexts: Conceptualization, assessment, and association with psychopathology. *Journal of Personality and Social Psychology, 60,* 456-470.

Highlen, P.S., & Bennett, B.B. (1979). Psychological characteristics of successful and nonsuccessful elite wrestlers: An exploratory study. *Journal of Sport Psychology, 1,* 123-137.

Mahoney, M.J., & Avener, M. (1977). Psychology of the elite athlete: An exploratory study. *Cognitive Therapy and Research, 1,* 135-141.

Mahoney, M.J., Gabriel, T.J., & Perkins, T.S. (1987). Psychological skills and exceptional athletic performance. *The Sport Psychologist, 1,* 181-199.

Martens, R. (1977). *Sport Competition Anxiety Test.* Champaign, IL: Human Kinetics.

Martens, R., Vealey, R.S., & Burton, D. (1990). *Competitive anxiety in sport.* Champaign, IL: Human Kinetics.

Mayer, J.D. (2005). A tale of two visions: Can a new view of personality integrate psychology? *American Psychologist, 60,* 294-307.

McAdams, D.P., & Pals, J.L. (2006). A new big five: Fundamental principles for an integrative science of personality. *American Psychologist, 61,* 204-217.

McCrae, R.R., & Costa, P.T. Jr. (1989). The structure of interpersonal traits: Wiggins' circumplex and the five-factor model. *Journal of Personality and Social Psychology, 56,* 586-595.

McNair, D.M., Lorr, M., & Droppleman, L.F. (1971). *Manual for the profile of mood states.* San Diego: Educational and Industrial Testing Service.

Meyers, Cooke, Cullen, and Liles 1979

Mischel, W. (1968). *Personality and adjustment.* New York: Wiley.

Mischel, W. (1973). Toward a cognitive social learning reconceptualization of personality. *Psychological Review, 80,* 252-283.

Morgan, W.P. (1978). Sport personology: The credulous-skeptical argument in perspective. In W.F. Straub (Ed.), *Sport psychology: An analysis of athlete behavior* (pp. 330-339). Ithaca, NY: Mouvement.

Morgan, W.P. (1980). The trait psychology controversy. *Research Quarterly for Exercise and Sport, 51,* 50-76.

Morgan, W.P., Brown, D.R., Raglin, J.S., O'Connor, P.J., & Ellickson, K.A. (1987). Psychological monitoring of overtraining and staleness. *British Journal of Sports Medicine, 21,* 107-114.

Motl, R.W., Dishman, R.K., Felton, G., & Pate, R.R. (2003). Self-motivation and physical activity among Black and White adolescent girls. *Medicine and Science in Sports and Exercise, 35,* 128-136.

Ogilvie, B.C. (1968). Psychological consistencies within the personality of high-level competitors. *Journal of the American Medical Association, 205,* 156-162.

Raglin, J.S. (1993). Overtraining and staleness: Psychometric monitoring of endurance athletes. In R.B. Singer, M. Murphey, & L. K. Tennant (Eds.), *Handbook of research on sports psychology* (pp. 840-850). New York: Macmillan.

Rowley, A.J., Landers, D., Kyllo, L.B., & Etnier, J.L. (1995). Does the Iceberg Profile discriminate between successful and less successful athletes? A meta analysis. *Journal of Sport & Exercise Psychology, 17* (2), 185-199.

Ryan, E.D. (1968). Reaction to "sport and personality dynamics". In the Proceedings of the National College Physical Education Association for Men (pp. 70-75).

Scheier, M.F., Carver, C.S., & Bridges, M.W. (1994). Distinguishing optimism from neuroticism (and trait anxiety, self-mastery, and self-esteem): A reevaluation of the Life Orientation Test. *Journal of Personality and Social Psychology, 67,* 1063-1078.

Seligman, M.E.P. (2005). Positive psychology, positive prevention and positive therapy. In C.R. Snyder & S.J. Lopez (Eds.), *Handbook of positive psychology* (pp. 3-9). New York: Oxford University Press.

Smith, R.E., Schutz, R.W, Smoll, F.L., & Ptacek, J.T. (1995). Development and validation of a multidimensional measure of sport-specific psychological skills: The Athletic Coping Skills Inventory-28. *Journal of Sport & Exercise Psychology, 17,* 379-398.

Smith, R.E., Smoll, F.L., & Schutz, R.W. (1990). Measurement and correlates of sport-specific cognitive and somatic trait anxiety: The Sport Anxiety Scale. *Anxiety Research, 2,* 263-280.

Snyder, C.R., Harris, C. et al. (1991). The will and the ways: Development and validation of an individual differences measure of hope. *Journal of Personality and Social Psychology, 60,* 570-585.

Snyder, C.R., Rand, K.L., & Sigmon, D.R. (2005). Hope theory: A member of the positive psychology family. In C.R. Snyder & S.J. Lopez (Eds.), *Handbook of positive psychology* (pp. 257-276). New York: Oxford University Press.

Spielberger, C.D. (1966). *Anxiety and behavior.* New York: Academic Press.

Thomas, P.R., Murphy, S.M., & Hardy, L. (1999). Test of performance strategies: Development and preliminary validation of a comprehensive measure of athletes' psychological skills. *Journal of Sports Sciences, 17,* 1-15.

Tutko, T.A., Lyon, L.P., & Ogilvie, B.C. (1969). *Athletic Motivation Inventory.* San Jose, CA: Institute for the Study of Athletic Motivation.

Vanden Auweele, Y., De Cuyper, B.D., Van Mele, V., & Rzewnicki, R. (1993). Elite performance and personality: From description and prediction to diagnosis and intervention. In R.N. Singer, M. Murphey, & L.K. Tennant (Eds.), *Handbook of research on sport psychology* (pp. 257-289). New York: Macmillan.

Wallston, K.A., Wallston, B.S., & DeVellis, R. (1978). Development of the multidimensional health locus of control (MHLC) scales. *Health Education Monographs, 6,* 160-170.

Zuckerman, M. (1994). *Behavioral expressions and biosocial bases of sensation seeking.* New York: Cambridge University Press.

Chapter 5 Attention and Cognitive Skills

Abernethy, B. (2001). Attention. In R.N. Singer, H.A. Hausenblas, & C.M. Janelle (Eds.), *Handbook of sport psychology* (2nd ed., pp. 53-85). New York: Macmillan.

Abernethy, B., & Russell, D.G. (1987). Expert-novice differences in an applied selective attention task. *Journal of Sport Psychology, 9,* 326-345.

Allard, F., Graham, S., & Paarsalu, M.T. (1980). Perception in sport: Basketball. *Journal of Sport Psychology, 2,* 14-21.

Beilock, S.L., & Carr, T.H. (2001). On the fragility of skilled performance: What governs choking under pressure? *Journal of Experimental Psychology: General, 130,* 701-725.

Beilock, S.L., Wierenga, S.A., & Carr, T.H. (2003). Memory and expertise: What do experienced athletes remember? In J.L. Starkes & A. Ericsson (Eds.), *Expert performance in sports* (pp. 295-320). Champaign, IL: Human Kinetics.

Boutcher, S., & Zinsser, N.W. (1990). Cardiac deceleration of elite and beginning golfers during putting. *Journal of Sport & Exercise Psychology, 12,* 37-47.

Boutcher, S.H. (2002). Attentional processes and sport performance. In T.S. Horn (Ed.), *Advances in sport psychology* (2nd ed., pp. 441-457). Champaign, IL: Human Kinetics.

Boutcher, S.H., & Crews, D.J. (1987). The effect of a preshot attentional routine on a well-learned skill. *International Journal of Sport Psychology, 18,* 30-39.

Burton, D. (1989). Winning isn't everything: Examining the impact of performance goals on collegiate swimmers' cognitions and performance. *The Sport Psychologist, 2,* 105-132.

Burton, D., & Naylor, S. (2002). The Jekyll/Hyde nature of goals: Revisiting and updating goal setting in sport. In T.S. Horn (Ed.), *Advances in sport psychology* (2nd ed., pp. 459-499). Champaign, IL: Human Kinetics.

Chambers, K.L., & Vickers, J.N. (2006). Effects of bandwidth feedback and questioning on the performance of competitive swimmers. *The Sport Psychologist, 20,* 184-197.

Chase, W.G., & Simon, H.A. (1973). Perception in chess. *Cognitive Psychology, 4,* 55-81.

Cote, J., Baker, J., & Abernethy, B. (2003). A developmental framework for the acquisition of expertise in team sport. In J.L. Starkes & A. Ericsson (Eds.), *Expert performance in sports* (pp. 89-114).Champaign, IL: Human Kinetics.

Crews, D.J., & Landers, D.M. (1991). *Cardiac pattern as an indicator of attention: A test of two hypothesis.* Manuscript submitted for publication.

Dewey, D., Brawley, L.R., & Allard, F. (1989). Do the TAIS attentional style scales predict how visual information is processed? *Journal of Sport & Exercise Psychology, 11,* 171-186.

Dijksterhuis, A., & Nordgren, L.F. (2006). A theory of unconscious thought. *Perspectives on Psychological Science, 1,* 95-109.

Easterbrook, J.A. (1959). The effect of emotion on cue utilization and the organization of behavior. *Psychological Review, 66,* 183-201.

Ellis, A. (1982). Self-direction in sport and life. *Rational Living, 17,* 27-33.

Feltz, D.L., & Landers, D.M. (1983). The effects of mental practice on motor skill learning and performance: A meta-analysis. *Journal of Sport Psychology, 5,* 25-57.

Gauvin, L. (1990). An experiential perspective on the motivational features of exercise and lifestyle. *Canadian Journal of Sport Sciences, 15,* 51-58.

Gill, D.L., & Strom, E.H. (1985). The effect of attentional focus on performance of an endurance task. *International Journal of Sport Psychology, 16,* 217-223.

Gould, D. (2006). Goal setting for peak performance. In J.M. Williams (Ed.), *Applied sport psychology: Personal growth to peak performance* (5th ed., pp. 240-259). Boston: McGraw-Hill.

Gould, D., Damarjian, N., & Greenleaf, C. (2002). Imagery training for peak performance. In J.L. Van Raalte and B.W. Brewer

(Eds.), *Exploring sport and exercise psychology* (2nd ed., pp. 49-74). Washington, DC: APA.

Gould, D., Tammen, V., Murphy, S., & May, J. (1989). An examination of U.S. Olympic sport psychology consultants and the services they provide. *The Sport Psychologist, 3,* 300-312.

Hall, C.R., Mack, D., Paivio, A., & Hausenblas, H.A. (1998). Imagery use in athletes: Development of the Sport Imagery Questionnaire. *International Journal of Sport Psychology, 29,* 73-89.

Hall, C.R., Pongrac, J., & Buckolz, E. (1985). The measurement of imagery ability. *Human Movement Science, 4,* 107-118.

Hall, C.R., Rodgers, W.M., & Barr, K.A.(1990). The use of imagery by athletes in selected sports. *The Sport Psychologist, 4,* 1-10.

Hatfield, B.D., & Hillman, C.H. (2001). The psychophysiology of sport: A mechanistic understanding of the psychology of superior performance. In R.N. Singer, H.A. Hausenblas, & C.M. Janelle (Eds.), *Handbook of sport psychology* (2nd ed., pp. 362-386). New York: Macmillan.

Hatfield, B.D., Landers, D.M., & Ray, W.J. (1984). Cognitive processes during self-paced motor performance: An electroencephalographic profile of skilled marksmen. *Journal of Sport Psychology, 6,* 42-59.

Hausenblas, H.A., Hall, C.R., Rodgers, W.M., & Munroe, K. (1999). Exercise imagery: Its nature and measurement. *Journal of Applied Sport Psychology, 11,* 171-180.

Ievleva, L., & Orlick, T. (1991). Mental links to enhanced healing: An exploratory study. *The Sport Psychologist, 5,* 25-40.

Jacobson, E. (1931). Electrical measurement of neuromuscular states during mental activities. *American Journal of Physiology, 96.*

James, W. (1890). *The principles of psychology* (Vol. 1). New York: Holt.

Janelle, C.M. (2002). Modification of visual attention parameters under conditions of heightened anxiety and arousal. *Journal of Sports Sciences, 20,* 237-251.

Janelle, C.M., & Hillman, C.H. (2003). Expert performance in sport: Current perspectives and critical issues. In J.L. Starkes & A. Ericsson (Eds.), *Expert performance in sports* (pp. 19-48). Champaign, IL: Human Kinetics.

Janelle, C.M., Singer, R.N., & Williams, A.M. (1999). External distraction and attentional narrowing: Visual search evidence. *Journal of Sport & Exercise Psychology, 21,* 70-91.

Kyllo, L.B., & Landers, D.M. (1995). Goal setting in sport and exercise: A research synthesis to resolve the controversy. *Journal of Sport & Exercise Psychology, 17,* 117-137.

Landers, D.M. (1980). The arousal/performance relationship revisited. *Research Quarterly for Exercise and Sport, 51,* 77-90.

Landers, D.M. (1981). Arousal, attention and skilled performance: Further considerations. *Quest, 33,* 271-283.

Landers, D.M., Christina, B.D., Hatfield, L.A., Doyle, L.A., & Daniels, F.S. (1980). Moving competitive shooting into the scientists' lab. *American Rifleman, 128,* 36-37, 76-77.

Lang, P.J. (1977). Imagery in therapy: An information processing analysis of fear. *Behavior Therapy, 8,* 862-886.

Lang, P.J. (1979). A bio-informational theory of emotional imagery. *Psychophysiology, 16,* 495-512.

Locke, E.A., & Latham, G.P. (1990). *A theory of goal setting and task performance.* Englewood Cliffs, NJ: Prentice Hall.

Locke, E.A., Saari, L.M., Shaw, K.N., & Latham, G.P. (1981). Goal setting and task performance: 1969-1980. *Psychological Bulletin, 90,* 125-152.

Mahoney, M.J., & Avener, M. (1977). Psychology of the elite athlete: An exploratory study. *Cognitive Therapy and Research, 1,* 135-141.

Martin, K.A., Moritz, S.E., & Hall, C.R. (1999). Imagery use in sport: A literature review and applied model. *The Sport Psychologist, 13,* 245-268.

McPherson, S.L. (2000). Expert-novice differences in planning strategies during singles tennis competition. *Journal of Sport & Exercise Psychology, 22,* 39-62.

McPherson, S.L., & Kernodle, M.W. (2003).Tactics, the neglected attribute of expertise: Problem representations and performance skills in tennis. In J.L. Starkes & A. Ericsson (Eds.), *Expert performance in sports* (pp. 137-167). Champaign, IL: Human Kinetics.

Mento, A.J., Steel, R.P., & Karren, R.J. (1987). A meta-analytic study of the effects of goal setting on task performance: 1966-1984. *Organizational Behavior and Human Decision Processes, 39,* 52-83.

Morgan, W.P. (1981). Psychophysiology of self-awareness during vigorous physical activity. *Research Quarterly for Exercise and Sport, 52,* 385-427.

Morgan, W.P., & Pollock, M.L. (1977). Psychologic characterization of the elite distance runner. *Annals of the New York Academy of Sciences, 301,* 382-403.

Morgan, W.P., Horstman, D.H., Cymerman, A., & Stokes, J. (1983). Facilitation of physical performance by means of a cognitive strategy. *Cognitive Therapy and Research, 7,* 251-264.

Nideffer, R.M. (1976a). *The inner athlete.* New York: Crowell.

Nideffer, R.M. (1993). Concentration and attention control training. In J.M. Williams (Ed.), *Applied sport psychology: Personal growth to peak performance,* (2nd ed., pp. 243-261). Mountain View, CA: Mayfield.

Nideffer, R.M.S. (1976b). Test of attentional and interpersonal style. *Journal of Personality and Social Psychology, 34,* 394-404.

Orlick, T., & Partington, J. (1988). Mental links to excellence. *The Sport Psychologist, 2,* 105-130.

Schomer, H. (1987). Mental strategy training programme for marathon runners. *International Journal of Sport Psychology, 18,* 133-151.

Shaffer, S.M., & Wiese-Bjornstal, D.M. (1999). Psychosocial interventions in sports medicine. In R. Ray & D.M. Wiese-Bjornstal (Eds.), *Counseling in sports medicine* (pp. 41-54). Champaign, IL: Human Kinetics.

Sheehan, P.W., Ashton, R., & White, K. (1983). Assessment of mental imagery. In A.A. Sheikh (Ed.), *Imagery: Current theory, research, and application* (pp. 189-221). New York: Wiley.

Silva, J.M., & Applebaum, M.S. (1989). Association-dissociation patterns of United States Olympic marathon trial contestants. *Cognition—Therapy and Research, 13,* 185-192.

Smith, A.L., Gill, D.L., Crews, D.J., Hopewell, R., & Morgan, D.W. (1995). Attentional strategy use by experienced distance runners: Physiological and psychological effects. *Research Quarterly for Exercise and Sport, 66,* 142-150.

Soberlak, P., & Cote, J. (2003). The developmental activities of elite ice hockey players. *Journal of Applied Sport Psychology, 15,* 41-49.

Starkes, J.L., & Ericsson, A. (Eds.). (2003). *Expert performance in sports.* Champaign, IL: Human Kinetics.

Starkes, J.L., Helsen, W., & Jack, R. (2001). Expert performance in sport and dance. In R.N. Singer, H.A. Hausenblas, & C.M. Janelle (Eds.). *Handbook of sport psychology* (2nd ed.) (pp. 174-201). New York: Macmillan.

Suinn, R.S. (1983). Imagery and sports. In A.A. Sheikh (Ed.), *Imagery: Current theory, research, and application* (pp. 507-534). New York: Wiley.

Van Schoyck, S.R., & Grasha, A.F. (1981). Attentional style variations and athletic ability: The advantages of a sports-specific test. *Journal of Sport Psychology, 3,* 149-165.

Vealey, R.S., & Greenleaf, C.A. (2006). Seeing is believing: Understanding and using imagery in sport. In J.M. Williams (Ed.), *Applied sport psychology: Personal growth to peak performance* (5th ed., pp. 306-348). Boston: McGraw-Hill.

Vickers, J.N. (1996). Visual control when aiming at a far target. *Journal of Experimental Psychology: Human Perception and Performance, 22,* 342-354.

Vickers, J.N. (2004). The quiet eye: It's the difference between q good putter and a poor one. *Golf Digest,* January, 96-101.

Vickers, J.N. (2007). *Perception, cognition and decision training: The quiet eye in action.* Champaign, IL: Human Kinetics.

Weinberg, R. (2002). Goal setting in sport and exercise: Research to practice. In J.L. Van Raalte and B.W. Brewer (Eds.), *Exploring sport and exercise psychology* (2nd ed., pp. 25-48). Washington, DC: APA.

Weinberg, R.S., Burton, D., Yukelson, D., & Weigand, D. (1993). Goal setting in competitive sport: An exploratory investigation of practices of collegiate athletes. *The Sport Psychologist, 7,* 275-289.

Williams, A.M., Ward, P., & Chapman, C. (2003). Training perceptual skill in field hockey: Is there transfer from the laboratory to the field? *Research Quarterly for Exercise and Sport, 74,* 98-103.

Williams, J M., & Leffingwell, T.R. (2002). Cognitive strategies in sport and exercise psychology. In J.L. Van Raalte and B.W. Brewer (Eds.), *Exploring sport and exercise psychology* (2nd ed., pp. 75-98). Washington, DC: APA.

Wilson, V.E., Peper, E., & Schmidt, A. (2006). Strategies for training concentration. In J.M. Williams (Ed.), *Applied sport psychology: Personal growth to peak performance* (5th ed., pp. 404-424). Boston: McGraw-Hill.

Zinsser, N., Bunker, L., & Williams, J.M. (2006). Cognitive techniques for building confidence and enhancing performance. In J.M. Williams (Ed.), *Applied sport psychology: Personal growth to peak performance* (5th ed., pp. 349-381). Boston: McGraw-Hill.

Chapter 6 Self-Perceptions

Anderson, C. B. (2004). Athletic identity and its relation to exercise behavior: Scale develoment and initial validation. *Journal of Sport & Exercise Psychology, 26,* 39-56.

Asci, F.H. (2003). The effects of physical fitness training on trait anxiety and physical self-concept on female university students. *Psychology Sport and Exercise, 4,* 255-264.

Bandura, A. (1977a). Self-efficacy: Toward a unifying theory of behavioral change. *Psychological Review, 84,* 191-215.

Bandura, A. (1977b). *Social learning theory.* Englewood Cliffs, NJ: Prentice-Hall.

Bandura, A. (1982). Self-efficacy mechanism in human agency. *American Psychologist, 37,* 122-147.

Bandura, A. (1986). *Social foundations of thought and action: A social cognitive theory.* Englewood Cliffs, NJ: Prentice-Hall.

Bandura, A. (1997). *Self-efficacy: The exercise of control.* New York: Freeman.

Berger, B.G., & McInman, A. (1993). Exercise and the quality of life. In R.N. Singer, M. Murphey, & L.K. Tennant (Eds.), *Handbook of research on sport psychology* (pp. 729-760.). New York: Macmillan.

Berger, B.G., Pargman, D., & Weinberg, R.S. (2007). *Foundation of exercise psychology.* Morgantown, WV: Fitness Information Technology.

Brewer, B.W., Van Raalte, J.L., & Linder, D.W. (1993). Athletic identity: Hercules' muscles or Achilles heel? *International Journal of Sport Psychology, 24,* 237-254.

Brone, R., & Reznikoff, M. (1989). Strength gains, locus of control, and self-description of college football players. *Perceptual and Motor Skills, 69,* 483-493.

Brown, T. N., Jackson, J. S., Brown, K. T., Sellers, R. M., Keiper, S., & Manuel, W. J. (2003). "There's no race on the playing field". *Journal of Sport & Social Issues 27,* 162-183.

Cooley, C.H. (1902). *Human nature and the social order.* New York: Scribner.

Coopersmith, S. (1967). *The antecedents of self-esteem.* San Francisco: Freeman.

Craft, L. L., Magyar, T. M., Becker, B. J., & Feltz, D. L. (2003). The relationship between the Competitive State Anxiety Inventory-2 and sport performance: A meta-analysis. *Journal of Sport & Exercise Psychology, 25,* 44-65.

Crocker, P. R. E., & Kowalski, K. C. (2000). Children's physical activity and physical self-perceptions. *Journal of Sports Sciences, 18,* 383-394.

Dzewaltowski, D.A. (1989). Toward a model of exercise motivation. *Journal of Sport & Exercise Psychology, 11,* 251-269.

Dzewaltowski, D.A., Noble, J.M., & Shaw, J.M. (1990). Physical activity participation: Social cognitive theory versus the theories of reasoned action and planned behavior. *Journal of Sport & Exercise Psychology, 12,* 388-405.

Ehrenreich, B. (1996, July). The real swimsuit issue. *Time,* p. 68.

Estabrooks, P., & Courneya, K. S. (1997). Relationships among self-schema, intention, and exercise behavior. *Journal of Sport & Exercise Psychology, 11,* 408-430.

Ewart, C.K., Stewart, K.J., Gillian, R.E., Keleman, M.H., Valenti, S.A., Manley, J.D., & Kaleman, M.D. (1986). Usefulness of self-efficacy in predicting overexertion during programmed exercise in coronary artery disease. *American Journal of Cardiology, 57,* 557-561.

Ewart, C.K., Taylor, C.B., Reese, L.B., & DeBusk, R.F. (1983). Effects of early post myocardial infarction exercise testing on self-perception and subsequent physical activity. *American Journal of Cardiology, 51,* 1076-1080.

Feltz, D. L., & Chase, M. A. (1998). The measurement of self-efficacy and confidence in sport. In J. L. Duda (Ed.), *Advances in sport and exercise psychology measurement* (pp. 65-80). Morgantown, WV: Fitness Information Technology.

Feltz, D. L., & Lrigg, C. D. (2001). Self-efficacy beliefs of atheltes, teams, and coaches. In R. N. Singer, H. A. Hausenblas & C. M. Janelle (Eds.), *Handbook of sport psychology* (pp.340-361). New York: Wiley & Sons.

Feltz, D. L., & Riessinger, C. A. (1990). Effects in vivo emotive imagery and performance feedback on self-efficacy and muscular endurance. *Journal of Sport & Exercise Psychology, 12,* 132-143.

Feltz, D.L. (1984). Path analysis of the causal elements in Bandura's theory of self-efficacy and an anxiety-based model of avoidance behavior. *Journal of Personality and Social Psychology, 42,* 764-781.

Folkins, C.H., & Sime, W.E. (1981). Physical fitness training and mental health. *American Psychologist, 36,* 373-389.

Fox, K. R. (1998). Advances in the measurement of the physical self. In J. L. Duda (Ed.), *Advances in sport and exercise psychology measurement.* Morgantown, WV: Fitness Information Technology.

Fox, K.H. (1990). *The Physical Self-Perception Profile manual.* DeKalb, IL: Northern Illinois University, Office for Health Promotion.

Fox, K.R., & Corbin, C.B. (1989). The Physical Self-Perception Profile: Development and preliminary validation. *Journal of Sport & Exercise Psychology, 11,* 408-430.

George, T. R., Feltz, D. L., & Chase, M. A. (1992). The effects of modle similarity on self-efficacy and muscular endurance:

A second look. *Journal of Sport & Exercise Psychology, 14,* 237-248.

Georgiadis, M., Biddle, S., & Chatzisarantis, N. (2001). The mediating role of self-determination in the relationship between goal orientations and physical self-worth in Greek exercisers. *European Journal of Sport Science, 1,* 1-9.

Gill, D. L. (2002). Gender and sport behavior. In T. S. Horn (Ed.), *Advances in Sport Psychology* (2nd ed.). Champaign, Il: Human Kinetics.

Gill, D. L. (2007). Gender and cultural diversity. In G. Tenenbaum & R. C. Eklund (Eds.), *Handbook of Sport Psychology* (3rd. ed.). New York: Wiley & Sons.

Gould, D., Weiss, M., & Weinberg, R. (1981). Psychological characteristics of successful and nonsuccessful Big Ten wrestlers. *Journal of Sport Psychology, 3,* 69-81.

Hart, E.A., Leary, M.R., & Rejeski, W.J. (1989). The measurement of social physique anxiety. *Journal of Sport & Exercise Psychology, 11,* 94-104.

Harter, S. (1983). Developmental perspectives on the self-system. In E.M. Hetherington (Ed.), *Handbook of child psychology: Social and personality development* (Vol. 4, pp. 275-385). New York: Wiley.

Harter, S. (1990). Causes, correlates and the functional role of global self-worth: A life-span perspective. In R.J. Sternberg & J. Kolligan (Eds.), *Competence considered* (pp. 67-97). New Haven, CT: Yale University Press.

Harter, S. (1999). *Construction of the self: A developmental perspective.* New York: Guilford Press.

Horn, T. S. (2004). Developmental perspectives on self-perceptions in children and adolescents. In M. R. Weiss (Ed.), *Developmental sport and exercise psychology: A lifespan perspective* (pp. 101-143). Morgantown, WV: Fitness Information Technology.

Horton, R. S., & Mack, D. E. (2000). Athletic identy in marathon runners: Functional focus or dysfuncational commitment? *Journal of Sport Behavior, 23,* 101-109.

James, W. (1890). *The principles of psychology* (Vol. 1). New York: Holt.

James, W. (1892). *Psychology: Briefer course.* New York: Holt.

Kaplan, R.M., Atkins, C.J., & Reinsch, S. (1984). Specific efficacy expectations mediate exercise compliance in patients with COPD. *Health Psychology, 3,* 223-242.

Kaplan, R.M., Ries, A.L., Prewitt, L.M., & Eakin, E. (1994). Self-efficacy expectations predict survival for patients with chronic obstructive pulmonary disease. *Health Psychology, 13,* 366-368.

Kendzierski, D. (1988). Self-schemata and exercise. *Basic and Applied Social Psychology, 9,* 45-59.

Kendzierski, D. (1994). Schema theory: An information processing focus. In R.K. Dishman (Ed.), *Advances in exercise adherence* (pp. 137-159). Champaign, IL: Human Kinetics.

Kendzierski, D., Furr, R. M., & Schiavoni, J. (1998). Physical activity self-definitions:Correlates and perceived criteria. *Journal of Sport & Exercise Psychology, 20,* 176-193.

Kowalski, K.C., Crocker, P.R.E., Kowalski, N.P., Chad, K.E., & Humbert, M.L. (2006). Examining the physical self in adolescent girls over time: Further evidence against the hierarchical model *Journal of Sport and Exercise Psychology, 25,* 5-18.

Kroichick, R. (2001, August 27). License to thrill. *The Sporting News* [Online]. www.encyclopedia.com.

Lally, P., & Kerr, G.A. (2005). The career planning, athletic identity, and student role identity of intercollegiate student athletes. *Research Quarterly for Exercise and Sport, 76,* 275-283.

Leary, M.R. (1992). Self-presentational process in exercise and sport. *Journal of Sport and Exercise Psychology, 14,* 339-351.

Mahoney, M.J., & Avener, M. (1977). Psychology of the elite athlete: An exploratory study. *Cognitive Therapy and Research, 1,* 135-141.

Markus, H. (1977). Self-schemata and processing information about the self. *Journal of Personality and Social Psychology, 35,* 63-78.

Markus, H., & Nurius, P. (1986). Possible selves. *American Psychologist, 41,* 954-969.

Markus, H., Cross, S., & Wurf, E. (1990). The roel of the self-system in competence. In R. J. Sternberg & J. K. Jr. (Eds.), *Competence Considered* (pp. 205-225). New Haven:CT: Yale University Press.

Marsh, H. W. (1997). The measurement of physical self-concept-A construct validity approach. In F. K.R. (Ed.), *The Physical Self.* Champaign, IL: Human Kinetics.

Marsh, H. W., & Craven, R. G. (1997). Academic self-concept: Beyond the dustbowl. In G. Phye (Ed.), *Handbook of classroom assessment: Learning, achievement, and adjustment.* Orlando, FL: Academic Press.

Marsh, H. W., & Craven, R. G. (2006). Reciprocal effects of self-concept and performance form a multidimensional persepective. *Perspectives on Psychological Science, 1,* 133-163.

Marsh, H. W., Chanal, J. P., & Sarrazin, P. G. (2006). Self-belief does make a difference: A reciprocal effects model of the causal ordering of physical self-concept and gymnastics performance. *Journal of Sports Sciences, 24,* 101-111.

Marsh, H.W. (1990). A multidimensional, hierarchical self-concept: Theoretical and empirical justification. *Educational Psychology Review, 2,* 77-172.

Marsh, H.W. (1996). Construct validity of physical self-description questionnaire responses: Relations to external criteria. *Journal of Sport & Exercise Psychology, 18,* 111-113.

Marsh, H.W., Richards, G.E., Johnson, S., Roche, L., & Tremayne, P. (1994). Physical Self-Description Questionnaire: Psychometric properties and multitrait-multimethod analysis of relations to existing instruments. *Journal of Sport & Exercise Psychology, 16,* 270-305.

Martin Ginis, K. A., Lindwall, M., & Prapavessis, H. (in press). Who cares what other people think. In G. Tenenbaum & R. Eklund (Eds.), *Handbook of sport psychology* (3rd ed.). New York: Wiley Press.

McAuley, E. (1992). Understanding exercise behavior: A self-efficacy perspective. In G.C. Roberts (Ed.), *Motivation in sport and exercise* (pp. 107-127). Champaign, IL: Human Kinetics.

McAuley, E. (1993). Self-referent thought in sport and physical activity. In T.S. Horn (Ed.), *Advances in sport psychology* (pp. 101-118). Champaign, IL: Human Kinetics.

McAuley, E., Katula, J., Mihalko, S. L., Blissmer, B., Duncan, T., Pena, M. M., et al. (1999). Mode of physical activity differentially influences self-efficacy in older adults: Latent growth curve analysis. *Journal of Gerontology, 54B,* P283-P292.

McAuley, E., Lox, C. L., & Duncan, T. (1993). Long-term maintenance of exercise, self-efficacy, and physiological changes in older adults. *Journal of Gerontology, 48,* P218-P223.

McAuley, E., Pena, M. M., & Jerome, G. J. (2001). Self-efficacy as a determinant and outcome of exercise. In G. C. Roberts (Ed.), *Advances in motivation in sport and exercise* (pp. 235-261). Champaign, IL: Human Kinetics.

McCullaugh, P., & Weiss, M. R. (2001). Modeling: Considerations for motort skill performance and psychological responses. In R. N. Singer, H. A. Hausenblas & C. M. Janelle (Eds.), *Handbook of sport psychology* (2nd ed., pp. 205-238). New York: Wiley & Sons.

Meyers, N. D., & Feltz, D. L. (2007). From self-efficacy to collective efficacy. In G. Tenenbaum & R. C. Elkund (Eds.), *Handbook of Sport Psychology*. New York: Wiley & Sons.

Oyserman, D., & Markus, H. (1990). Possible selves and delinquency. *Journal of Personality and Social Psychology, 59,* 112-125.

Oyserman, D., Bybee, D., & Terry, K. (2006). Possible selves and academic outcomes: How and when possible selves impel action. *Journal of Personality and Social Psychology, 90,* 188-204.

Prapavessis, H., Grove, J. R., & Eklund, R. (2004). Self-presentational issues in competition in sport. *Journal of Applied Sport Psychology, 16,* 19-40.

Ram, N., & McCullaugh, P. (2003). Self-modeling: influence on psychological responses and physical performance. *The Sport Psychologist, 17,* 220-241.

Reel, J.J., & Gill, D.L. (1996). Psychosocial factors related to eating disorders among high school and college female cheerleaders. *The Sport Psychologist, 10,* 195-206.

Reis, J. (2007, February 13). Davis' swagger commands respect. *The Daily Collegian Online* [Online]. www.collegian.psu.edu/archive/2007.

Ries, A. L., Kaplan, R. M., Limberg, T. M., & Prewitt, L. M. (1995). Effects of pulmonary rehabilitation on physiologic and pyschosocial outcomes in patients with chronic obstructive pulmonary disease. *Annals of Internal Medicine, 122,* 823-832.

Rodin, J., & Larson, L. (1992). Social factors and the ideal body shape. In K.D. Brownell, J. Rodin, & J.H. Wilmore (Eds.), *Eating, body weight, and performance in athletes* (pp. 146-158). Philadelphia: Lea & Febiger.

Rudolph, D. L., & McAuley, E. (1995). Self-efficacy and salivary cortisol responses to acute exercise in physically active and lesss active adults. *Journal of Sport & Exercise Psychology, 17,* 206-213.

Ruvolo, A. P., & Markus, H. (1992). Possible selves and performance: The power of self-relevant imagery. *Social Cognition, 10*(1), 95-124.

Ryckman, R.M., Robbins, M.A., Thornton, B., & Cantrell, P. (1982). Development and validation of a physical self-efficacy scale. *Journal of Personality and Social Psychology, 42,* 891-900.

Sallis, J.F., Haskell, W.L., Fortmann, S.P., Vranizan, K.M., Taylor, C.B., & Solomon, D.S. (1986). Predictors of adoption and maintenance of physical activity in a community sample. *Preventive Medicine, 15,* 331-341.

Secord, P.F., & Jourard, S.M. (1953). The appraisal of body cathexis: Body cathexis and the self. *Journal of Consulting Psychology, 17,* 343-347.

Shavelson, R.J., Hubner, J.J., & Stanton, G.C. (1976). Self-concept: Validation of construct interpretations. *Review of Educational Research, 46,* 407-441.

Sonstroem, R.J., & Morgan, W.P. (1989). Exercise and self-esteem: Rationale and model. *Medicine and Science in Sports and Exercise, 21,* 329-337.

Sonstroem, R.J., Speliotis, E.D., & Fava, J.L. (1992). Perceived physical competence in adults: An examination of the Physical Self-Perception Scale. *Journal of Sport & Exercise Psychology, 10,* 207-221.

Starek, J., & McCullaugh, P. (1999). The effect of self-modeling on the performance of beginning swimmers. *The Sport Psychologist, 13,* 269-287.

Stein, K. F., Roeser, R., & Markus, H. (1998). Self-Schemas and possibile shelves as preditors and outcomes of risky behaviors in adolescents. *Nursing Research, 47*(2), 96-106.

Taylor, A.H., & Fox, K.R. (2005). Effectiveness of primary care exercise referral intervention for changing physical self-perceptions over 9 months. *Health Psychology, 24,* 11-24.

Taylor, C.B., Bandura, A., Ewart, C.K., Miller, N.H., and DeBusk, R.T. (1985). Exercise testing to enhance wives' confidence in their husbands' cardiac capabilities soon after clinically uncomplicated acute myocardial infarction. American Journal of *Cardiology 55,* 6335-6638.

Treasure, D. C., Monson, J., & Lox, C. L. (1996). Relationship between self-efficacy, wrestling performance and affect prior to competition. . *The Sport Psychologist, 10,* 73-83.

Tremblay, M. S., Inman, J. W., & Willms, J. D. (2000). The relationship between physical activity, self-esteem, and academic achievement in 12-year old children. *Pediatric Exercise Science, 12,* 312-323.

Tucker, L.A. (1987). Effect of weight training on body attitudes: Who benefits most? *Journal of Sports Medicine and Physical Fitness, 27,* 70-78.

Vealey, R. S. (2001). Understanding and enhancing self-confidence in athletes. In G. Tenenbaum & R. Elkund (Eds.), *Handbook of sport psychology* (3rd ed., pp. 550-565). New York: Wiley & Sons.

Vealey, R.S. (1986). Conceptualization of sport-confidence and competitive orientation: Preliminary investigation and instrument development. *Journal of Sport Psychology, 8,* 221-246.

Weise-Bjornstal, D. M. (2004). From skinned knees and pee-wees to menisci and masters: Developmental sport injury psychology. In M. R. Weiss (Ed.), *Developmental sport and exericse psychology: A lifespan perspective* (pp. 525-568). Morgantown, WV: Fitness Information Technology.

Weiss, M. R., & Ferrer-Caja, E. (2002). Motivational orientations and sport behavior. In T. S. Horn (Ed.), *Advances in Sport Psychology* (2nd ed., pp. 101-183). Champaign, IL: Human Kinetics.

Weiss, M. R., McCullaugh, P., Smith, A. L., & Berlant, A. R. (1998). Observational learning and the fearful child: Influence of peer models on swimming skill performance and psychological responses. *Research Quarterly for Exercise & Sport, 69,* 380-394.

Whaley, D. (2004). Seeing isn't always believing: Self-perceptions and physical activity behaviors in adults. In M. R. Weiss (Ed.), *Developmental sport and exercise psychology: A lifespan perspective* (pp. 289-311). Morgantown,WV: Fitness Information Technology.

Winfrey, M. L., & Weeks, D. L. (1993). Effects of self-modeling on self-efficacy and balance beam performance. *Perceptual and motor skills, 77,* 907-913.

Yin, Z., & Boyd, M. P. (2000). Behavioral and cognitive correlates of exercise self-schema. *The Journal of Psychology, 134,* 269-282.

Chapter 7 Behavioral Approaches

Brobst, B., & Ward, P. (2002). Effects of public posting, goal setting, and oral feedback on the skills of female soccer players. *Journal of Applied Behavior Analysis, 35,* 247-257.

Coatsworth, J.D., & Conroy, D.E. (2006). Enhancing the self-esteem of youth swimmers through coach training: Gender and age effects. *Psychology of Sport and Exercise, 7,* 173-192.

Critchfield, T.S., & Vargas, E.A. (1991). Self-recording, instructions and public self-graphing: Effects on swimming in the absence of coach verbal interaction. *Behavior Modification, 15,* 95-112.

Fitterling, J.M., & Ayllon, T. (1983). Behavioral coaching in classical ballet. *Behavior Modification, 3,* 345-368.

Gallimore, R., & Tharp, R. (2004). What a coach can teach a teacher, 1975-2004: Reflections and reanalysis of John

Wooden's teaching practices. *The Sport Psychologist, 18,* 119-137.

Kauss, D.R. (1980). *Peak performance.* Englewood Cliffs, NJ: Prentice-Hall.

Komaki, J., & Barnett, F.T. (1977). A behavioral approach to coaching football: Improving the play execution of the offensive backfield on a youth football team. *Journal of Applied Behavior Analysis, 10,* 657-664.

Malott, R. W., & Suarez, E. T. (2004). *Principles of behavior, fifth edition.* Upper Saddle River, NJ: Pearson.

Martin, G. L., Vause, T., & Schwartzman, L. (2005). Experimental studies of psychological interventions with athletes in competitions: Why so few? *Behavior Modification, 29,* 616-641.

Martin, J.E., Dubbert, P.M., Katell, A.D., Thompson, J.K., Raczynski, J.R., Lake, M., Smith, P.O., Webster, J.S., Sikora, T., & Cohen, R.E. (1984). Behavioral control of exercise in sedentary adults: Studies 1 through 6. *Journal of Consulting and Clinical Psychology, 52,* 795-811.

McKenzie, T., & Rushall, B. (1974). Effects of self-recording on attendance and performance in a competitive swimming training environment. *Journal of Applied Behavior Analysis, 7,* 199-206.

Polaha, J., Allen, K., & Studley, B. (2004). Self-monitoring as an intervention to decrease swimmers' stroke counts. *Behavior Modification, 28,* 261-275.

Smith, R.E. & Smoll, F.L. (1997). Coaching the coaches: Youth sports as a scientific and applied behavioral setting. *Current Directions in Psychological Science, 6,* 16-21.

Smith, R.E., Smoll, F.L., & Curtis, B. (1978). Coaching behaviors in little league baseball. In F.L. Smoll & R.E. Smith (Eds.), *Psychological perspectives in youth sports* (pp. 173-201). Washington, DC: Hemisphere.

Smith, R.E., Smoll, F.L., & Curtis, B. (1979). Coach effectiveness training: A cognitive-behavioral approach to enhancing relationship skills in youth sport coaches. *Journal of Sport Psychology, 1,* 59-75.

Smith, R.E., Smoll, F.L., & Hunt, E. (1977). A system for the behavioral assessment of athletic coaches. *Research Quarterly, 48,* 401-407.

Smoll, F.L., & Smith, R.E. (1984). Leadership research in youth sports. In J.M. Silva & R.S. Weinberg (Eds.), *Psychological foundations of sport* (pp. 371-386). Champaign, IL: Human Kinetics.

Spiegler, M.D., & Guevremont, D.C. (2003). *Contemporary behavior therapy* (4th ed.). Belmont, CA: Wadsworth/Thompson Learning.

Tharp, R.G., & Gallimore, R. (1976, January). What a coach can teach a teacher. *Psychology Today, 9,* 74-78.

Chapter 8 Motivational Orientations

Ames, C. (1984). Conceptions of motivation within competitive and noncompetitive goal structures. In R. Schwarzer (Ed.), *Selfrelated cognitions in anxiety and motivation* (pp. 205-241). Hillsdale, NJ: Erlbaum.

Ames, C. (1992). Achievement goals, motivational climate, and motivational processes. In G.C. Roberts (Ed.), *Motivation in sport and exercise* (pp. 161-176). Champaign, IL: Human Kinetics.

Ames, C., & Ames, R. (1981). Competitive versus individualistic goal structures: The salience of past performance information for causal attributions and affect. *Journal of Educational Psychology, 73,* 411-418.

Ames, C., & Archer, J. (1988). Achievement goals in the classroom: Students' learning strategies and motivation processes. *Journal of Educational Psychology, 80,* 260-267.

Atkinson, J.W. (1964). *An introduction to motivation.* Princeton, NJ: Van Nostrand.

Atkinson, J.W. (1974). The mainsprings of achievement-oriented

activity. In J.W. Atkinson & J.O. Raynor (Eds.), *Motivation and achievement* (pp. 13-41). New York: Halstead.

Biddle, S. J. H. (2001). Enhancing motivation in physical education. In G. C. Roberts (Ed.), *Advances in motivation in sport and exercise* (pp. 101-127). Champaign, IL: Human Kinetics.

Biddle, S. J. H., Wang, J. C. K., Kavussanu, M., & Spray, C. (2003). Correlates of achievment goal orientations in physical activity: A systematic review of research. *European Journal of Sports Science, 3,* 1-19.

Carr, S. (2006). An examination of multiple goals in children's physical education: Motivational effects of goal profiles and the role of perceived climate in multiple development. *Journal of Sports Sciences, 24,* 281-297.

Cury, F., Da Fonseca, D., Rufo, M., Peres, C., & Sarrazin, P. (2003). The trichotomous model and investment in learning to prepare for a sport test: A mediatinoal anlaysis. *British Journal of Educational Psychology, 73,* 529-543.

Cury, F., DaFonseca, D., Rufo, M., & Sarrazin, P. G. (2002). Perceptions of competence, implicit theory of ability, perceptions of motivational climate, and achievement goals: A test of the trichotomous conceptualization of endorsement of achievment motivation in the physical education setting. *Perceptual and Motor Skills, 95,* 233-244.

Cury, F., Sarrazin, P., & Famose, J. P. (1997). Achievement goals, perceived ability and active search for information. *European Yearbook of Sport Psychology, 1,* 166-183.

Digelidis, N., Papaioannou, A., Laparidis, K., & Christodoulisdis, T. (2003). A one-year intervention in 7th grade physical education classess aiming to change motivational climate and attitudes toward exercise. *Psychology of Sport and Exercise, 4,* 195-210.

Dishman, R.K. (1986). Exercise compliance: A new view for public health. *Physician and Sportsmedicine, 14,* 127-145.

Duda, J. L. (1997). Perpetuating myths: A response to Hardy's 1996 Coleman Griffith Address. *Journal of Applied Sport Psychology, 9,* 303-309.

Duda, J. L. (2005). Motivation in sport: The relevance of competence and achievement motivation. In A. J. Elliot & C. S. Dweck (Eds.), *Handbook of competence and motivation.* New York The Guilford Press.

Duda, J. L., & Whitehead, J. R. (1998). Measurement of goal perspectives in the physical domain. In J. L. Duda (Ed.), *Advances in sport and exercise psychology measurement.* Champaign, IL: Human Kinetics.

Dweck, C.S. (2000). *Self-theories: their role in motivation, personality, and development.* Philadelphia: Psychology Press.

Dweck, C.S., & Leggett, E.L. (1988). A social-cognitive approach to motivation and personality. *Psychological Review, 95,* 256-259.

Elliot, A. J. (1999). Approach and avoidance motivation and achievement goals. *Educational Psychologist, 34,* 169-189.

Elliot, A. J., & Church, M. A. (1996). A hierarchical model of approach and avoidance achievement motivation. *Journal of Personality and Social Psychology, 72,* 218-232.

Fox, K. R. (1998). Advances in the measurement of the physical self. In J. L. Duda (Ed.), *Advances in sport and exercise psychology measurement.* Morgantown, WV: Fitness Information Technology.

Fry, M. D. (2000a). A developmental analysis of children's and adolescents understanding of luck and ability in the physical domain. *Journal of Sport & Exercise Psychology, 22,* 145-166.

Fry, M. D. (2000b). A developmental examination of children's understanding of task difficulty in the physical domain. *Journal of Applied Sport Psychology, 12,* 180-202.

Fry, M. D., & Duda, J. L. (1997). A developmental examination of children's understanding of effort and ability in teh physical and academic domains. *Research Quarterly for Exercise and Sport, 68,* 331-344.

Gill, D.L. (1993). Competitiveness and competitive orientation in sport. In R.A. Singer, M. Murphey, & L.K. Tennant (Eds.), *Handbook of research on sport psychology* (pp. 314-327). New York: Macmillan.

Gill, D.L., & Deeter, T.E. (1988). Development of the Sport Orientation Questionnaire. *Research Quarterly for Exercise and Sport, 59,* 191-202.

Gill, D.L., & Dzewaltowski, D.A. (1988). Competitive orientations among intercollegiate athletes: Is winning the only thing? *The Sport Psychologist, 2,* 212-221.

Gill, D.L., Gross, J.B., & Huddleston, S. (1983). Participation motivation in youth sports. *International Journal of Sport Psychology, 14,* 1-14.

Gould, D., Feltz, D., & Weiss, M. (1985). Motives for participating in competitive youth swimming. *International Journal of Sport Psychology, 6,* 126-140.

Gould, D., Feltz, D., Horn, T., & Weiss, M. (1982). Reasons for attrition in competitive youth swimming. *Journal of Sport Behavior, 5,* 155-165.

Hardy, L. (1997). Three myths about applied consultancy work. *Journal of Applied Sport Psychology, 9,* 277-294.

Horn, T. S. (2004). Developmental perspectives on self-perceptions in children and adolescents. In M. R. Weiss (Ed.), *Developmental sport and exercise psychology: A lifespan perspective* (pp. 101-143). Morgantown, WV: Fitness Information Technology.

Kang, L., Gill, D.L., Acevedo, E.D., & Deeter, T.E. (1990). Competitive orientations among athletes and nonathletes in Taiwan. *International Journal of Sport Psychology, 21,* 146-152.

Klint, K.A., & Weiss, M.R. (1986). Dropping in and dropping out: Participation motives of current and former youth gymnasts. *Canadian Journal of Applied Sport Science, 11,* 106-114.

Lee, A., Carter, J. A., & Xiang, P. (1995). Children's conceptions of ability in physical education. *Journal of Teaching Physical Education, 14,* 384-393.

Maehr, M.L., & Nicholls, J.G. (1980). Culture and achievement motivation: A second look. In N. Warren (Ed.), *Studies in cross-cultural psychology* (Vol. 3, pp. 221-267). New York: Academic Press.

Magyar, T.M., & Feltz, D.L. (2003). The influence of dispositional and situational tendencies on adolescent girls' sport confidence sources. *Psychology of Sport and Exercise, 4,* 175-190.

Martens, R. (1977). *Sport Competition Anxiety Test.* Champaign, IL: Human Kinetics.

Martens, R., Vealey, R.S., & Burton, D. (1990). *Competitive anxiety in sport.* Champaign, IL: Human Kinetics.

Martinek, T., & Griffith, J.B. (1994). Learned helplessness in physical education: A developmental study of causal attributions and task persistence. *Journal of Teaching in Physical Education, 13,* 108-122.

Martinek, T., & Williams, L. (1997). Goal orientation and task persistence in learned helplessness and mastery oriented students in middle school physical education classes. *International Sports Journal, 1,* 63-76.

Murray, H.A. (1938). *Explorations in personality.* New York: Oxford University Press.

Nicholls, J.G. (1989). *The competitive ethos and democratic education.* Cambridge, MA: Harvard University Press.

Ommundsen, Y. (2004). Self-handicapping related to task and performance-approache and avoidance goals in physical education. *Journal of Applied Sport Psychology, 16,* 183-197.

Ommundsen, Y., & Pedersen, B. H. (1999). The role of achievement goal orientations and perceive ability upon somatic and cogntive indicees of sport competition trait anxiety. *Scandinavian Journal of Medicine and Science in Sports, 9,* 333-343.

Passer, M.W. (1988). Determinants and consequences of children's competitive stress. In F.Smoll, R. Magill, & M. Ash (Eds.), *Children in sport* (3rd ed., pp. 203-228). Champaign, IL: Human Kinetics.

Sapp, M., & Haubenstricker, J. (1978, April). *Motivation for joining and reasons for not continuing in youth sport programs in Michigan.* Paper presented at the meeting of the American Alliance for Health, Physical Education, Recreation and Dance, Kansa City, MO.

Scanlan, T.K. (1988). Social evaluation and the competitive process. In F.L. Smoll, R.A. Magill, & M.J. Ash (Eds.), *Children in sport.* Champaign, IL: Human Kinetics.

Skorkilis, E. K. (2003). Comparison of sport achievement orientation of male professional, amateur, and wheelchair basketball athletes. *Perceptual and Motor Skills, 97,* 483-490.

Skorkilis, E. K., Sherrill, C., Yilla, C., Koutsouki, D., & Stavrou, N. A. (2002). Use of the Sport Orientation Questionnaire with wheelchair athletes: Examination of evidence for validity. *Perceptual and Motor Skills, 95,* 197-207.

Solmon, M. (1996). Impact of motivational climate on students' behaviors and perceptions in a physical education setting. *Journal of Educational Psychology, 88*(4), 731-738.

Spence, J.T., & Helmreich, R.L. (1978). *Masculinity and femininity: Their psychological dimensions, correlates, and antecedents.* Austin, TX: University of Texas Press.

Spence, J.T., & Helmreich, R.L. (1983). Achievement-related motives and behaviors. In J.T. Spence (Ed.), *Achievement and achievement motives* (pp. 7-74). San Francisco: Freeman.

Spink, K.S., & Roberts, G.C. (1980). Ambiguity of outcome and causal attributions. *Journal of Sport Psychology, 2,* 237-244.

Standage, M., & Treasure, D. C. (2002). Relationship among achievement goal orientations and multidimensional situational motivation in physical education *British Journal of Educational Psychology, 72,* 87-103.

Standage, M., Duda, J. L., & Ntoumanis, N. (2003). Predicting motivational regulations in physical education: The interplay between dispositional goal orientations, motivational climate and perceived competence. *Journal of Sports Sciences, 21,* 631-647.

Stephens, D. E. (2000). Goal orientation profiles and beliefs about the causes of success in girls' basketball. *International Sports Journal, 4,* 139-149.

Treasure, D. C. (2001). Enhancing young peoples' motivation in youth sport. In G. C. Roberts (Ed.), *Advances in motivation in sport and exercise* (pp. 79-100). Champaign, IL: Human Kinetics.

Vazou, S., Ntoumanis, N., & Duda, J. L. (2006). Predicting young ahtletes' motivational indices as a function of their perceptions of the coach- and peer-created climate. *Psychology of Sport and Exercise, 7,* 215-233.

Veroff, J. (1969). Social comparison and the development of achievement motivation. In C. Smith (Ed.), *Achievement related motives in children* (pp. 46-110). New York: Russell Sage Foundation.

Waldron, J. J., & Krane, V. (2005). Motivational climate and goal orientation in adolescent female softball players. *Journal of sport Behavior, 28,* 378-392.

Wang, J. C. K., & Biddle, S. J. H. (2001). Young people's motivational profiles in physical activity: A cluster analysis. *Journal of Sport & Exercise Psychology, 23,* 1-22.

Weiner, B. (1974). The provision of social relationships. In Z. Rubin (Ed.), *Doing unto others* (pp. 17-26). Englewood Cliffs, NJ: Prentice-Hall.

Weingarten, Furst, Tenebaum, and Schaefer 1984

Weiss, M. R., & Ferrer-Caja, E. (2002). Motivational orientations and sport behavior. In T. S. Horn (Ed.), *Advances in Sport Psychology* (2nd ed., pp. 101-183). Champaign, IL: Human Kinetics.

Weiss, M. R., & Williams, L. (2004). The *why* of youth sport: A developmental perspective on motivational processes. In M. R. Weiss (Ed.), *Developmental sport and exercise psychology: A lifespa perspective* (pp. 223-268). Morgantown:WV: Fitness Information Technology.

White, A. & Coakley, J. (1986). *Making decisions: The response of young people in the Medway Towns to the 'Ever Thought of Sport?' campaign.* London: Sports Council.

White, S. A. (1996). Goal orientations and perceptions of the motivational climate intiated by parents. *Pediatric Exercise Science, 8,* 122-129.

Williams, L. (1998). Contextual influences and goal perspectives among female youth sport participants. *Research Quarterly for Exercise and Sport, 69,* 47-57.

Williams, L., & Gill, D. (1995). The role of perceived competence in the motivation of physical activity. *Journal of Sport & Exercise Psychology, 17,* 363-378.

Xiang, P., & Lee, A. (1998). The development of self-perceptions of ability and achievement goals and their relations in physical education. *Research Quarterly for Exercise and Sport, 69,* 231-241.

Xiang, P., Lee, A., & Shen, J. (2001). Conceptions of ability and achievment goals in physical education: Comparisons of American and Chinese students. *Contemporary Educational Psychology, 26,* 348-365.

Xiang, P., Lee, A., & Williamson, L. (2001). Conceptions of ability in physical education: Children and adolescents. *Journal of Teaching Physical Education, 20,* 282-294.

Chapter 9 Cognitive Approaches to Motivation

Amorose, A. J., & Horn, T. S. (2000). Intrinsic motivation: Relationships with collegiate athletes' gender, scholarship status, and perceptions of their coaches behavior. *Journal of Sport and Exercise Psychology, 22,* 63-84.

Atkinson, J.W. (1974). The mainsprings of achievement-oriented activity. In J.W. Atkinson & J.O. Raynor (Eds.), *Motivation and achievement* (pp. 13-41). New York: Halstead.

Biddle, S. (1993). Attribution research and sport psychology. In R.N. Singer, M. Murphey, & L.K. Tennant (Eds.), *Handbook on research on sport psychology* (pp. 437-464). New York: Macmillan.

Biddle, S.J.H., Hanarahan, S.J., & Sellars, C.N. (2001). Attribuions: Past, present, and future. In R.N. Singer, Hausenblass, H.A., & Janelle, C.M. (Eds.), H*andbook of sport psychology* (2nd ed) (pp. 444-471). New York: John Wiley & Sons.

Black, S. J., & Weiss, M. R. (1992). The relationship among perceived coaching behaviors behaviors, perceptions of ability, and motivation in competitive age-group swimmers. *Journal of Sport & Exercise Psychology, 14,* 309-325.

Bukowski, W.M., & Moore, D. (1980). Winners' and losers' attributions for success and failure in a series of athletic events. *Journal of Sport Psychology, 2,* 195-210.

Cox, A. E. (2006). *Perceived Classroom Climate and Motivation in Physical Education during the Move to Middle School.* Unpublished doctoral dissertation, Purdue University, West Lafayette, IN.

Curtis, (1992). Altering beliefs about the importance of strategy: An attributional intervention. *Journal of Applied Social Psychology, 22,* 953-972.

Deci, E. L., & Ryan, R. M. (2000). The "what" and "why" of goal pursuits: Human needs and the self-determination of behavior. *Psychological Inquiry, 11,* 227-268.

Deci, E.L., & Ryan, R.M. (1985). *Intrinsic motivation and self-determination in human behavior.* New York: Plenum Press.

Deci, E.L., Betley, G., Kahle, J., Abrams, L., & Porac, J. (1981). When trying to win: Competition and intrinsic motivation. *Personality and Social Psychology Bulletin, 7,* 79-83.

Dieser, R. B., & Ruddel, E. (2002). Effects of attribution retraining during therapeutic recreation on attributions and explanatory styles of adolescents with depression. *Therapeutic Recreation Journal, 36,* 35-47.

Duda, J.L., Chi, L., Newton, M., Walling, M.D., & Catley, D. (1995). Task and ego orientation and intrinsic motivation in sport. *International Journal of Sport Psychology, 26,* 40-63.

Dweck, C.S. (1975). The role of expectations and attributions in the alleviation of learned helplessness. *Journal of Personal and Social Psychology, 31,* 674-685.

Dweck, C.S. (2000). *Self-theories: their role in motivation, personality, and development.* Philadelphia: Psychology Press.

Ferrer-Caja, E., & Weiss, M. R. (2000). Predictors of intrinsic motivation among adolescent students in physical education. *Research Quarterly for Exercise and Sport, 71,* 267-279.

Frederick, C.M., & Ryan, R.M. (1995). Self-determination in sport: A review using Cognitive Evaluation Theory. *International Journal of Sport Psychology, 26,* 5-23.

Gill, D.L., Ruder, M.K., & Gross, J.B. (1982). Open-ended attributions in team competition. *Journal of Sport Psychology, 4,* 159-169.

Goudas, M., Biddle, S. J. H., & Fox, K. R. (1994). Received locus of causality, goal orientations, and perceived competence in school physical education classes. *British Journal of Educational Psychology, 64,* 453-463.

Graham, T. R., Kowalski, K. C., & Crocker, P. R. E. (2002). The contributions of goal characteristics and causal attributions to emotional experience in youth sport participants. *Psychology of Sport and Exercise, 4,* 273-291.

Grove, J.R., Hanrahan, S.J., & McInman, A. (1991). Success/failure bias in attributions across involvement categories in sport. *Personality and Social Psychology Bulletin, 17,* 93-97.

Hamilton, P. R., & Jordan, J. S. (2000). Most and least successful performances: Perceptions of causal attributions in high school track athletes. *Journal of Sport Behavior, 23,* 245-254

Hollembeak, J., & Amorose, A.J. (2005). Perceived coaching behaviors and college athletes' intrinsic motivation: A test of self-determination theory. *Journal of Applied Sport Psychology, 17,* 20-36.

Holt, N. L., & Morley, D. (2004). Gender difference in psychosocial factors associated with athletic success during childhood. *The Sport Psychologist, 18,* 138-153.

Johnson, L., & Biddle, S.J.H. (1988). Persistence after failure: An exploratory look at "learned helplessness" in motor performance. *British Journal of Physical Education Research Supplement, 5,* 7-10.

Lepper, M.R., & Greene, D. (1975). Turning play into work: Effects of adult surveillance and extrinsic rewards on children's intrinsic motivation. *Journal of Personality and Social Psychology, 31,* 479-486.

Mark, M.M., Mutrie, N., Brooks, D.R., & Harris, D.V. (1984). Causal attributions of winners and losers in individual competitive sports: Toward a reformulation of the self-serving bias. *Journal of Sport Psychology, 6,* 184-196.

Martinek, T., & Griffith, J.B. (1994). Learned helplessness in physical education: A developmental study of causal attributions and task persistence. *Journal of Teaching in Physical Education, 13,* 108-122.

Martinek, T., & Williams, L. (1997). Goal orientation and task persistence in learned helplessness and mastery oriented students in middle school physical education classes. *International Sports Journal, 1,* 63-76.

McAuley, E. (1985). Modeling status as a determinant of attention in observational learning and performance. *Journal of Sport Psychology, 7,* 283-295.

McAuley, E., & Duncan, T.E. (1989). Causal attributions and affective reactions to disconfirming outcomes in motor performance. *Journal of Sport & Exercise Psychology, 11,* 187-200.

McAuley, E., & Gross, J.B. (1983). Perceptions of causality I sport: An application of the Causal Dimension Scale. *Journal of Sport & Exercise Psychology, 5,* 72-76.

McAuley, E., & Tammen, V.V. (1989). The effects of subjective and objective competitive outcomes on intrinsic motivation. *Journal of Sport & Exercise Psychology, 11,* 84-93.

Orbach, I., Singer, R. N., & Murphey, M. (1997). Changing attributional style with an attribution tranining technique reated to basketball dribbling. *The Sport Psychologist, 11,* 294-304.

Orbach, I., Singer, R. N., & Price, S. (1999). An attribution training program and achievement in sport. *The Sport Psychologist, 13,* 69-82.

Prapavessis, H., & Carron, A.V. (1988). Learned helplessness in sport. *The Sport Psychologist, 2,* 189-201.

Roberts, G.C., & Pascuzzi, D. (1979). Causal attributions in sport: Some theoretical implications. *Journal of Sport Psychology, 1,* 203-211.

Robinson, D.W. (1990). An attributional analysis of student demoralization in physical education settings. *Quest, 42,* 27-39.

Robinson, D.W., & Howe, B.L. (1989). Appraisal variable/affect relationships in youth sport: A test of Weiner's attributional model. *Journal of Sport & Exercise Psychology, 11,* 431-443.

Rutherford, W.J., Corbin, C.B., & Chase, L.A. (1992). Factors influencing intrinsic motivation toward physical activity. *Health Values, 16,* 19-24.

Ryan, E.D. (1977). Attribution, intrinsic motivation, and athletics. In L.I. Gedvilas & M.E. Kneer (Eds.), *Proceedings of the NAPECW/NCPEAM National Conference, 1977* (pp. 346-353). Chicago: University of Illinois at Chicago Circle, Office of Publications Services.

Ryan, E.D. (1980). Attribution, intrinsic motivation, and athletics: A replication and extension. In C.H. Nadeau, W.R. Halliwell, K.M. Newell, & G.C. Roberts (Eds.), *Psychology of motor behavior and sport—1979* (pp. 19-26). Champaign, IL: Human Kinetics.

Ryan, R.M., Vallerand, R.J., & Deci, E.L. (1984). Intrinsic motivation in sport: A cognitive evaluation theory interpretation. In W.F. Straub & J.M. Williams (Eds.), *Cognitive sport psychology* (pp. 231-242). Lansing, NY: Sport Sciences Associates.

Spink, K.S., & Roberts, G.C. (1980). Ambiguity of outcome and causal attributions. *Journal of Sport Psychology, 2,* 237-244.

Standage, M., Duda, J. L., & Ntoumanis, N. (2003). A model of contextual motivation in physical education: Using constructs from self-determination and achievement goal theories to predict physical activity intentions. *Journal of Educational Psychology, 95,* 419-439.

Tammen, V.V., & Murphy, S. (1990). *The effects of four competitive outcomes on elite athletes' intrinsic motivation.* Paper presented at the annual conference of the Association for the Advancement of Applied Sport Psychology, San Antonio.

Vallerand, R.J. (1983). The effect of differential amounts of positive verbal feedback on the intrinsic motivation of male hockey players. *Journal of Sport Psychology, 5,* 101-107.

Vallerand, R.J. (2007). Intrinsic and extrinsic motivation in sport and physical activity. In G. Tenenbaum & R.C. Eklund (Eds.), *Handbook of sport psychology* (3rd ed., pp. 59-83). New York: Wiley.

Vallerand, R.J., & Reid, G. (1984). On the causal effects of perceived competence on intrinsic motivation: A test of cognitive evaluation theory. *Journal of Sport Psychology, 6,* 94-102.

Vallerand.R.J., & Blanchard, C. M. (2000). The study of emotion in sport and exercise. In Y. L. Hanin (Ed.), *Emotions in Sport.* Champaign, IL: Human Kinetics.

Vlachopoulos, S., Biddle, S., & Fox, K. (1996). A social-cognitive investigation into the mechanism of affect generation in children's physical activity. *Journal of Sport & Exercise Psychology, 18,* 174-193.

Wagner, S.L., Lounsbury, J.W., & Fitzgerald, L.G. (1989). Attribute factors associated with work/leisure perception. *Journal of Leisure Research, 21,* 155-166.

Walling, M., & Martinek, T. (1995). Learned helplessness: A case study of a middle school student. *Journal of Teaching in Physical Education, 14,* 454-466.

Weinberg, R.S. (1984). The relationship between extrinsic rewards and intrinsic motivation. In J.M. Silva & R.S. Weinberg (Eds.), *Psychological foundations of sport* (pp. 177-189). Champaign, IL: Human Kinetics.

Weinberg, R.S., & Ragan, J. (1979). Effects of competition, success/failure, and sex on intrinsic motivation. *Research Quarterly for Exercise and Sport, 50,* 503-510.

Weiner, B. (1979). A theory of motivation for some classroom experiences. *Journal of Educational Psychology, 71,* 3-25.

Weiner, B. (1986). *An attributional theory of motivation and emotion.* New York: Springer-Verlag.

Weiner, B. (1992). *Human motivation.* Newbury Park, CA: Sage.

Weiner, B., Frieze, I., Kukla, A., Reed, L., Rest, S., & Rosenbaum, R.M.S. (1972). Perceiving the causes of success and failure. In E.E. Jones, D.E. Kanouse, H.H. Kelley, R.E. Nisbett, S. Valins, & B. Weiner (Eds.), *Attribution: Perceiving the causes of behavior* (pp. 95-120). Morristown, NJ: General Learning Press.

Weiss, M. R., & Ferrer-Caja, E. (2002). Motivational orientations and sport behavior. In T. S. Horn (Ed.), *Advances in Sport Psychology* (2nd ed., pp. 101-183). Champaign, IL: Human Kinetics.

Whitehead, J. R., & Corbin, C. B. (1991). Youth fitness testing: The effects of percentile-based evaluation feedback on intrinsic motivation. *Research Quarterly for Exercise and Sport, 62,* 225-231.

Williams, L., & Gill, D. (1995). The role of perceived competence in the motivation of physical activity. *Journal of Sport & Exercise Psychology, 17,* 363-378.

Chapter 10 Participation Motivation

Ajzen, I. (1985). From intentions to actions: A theory of focus on these important subgroups. In J. Kuhl & J. Reckman (Eds.), *Actioncontrol: From cognition to behavior* (pp. 11-39). Heidelberg: Springer.

Blumenthal, J.A., O'Toole, L.C., & Chang, J.L. (1984). Is running an analogue of anorexia nervosa? *Journal of the American Medical Association, 252* (4), 520-523.

Blumenthal, J.A., Rose, S., & Chang, J.L. (1985). Anorexia nervosa and exercise: Implications from recent findings. *Sports Medicine, 2,* 237-247.

Brawley, L.R., & Rodgers, W.M. (1992). Social psychological aspects of fitness promotion. In P. Seraganian (Ed.), *Exercise psychology.* New York: Wiley.

Brownell, K.D. (1989). *The LEARN program for weight control.* Dallas: Brownell & Hager.

Brownell, K.D., Marlatt, G.A., Lichtenstein, E., & Wilson, G.T. (1986). Understanding and preventing relapse. *American Psychologist, 41,* 765-782.

Buckworth, J., & Dishman, R.K. (2002). *Exercise psychology.* Champaign, IL: Human Kinetics.

Cardinal, B.J., Kosma, M., & McCubbin, J.A. (2004). Factors influencing the exercise behavior of adults with physical disabilities. *Medicine and Science in Sports and Exercise, 36,* 868-875.

Cohen, D.A., Ashwood, S., Scott, M., Overton, A., Evenson, K.R., Woorhees, C.C., Bedino-Rung, A., & McKenzie, T.L. (2006). Proximity to school and physical activity among middle school girls: The trial of activity for adolescent girls study. *Journal of Physical Activity and Health, 3*(Suppl. 1), S129-S138.

Corbin, C.B., Welk, G.J., Corbin, W.R. & Welk, K.A. (2008). *Concepts of fitness and wellness* (7th ed.). Boston: McGraw-Hill.

Courneya, K.S., Estabrooks, P.A., & Nigg, C.R. (1997). Predicting change in exercise stage over a 3-year period: An application of the theory of planned behavior. *Avante, 3,* 1-13.

Courneya, K.S., Plotnikoff, R.C., Hotz, S.B., & Birkett, N.J. (2000). Social support and the theory of planned behavior in the exercise domain. *American Journal of Health Promotion, 14,* 300-308.

Dallow, C.B., & Anderson, J. (2003). Using self-efficacy and the transtheoretical model to develop a physical activity intervention for obese women. *American Journal of Health Promotion, 17,* 373-381.

Deci, E.L., & Ryan, R.M. (1985). *Intrinsic motivation and self-determination in human behavior.* New York: Plenum Press.

Downs, D.S., & Hausenblas, H.A. (2005). The theories of reasoned action and planned behavior applied to exercise: A meta-analytic update. *Journal of Physical Activity and Health, 2,* 76-97.

Duda, J.L., & Tappe, M.K. (1988). Predictors of personal investment in physical activity among middle-aged and older adults. *Perceptual and Motor Skills, 66,* 3543-3549.

Duda, J.L., & Tappe, M.K. (1989). The Personal Incentives for Exercise Questionnaire: Preliminary development. *Perceptual and Motor Skills, 68,* 1122.

Dunn, A.L., Marcus, B.H., Kampert, J.B., Garcia, M.E., Kohl, H.W., & Blair, S.N. (1999). Reduction in cardiovascular disease risk factors: 6-month results from Project Active. *Preventive Medicine, 26,* 883-892.

Dzewaltowski, D.A. (1989). Toward a model of exercise motivation. *Journal of Sport & Exercise Psychology, 11,* 251-269.

Dzewaltowski, D.A., Noble, J.M., & Shaw, J.M. (1990). Physical activity participation: Social cognitive theory versus the theories of reasoned action and planned behavior. *Journal of Sport & Exercise Psychology, 12,* 388-405.

Fishbein, M., & Ajzen, I. (1974). Attitudes toward objects as predictors of single and multiple behavioral criteria. *Psychological Review, 81,* 59-74.

Gill, D.L., Dowd, D.A., Williams, L., Beaudoin, C.M., & Martin, J.J. (1996). Competitive orientation and motives of adult sport and exercise participants. *Journal of Sport Behavior, 19,* 307-318.

Gill, D.L., Gross, J.B., & Huddleston, S. (1983). Participation motivation in youth sports. *International Journal of Sport Psychology, 14,* 1-14.

Godin, G. (1993). The theories of reasoned action and planned behavior: Overview of findings, emerging research problems, and usefulness for exercise promotion. *Journal of Applied Sport Psychology, 5,* 141-157.

Grodesky, J.M., Kosma, M., & Solmon, M.A. (2006). Understanding older adults' physical activity behavior: A multi-theoretical approach. *Quest, 58,* 310-329.

Hagger, M.S., Chatzisarantis, N.L.D., & Biddle, S.J.H. (2002). A meta-analytic review of the theories of reasoned action and planned behavior in physical activity. *Journal of Sport & Exercise Psychology, 24,* 3-32.

Hausenblas, H.A., & Symons Downs, D. (2002a). Exercise dependence: A systematic review. *Psychology of Sport and Exercise, 3,* 89-123.

Hausenblas, H.A., & Symons Downs, D. (2002b). How much is too much? The development and validation of the Exercise Dependence Scale. *Psychology and Health, 17,* 387-404.

Heath, G.W., Brownson, R.C., Kruger, J., Miles, R., Powell, K.E., Ramsey, L.T. and the Task Force on Community Preventive Services. (2006). The effectiveness of urban design and land use and transport policies and practices to increase physical activity: A systematic review. *Journal of Physical Activity and Health, 3*(Suppl. 1), S55-S76.

Janis, I.L., & Mann, L. (1977). *Decision making: A psychological analysis of conflict, choice and commitment.* New York: Free Press.

Jordan, P.J., Nigg, C.R., Norman, G.J., Rossi, J.S., & Benisovich, S.V. (2002). Does the transtheoretical model need an attitude adjustment? Integrating attitude with decisional balance as predictors of state of change for exercise. *Psychology of Sport and Exercise, 3,* 65-85.

Kagan, D.M., & Squires, R.L. (1985). Addictive aspects of physical exercise. *Journal of Sports Medicine, 25,* 227-237.

Kesaniemi, Y.K., Danforth, E., Jr., Jensen, M.D., Kopelman, P.G., Lefebre, P., & Reeder, B.A. (2001). Dose-response issues concerning physical activity and health: An evidence-based symposium. *Medicine and Science in Sports and Exercise, 33*(Suppl. 6), S351-S358.

Kraft, M.K., Sallis, J.F., Moudon, A.V., & Linton, L.S. (2006). The second Active Living Research Conference: Signs of maturity. *Journal of Physical Activity and Health, 3*(Suppl. 1), S1-S5.

Landry, J.B., & Solmon, M.A. (2002). Self-determination theory as an organizing framework to investigate women's physical activity behavior. *Quest, 54,* 332-354.

Landry, J.B., & Solmon, M.A. (2004). African-American women's self-determination theory across stages of change for exercise. *Journal of Sport & Exercise Psychology, 26,* 457-469.

Lox, C.L., Martin, K.A., & Petruzzello, S.J. (2006). *The psychology of exercise* (2nd ed.). Scottsdale, AZ: Holcomb Hathaway.

Lubans, D., & Sylva, K. (2006). Controlled evaluation of a physical activity intervention for senior school students: Effects of the Lifetime Activity Program. *Journal of Sport and Exercise Psychology, 28,* 252-268.

Marcus, B.H., & Forsyth, L.H. (2003). *Motivating people to be physically active.* Champaign, IL: Human Kinetics.

Marcus, B.H., & Owen, N. (1992). Motivational readiness, self-efficacy and decision-making for exercise. *Journal of Applied Social Psychology, 22,* 3-16.

Marcus, B.H., Bock, B.C. Pinto, B.M. Napolitano, M.A. & Clark, M.M. (2002). Exercise initiation, adoption and maintenance in adults: Theoretical models and empirical support. In J.L. VanRaalte & B.W. Brewer (Eds.), *Exploring sport and exercise psychology* (2nd ed., pp. 185-208). Washington, DC: APA.

Marcus, B.H., Dubbert, P.M., Forsyth, L.H., McKenzie, T.L., Stone, E.J., Dunn, A.L., & Blair, S.N. (2000). Physical activity behavior change: Issues in adoption and maintenance. *Health psychology, 19,* (Suppl. 1), 32-41.

Marcus, B.H., Eaton, C.A., Rossi, J.S., & Harlow, L.L. (1994). Self-efficacy, decision making and stages of change: An integrative model of physical exercise. *Journal of Applied Social Psychology, 24,* 489-508.

Marcus, B.H., Emmons, K.M., Simkin, L.R., Taylor, E.R., Linnan, L., Rossi, J.S., & Abrams, D.B. (1994). Comparison of stage-matched versus standard care physical activity interventions at the workplace. *Annals of Behavioral Medicine, 16,* S035.

Marcus, B.H., Pinto, B.M., Simkin, L.R., Audrain, J.E., & Taylor, E.R. (1994). Application of theoretical models to exercise behavior among employed women. *American Journal of Health Promotion, 9,* 49-55.

Marcus, B.H., Rakowski, W., & Rossi, J.S. (1992). Assessing motivational readiness and decision-making for exercise. *Health Psychology, 11,* 257-261.

Marcus, B.H., Rossi, J.S., Selby, V.C., Niaura, R.S., & Abrams, D.B. (1992). The stages and processes of exercise adoption and maintenance in a worksite sample. *Health Psychology, 11,* 386-395.

Marcus, B.H., Selby, V.C., Niaura, R.S., & Rossi, J.S. (1992). Self-efficacy and the stages of exercise behavior change. *Research Quarterly for Exercise and Sport, 63,* 60-66.

Marlatt, G.A., & Gordon, J.R. (1985). *Relapse prevention: Maintenance strategies in addictive behavior change.* New York: Guilford.

Martin, J.E. & Dubbert, P.M. (1984). Behavioral management strategies for improving health and fitness. *Journal of Cardiac Rehabilitation, 4,* 200-208.

McAuley, E. (1992). Understanding exercise behavior: A self-efficacy perspective. In G.C. Roberts (Ed.), *Motivation in sport and exercise* (pp. 107-127). Champaign, IL: Human Kinetics.

McAuley, E., & Courneya, K.S. (1993). Adherence to exercise and physical activity as health-promoting behaviors: Attitudinal and self-efficacy influences. *Applied & Preventive Psychology, 2,* 65-77.

McAuley, E., Jerome, G.J., Marquez, D.X., Elavsky, S., & Blissmer, B. (2003). Exercise self-efficacy in older adults: Social, affective and behavioral influences. *Annals of Behavioral Medicine, 25,* 1-7.

Morgan, W.P. (1979). Negative addiction in runners. *Physician and Sportsmedicine, 7* (2), 57-70.

Nigg, C.R., & Courneya, K.S. (1998). Transtheoretical model: Examining adolescent exercise behavior. *Journal of Adolescent Health, 22,* 214-224.

Oman, R.F., & McAuley, E. (1993). Intrinsic motivation and exercise behavior. *Journal of Health Education, 24*(4), 232-238.

Pate, R.R., Pratt, M., Blair, S.N., et al. (1995). Physical activity and public health: A recommendation from the Centers for Disease Control and Prevention and the American College of Sports Medicine. *Journal of the American Medical Association, 273*(5), 402-407.

Pierce, E.F. (1994). Exercise dependence syndrome in runners. *Sports Medicine, 18,* 149-155.

Prochaska, J.O., & DiClemente, C.C. (1983). Stages and processes of self-change of smoking: Towards an integrative model of change. *Journal of Consulting and Clinical Psychology, 51,* 390-395.

Prochaska, J.O., Velicer, W.F., Rossi, J.S., Goldstein, M.G., Marcus, B.H., Rakowski, W., Fiore, C., Harlow, L.L., Redding, C.A., Rosenbloom, D., & Rossi, S.R. (1994). Stages of change and decisional balance for twelve problem behaviors. *Health Psychology, 13,* 39-46.

Raglin, J.S., & Moger, L. (1999). Adverse consequences of physical activity: When more is too much. In J. Rippe (Ed.), *Lifestyle medicine* (pp. 998-1004). Malden, MA: Blackwell Scientific.

Robbins, J.M., & Joseph, P. (1985). Experiencing exercise with-drawal: Possible consequences of therapeutic and mastery running. *Journal of Sport Psychology, 7,* 23-39.

Rosenstock, I.M. (1974). Historical origins of the health belief model. *Health Education Monographs, 2,* 328-335.

Ryan, R.M., & Deci, E.L. (2000). Self-determination theory and the facilitation of intrinsic motivation, social development, and well-being. *American Psychologist, 55,* 68-78.

Sachs, M.L. (1981). Running addiction. In M. Sacks & M. Sachs (Eds.), *Psychology of running* (pp. 116-127). Champaign, IL: Human Kinetics.

Sallis, J.F., Bauman, A., & Pratt, M. (1998). Environmental and policy interventions to promote physical activity. *American Journal of Preventive Medicine, 15,* 379-397.

Sallis, J.F., Haskell, W.L., Fortmann, S.P., Vranizan, K.M., Taylor, C.B., & Solomon, D.S. (1986). Predictors of adoption and maintenance of physical activity in a community sample. *Preventive Medicine, 15,* 331-341.

Sallis, J.F., Hovell, M.F., Hofstetter, C.R., Elder, J.P., Faucher, P., Spry, V.M., Barrington, E., & Hackley, M. (1990). Lifetime history of relapse from exercise. *Addictive Behaviors, 15,* 573-579.

Taylor, W.C., Carlos Postoin, W.S., Jones, L., & Kraft, A.K. (2006). Environmental justice: Obesity, physical activity and healthy eating. *Journal of Physical Activity and Health, 3*(Suppl. 1), S30-S54.

Thompson, J.K., & Blanton, P. (1987). Energy conservation and exercise dependence: A sympathetic arousal hypothesis. *Medicine and Science in Sports and Exercise, 19,* 91-99.

U.S. Department of Health and Human Services (USDHHS). (1996). *Physical activity and health: A report of the Surgeon General.* Atlanta: USDHHS, CDC.

Wankel, L.M. (1984). Decision-making an social support strategies for increasing exercise involvement. *Journal of Cardiac Rehabilitation, 4,* 124-135.

Yates, A., Leehey, K., & Shisslak, C.M. (1983). Running—an analogue of anorexia. *New England Journal of Medicine, 308,* 251-255.

Chapter 11 Emotion Models and Research

Apter, M.J. (1984). Reversal theory and personality: A review. *Journal of Research in Personality, 18,* 265-288.

Borg, G. (1973). Psychophysical basis of perceived exertion. *Medicine and Science in Sports and Exercise, 14,* 377-81.

Borg, G. (1998). *Borg's perceived exertion and pain scales.* Champaign, IL: Human Kinetics.

Boutcher, S. (1993). Emotion and aerobic exercise. In R.N. Singer, M. Murphey, & L.K. Tennant (Eds.), *Handbook of research on sport psychology* (pp. 799-814). New York: Macmillan.

Broocks, A., Bandelow, B., Pekrun, G., Georege, A., Meyer, T., Bartmenn, U., Hillmer-Vogel, U., & Ruther, E. (1998). Comparison of aerobic exercise, chloripramine, and placebo in the treatment of panic disorder. *american Journal of Psychiatry, 155,* 603-609.

Burton, D. (1988). Do anxious swimmers swim slower? Reexamining the elusive anxiety-performance relationship. *Journal of Sport & Exercise Psychology, 10,* 26-37.

Cannon, W.B. (1929). *Bodily changes in pain, hunger, fear and rage* (2nd ed.). New York: Appleton-Century-Crofts.

Colcombe, S., & Kramer, A.F. (2003). Fitness effects on the cognitive function of older adults: A meta-analytic study. *Psychological Science, 14,* 125-130.

Courneya, K.S., Friedenreich, C.M., Sela, R.A., Quinney, A., Rhodes, R.E., & Handman, M. (2003). The group psycho-therapy and home-based (GROUP-HOPE) trial in cancer survivors: Physical fitness and quality of life outcomes. *Psycho-Oncology, 12,* 357-374.

Courneya, K.S., Mackey, J.R., & Jones, L.W. (2000). Coping with cancer: Can exercise help? *The Physician and Sportsmedicine, 28,* 49-51, 55-56, 66-68, 71, 73.

Craft, L.L., & Landers, D.M. (1998). The effect of exercise on clinical depression and depression resulting from mental illness: A meta-analysis. *Journal of Sport & Exercise Psychology, 20,* 339-357.

Crews, D.J., & Landers, D.M. (1987). A meta-analytic review of aerobic fitness and reactivity to psychosocial stressors. *Medicine and Science in Sports and Exercise, 19,* S114-S120.

Crocker, P.R.E. (1997). A confirmatory factor analysis of the Positive Affect Negative Affect Schedule (PANAS) with a youth sport sample. *Journal of Sport & Exercise Psychology, 19,* 91-97.

Crocker, P.R.E., & Graham, T.R. (1995). Coping by competitive athletes with performance stress: Gender differences and relationships with affect. *The Sport Psychologist, 9,* 325-338.

Crocker, P.R.E., Bouffard, M., & Gessaroli, M.E. (1995). Measuring enjoyment in youth sport settings: A confirmatory factor analysis of the Physical Activity Enjoyment Scale. *Journal of Sport & Exercise Psychology, 17,* 200-205.

Csikszentmihalyi, M. (1975). *Beyond boredom and anxiety.* San Francisco: Jossey-Bass.

Csikszentmihalyi, M. (1990). *Flow: The psychology of optimal experience.* New York: Harper & Row.

Diener, E. (1984). Subjective well-being. *Psychological Bulletin, 95*(3), 542-575.

Diener, E., Emmons, R. A., Larsen, R. J., & Griffin, S. (1985). The Satisfaction with Life Scale. *Journal of Personality Assessment, 49*(1), 71-75.

Edwards, T., & Hardy, L. (1996). The interactive effects of intensity and direction of cognitive and somatic anxiety and self-confidence upon performance. *Journal of Sport & Exercise Psychology, 18,* 296-312.

Ekkekakis, P., & Petruzzello, S.J. (1999). Acute aerobic exercise and affect: Current status, problems and prospects regarding dose-response. *Sports Medicine, 28,* 337-374.

Ekkekakis, P., & Petruzzello, S.J. (2002). Analysis of the affect measurement conundrum in exercise psychology. *Psychology of Sport and Exercise, 3,* 35-63.

Emery, C.F., Schein, R.L., Hauck, E.R., & MacIntyre, N.R. (1998). Psychological and cognitive outcomes of a randomized trial of exercise among patients with chronic obstructive pulmonary disease. *Health Psychology, 17,* 232-240.

Etnier, J.L., Salazar, W., Landers, D.M., Petruzzello, S.J., Han, M., & Nowell, P. (1997). The influence of physical fitness and exercise upon cognitive functioning: A meta-analysis. *Journal of Sport & Exercise Psychology, 19,* 249-277.

Fenz, W.D. (1975). Coping mechanisms and performance under stress. In D.M. Landers, R.W. Christina, & D.V. Harris (Eds.), *Psychology of sport and motor behavior-II* (pp. 3-24). University Park, PA: Pennsylvania State University.

Fenz, W.D. (1988). Learning to anticipate stressful events. *Journal of Sport & Exercise Psychology, 10,* 223-228.

Folkins, C.H., & Sime, W.E. (1981). Physical fitness training and mental health. *American Psychologist, 36,* 373-389.

Fredrickson, B.L. (2005). Positive emotions. In C.R. Snyder & S.J. Lopez (Eds.), *Handbook of positive psychology* (pp. 120-134). New York: Oxford University Press.

Gauvin, L. & Brawley, L.R. (1993). Alternative psychological models and methodologies for the study of exercise and affect. In P. Seraganian (Ed.), *Exercise psychology: The influence of physical exercise on psychological processes* (pp. 146-171). New York: Wiley.

Gill, D.L., Chang, Y.K., Murphy, K.J., & Holder, K.M. (2006). Quality of life assessment in physical activity and health promotion. *Medicine and Science in Sports and Exercise, 38* (Suppl. 5), S370-S371.

Goodwin, R.D. (2003). Association between physical activity and mental disorders among adults in the United States. *Preventive Medicine, 36,* 698-703.

Gould, D., Petlichkoff, L., & Weinberg, R.S. (1984). Antecedents of, temporal changes in, and relationships between CSAI-2 subcomponents. *Journal of Sport Psychology, 6,* 289-304.

Gould, D., Petlichkoff, L., Simons, J., & Vevera, M. (1987). Relationship between Competitive State Anxiety-2 subscale scores and pistol shooting performance. *Journal of Sport Psychology, 9,* 33-42.

Hanin, Y. (1989). Interpersonal and intragroup anxiety in sports. In D. Hackfort & C.D. Spielberger (Eds.), *Anxiety in sports: An international perspective* (pp. 19-28). Washington, DC: Hemisphere.

Hanin, Y. (1995). Individual zones of optimal functioning (IZOF) model: An idiographic approach to anxiety. In K. Henschen & W. Straub (Eds.), *Sport psychology: An analysis of athlete behavior* (pp. 103-119). Longmeadow, MA: Mouvement.

Hanin, Y., & Syrja, P. (1996). Predicted, actual, and recalled affect in Olympic-level soccer players: Idiographic assessments on individualized scales. *Journal of Sport & Exercise Psychology, 18,* 325-335.

Hardy, C.J., & Rejeski, W.J. (1989). Not what, but how one feels: The measurement of affect during exercise. *Journal of Sport & Exercise Psychology, 11,* 304-317.

Hardy, L. (1990). A catastrophe model of performance in sport. In J.G. Jones & L. Hardy (Eds.), *Stress and performance in sport* (pp. 81-106). Chichester, England: Wiley.

Hardy, L. (1996). Testing the predictions of the cusp catastrophe model of anxiety and performance. *The Sport Psychologist, 10,* 140-156.

Hardy, L., & Parfitt, C.G. (1991). A catastrophe model of anxiety and performance. *British Journal of Psychology, 82,* 163-178.

Hardy, L., Parfitt, C.G., & Pates, J. (1994). Performance catastrophes in sport. *Journal of Sport Sciences, 12,* 327-334.

Heller, T., Hsieh, K., & Rimmer, J.H. (2004). Attributional and psychosocial outcomes of a fitness and health education program on adults with Down syndrome. *American Journal of Mental Retardation, 109,* 175-185.

Holmes, D.S. (1993). Aerobic fitness and the response to psychological stress. In P. Seragapian (Ed.), *Exercise psychology: The influence of physical exercise on psychological processes* (pp. 39-63). New York: Wiley.

Hong, S., & Mills, P.J. (2006). Physical activity and psychoneuroimmunology. In E.O. Acevedo & P. Ekkekakis (Eds.), *Psychobiology of physical activity* (pp. 177-188). Champaign, IL: Human Kinetics.

Hull, C.L. (1943). *Principles of behavior.* New York: Appleton-Century-Crofts.

Jackson, S.A. (1995). Factors influencing the occurrence of flow state in elite athletes. *Journal of Applied Sport Psychology, 7,* 138-166.

Jackson, S.A., & Marsh, H.W. (1996). Development and validation of a scale to measure optimal experience: The flow state scale. *Journal of Sport & Exercise Psychology, 18,* 17-35.

Kendzierski, D., & DeCarlo, K.J. (1991). Physical activity enjoyment scale: Two validation studies. *Journal of Sport & Exercise Psychology, 13,* 50-64.

Kerr, J. (1990). Stress and sport: Reversal theory. In J.G. Jones & L. Hardy (Eds.), *Stress and performance in sport* (pp. 107-131). Chichester: Wiley.

Kerr, J.H. (1985). The experience of arousal: A new basis for studying arousal effects in sport. *Journal of Sport Sciences, 3,* 169-179.

Kimiecik, J.C., & Harris, A.T. (1996). What is enjoyment? A conceptual/definitional analysis with implications for sport and exercise psychology. *Journal of Sport & Exercise Psychology, 18,* 247-263.

Kleinginna, P.R., & Kleinginna, A.M. (1981). A categorized list of emotional definitions, with suggestions for a consensual definition. *Motivation and Emotion, 5,* 345-379.

Kramer, A.F., & Hillman, C.H. (2006). Aging, physical activity and neurocognitive function. In E.O. Acevedo & P. Ekkekakis (Eds.), *Psychobiology of physical activity* (pp. 45-59). Champaign, IL: Human Kinetics.

Landers, D.M. (1978). Motivation and performance: The role of arousal and attentional factors. In W.F. Straub (Ed.), *Sport psychology: An analysis of athlete behavior* (pp. 91-103). Ithaca, NY: Mouvement.

Landers, D.M., & Petruzzello, S.J. (1994). Physical activity, fitness and anxiety. In C. Bouchard, R.J. Shepard, & T. Stephens (Eds.), *Physical activity, fitness and health: International proceedings and consensus statement* (pp. 868-882). Champaign, IL: Human Kinetics.

Lange, C.G. (1885). *Om sindsbevaegelser. et psyko. fysidog. studie.* Copenhagen: Kronar.

LaPerriere, A.R., Antoni, M.H., Schneiderman, N., Ironson, G., Klimas, N., Caralis, P., & Fletcher, M.A. (1990). Exercise intervention attenuates emotional distress and natural killer cell decrements following notification of positive serologic status for HIV-1. *Biofeedback and Self-Regulation, 15,* 229-242.

LaPerriere, A.R., Fletcher, M.A., Antoni, M.H., Klimas, N.G., Ironson, G., & Schneiderman, N. (1991). Aerobic exercise training in an AIDS risk group. *International Journal of Sports Medicine, 12,* S53-S57.

Latimer, A.E., & Martin Ginis, K.A. (2005). The theory of planned behavior in prediction of leisure time physical activity among individuals with spinal cord injury. *Rehabilitation Psychology, 50,* 389-396.

Lazarus, R.S. (1966). *Psychological stress and the coping process.* New York: McGraw-Hill.

Lazarus, R.S. (1991). *Emotion and adaptation.* New York: Oxford University Press.

Lazarus, R.S. (1993). From psychological stress to the emotions: A history of changing outlooks. *Annual Review of Psychology, 44,* 1-21.

Lee, C., & Russell, A. (2003). Effects of physical activity on emotional well-being among older Australian women: Cross-sectional and longitudinal analyses. *Journal of Psychosomatic-Research, 54*(2), 155-160.

Long, B.C., & van Stavel, R. (1995). Effects of exercise training on anxiety: A meta-analysis. *Journal of Applied Sport Psychology, 7,* 167-189.

Lox, C.L., Martin Ginis, K.A., & Petruzzello, S.J. (2006). *The psychology of exercise: Integrating theory and practice* (2nd ed.). Scottsdale, AZ: Holcomb Hathaway.

Lox, C.L., McAuley, E., & Tucker, R.S. (1995). Exercise as an intervention for enhancing subjective well-being in an HIV-1 population. *Journal of Sport & Exercise Psychology, 17,* 345-362.

Mahoney, M.J. (1979). Cognitive skills and athletic performance. In P.C. Kendall & S.D. Hollon (Eds.), *Cognitive-behavioral intervention: Theory, research, and procedures* (pp. 423-443). New York: Academic Press.

Mahoney, M.J., & Avener, M. (1977). Psychology of the elite athlete: An exploratory study. *Cognitive Therapy and Research, 1,* 135-141.

Martens, R. & Landers, D.M. (1970). Motor performance under stress: A test of the inverted-U hypothesis. *Journal of Personality and Social Psychology, 16,* 29-37.

Martens, R., Vealey, R.S., & Burton, D. (1990). *Competitive anxiety in sport.* Champaign, IL: Human Kinetics.

Martin Ginis, K.A., Latimer, A.E., McKechnie, K., Ditor, D.S., McCartney, N., Hicks, A.L., Bugaresti, J., & Craven, C. (2003). Using physical activity to enhance subjective well-being among people with spinal cord injury. *Rehabilitation Psychology, 48,* 157-164.

McAuley, E., & Courneya, K.S. (1994). The subjective exercise experience scale (SEES): Development and preliminary validation. *Journal of Sport & Exercise Psychology, 16,* 163-177.

McAuley, E., & Elavsky, S. (2005). Physical activity, aging, and quality of life: Implications for measurement. In W. Zhu (Ed.), *Measurement issues and challenges in aging and physical activity research* (pp. 57-68). Champaign, IL: Human Kinetics.

McNair, D.M., Lorr, M., & Droppleman, L.F. (1971). *Manual for the profile of mood states.* San Diego: Educational and Industrial Testing Service.

Meyer, T., Broocks, A., Bandelow, B., Hillmer-Vogel, U., & Ruther, E. (1998). Endurance training in panic patients: Spiroergometric and clinical effects. *International Journal of Sports Medicine, 19,* 496-502.

Mobily, K.E., Rubenstein, L.M., Lemke, J.H., O'Hara, M.W., & Wallace, R.B. (1996). Walking and depression in a cohort of older adults: The Iowa 65+ Rural Health study. *Journal of Aging and Physical Activity, 4,* 119-135.

Morgan, W.P. (1994). Psychological components of effort sense. *Medicine and Science in Sports and Exercise, 26,* 1071-1077.

Morris, L.W., Davis, M.A., & Hutchings, C.H. (1981). Cognitive and emotional components of anxiety: Literature review and a revised worry-emotionality scale. *Journal of Educational Psychology, 73,* 541-555.

Motl, R.W., Birnbaum, A.S., Kubik, M.Y., & Dishman, R.K. (2004). Naturally occurring changes in physical activity are inversely related to depressive symptoms during early adolescence. *Psychosomatic Medicine, 66,* 336-342.

Nakamura, J., & Csikszentimihalyi, M. (2005). The concept of flow. In C.R. Snyder & S.J. Lopez (Eds.), *Handbook of positive psychology* (pp. 89-105). New York: Oxford University Press.

North, T.S., McCullagh, P., & Tran, Z.V. (1990). Effects of exercise on depression. *Exercise and Sport Sciences Reviews, 18,* 379-415.

O'Connor, R. (2004). *Measuring quality of life in health.* London: Elsevier Limited.

Petruzzello, S., Landers, D.M., Hatfield, B.D., Kubitz, K.A., and Salazar, W. (1991). A meta-analysis on the anxiety-reducing effects of acute and chronic exercise: Outcomes and mechanism. *Sports Medicine, 11,* 143-182.

Plutchik, R. (2003). *Emotions and life.* Washington, DC: APA.

Reeve, J. (2005). *Understanding motivation and emotion* (4th ed.). Hoboken, NJ: Wiley.

Rejeski, W.J., Best, D.L., Griffith, P., & Kenney, E. (1987). Sex-role orientation and the responses of men to exercise stress. *Research Quarterly for Exercise and Sport, 58,* 260-264.

Rejeski, W.J., Brawley, L.R., & Shumaker, S.A. (1996). Physical activity and health-related quality of life. *Exercise and Sport Sciences Reviews, 24,* 71-108.

Robertson, R.J., & Noble, B.J. (1997). Perception of physical exertion: Methods, mediators, and applications. *Exercise and Sport Sciences Reviews, 25,* 407-452.

Russell, J.A. (1980). A circumplex model of affect. *Journal of Personality and Social Psychology, 57,* 491-502.

Russell, J.A., Weiss, A., & Mendelsohn, G.A. (1989). Affect grid: A single item scale of pleasure and arousal. *Journal of Personality and Social Psychology, 39,* 1161-1178.

Scanlan, T.K., & Simons, J.P. (1992). The construct of sport enjoyment. In G. Roberts (Ed.), *Motivation in sport and exercise* (pp. 199-215). Champaign, IL: Human Kinetics.

Scanlan, T.K., Simons, J.P., Carpenter, P.J., Schmidt, G.W., & Keeler, B. (1993). The Sport Commitment Model: Measurement development for the youth-sport domain. *Journal of Sport & Exercise Psychology, 15*, 16-38.

Scanlan, T.K., Stein, G.L., & Ravizza, K. (1989). An in-depth study of former elite figure skaters: 2. Sources of enjoyment. *Journal of Sport & Exercise Psychology, 11*, 65-83.

Scanlan, T.K., Babkes, M.L., & Scanlan, L.A. (2005). Participation in sport: A developmental glimpse at emotion. In J.L. Mahoney, R.W. Larson, & J.S. Eccles (Eds.), *Organized activities as contexts of development* (pp. 275-309). Mahwah, NJ: Erlbaum.

Schachter, S., & Singer, J. (1962). Cognitive, social and physiological determinants of emotional state. *Psychological Review, 69*, 378-399.

Schechtman, K.B., & Ory, M.G. (2001). The effects of exercise on the quality of life of frail older adults: A preplanned meta-analysis of the FICSIT trials. *Annals of Behavioral Medicine, 23*(3), 186-197.

Schmitz, N., Kruse, J., & Kugler, J. (2004). The association between physical exercise and health-related quality of life in subjects with mental disorders: Results from a cross-sectional survey. *Preventive Medicine, 39*(6), 1200-1207.

Segar, M.L., Katch, V.L., Roth, R.S., Weinstein Garcia, A., Portner, T.I., Glickman, S.G., Haslanger, S., & Wilkins, E.G. (1998). The effect of aerobic exercise on self-esteem and depressive and anxiety symptoms among breast cancer survivors. *Journal of Rheumatology, 10*, 2473-2481.

Selye, H. (1956). *The stress of life.* New York: McGraw-Hill.

Sonstroem, R.J., & Bernardo, P.B. (1982). Intraindividual pregame state anxiety and basketball performance: A re-examination of the inverted-U curve. *Journal of Sport Psychology, 4*, 235-245.

Spence, K.W. (1956). *Behavior theory and conditioning.* New Haven, CT: Yale University Press.

Spielberger, C.D., Gorsuch, R.L., & Lushene, R.E. (1970). *Manual for the State-Trait Anxiety Inventory.* Palo Alto, CA: Consulting Psychologists Press.

Stathi, A., Fox, K.R., & McKenna, J. (2002). Physical activity and dimensions of subjective well-being in older adults. *Journal of Aging and Physical Activity, 10*(1), 76-92

Stewart, A.L., & King, A.C. (1991). Evaluating the efficacy of physical activity for influencing quality-of-life outcomes in older adults. *Annals of Behavioral Medicine, 13*(3), 108-116.

Tuson, K.M., & Sinyor, D. (1993). On the affective benefits of aerobic exercise: Taking stock after twenty years of research. In P. Seraganian (Ed.), *Exercise psychology: The influence of physical exercise on psychological processes* (pp. 80-121). New York: Wiley.

Wankel, L.M., & Sefton, J.M. (1989). A season-long investigation of fun in youth sports. *Journal of Sport & Exercise Psychology, 11*, 355-366.

Ware, J.E. (2000). SF-36 health survey update. *Spine, 25*(24), 3130-3139.

Watson, D., & Tellegen, A. (1985). Toward a consensual analysis of mood. *Psychological Bulletin, 98*, 219-235.

Watson, D., Clark, L.A., & Tellegen, A. (1988). Development and validation of brief measures of positive and negative affect. The PANAS scales. *Journal of Personality and Social Psychology, 54*, 1063-1070.

Yerkes, R.M., & Dodson, J.D. (1908). The relation of strength of stimulus to rapidity of habit formation. *Journal of Comparative and Neurological Psychology, 18*, 459-482.

Chapter 12 Emotion Control and Stress Management

Anderson, M., & Williams, J. (1988). A model of stress and athletic injury: Prediction and prevention. *Journal of Sport and Exercise Psychology, 10*, 294-306.

Benson, H. (1976). *The relaxation response.* New York: William Morrow.

Bernstein, D.A., & Borkovec, T.D. (1973). *Progressive relaxation: A manual for the helping professions.* Champaign, IL: Research Press.

Bramwell, S.T., Masuda, M., Wagner, N.H., & Holmes, T.H. (1975). Psychological factors in athletic injuries: Development and application of the Social and Athletic Readjustment Scale (SARRS). *Journal of Human Stress, 1*, 6-20.

Callahan, T. (1984, July 30). No limit to what he can do. *Time,* pp. 52-59.

Carver, C.S., Scheier, M.F., & Weintraub, J.K. (1989). Assessing coping strategies: A theoretically based approach. *Journal of Personality and Social Psychology, 56*, 267-283.

Fenz, W.D. (1975). Coping mechanisms and performance under stress. In D.M. Landers, R.W. Christina, & D.V. Harris (Eds.), *Psychology of sport and motor behavior-II* (pp. 3-24). University Park, PA: Pennsylvania State University.

Fenz, W.D. (1988). Learning to anticipate stressful events. *Journal of Sport & Exercise Psychology, 10*, 223-228.

Holmes, T.H., & Rahe, R.J. (1967). The Social and Readjustment Scale. *Journal of Psychosomatic Research, 11*, 213-218.

Jacobson, E. (1938). *Progressive relaxation.* Chicago: University of Chicago Press.

Kelley, B.C. (1994). A model of stress and burnout in collegiate coaches: Effects of gender and time of season. *Research Quarterly for Exercise and Sport, 65*, 48-58.

Kelley, B.C., & Gill, D.L. (1993). An examination of personal/situational variable, stress appraisal, and burnout in collegiate teacher-coaches. *Research Quarterly for Exercise and Sport, 64*, 94-102.

Kobasa, S.C. (1988). *The Hardiness Test* (3rd ed.). New York: Hardiness Institute.

Kobasa, S.C., Maddi, S.R., & Courington, S. (1981). Personality and constitution as mediators in the stress-illness relationship. *Journal of Health and Social Behavior, 22*, 368-378.

Lauer, L.L. (2005). Playing tough and clean hockey: Developing emotional management skills to reduce individual player aggression. Unpublished doctoral dissertation, University of North Carolina at Greensboro.

Lazarus, R.S., & Folkman, S. (1984). *Stress, appraisal and coping.* New York: Springer.

Lazarus, R.S., & Folkman, S. (1985). If it changes, it must be a process: Study of emotion and coping during three stages of a college examination. *Journal of Personality and Social Psychology, 48*, 150-170.

Mahoney, M.J. (1979). Cognitive skills and athletic performance. In P.C. Kendall & S.D. Hollon (Eds.), *Cognitive-behavioral intervention: Theory, research, and procedures* (pp. 423-443). New York: Academic Press.

Maslach, C., & Jackson, S.E. (1986). *Maslach Burnout Inventory manual* (6th ed.). Palo Alto, CA: Consulting Psychologists Press.

Mayer, J.D., & Salovey, P. (1997). What is emotional intelligence? In P. Salovey & D. Sluyter (Eds.), *Emotional development and emotional intelligence: Implications for educators* (pp. 3-31). New York: Basic Books.

Meichenbaum, D. (1977). *Cognitive-behavior modification.* New York: Plenum.

Nideffer, R.M. (1993). Concentration and attention control training. In J.M. Williams (Ed.), *Applied sport psychology:*

Personal growth to peak performance, (2nd ed., pp. 243-261). Mountain View, CA: Mayfield.

Raedke, T.D., & Smith, A.L. (2004). Coping resources and athlete burnout: An examination of stress mediated ad moderation hypotheses. *Journal of Sport & Exercise Psychology, 26,* 525-541.

Salovey, P., Mayer, J.D., & Caruso, D. (2005). The positive psychology of emotional intelligence. In C.R. Snyder & S.J. Lopez (Eds.), *Handbook of positive psychology* (pp. 159-171). New York: Oxford University Press.

Smith, R.E. (1980). A cognitive-affective approach to stress management training for athletes. In A. Nadeau (Ed.), *Psychology of motor behavior and sport* (pp. 54-72). Champaign, IL: Human Kinetics.

Smith, R.E. (1986). Toward a cognitive-affective model of athletic burnout. *Journal of Sport & Exercise Psychology, 8,* 36-50.

Suinn, R. (1993). Imagery: In R.N. Singer, M. Murphey, & L.K. Tennant (Eds.), *Handbook of research on sports psychology* (pp. 492-510). New York: Macmillan.

Suinn, R.S. (1976, July). Body thinking: Psychology for Olympic champs. *Psychology Today, 10,* 38-43.

Suinn, R.S. (1983). Imagery and sports. In A.A. Sheikh (Ed.), *Imagery: Current theory, research, and application* (pp. 507-534). New York: Wiley.

Udry, E. (1997). Coping and social support among injured athletes following surgery. *Journal of Sport & Exercise Psychology, 19,* 71-90.

Udry, E., & Anderson, M.B. (2002). Athletic injury and sport behavior. In T.S. Horn (Ed.), *Advances in sport psychology* (2nd ed., pp. 529-553). Champaign, IL: Human Kinetics.

Vealey, R.S., Udry, E.M., Zimmerman, V., & Soliday, J. (1992). Intrapersonal and situational predictors of coaching burnout. *Journal of Sport & Exercise Psychology, 14,* 40-58.

Weinberg, R.S. (1977). Anxiety and motor behavior: A new direction. In R.W. Christina & D.M. Landers (Eds.), *Psychology of motor behavior and sport—1976* (Vol. 2, pp. 132-139). Champaign, IL: Human Kinetics.

Wiese-Bjornstal, D.M., Smith, A.M., Shaffer, S.M., & Morrey, M.A. (1998). An integrated model of response to sport injury: Psychological and sociological dynamics. *Journal of Applied Sport Psychology, 10,* 46-69.

Williams, J.M., & Anderson, M.B. (1998). Psychosocial antecedents of sport injury: Review and critique of the stress and injury model. *Journal of Applied Sport Psychology, 10,* 5-25.

Williams, J.M., & Harris, D.V. (2006). Relaxation and energizing techniques for regulation of arousal. In J.M. Williams (Ed.), *Applied sport psychology: Personal growth to peak performance* (5th ed., pp. 285-305). Boston: McGraw-Hill.

Ziegler, S.G. (1978). An overview of anxiety management strategies in sport. In W.F. Straub (Ed.), *Sport psychology: An analysis of athlete behavior* (pp. 257-264). Ithaca, NY: Mouvement.

Chapter 13 Social Influence

Albert, E. (1991). Riding a line: Competition and cooperation in the sport of bicycle racing. *Sociology of Sport Journal, 8,* 341-361.

Allport, F.H. (1924). *Social psychology.* Boston: Houghton Mifflin.

Bandura, A. & Jeffery, R.W. (1973). Role of symbolic coding and rehearsal processes in observational learning. *Journal of Personality and Social Psychology, 37,* 122-130.

Bandura, A. (1977). *Social learning theory.* Englewood Cliffs, NJ: Prentice-Hall.

Bandura, A. (1986). *Social foundations of thought and action: A social cognitive theory.* Englewood Cliffs, NJ: Prentice-Hall.

Baron, R., Moore, D., & Sanders, G.S. (1978). Distraction as a source of drive in social facilitation research. *Journal of Personality and Social Psychology, 36,* 816-824.

Baumeister, R.F. & Steinhilber, A. (1984). Paradoxical effects of supportive audiences on performance under pressure: The home field disadvantage in sports championships. *Journal of Personality and Social Psychology, 47,* 85-93.

Baumeister, R.F. (1984). Choking under pressure: Self-consciousness and paradoxical effects of incentives on skillful performance. *Journal of Personality and Social Psychology, 47,* 85-93.

Bray, S.R., Gyurcsik, N.C., Culos-Reed, S.N., Dawson, K.A., & Martin, K.A. (2001). An exploratory investigation of the relationship between proxy efficacy, self-efficacy and exercise attendance. *Journal of Health Psychology, 6,* 425-434.

Bray, S.R., Gyurcsik, N.C., Martin Ginis, K.A., & Culos-Reed, S.N. (2004). The Proxy Efficacy, Exercise Questionnaire: Development of an instrument to assess female exercisers' proxy efficacy beliefs in structured group exercise classes. *Journal of Sport & Exercise Psychology, 26,* 442-456.

Brustad, R.J. (1993). Who will go out and play? Parental and psychological influences on children's attraction to physical activity. *Pediatric Exercise Science, 5,* 210-223.

Brustad, R.J. (1996). Attraction to physical activity in urban schoolchildren: Parental socialization and gender influences. *Research Quarterly for Exercise and Sport, 67,* 316-323.

Brustad, R.J. (1998, June). *Parental influence on youth motivation in physical activity.* Paper presented at the annual meeting of the North American Society for the Psychology of Sport and Physical Activity, St. Charles, IL.

Bryan, J.H. (1969, December). How adults teach hypocrisy. *Psychology Today, 3,* 50-52, 65.

Bryan, J.H., & Walbek, N.H. (1970). Preaching and practicing generosity: Some determinants of sharing in children. *Child Development, 41,* 329-354.

Carron, A. V., Loughhead, T. M., & Bray, S. R. (2005). The home advantage in sport competitions: Courneya and Carron's (1992) conceptual framework a decade later. *Journal of Sports Sciences, 23,* 395-407.

Carron, A.V., Hausenblas, H.A., & Mack, D. (1996). Social influence: A meta-analysis. *Journal of Sport & Exercise Psychology, 18,* 1-16.

Chelladurai, P. (1993). Leadership. In R.N. Singer, M. Murphey, & L.K. Tennant (Eds.), *Handbook of research on sport psychology.* New York: Macmillan.

Coakley, J. (1993). Social determinants of intensive training and participation in youth sports. In B.R. Cahill & A.J. Pearl (Eds.), *Intensive participation in children's sports* (pp. 77-94). Champaign, IL: Human Kinetics.

Cottrell, N.B. (1968). Performance in the presence of other human beings: Mere presence, audience, and affiliation effects. In E.C. Simmer, R.A. Hope, & G.A. Milton (Eds.), *Social facilitation and imitative behavior* (pp. 91-110). Boston: Allyn & Bacon.

Courneya, K.S., & Carron, A.V. (1992). The home advantage in sport competitions: A literature review. *Journal of Sport & Exercise Psychology, 14,* 13-27.

Dempsey, J.M., Kimiecik, J.C., & Horn, T.S. (1996). Parental influence on children's moderate to vigorous physical activity participation: An expectancy-value approach. *Pediatric and Exercise Science, 5,* 151-167.

Deutsch, M. (1949). A theory of cooperation and competition. *Human Relations, 2,* 129-152.

Dorrick, P.W. (1999). A review of self-modeling and related interventions. *Applied and Preventive Psychology, 8*, 23-39.

Eccles, J.S. (2004). Schools, academic motivation, and stage-environment fit. In R.M. Learner & L. Steinberg (Eds.), *Handbook of Adolescent Psychology*, (2nd ed., pp. 125-153). Hoboken, NJ: Wiley.

Eccles, J.S., & Harrold, R.D. (1991). Gender differences in sport involvement: Applying the Eccles' expectancy-value model. *Journal of Applied Sport Psychology, 3*, 7-35.

Eccles, J.S., Wigfield, A., & Schiefele, U. (1998). Motivatioin to succeed. In W. Damon & N. Eisenberg (Eds.), *Handbook of Child Psychology* (vol. 3). New York: John Wiley & Sons, Inc.

Evans, J., & Roberts, G.C. (1987). Physical competence and the development of children's peer relations. *Quest, 39*, 23-35.

Feltz, D.L. & Landers, D.M. (1977). Informational-motivational components of a model's demonstration. *Research Quarterly for Exercise and Sport, 48*, 525-533.

Feltz, D.L. (1982). The effects of age and number of demonstrations on modeling of form and performance. *Research Quarterly for Exercise and Sport, 53*, 291-296.

Feltz, D.L., Landers, D.L., & Raeder, U. (1979). Enhancing self-efficacy in high avoidance motor tasks: A comparison of modeling techniques. *Journal of Sport Psychology, 1*, 112-122.

Fredricks, J. A., & Eccles, J. S. (2002). Childrens' competence and value beliefs from childhood through adolescence: Growth trajectories in two male-sex-types domain. *Developmental Psychology, 38*, 519-533.

Fredricks, J. A., & Eccles, J. S. (2004). Parental influences on youth involvement in sports. In M. R. Weiss (Ed.), *Developmental sport and exercise psychology: A lifespan perspective* (pp. 145-164). Morgantown, WV: Fitness Information Technology.

Fredricks, J. A., & Eccles, J. S. (2005). Family socialization, gender, and sport motivation and involvement. *Journal of Sport and Exercise Psychology, 27*, 3-31.

Geen, R.G., & Gange, J.G. (1977). Drive theory of social facilitation: Twelve years of theory and research. *Psychological Bulletin, 84*, 1267-1288.

Gill, D.L. (1977). The influence of group success-failure and relative ability on intrapersonal variables. *Research Quarterly, 48*, 685-694.

Gill, D.L. and Martens, R. (1975). The informational and motivational influence of social reinforcement on motor performance. *Journal of Motor Behavior, 7*, 171-182.

Gill, D.L., Gross, J.B., & Huddleston, S. (1983). Participation motivation in youth sports. *International Journal of Sport Psychology, 14*, 1-14.

Gould, D. & Weiss, M.R. (1981). The effects of model similarity and model talk on self-efficacy and muscular endurance. *Journal of Sport Psychology, 3*, 17-29.

Gould, D. (1978). *The influence of motor task types o model effectiveness*. Unpublished doctoral dissertation, University of Illinois at Urbana-Champaign.

Greendorfer, S. (1997). Role of socializing agents in female sport involvement. *Research Quarterly for Exercise and Sport, 48*, 305-310.

Greendorfer, S.L., Lewko, J.H., & Rosengren, K.S. (1996). Family and gender-based influences in sport socialization of children and adolescents. In F.L. Smoll & R.E. Smith (Eds.), *Children and youth in sport: A biopsychosocial perspective*. Madison, WI: Brown & Benchmark.

Gross, J.B., & Gill, D.L. (1982). Competition and instructional set effects on the speed and accuracy of a throwing task. *Research Quarterly for Exercise and Sport, 53*, 125-132.

Harney, D.M., & Parker, R. (1972). Effects of social reinforcement, subject sex, and experimenter sex on children's motor performance. *Research Quarterly, 43*, 187-196.

Hertz-Lazarowitz, R., & Miller, N. (Eds.). (1992). *Interaction in cooperative groups.* New York: Cambridge University Press.

Holland, A., & Andre, T. (1994). Athletic participation and the social status of adolescent males and females. *Youth & Society, 25*, 388-407.

Horn, T.S., & Horn, J.L. (2007). Family influences on children's sport and physical activity participation, behavior, and psychosocial responses. In G. Tenenbaum & R.C. Eklund (Eds.), *Handbook of sport psychology* (3rd ed., pp. 685-711). New York: Wiley.

Horn, T.S., & Weiss, M.R. (1991). A developmental analysis of children's self-ability judgments in the physical domain. *Pediatric Exercise Science, 3*, 310-326.

Johnson, D.W., & Johnson, R.T. (1992). Positive interdependence: Key to effective cooperation. In R. Hertz-Lazarowitz & N. Miller (Eds.), *Interaction in cooperative groups* (pp. 174-199). New York: Cambridge University Press.

Kimiecik, J.C., & Horn, T.S. (1998). Parental beliefs and children's moderate-to-vigorous physical activity. *Research Quarterly for Exercise and Sport, 69*, 163-175.

Kimiecik, J.C., Horn, T.S., & Shurin, C.S. (1996). Relationships among children's beliefs, perceptions of their parent's beliefs, and their moderate-to-vigorous physical activity. *Research Quarterly for Exercise and Sport, 67*, 324-336.

Landers, D.M. (1980). The arousal/performance relationship revisited. *Research Quarterly for Exercise and Sport, 51*, 77-90.

Landers, D.M., & McCullagh, P.D. (1976). Social facilitation of motor performance. In J. Keough & R.S. Hutton (Eds.), *Exercise and Sport Sciences Reviews* (Vol. 4, pp. 125-162). Santa Barbara, CA: Journal Publishing Affiliates.

Lirgg, C.D., & Feltz, D.L. (1991). Teacher versus peer models revisited: Effects on motor performance and self-efficacy. *Research Quarterly for Exercise and Sport, 62*, 217-224.

Lox, C.L., Martin Ginis, K.A., & Petruzzello, S.J. (2006). *The psychology of exercise* (2nd ed.). Scottsdale, AZ: Holcomb Hathaway.

Martens, R. & Landers, D.M. (1972). Evaluation potential as a determinant of coaction effects. *Journal of Experimental Social Psychology, 8*, 347-359.

Martens, R. (1969). Effect of an audience on learning and performance of a complex motor skill. *Journal of Personality and Social Psychology, 12*, 252-260.

Martens, R. (1972). Social reinforcement effects on motor performance as a function of socio-economic status. *Perceptual and Motor Skills, 35*, 215-218.

Martens, R. (1979). From smocks to jocks. *Journal of Sport Psychology, 1*, 94-99.

Martens, R., & White, V. (1975). Influence of win-loss ratio on performance, satisfaction and preference for opponents. *Journal of Experimental Social Psychology, 11*, 343-362.

Martens, R., Burwitz, L., & Zuckerman, J. (1976). Modeling effects on motor performance. *Research Quarterly for Exercise and Sport, 47*, 277-291.

McAuley, E. (1985). Modeling status as a determinant of attention in observational learning and performance. *Journal of Sport Psychology, 7*, 283-295.

McCullagh, P. (1987). Model similarity effects on motor performance. *Journal of Sport Psychology, 9*, 249-260.

McCullagh, P., & Weiss, M. R. (2001). Modeling: Considerations for motor skill and psychological responses. In R. N. Singer, H. A. Hausenblas, and Janelle, C. M. (Eds.),

Handbook of Sport Psychology (pp. 205-238). NY: John Wiley & Sons.

McCullagh, P., & Weiss, M.R. (2002). Observational learning: The forgotten psychological method in sport psychology. In J.L. Van Raalte & B.W. Brewer (Eds.), *Exploring sport and exercise psychology* (pp. 131-149). Washington, D.C.: American Psychological Association.

McCullagh, P., Stiehl, J., & Weiss, M.R. (1990). Developmental modeling effects on the quantitative and qualitative aspects of motor performance. *Research Quarterly for Exercise and Sport, 61,* 344-350.

McDonough, M.H., & Crocker, P.R.E. (2005). Sport participation motivation in young adolescent girls: The role of friendship quality and self-concept. *Research Quarterly for Exercise and Sport, 76,* 456-467.

Minas, S.C. (1980). Acquisition of a motor skill following guided mental and physical practice. *Journal of Human Movement Studies, 6,* 127-141.

Obermeier, G.E., Landers, D.M., & Ester, M.A. (1977). Social facilitation of speed events: The coaction effect in racing dogs and trackmen. In R.W. Christina & D.M. Landers (Eds.), *Psychology of motor behavior and sport—1976* (Vol. 2, pp. 9-23). Champaign, IL: Human Kinetics.

Ram, N., & McCullagh, P. (2003). Self-modeling: influence on psychological responses and physical performance. *The Sport Psychologist, 17,* 220-241.

Romance, T.J., Weiss, M.R., & Bockoven, J. (1986). A program to promote moral development through elementary school physical education. *Journal of Teaching in Physical Education, 5,* 126-136.

Schwartz, B., & Barsky, S.F. (1977). The home advantage. *Social Forces, 55,* 641-661.

Smith, A. L. (1999). Perceptions of peer relationships and physical activity participation in early adolescents. *Journal of Sport and Exercise Psychology, 21,* 329-350.

Smith, A. L. (2003). Peer relationships in physical activity contexts: A road less traveled in youth sport and exercise psychology research. *Psychology of Sport and Exercise, 4,* 25-39.

Smith, A. L., Ullrich-French, S., Walker, E. II, & Hurley, K. S. (2006). Peer relationship profiles and motivation in youth sport. Journal of Sport and Exercise Psychology, 28, 362-382.

Smith, R.E. & Smoll, F.L. (1997). Coaching the coaches: Youth sports as a scientific and applied behavioral setting. *Current Directions in Psychological Science, 6,* 16-21.

Stanne, M. (1993). *The impact of social interdependence on motor performance, social, & self acceptance: A meta-analysis.* Unpublished doctoral dissertation, University of Minnesota.

Starek, J., & McCullagh, P. (1999). The effect of self-modeling on the performance of beginning swimmers. *The Sport Psychologist, 13,* 269-287

Starkes, J.L., & Allard, F. (1983). Perception in volleyball: The effects of competitive stress. *Journal of Sport Psychology, 5,* 189-196.

Stuart, M. E. (2003). Sources of subjective task value in sport: An examination of adolescents with high or low value for sport. *Journal of Applied Sport Psychology, 15,* 239-255.

Triplett, N. (1898). The dynamogenic factors in pacemaking and competition. *American Journal of Psychology, 9,* 507-553.

Turner, E.E., Rejeski, W.J., & Brawley (1997). Psychological benefits of physical activity are influenced by the social environment. *Journal of Sport & Exercise Psychology, 19,* 119-130.

Ullrich-French, S., & Smith, A. L. (2006). Perceptions of relationships with parents and peers in youth sport: Independent and combined prediction of motivational outcomes. *Psychology of Sport and Exercise,* 7, 193-214.

Varca, P.E. (1980). An analysis of home and away game performance of male college basketball teams. *Journal of Sport Psychology, 2,* 245-257.

Voyer, D., Kinch, S., & Wright, E. F. (2006). The home disadvantage: Examination of the self-image redefinition hypothesis. *Journal of Sport Behavior, 29,* 270-279.

Weiss, M.R. & Frazer, K.M. (1995). Initial, continued, and sustained motivation in adolescent female athletes: A season-long analysis. *Pediatric Exercise Science, 7,* 314-329.

Weiss, M.R. (1983). Modeling and motor performance: A developmental perspective. *Research Quarterly for Exercise and Sport, 54,* 190-197.

Weiss, M.R., & Klint, K.A. (1987). "Show and tell" I the gymnasium: Developmental differences in modeling and verbal rehearsal effects on motor skill learning and performance. *Research Quarterly for Exercise and Sport, 58,* 234-241.

Weiss, M.R., & Smith, A.L. (1999). Quality of sport friendship: Measurement development and validation. *Journal of Sport & Exercise Psychology, 21,* 145-166.

Weiss, M.R., & Smith, A.L. (2002). Friendship quality in youth sport: Relationship to age, gender, and motivation. *Journal of Sport & Exercise Psychology, 24,* 420-437

Weiss, M.R., & Stuntz, C.P. (2004). A little friendly competition: Peer relationships and psychosocial development in youth sport and physical activity contexts. In M.R. Weiss (Ed.), *Developmental sport and exercise psychology: A lifespan perspective* (pp. 165-196). Morgantown, WV: Fitness Information Technology.

Weiss, M.R., Ebbeck, V., & Horn, T.S. (1997). Children's self-perceptions and sources of physical competence information: A cluster analysis. *Journal of Sport & Exercise Psychology, 19,* 64-83.

Weiss, M.R., McCullaugh, P., Smith, A.L., & Berlant, A.R. (1998). Observational learning and the fearful child: Influence of peer models on swimming skill performance and psychological responses. *Research Quarterly for Exercise and Sport, 69,* 380-394.

Weiss, M.R., Smith, A.L., & Theeboom, M. (1996). "That's what friends are for": Children's and teenagers' perceptions of peer relationships in the sport domain. *Journal of Sport & Exercise Psychology, 18,* 347-379.

Winfrey, M. L., & Weeks, D. L. (1993). Effects of self-modeling on self-efficacy and balance beam performance. *Perceptual and motor skills, 77,* 907-913.

Xiang, P., McBride, R., & Bruene, A. (2003). Relations of parents' beliefs to children's motivation in an elementary physical education running program. *Journal of Teaching in Physical Education, 22,* 410-425.

Zajonc, R.B. (1965). Social facilitation. *Science, 149,* 269-274.

Chapter 14 Aggression and Character Development

Ardrey, R. (1966). *The territorial imperative.* New York: Atheneum.

Argentine footballer shot in riot [Electronic (2005, August). Version]. *BBC News* from Retrieved December 2, 2006 from, http://news.bbc.co.uk/2/hi/americas/4238844.stm).

Arms, R.L., Russell, G.W., & Sandilands, M.L. (1979). Effects of viewing aggressive sports on the hostility of spectators. *Social Psychology Quarterly, 42,* 275-279.

Bandura, A. (1965). Influence of models' reinforcement contingencies on the acquisition of imitative responses. *Journal of Personality and Social Psychology, 1,* 589-595.

Bandura, A. (1973). *Aggression: A social learning analysis.* Englewood Cliffs, NJ: Prentice-Hall.

Bandura, A. (1986). *Social foundations of thought and action: A social cognitive theory.* Englewood Cliffs, NJ: Prentice-Hall.

Bandura, A., Ross, D., & Ross, S.A. (1963a). Imitation of film-mediated aggressive models. *Journal of Abnormal and Social Psychology, 66,* 3-11.

Bandura, A., Ross, D., & Ross, S.A. (1963b). Vicarious reinforcement and imitative learning. *Journal of Abnormal and Social Psychology, 67,* 601-607.

Baron, R.A., & Richardson, D.R. (1994). *Human aggression.* New York: Plenum Press.

Berkowitz, L. (1962). *Aggression: A social psychological analysis.* New York: McGraw-Hill.

Berkowitz, L. (1970). Experimental investigations of hostility catharsis. *Journal of Consulting and Clinical Psychology, 35,* 1-7.

Berkowitz, L. (1993). *Aggression: Its causes, consequences, and control.* Philadelphia: Temple University Press.

Bjorkqvist, K., Osterman, K., & Kaukiainen, A. (1992). The development of direct and indirect aggressive strategies in males and females. In K. Bjorkqvist & P. Niemela (Eds.), *Of mice and women: Aspects of female aggression* (pp. 51-64). New York: Academic Press.

Bredemeier, B.J., & Shields, D.L. (1986a). Athletic aggression: An issue of contextual morality. Sociology of Sport Journal, 3, 152-158.

Bredemeier, B.J., & Shields, D.L. (1986b). Game reasoning and interactional morality. Journal of Genetic Psychology, 147, 257-275.

Bredemeier, B.J., Weiss, M.R., Shields, D.L., and Cooper, B.A.B. (1986). The relationship of sport involvement with children's moral reasoning and aggression tendencies. *Journal of Sport Psychology, 8,* 304-318.

Bredemeier, B.J.L. (1994). Children's moral reasoning and their assertive, aggressive, and submissive tendencies in sport and daily life. *Journal of Sport & Exercise Psychology, 16,* 1-14.

Bredemeier, B.J.L., & Shields, D.L.L. (1995). *Character development and physical activity.* Champaign, IL: Human Kinetics.

Bushman, B. J., & Anderson, C. A. (2001). Is it time to pull the plug on hostile versus instrumental aggression dichotomy? *Psychological Review, 108,* 273-279.

Butterfield, F. (2003, July). A fatality, parental violence and youth sports [Electronic Version]. *New York Times* from Retrieved December 2, 2006 from, (http://query.nytimes.com/gst/fullpage. html?sec=health&res=9500E1DA1338F932A25754C0A9669C8B63&n=Top%2fReference%2fTimes%20Topics%2fPeople%2fJ%2fJunta%2c%20Thomas).

DeBusk, M., & Hellison, D.R. (1989). Implementing a physical education self-responsibility model for delinquency-prone youth. *Journal of Teaching Physical Education, 8,* 104-112.

Dollard, J., Dobb, J., Miller, N., Mower, O., & Sears, R. (1939). *Frustration and aggression.* New Haven, CT: Yale University Press.

Duda, J.L., Olson, L.K., & Templin, T.J. (1991). The relationship of task and ego orientation to sportsmanship attitudes and perceived legitimacy of injurious acts. *Research Quarterly for Exercise and Sport, 62,* 79-87.

Geen, R.G., Stonner, D., & Shope, G.L. (1975). The facilitation of aggression by aggression: Evidence against the catharsis hypothesis. *Journal of Personality and Social Psychology, 31,* 721-726.

Gibbons, S. L., & Ebbeck, V. (1997). The effect of different teaching strategies on moral development of physical education students. *Journal of Teaching Physical Education, 17,* 85-98.

Gibbons, S.L., Ebbeck, V., & Weiss, M.R. (1995). Fair play for kids: Effects on the moral development of children in physical education. *Research Quarterly for Exercise and Sport, 66,* 247-255.

Gill, D.L. (1986). *Psychological dynamics of sport.* Champaign, IL: Human Kinetics.

Goldstein, J., & Arms, R. (1971). Effects of observing athletic contests on hostility. *Sociometry, 54,* 83-91.

Haan, N. (1991). Moral development and action from a social constructivist perspective. In W.M. Kurtines & J.L. Gerwitz (Eds.), *Handbook of moral behavior and development: Vol. 1. Theory.* Hillsdale, NJ: Erlbaum.

Hellison, D., & Walsh, D. (2002). Responsibility-based youth programs evaluation: Investigating the investigations. *Quest, 54,* 292-307.

Hellison, D.R. (1995). *Teaching responsibility through physical activity.* Champaign, IL: Human Kinetics.

Hellison, D.R., & Templin, T.J. (1991). *A reflective approach to teaching physical education.* Champaign, IL: Human Kinetics.

Kirker, B., Tenenbaum, G., & Mattson, J. (2000). An investigation of the dynamics of aggression: Direct observation in ice hockey and basketball. *Research Quarterly for Exercise & Sport, 71,* 373-386.

Konecni, V.J. (1975). Annoyance, type, and duration of post-annoyance activity, and aggression: the "cathartic" effect. *Journal of Experimental Psychology: General, 104,* 76-102.

Koss, M.P., & Gaines, J.A. (1993). The prediction of sexual aggression by alcohol use, athletic participation, and fraternity affiliation. *Journal of Interpersonal Violence, 8,* 84-108.

Lauer, L.L. (2005). Playing tough and clean hockey: Developing emotional management skills to reduce individual player aggression. Unpublished doctoral dissertation, University of North Carolina at Greensboro.

Lorentzen, R., Werden, D., and Pietila, T. (1988). Incidence, nature, and causes of ice hockey injuries. *The American Journal of Sports Medicine, 16*(4), 392-396.

Lorenz, K. (1966). *On aggression.* New York: Harcourt, Brace, & World.

Martinek, T., Schilling, T. A., & Johnson, D. (2001). Transferring personal and social responsibility of underserved youth to the classroom. *The Urban Review, 33*(1), 29-45

Morra, N., & Smith, M.D. (1996). Interpersonal sources of violence in hockey: The influence of the media, parents, coaches, and game officials. In F.L. Smoll & R.E. Smith (Eds.), *Children and youth in sport: A biopsychosocial perspective* (pp. 142-155). Madison, WI: Brown & Benchmark.

Mummendey, A., & Mummendey, H.D. (1983). Aggressive behavior of soccer players as social interaction. In J.H. Goldstein (Ed.), *Sports violence.* New York: Springer-Verlag.

Notebook: Cowboys C Gurode needs stitches after being kicked [Electronic (2006, October). Version]. *USA Today.* from Retrieved December 2, 2006, from http://www.usatoday.com/sports/football/nfl/2006-10-01-injury-notes_x.htm?csp=34

Ryan, E.D. (1970). The cathartic effect of vigorous motor activity on aggressive behavior. *Research Quarterly, 41,* 542-551.

Ryan, K.R., Williams, J.M., & Wimer, B. (1990). Athletic aggression: Perceived legitimacy and behavioral intentions in girl's high school basketball. *Journal of Sport & Exercise Psychology, 12,* 48-55.

Schilling, T. A. (2001). An investigation of commitment among participants in an extended day physical activity program. *Research Quarterly for Exercise & Sport, 72,* 355-365.

Silva, J.M. (1983). The perceived legitimacy of rule violating behavior in sport. *Journal of Sport Psychology, 5,* 438-448.

Smith, M.D. (1988). Interpersonal sources of violence in hockey: The influence of parents, coaches, and teammates. In F.L. Smoll, R.A. Magill, & M.J. Ash (Eds.), *Children in sport* (3rd ed., pp. 301-313). Champaign, IL: Human Kinetics.

Stephens, D. E. (2001). Predictors of aggressive tendencies in girls' basketball: An examination of beginning and advanced participants in a summer skills camp. *Research Quarterly for Exercise & Sport, 72,* 257-266.

Stephens, D. E. (2004). Moral atmosphere and aggression in collegiate intramural sport. *International Sports Journal, 8,* 66-75.

Stephens, D. E., & Kavanagh, B. (2003). Aggression in Canadian youth ice hockey: The role of moral atmosphere. *International Journal of Sport Psychology, 7,* 109-119.

Storr, A. (1968). *Human aggression.* New York: Atheneum.

Tator, C., Carson, J.D., and Cushman, R. (2000). Hockey injuries of the spine in Canada, 1966-1996. *CMAJ: Canadian Medical Association Journal, 162*(6), 787.

Watson, G.G. (1986). Approach-avoidance behaviour in team sports: An application to leading Australian national hockey players. *International Journal of Sport Psychology, 17,* 136-155.

Weiss, M. R., & Smith, A. L. (2002). Moral development in sport and physical activity. In T.S. Horn (Ed.), *Advances in sport psychology* (pp. 243-280). Champaign, IL: Human Kinetics.

Widmeyer, W. N., Dorsch, K. D., Bray, S. R., & McGuire, E. J. (2002). The nature, prevalence, and consequences of agression. In J. M. Silva & D. E. Stevens (Eds.), *Psychological foundations of sport* (pp. 328-351). Boston: Allyn & Bacon.

Wulf, S. (1993, August 16). Basebrawl: Nolan Ryan's pummeling of Robin Ventura epitomizes a season marred by bench-clearing incidents. *Sports Illustrated, 79,* 12-17.

Zillmann, D., Johnson, R.C., & Day, K.D. (1974). Provoked and unprovoked aggressiveness in athletes. *Journal of Research in Personality, 8,* 139-152.

Zillmann, D., Katcher, A.H., & Milavsky, B. (1972). Excitation transfer from physical exercise to subsequent aggressive behavior. *Journal of Experimental Social Psychology, 8,* 247-259.

Chapter 15 Group Dynamics and Interpersonal Relationships

Bakeman, R., & Helmreich, R. (1975). Cohesiveness and performance: Covariation and causality in an undersea environment. *Journal of Experimental Social Psychology, 11,* 478-489.

Barrow, J.C. (1977). The variables of leadership: A review and conceptual framework. *Academy of Management Review, 74,* 231-251.

Bird, A.M. (1977). Development of a model for predicting team performance. *Research Quarterly, 48,* 24-32.

Brawley, L.R., & Paskevich, D.M. (1997). Conducting team building research in the context of sport and exercise. *Journal of Applied Sport Psychology, 9,* 11-40.

Brawley, L.R., Carron, A.V., & Widmeyer, W.N. (1987). Assessing cohesion of teams: Validity of the Group Environment Questionnaire. *Journal of Sport Psychology, 9,* 275-294.

Carron, A.V. (1982). Cohesiveness in sport groups: Interpretations and considerations. *Journal of Sport Psychology, 4,* 123-138.

Carron, A.V., & Ball, J.R. (1977). Cause-effect characteristics of cohesiveness and participation motivation in intercollegiate hockey. *International Review of Sport Sociology, 12,* 49-60.

Carron, A.V., & Spink, K.S. (1993). Team building in an exercise setting. *The Sport Psychologist, 7,* 8-18.

Carron, A.V., Brawley, L.R. & Widemeyer, W.N. (1998). The measurement of cohesiveness in sport groups. In J.L. Duda (Ed), Advancements in sport and exercise psychology measurement (pp. 213-226). Morgantown, WV: Fitness Information Technology.

Carron, A.V., Brawley, L.R., & Widmeyer, W.N. (2002). *The Group Environment Questionnaire: Test Manual.* Morgantown, WV: Fitness Information Technology.

Carron, A.V., Colman, M.M., Wheeler, J., & Stevens, D. (2002). Cohesion and performance in sport: A meta-analysis. *Journal of Sport & Exercise Psychology, 24,* 168-188.

Carron, A.V., Hausenblas, H.A., & Eys, M.A. (2005). *Group dynamics in sport* (3rd ed.). Morgantown, WV: Fitness Information Technology.

Carron, A.V., Hausenblas, H.A., & Mack, D. (1996). Social influence: A meta-analysis. *Journal of Sport & Exercise Psychology, 18,* 1-16.

Carron, A.V., Spink, K.S., & Prapavessis, H. (1997). Team building and cohesiveness in the sport and exercise setting: Use of indirect interventions. *Journal of Applied Sport Psychology, 9,* 61-72.

Carron, A.V., Widmeyer, W.N., & Brawley, L.R. (1985). The development of an instrument to assess cohesion in sport teams: The Group Environment Questionnaire. *Journal of Sport Psychology, 7,* 244-266.

Carron, A.V., Widmeyer, W.N., & Brawley, L.R. (1988). Group cohesion and individual adherence to physical activity. *Journal of Sport & Exercise Psychology, 10,* 119-126.

Chelladurai, P. (1984). Leadership in sports. In J.M. Silva & R.S. Weinberg (Eds.), *Psychological foundations of sport* (pp. 329-339). Champaign, IL: Human Kinetics.

Chelladurai, P., & Haggerty, T. (1978). A normative model of decision- making styles in coaching. *Athletic Administration, 13,* 6-9.

Chelladurai, P., & Saleh, S.D. (1980). Dimensions of leader behavior in sports: Development of a leadership scale. *Journal of Sport Psychology, 2,* 34-45.

Chelladurai, P., & Turner, B.A. (2006). Styles of decision-making in coaching. In J.M. Williams (Ed.), *Applied sport psychology: Personal growth to peak performance* (5th ed., pp. 140-154). Boston: McGraw-Hill.

Chelladurai, P., Haggerty, T.R., & Baxter, P.R. (1989). Decision style choices of university basketball coaches and players. *Journal of Sport & Exercise Psychology, 11,* 201-215.

Cohen, S. (2004). Social relationships and health. *American Psychologist, 59,* 673-684.

Crace, R.K., & Hardy, C.J. (1997). Individual values and the team building process. *Journal of Applied Sport Psychology, 9,* 41-60.

Cutrona, C.E. & Russell, D.W. (1987). The provisions of social relationships and adaptation to stress. In W.H. Jones and D. Perlman (Eds.), *Advances in personal relationships* (Vol. 1, pp. 37-67). Greenwich, CT: JAI Press.

Duncan, T.E., & McAuley, E. (1993). Social support and efficacy cognitions in exercise adherence: A latent growth curve analysis. *Journal of Behavioral Medicine, 16* (2), 199-218.

Estabrooks, P.A., & Carron, A.V. (2000).The physical activity group environment questionnaire: An instrument for the assessment of cohesion in exercise classes. *Group Dynamics, 4,* 230-243.

Eys, M.A., Burke, S.M., Carron, A.V., & Dennis, P.W. (2006). The sport team as an effective group. In J.M. Williams (Ed.), *Applied sport psychology: Personal growth to peak performance* (5th ed., pp. 157-173). Boston: McGraw-Hill.

Festinger, L., Schachter, S., & Back, K. (1950). *Social pressures in informal groups.* New York: Harper & Row.

Fiedler, F.E. (1967). *A theory of leadership effectiveness.* New York: McGraw-Hill.

Gammage, K.L., Carron, A.V., & Estabrooks, P.A. (2001). Team cohesion and individual productivity: The influence of the morn for productivity and the identifiability of individual effort. *Small Group Research, 32,* 3-18.

Gill, D.L. (1979). The prediction of group motor performance from individual member abilities. *Journal of Motor Behavior, 11,* 113-122.

Glenn, S.D., & Horn, T.S. (1993). Psychological and personal predictors of leadership behavior in female soccer athletes. *Journal of Applied Sport Psychology, 5,* 17-34.

Hardy, C.J., & Crace, R.K. (1993). The dimensions of social support when dealing with sport injuries. In D. Pargman (Ed.), *Psychological bases of sport injuries* (pp. 121-144). Morgantown, WV: Fitness Technology.

Hardy, C.J., & Crace, R.K. (1997). Foundations of team building: Introduction to the team building primer. *Journal of Applied Sport Psychology, 9,* 1-10.

Ingham, A.G., Levinger, G., Graves, J., & Peckham, V. (1974). The Ringelmann effect: Studies of group size and group performance. *Journal of Experimental Social Psychology, 10,* 371-384.

Jones, M.B. (1974). Regressing group on individual effectiveness. *Organizational Behavior and Human Performance, 11,* 426-451.

Karau, S.J. & Williams, K.D. (1993). Social loafing: A meta-analytic review and theoretical integration. *Journal of Personality and Social Psychology, 65,* 681-706.

Karau, S.J., & Williams, K.D. (1995). Social loafing: Research findings, implications, and future directions. *Psychological Science, 4* (5), 134-139.

Kelley, B.C., & Gill, D.L. (1993). An examination of personal/situational variable, stress appraisal, and burnout in collegiate teacher-coaches. *Research Quarterly for Exercise and Sport, 64,* 94-102.

Kravitz, D.A., & Martin, B. (1986). Ringelmann rediscovered: The original article. *Journal of Personality and Social Psychology, 50,* 936-941.

Landers, D.M. (1974). Taxonomic considerations in measuring group performance and the analysis of selected group motor performance tasks. In M.G. Wade & R. Martens (Eds.), *Psychology of motor behavior and sport.* Champaign, Illinois: Human Kinetics.

Landers, D.M., & Lueschen, G. (1974). Team performance outcome and the cohesiveness of competitive coacting groups. *International Review of Sport Sociology, 9,* 57-71.

Landers, D.M., Wilkinson, M.O., Hatfield, B.D., & Barber, H. (1982). Causality and the cohesion-performance relationship. *Journal of Sport Psychology, 4,* 170-183.

Latane, B., Harkins, S.G., & Williams, K.D. (1980). *Many hands make light the work: Social loafing as a social disease.* Unpublished manuscript, Ohio Stat University, Columbus.

Latane, B., Williams, K.D., & Harkins, S.G. (1979). Many hands make light the work: The causes and consequences of social loafing. *Journal of Personality and Social Psychology, 37,* 823-832.

Loy, J.W., Curtis, J.E., & Sage, J.N. (1979). Relative centrality of playing position and leadership recruitment in team sports. In R.S. Hutton (Ed.), *Exercise and Sport Sciences Reviews* (Vol. 6, pp. 257-284). Santa Barbara, CA: Journal Publishing Affiliates.

Martens, R., & Peterson, J.A. (1971). Group cohesiveness as a determinant of success and member satisfaction in team performance. *International Review of Sport Sociology, 6,* 49-61.

Martens, R., Landers, D.M., & Loy, J.W. (1972). *Sport cohesiveness questionnaire.* Unpublished report, University of Illinois at Urbana-Champaign.

McGrath, J.E. (1984). *Groups: Interaction and performance.* Englewood Cliffs, NJ: Prentice-Hall.

Melnick, M.J., & Chemers, M.M. (1974). Effects of group structure on the success of basketball teams. *Research Quarterly, 45,* 1-8.

Mullen, B., & Copper, C. (1994). The relation between group cohesiveness and performance: An integration. *Psychological Bulletin, 115,* 210-227.

Peterson, J.A., & Martens, R. (1972). Success and residential affiliation as determinants of team cohesiveness. *Research Quarterly, 43,* 62-76.

Richman, J.M. & Rosenfeld, L.B. & Hardy, C.J. (1993). The social support survey: An initial evaluation of a clinical measure and practice model of the social support process. *Research on Social Work Practice, 3,* 288-311.

Rosenfeld, L.B. & Richman, J.R. (1997). Developing effective social support: Team building and the social support process. *Journal of Applied Social Psychology, 9,* 133-153.

Rosenfeld, L.B., Richman, J.M., & Hardy, C.J. (1989). An examination of social support networks among athletes: Description and relationship to stress. *The Sport Psychologist, 3,* 23-33.

Ruder, M.D., & Gill, D.L. (1982). Immediate effects of win-loss on perceptions of cohesion in intramural volleyball teams. *Journal of Sport Psychology, 4,* 227-234.

Sarason, I.G., Levine, H., Basham, R., & Sarason, B. (1983). Concomitants of social support: The social support questionnaire. *Journal of Personality and Social Psychology, 44,* 127-139.

Sarason, I.G., Sarason, B.R., & Pierce, G.R. (1990). Social support, personality and performance. *Journal of Applied Sport Psychology, 2,* 117-127.

Schachter, S., Ellerton, N., McBride, D., & Gregory, D. (1951). An experimental study of cohesiveness and productivity. *Human Relations, 4,* 229-238.

Shaffer, S.M., & Wiese-Bjornstal, D.M. (1999). Psychosocial interventions in sports medicine. In R. Ray & D.M. Wiese-Bjornstal (Eds.), *Counseling in sports medicine* (pp. 41-54). Champaign, IL: Human Kinetics.

Shumaker, S.A., & Brownell, A. (1984). Toward a theory of social support: Closing conceptual gaps. *Journal of Social Issues, 40,* 11-36.

Smith, R.E. (1986). Toward a cognitive-affective model of athletic burnout. *Journal of Sport & Exercise Psychology, 8,* 36-50.

Spink, K.S., & Carron, A.V. (1992). Group cohesion and adherence in exercise classes. *Journal of Sport & Exercise Psychology, 14,* 78-86.

Spink, K.S., & Carron, A.V. (1993). The effects of team building on the adherence patterns of female exercise participants. *Journal of Sport & Exercise Psychology, 15,* 39-49.

Spink, K.S., & Carron, A.V. (1994). Group cohesion effects in exercise classes. *Small Group Research, 25,* 26-42.

Steiner, I.D. (1972). *Group process and productivity.* New York: Academic Press.

Widmeyer, W.N., Brawley, L.R., & Carron, A.V. (1990). Group size in sport. *Journal of Sport & Exercise Psychology, 12,* 177-190.

Widmeyer, W.N., Brawley, L.R., & Carron, A.V. (2002). Group dynamics in sport. In T.S. Horn (Ed.), *Advances in sport psychology* (2nd ed., pp. 285-308). Champaign, IL: Human Kinetics.

Wiese, D.M., & Weiss, M.R. (1987). Psychological rehabilitation and physical injury: Implication for the sports medicine team. *The Sport Psychologist, 1,* 318-330.

Wiest, W.M., Porter, L.W., & Ghiselli, E.E. (1961). Relationships between individual proficiency and team performance and efficiency. *Journal of Applied Psychology, 45,* 435-440.

Williams, J.M., & Hacker, C.M. (1982). Causal relationships among cohesion, satisfaction and performance in women's intercollegiate field hockey teams. *Journal of Sport Psychology, 4,* 324-337.

Williams, J.M., & Widmeyer, W.N. (1991). The cohesion-performance outcome relationship in a coacting sport. *Journal of Sport & Exercise Psychology, 13,* 364-371.

Williams, K., Harkins, S., & Latane, B. (1981). Identifiability and social loafing: Two cheering experiments. *Journal of Personality and Social Psychology, 40,* 303-311.

Williams, K.D., Nida, S.A., Baca, L.D., & Latane, B. (1989). Social loafing and swimming: Effects of identifiability on individual and relay performance for intercollegiate swimmers. *Basic and Applied Sport Psychology, 10,* 73-81.

Wright, A., & Cote, J. (2003). A retrospective analysis of leadership development through sport. *The Sport Psychologist, 17,* 268-291.

Yukelson, D. (1997). Principles of effective team building intervention in sport: A direct services approach at Penn State University. *Journal of Applied Sport Psychology, 9,* 73-96.

Yukelson, D., Weinberg, R., & Jackson, A. (1984). A multidimensional sport cohesion instrument for intercollegiate basketball teams. *Journal of Sport Psychology, 6,* 103-117.

Zander, A. (1971). *Motives and goals in groups.* New York: Academic Press.

Chapter 16 Gender, Diversity, and Cultural Competence

Adler, N.E., Boyce, T., Chesney, M.A., Choen, S., Folkman, S., Kahn, R.L., & Syme, S.L. (1994). Socioeconomic status and health: The challenge of the gradient. *American Psychologist, 49,* 15-24.

American Psychological Association (APA). (2003). Guidelines on multicultural education, training, research, practice and organizational change for psychologists. *American Psychologist* [Online], *58,* 377-402. www.apa.org/pi.

Ashmore, R.D. (1990). Sex, gender, and the individual. In L.A. Pervin (Ed.), *Handbook of personality theory and research* (pp. 486-526). New York: Guilford.

Barber, H., & Krane, V. (2005). The elephant in the locker room: Opening the dialogue about sexual orientation on women's sport teams. In M.B. Anderson (Ed.), *Sport psychology in practice* (pp. 265-285). Champaign, IL: Human Kinetics.

Basow, S.A., & Rubin, L.R. (1999). Gender influences and adolescent development. In N.G. Johnson, M.C. Roberts, & J. Worell (Eds.), *Beyond appearance: A new look at adolescent girls* (pp. 25-52). Washington, DC: APA.

Beilock, S.L., & McConnell, A.R. (2004). Stereotype threat and sport: Can athletic performance be threatened? *Journal of Sport & Exercise Psychology, 26,* 597-609

Bem, S.L. (1978a). Beyond androgyny: Some presumptuous prescriptions for a liberated sexual identity. In J. Sherman & F. Denmark (Eds.), *Psychology of women: Future directions for research* (pp. 1-23). New York: Psychological Dimensions.

Bem, S.L. (1993). *The lenses of gender.* New Haven, CT: Yale University Press.

Berman, E., DeSouza, M.J., & Kerr, G. (2005). A qualitative examination of weight concerns, eating and exercise behaviors in recreational exercisers. *Women in Sport and Physical Activity Journal, 14,* 24-38.

Bernard, J. (1981). *The female world.* New York: Free Press. Bernstein, D.A., & Borkovec, T.D. (1973). *Progressive relaxation: A manual for the helping professions.* Champaign, IL: Research Press.

Blinde, E.M., & McCallister, S.G. (1999). Women, disability, and sport and physical fitness activity: The intersection of gender and disability dynamics. *Research Quarterly for Exercise and Sport, 70,* 303-312.

Brackenridge, C. (1997). Playing safe: Assessing the risk of sexual abuse to elite child athletes. *International Review for the Sociology of Sport, 32,* 407-418.

Bringer, J.D., Brackenridge, C.H., & Johnston, L.H. (2001). A qualitative study of swimming coaches' attitudes towards sexual relationships in sport. In A. Papaioannou, M. Goudas, & Y. Theodorkis (Eds.), *International Society of Sport Psychology 10th World Congress of Sport Psychology: Programme and proceeding* (Vol. 4, pp. 187-189). Thessaloniki, Greece: Christodoulidi Publications.

Brooks, D., & Althouse, R. (2000). *Racism in college athletics: The African-American athlete's experience* (2nd ed.). Morgantown, WV: Fitness Information Technology.

Brown, R.D., & Harrison, J.M. (1986). The effects of a strength training program on the strength and self-concept of two female age groups. *Research Quarterly for Exercise and Sport, 57,* 315-320.

Carpenter, L.J., & Acosta, R.V. (2006). *Title IX.* Champaign, IL: Human Kinetics.

Caruso, C.M., & Gill, D.L. (1992). Strengthening physical self-perceptions through exercise. *Journal of Sports Medicine and Physical Fitness, 32,* 416-427.

Chambliss, H.O., Finley, C.E., & Blair, S.N. (2004). Attitudes toward obese individuals among exercise science students. *Medicine and Science in Sports and Exercise, 36,* 468-474.

Choi, P.Y.L. (2000). *Femininity and the physically active woman.* Philadelphia: Taylor & Francis.

Conception, R.Y., & Ebbeck, V. (2005). Examining the physical activity experience of survivors of domestic violence in relation to self-views. *Journal of Sport & Exercise Psychology, 27,* 197-211.

Contrada, R.J., Ashmore, R.D., Gary, M.L., Coups, E., Egeth, J.D., Sewell, A., Ewell, K., Goyal, T., & Chasse, V. (2000). Ethnicity-related sources of stress and their effects on well-being. *Current Directions in Psychological Science, 9,* 136-139.

Corbett, D., & Johnson, W. (2000). The African-American female in collegiate sport: Sexism and racism. In D. Brooks & R. Althouse (Eds.), *Racism in college athletics: The African-American athlete's experience* (2nd ed., pp. 199-225). Morgantown, WV: Fitness Information Technology.

Cox, B., & Thompson, S. (2000). Multiple bodies: Sportswomen, soccer and sexuality. *International Review for the Sociology of Sport, 35,* 5-20.

Crespo, C.J. (2005). Physical activity in minority populations: Overcoming a public health challenge. *The President's Council on Physical Fitness and Sports Research Digest, 6*(2).

Crespo, C.J., Ainsworth, B.E., Keteyian, S.J., Heath, G.W., & Smit, E. (1999). Prevalence of physical inactivity and its relations to social class in U.S. adults: Results from the Third National Health and Nutrition Examination Survey, 1988-1994. *Medicine and Science in Sports and Exercise, 31,* 1821-1827.

Cross, T., Bazron, B., Dennis, K., & Isaacs, M. (1999). *Towards a culturally competent system of care.* Washington, DC: National Institute of Mental Health, Child and Adolescent Service System Program Technical Assistance Center, Georgetown University Child Development Center.

D'Andrea, M., & Daniels, J. (2005). Respectful sport psychology: A multidimensional-multicultural competency model. *ESPNews, 19*(1), 9.

Danish, S.J., Fazio, R.J., Nellen, V.C., & Owens, S.S. (2002). Teaching life skills through sport: Community-based programs to enhance adolescent development. In J.L. VanRaalte & B.W. Brewer (Eds.), *Exploring sport and exercise psychology* (2nd ed., pp. 269-288). Washington, DC: APA.

Daubenmier, J.J. (2005). The relationship of yoga, body awareness, and body responsiveness to self-objectification and disordered eating. *Psychology of Women Quarterly, 29,* 207-219.

Davis, C. (1992). Body image, dieting behaviors, and personality factors: A study of high –performance female athletes. *International Journal of Sport Psychology, 23,* 179-192.

Deaux, K. (1984). From individual differences to social categories: Analysis of a decade's research on gender. *American Psychologist, 39,* 105-116.

Deaux, K., & Kite, M. (1993). Gender stereotypes. In F. L. Denmark & M. A. Paludi (Eds.), *Psychology of women: A handbook of issues and theories* (pp. 107-139). Westport, CT: Greenwood Press.

DePauw, K.P. (1997). The (in)visibility of disability: Cultural context and "sporting bodies." *Quest,49,* 416-430.

Devine, P.G. & Baker, S.M. (1991). Measurement of racial stereotype subtyping. *Personality and Social Psychology Bulletin, 17* (1), 44-50.

Duda, J.L. & Allison, M.T. (1990). Cross-cultural analysis in exercise and sport psychology: A void in the field. *Journal of Sport & Exercise Psychology, 12,* 114-131.

Duda, J.L. (1986). A cross-cultural analysis of achievement motivation in sport and the classroom. In L. VanderVelden and J. Humphrey (Eds.), *Psychology and sociology in sport: Current selected research* (Vol. I, pp. 115-134). New York: AMS Press.

Eccles, J. S., Barber, B., Jozefowicz, D., Malenchuk, O., & Vida, M. (1999). Self-evaluation of competence, task values and self-esteem. In N.G. Johnson, M. C. Roberts, & J. Worell (Ed.), *Beyond appearance: A new look at adolescent girls* (pp. 53-84). Washington, DC: APA.

Eccles, J.S. (1985). Sex differences in achievement patterns. In T. Sonderegger (Ed.), *Nebraska Symposium on Motivation, 1984: Psychology and gender* (pp. 97-132). Lincoln, NE: University of Nebraska Press.

Eccles, J.S., & Harrold, R.D. (1991). Gender differences in sport involvement: Applying the Eccles' expectancy-value model. *Journal of Applied Sport Psychology, 3,* 7-35.

Erkut, S., Fields, J.P., Sing, R., & Marx, F. (1996). Diversity in girls' experiences: Feeling good about who you are. In B.J. Ross Leadbeater & N. Way (Eds.), *Urban girls: Resisting stereotypes, creating identities* (pp. 53-64). New York: New York University Press.

Faith, M.S., Leone, M.A., Ayers, T.S., Heo, M., & Pietrobelli, A. (2002). Weight criticism during physical activity, coping skills, and reported physical activity in children. *Pediatrics, 110*(2), e23.

Fredericks, J.A., & Eccles, J.S. (2004). Parental influences on youth involvement in sports. In M.R. Weiss (Ed.), *Developmental sport and exercise psychology: A lifespan perspective.* (pp. 145-164). Morgantown, WV: Fitness Information Technology.

Fredericks, J.A., & Eccles, J.S. (2005). Family socialization, gender and sport motivation and involvement. *Journal of Sport and Exercise Psychology, 27,* 3-31.

Gill, D.L. (1993). Competitiveness and competitive orientation in sport. In R.A. Singer, M. Murphey, & L.K. Tennant (Eds.), *Handbook of research on sport psychology* (pp. 314-327). New York: Macmillan.

Gill, D.L. (2002). Gender and sport behavior. In T.S. Horn (Ed.), *Advances in sport psychology* (2nd ed., pp. 355-375). Champaign, IL: Human Kinetics.

Gill, D.L., & Deeter, T.E. (1988). Development of the Sport Orientation Questionnaire. *Research Quarterly for Exercise and Sport, 59,* 191-202.

Gill, D.L., Jamieson, K.M., & Kamphoff, C. (2005). *Final report: Promoting cultural competence among physical activity professionals.* American Association of University Women Scholar-in-Residence award, 2003-2004.

Gill, D.L., Morrow, R.G., Collins, K.E., Lucey, A.B., & Schultz, A.M. (2005). Climate for minorities in exercise and sport settings. *Journal of Sport and Exercise Psychology, 27*(Suppl.), S68.

Gill, D.L., Morrow, R.G., Collins, K.E., Lucey, A.B., & Schultz, A.M. (2006). Attitudes and sexual prejudice in sport and physical activity. *Journal of Sport Management, 20,* 554-564.

Greenleaf, C. (2002). Athletic body image: Exploratory interviews with former competitive female athletes. *Women in Sport and Physical Activity Journal, 11,* 63-74.

Greenleaf, C., & Weiller, K. (2005). Perceptions of youth obesity among physical educators. *Social Psychology of Education, 8,* 407-423.

Griffin, P.S. (1998). *Strong women, deep closets: Lesbians and homophobia in sport.* Champaign, IL: Human Kinetics.

Guthrie, R.V. (1998). *Even the rat was White: A historical view of psychology* (2nd ed.). Boston: Allyn & Bacon.

Hall, M.A. (1996). *Feminism and sporting bodies.* Champaign, IL: Human Kinetics.

Hall, R.L. (1998). Softly strong: African American women's use of exercise in therapy. In K.F. Hays (Ed.), *Integrating exercise, sports, movement and mind: Therapeutic unity* (pp. 81-100). The Haworth Press.

Hall, R.L. (2001). Shaking the foundation: Women of color in sport. *The Sport Psychologist, 15,* 386-400.

Harris, D.V., & Jennings, S.E. (1977). Self-perceptions of female distance runners. *Annals of the New York Academy of Sciences, 301,* 808-815.

Harris, O. (2000). African American predominance in sport. In D. Brooks & R. Althouse (Eds.), *Racism in college athletics: The African-American athlete's experience* (2nd ed., pp. 37-51). Morgantown, WV: Fitness Information Technology.

Hausenblas, H., & Fallon, E. (2002). Relationship among body image, exercise behavior, and exercise dependence symptoms. *International Journal of Eating Disorders, 32,* 179-185.

Hausenblas, H., & Mack, D.E. (1999). Social physique anxiety and eating disorders among female athletic and nonathletic populations. *Journal of Sport Behavior, 22,* 502-512.

Heesch, K.C., Brown, D.R., & Blanton, C.J. (2000). Perceived barriers to exercise and stage of exercise adoption in older women of different racial/ethnic groups. *Women and Health, 30,* 61-76.

Hellison, D., Cutforth, N., Kallusky, J., Martinek, T., Parker, M., & Stiehl, J. (2000). *Youth development and physical activity.* Champaign, IL: Human Kinetics.

Henderson, K.A., & Bedini, L.A. (1995). "I have a soul that dances like Tina Turner, but my body can't": Physical activity and women with disability impairments. *Research Quarterly for Exercise and Sport, 66,* 151-161.

Herek, G.M. (2000). Psychology of sexual prejudice. *Current directions in psychological science, 9,* 19-22.

Holloway, J.B., Beuter, A., & Duda, J.L. (1988). Self-efficacy and training for strength in adolescent girls. *Journal of Applied Social Psychology, 18,* 699-719.

Horner, M.S. (1972). Toward an understanding of achievement-related conflicts in women. *Journal of Social Issues, 28,* 157-176.

Human Rights Watch. (2001). Hatred in the hallways: Violence and discrimination against lesbian, gay, bisexual, and transgender students in U.S. schools. *American Journal of Health Education* [Online], *32,* 302-306. www.hrw.org/reports/2001/uslgbt/toc.htm.